PRESENTED TO

Paul & McPhee

ON

Christmas 2013

BY

Jesse H. Fry
180 Applewood Dr. Apt. 306
Lawrenceville, GA 30046-6481
770-542-8865

KENNETH
COPELAND
PUBLICATIONS

LIMITLESSLOVE

Discover the Love that knows no bounds & fuels your faith daily.

365~DAY DEVOTIONAL

KENNETH & GLORIA COPELAND

Limitless Love
A 365-Day Devotional

ISBN 978-1-60463-242-2   21-0033

18 17 16 15 14 13   6 5 4 3 2 1

Kenneth Copeland Publications
Fort Worth, TX 76192-0001

For more information about Kenneth Copeland Ministries, visit kcm.org or call 1-800-600-7395 (U.S. only) or +1-817-852-6000.

LIMITLESS LOVE

LIMITLESS**LOVE**

A Life Worth Living

"By this we know that we have come to know Him, if we keep His commandments. The one who says, 'I have come to know Him,' and does not keep His commandments, is a liar, and the truth is not in him; but whoever keeps His word, in him the love of God has truly been perfected. By this we know that we are in Him: the one who says he abides in Him ought himself to walk in the same manner as He walked."
1 John 2:3-6, *New American Standard*

A great many people claim to know God. They call themselves Christians and say, "The LORD told me this…" or "The LORD told me that…." Yet, it's not just what we say that proves we know Jesus, it's how we live. The Bible says if we are abiding in Him, we will live as He lived.

How *did* Jesus live? First and foremost, He lived a life of love.

Jesus didn't live for Himself. He didn't seek to do His own will. He lived to do the will of His Father. He lived to pour out His life for others.

You might say it this way: Jesus lived to give Himself away.

Worldly people don't understand that kind of life. They'll warn you against it. They'll say, "If you live like that, you'll be miserable…. You'll never have any fun…. You'll never get anywhere…. You'll be a weakling, and people will walk all over you!" But don't listen. They don't know what they're talking about.

Jesus lived like that and His life was wonderful! He walked the earth in total victory. He defeated Satan and destroyed his works at every turn. Everywhere He went He loved people. He made the blind see, the deaf hear and the lame walk. He cast out demons and raised the dead. He made people know the love of God.

No matter how the world tries to convince us that it's more rewarding to live in sin and selfishness than in love and obedience, Jesus proved it's not. He lived the most rewarding life in history.

If you'll live the life of love by faith in Jesus, you'll have the same kinds of experiences He had. Jesus said in John 14:12 you'll even do the works that He did. You won't be cheated out of the good things in life. On the contrary, you'll enjoy the most thrilling life of victory you could ever imagine. You'll experience God pouring His power out through you. You'll know the joy of The LORD.

Now, that's what I call a life worth living!

A Simple, Supernatural Secret

"He that hath my commandments, and keepeth them, he it is that loveth me: and he that loveth me shall be loved of my Father, and I will love him, and will manifest myself to him…. This is my commandment, That ye love one another, as I have loved you."

John 14:21, 15:12

Something about the manifest presence of The LORD is indescribable. Although we know God is with us always—when we can sense His presence and when we can't—every believer who has ever experienced the tangible presence of God hungers for it more and more.

That's why we often hear believers praying, "LORD, I want more of You!" Having tasted the sweet awareness of God's presence, they are seeking it with greater fervency than ever before. They want to experience His nearness and hear His voice. They don't just want to know theological facts about God, they want to have living contact with Him!

Some try to experience His presence by running from one meeting to another, seeking spectacular signs and wonders. Others pray for hours, begging and pleading for God to reveal Himself. Certainly, Holy Spirit-anointed meetings are wonderful and prayer is essential, but Jesus gave us the major key to His manifest presence that many people overlook—*the key of love.* In essence He said, "I will manifest Myself to those who believe in Me and keep the commandment of love."

Living a lifestyle of love is essential if you want to maintain vital contact with God. Every step in love is a step toward Him and every step out of love draws you away.

Years ago, Rufus Moseley caught sight of the revelation that if we live by the commandment of love, God's presence will always be with us. He said:

I knew this was the secret. If we abide in His love and always go in love, feeling and willing and giving out nothing but love and all possible love to all men and all things, we will always be in Him and under His anointing. It was made known to me that I could write editorials and do everything else that can be done in the loving Spirit of Jesus. I could even be in heavenly places while plowing with a mule, pruning trees, in courtrooms, in death cells, in all places of need, provided all was done in the spirit of love.[1]

What a wonderfully simple yet supernatural secret! The more we live by love, the more we'll experience the manifest presence of God. As we walk in love, we'll be increasingly able to sense our LORD Jesus walking with us everywhere we go! And since His presence brings fullness of joy (Psalm 16:11), that will make everything we do a delight!

---

[1] Rufus Moseley, *Manifest Victory* (Plainfield, NJ: Logos International, 9171) p. 117.

LIMITLESS LOVE

You're Not on Your Own

"Love endures long and is patient and kind; love never is envious nor boils over with jealousy, is not boastful or vainglorious, does not display itself haughtily. It is not conceited (arrogant and inflated with pride); it is not rude (unmannerly) and does not act unbecomingly. Love (God's love in us) does not insist on its own rights or its own way, for it is not self-seeking; it is not touchy or fretful or resentful; it takes no account of the evil done to it [it pays no attention to a suffered wrong]. It does not rejoice at injustice and unrighteousness, but rejoices when right and truth prevail. Love bears up under anything and everything that comes, is ever ready to believe the best of every person, its hopes are fadeless under all circumstances, and it endures everything [without weakening]. Love never fails."

1 Corinthians 13:4-8, *The Amplified Bible*

When you see in the Bible what it really means to live a life of love, your first thought may be that you could never do it. *How can I consistently be unselfish and kind to those who are harsh and thoughtless toward me?* you wonder. *How can I continually overlook insults and mistreatment, refusing to take account of a suffered wrong? It's just too hard to do!*

Frankly, you're right. Walking in love *is* hard for human beings to do. In fact, when we try to do it on our own, we find it's impossible.

But, thank God, we're not on our own! If we've been born again, Jesus Christ—the Greater One—lives within us by His Spirit. He makes us able. In fact, as we trust in Him, His own love will actually flow through us.

While weak, human attempts to walk in love will always fall short, Jesus' love within us will overcome every challenge, every situation, every hurt and offense. His love released in our lives will perfectly fulfill the description in 1 Corinthians 13. His love in us will never fail!

What can we do to tap into that love? Begin by meditating on what the Bible says about it. Fellowship with God in the truth of these verses by saying, "I thank You, LORD, that Your love in me endures long and is patient and kind. Your love in me is never envious, conceited or self-seeking. Your love within me is not touchy nor resentful but believes the best of every person…" (see 1 Corinthians 13:4-5, 7, *The Amplified Bible*).

As we renew our minds in this way, the God-kind of love will begin to dominate our thought lives. Faith will grow strong in our hearts, giving us confidence, not in ourselves, but in the One who dwells within us. As we act on that faith, we'll be empowered to respond in love to every kind of meanness, selfishness, persecution and hurt that comes our way.

We'll find as we practice the walk of love that was so impossible to our flesh, it becomes the natural outflow of our spirits that have been born again in the image of Jesus. We'll find we are truly able to love others with His mighty love!

LIMITLESS**LOVE**

Abide and Bear Fruit

"But the fruit of the [Holy] Spirit [the work which His presence within accomplishes] is love, joy (gladness), peace, patience (an even temper, forbearance), kindness, goodness (benevolence), faithfulness, gentleness (meekness, humility), self-control (self-restraint, continence)...."
Galatians 5:22-23, *The Amplified Bible*

As you set your sights on living a life of love, you will be encouraged to know that love isn't something you have to struggle to attain. It's not a work produced by your own efforts. On the contrary, the Bible lists love as the very first "fruit of the spirit." It is the natural outgrowth of the life of God in you.

Actually, all the fruit of the spirit is put within you the moment you were born again. It will forever be a part of your reborn spirit because your spirit is made in the image of God. He put His own, divine nature inside you, and the fruit of the spirit is characteristic of His nature.

"If that's true," you might ask, "why haven't I seen more evidence of it in my life? I've tried very hard to be more loving and kind. I've struggled and I just can't seem to do it."

That's because fruit bearing doesn't come that way. Have you ever seen the branch of an apple tree struggling, straining and trying with all its might to bear apples? Certainly not! All the branch has to do is stay connected to the tree. As it draws life from the tree, apples come forth naturally!

According to Jesus, the same is true for us. He said, "I am the vine, you are the branches; he who abides in Me, and I in him, he bears much fruit; for apart from Me you can do nothing" (John 15:5, *New American Standard*).

As we abide in Jesus, spending time in fellowship with Him in prayer and in His WORD, His life will flow through us and bear fruit in our lives. The force of His Spirit will cause the love inside us to develop on the outside!

Praise God, we *can* live the life of love––not by putting forth great effort in trying to do it, but simply by abiding in Jesus. When we focus our efforts on doing what it takes to stay in union and communion with Him, we will bear fruit abundantly. Just as the grape is the natural result of abiding connected to the vine, love is the supernatural result of abiding connected to Jesus. He is the love vine!

LIMITLESS*LOVE*

Your No. 1 Priority

"Abide in Me, and I in you. As the branch cannot bear fruit of itself, unless
it abides in the vine, so neither can you unless you abide in Me."
John 15:4, *New American Standard*

Once you understand that love, as a fruit of the spirit, will only grow in your life as you abide in Jesus, you'll be more diligent to spend time with Him. You won't try to live from Sunday to Sunday, fellowshiping with Him once a week and ignoring Him the rest of the time. You'll draw near to Him daily, realizing the supernatural life of love comes only from consistent communion with Him.

Actually, true, unbroken communion with The LORD comes from walking with Him all day long. I've found when I set aside time each day to focus exclusively on Him, I can more easily stay tuned in to Him during my other activities. By tending to my union with Jesus first thing every morning, I can more easily maintain that union throughout my day.

This is very important because Jesus said, "If a man abide not in me, he is cast forth as a branch, and is withered..." (John 15:6). The word *wither* means "to shrivel, to lose or cause to lose energy, force or freshness."

The moment a branch is broken off the vine, it begins to die. It doesn't matter how close it is to the vine, if the union has been broken, there will be no energy going into it. There will be no sap flowing from the vine into the branch.

That's a vivid picture of what happens to us if we don't stay in vital contact and living union with The LORD. When we become too busy to spend time with God in prayer and His WORD, when we become preoccupied with natural, earthly things and disconnect from communion with Him, we immediately begin to wither.

We still belong to Him. We still have His life within us, but His energy is not flowing through us, so we can't produce anything.

I don't want to live that way, even for a day! Do you?

Glory to God, we don't have to! If we'll just make our time with The LORD our No. 1 priority every day, we can produce fruit in Him. As a result, we'll not only live BLESSED, we'll be able to share THE BLESSING with those around us. When they are in need of love, they'll always be able to find it flowing through us.

LIMITLESS**LOVE**

The Choice Is Yours

"Neither yield ye your members as instruments of unrighteousness unto sin: but yield yourselves unto God, as those that are alive from the dead, and your members as instruments of righteousness unto God. For sin shall not have dominion over you...."
Romans 6:13-14

Although the life of Jesus in us produces the fruit of love, don't make the mistake of thinking you can just sit back and let Him do everything. He won't grow the fruit for you any more than the apple tree will take up the responsibility of the branch and grow apples straight from the trunk of the tree.

Jesus provides you with the power and the life. Then you must do your part by choosing to yield to that life. By an act of your will, you must let what He has put inside you manifest itself on the outside.

When someone says something ugly to you, for example, you have to make a decision: Will you yield to the irritation of your flesh and say something unkind in return? Or will you yield to your spirit and respond in love?

The answer to those questions will be determined by two factors. The first, of course, is the choice you make. The second is the condition of your heart.

If you've been neglecting your time with God, spending hours in front of the world's entertainment instead of attending to The WORD, you may find yourself too weak to obey the voice of the Spirit. Although your heart's desire is to act lovingly, your flesh will win the struggle with your undernourished spirit and lash out in anger toward the one who wronged you.

But, if you have been daily abiding in fellowship with The LORD, your heart will be strong and full of the spiritual energy necessary to overrule the flesh and let love flow. You'll be well able to make the right choice and Jesus' love will reach others through you! That love could be the avenue through which they discover the love of Jesus for themselves. We are living love letters from God to others (2 Corinthians 3:2-3).

LIMITLESS**LOVE**

Dare to Believe God's Love

"Whoever confesses that Jesus is the Son of God, God abides in him, and he in God. And we have come to know and have believed the love which God has for us. God is love, and the one who abides in love abides in God, and God abides in him…. And this commandment we have from Him, that the one who loves God should love his brother also."
1 John 4:15-16, 21, *New American Standard*

To effectively love others, you must first believe God loves you.

"That's no problem," you might say. "I know God loves me."

Maybe so, but according to these verses, just knowing it is not enough. We also need to believe it. To *believe* means "to have firm faith in something; to accept it as true, genuine, or real; to have an unshakable conviction of its goodness, efficacy and ability."

As Christians, we should have more than a mental understanding that God loves us. We should be firmly grounded in that love. We should believe it to be so good and genuine, so trustworthy and strong that it will keep us safe from harm in every situation. No matter what anyone else may say or do to us, we should rest securely in the fact that we are fully and forever loved.

Maybe that kind of confident love doesn't come easily for you. Maybe you've been abused and criticized so much in the past that you naturally think of yourself as unlovable. If so, allow The WORD of God to change how you see yourself. Instead of filling your thoughts with the unkind words others have said to you, fill your thoughts with the tender words of God.

Set your mind on verses like 1 John 3:1: "Behold, what manner of love the Father hath bestowed upon us, that we should be called the sons of God." Then fellowship with The LORD over the truth of those verses. Thank Him for loving you with such a great love. Praise Him for caring for you so much that He called you to be His very own child.

Agree with The WORD and begin to see yourself as the Father sees you. Acknowledge that regardless of your past experiences, whatever He says about you as His child is true. And since He says you are loved, choose to believe it.

As you do, you'll begin to see by revelation of the Spirit that God actually is your Father and He does care for you. You'll be able to say just like the Apostle John did, "I know and believe the love God has for me!"

As a result, the love of God will become a reality in your life. You'll find that God's love is not only coming *to* you, it's flowing *through* you…and before you know it, you'll be living the life of love!

LIMITLESS**LOVE**

Two Reasons to Forgive

*"But I say unto you, Love your enemies, bless them that curse you,
do good to them that hate you, and pray for them which despitefully
use you, and persecute you; that ye may be the children
of your Father which is in heaven…."*
Matthew 5:44-45

One of the most common obstacles the devil uses to block the pathway of love is the hurt that comes when other people mistreat us. He'll tempt us to keep an account of those suffered wrongs. He'll pressure us to become bitter, resentful and unforgiving. But when he does, we must tell him *no.* We must choose to drop our offenses, forgive everyone who has harmed us and let bitterness go.

If you've suffered serious abuse, you may think that's impossible to do. But it's not. The power to forgive is an awesome power. God has it and He has given it to you! His power within you will enable you to do it.

When you do, no matter how terrible the pain of those experiences may have been, you'll find the love of God is more powerful. And as you begin to walk in love and forgiveness, giving up the resentment you've harbored against those who have hurt you, the love of God will overcome the damage that abuse caused in your life.

"But Gloria," you may say, "the people who mistreated me did something very wrong. I've been miserable for years because of them. Why should I just drop my resentment and let them go free?"

You should do it, first of all because Jesus did that for you. Even before you repented and asked Him to be your Savior, Jesus went to the cross and shed His own blood, so you wouldn't have to pay the penalty for your own sin. Even though you were guilty, He dropped the charges against you so you could go free. That alone is reason enough for you to forgive others.

But there's another reason. You should forgive those who have done you wrong because if you don't, you're the one who is going to suffer for it—not the people who hurt you. Unforgiveness is like drinking poison and expecting someone else to die. It really doesn't affect the other person at all.

On the other hand, if you forgive and let the love of God flow into that area of your life, it will restore you—spirit, soul and body.

What's more, as you continue to yield to love, you'll continually live in victory. So when the devil comes back and tries to bring hurt to you again, that hurt will not be able to gain a place in you. The love of God will completely protect you and keep you free, free, free!

LIMITLESS**LOVE**

The Enemies of Love

"There hath no temptation taken you but such as is common to man: but God is faithful, who will not suffer you to be tempted above that ye are able; but will with the temptation also make a way to escape, that ye may be able to bear it."
1 Corinthians 10:13

Love is the one commandment of the new covenant. It's the unfailing key to our supernatural success. That's why Satan works furiously day in and day out to deceive and pressure us into stepping out of love. He constantly sends situations our way to tempt us to yield to things like selfishness, pride, jealousy, envy and strife.

Of course, none of us likes to think about those things. But the Bible talks about them, and we need to keep in mind what it says. We can't afford to be ignorant of the devil's devices (2 Corinthians 2:11), because if we're ignorant or unaware, we're more likely to fall prey to them. We need to study The WORD, learn what love is—and what it is not—so when the devil tempts us, we can quickly recognize his strategies and say, "No, devil! I refuse to do that. Get out, in the Name of Jesus." When we do that, we make the choice for victory!

Some people don't realize that resisting temptation is that simple. (Notice, I didn't say easy, I said *simple*.) But it is!

Temptation is nothing more than a solicitation to do evil. That's actually one of the dictionary definitions of the word.[2] In times of temptation, the devil comes to you like a solicitor, or a salesman, and makes a presentation. He brings an influence into your life and puts an opportunity in front of you to sin.

You can say *yes* to a salesman if you want what he's offering, or *no* if you don't think it would be to your advantage. You can either accept or reject the devil's solicitations the same way.

One reason we fail to reject the devil's solicitations at times is that we don't recognize temptation for what it is. We buy the devil's line before we even realize he's selling it to us. That's why we need to study the enemies of love. The more we know about them, and engraft into our hearts what The WORD has to say about them, the easier it will be for us to detect the devil's devices.

Then, instead of falling into his traps, we'll take another route. We'll look to God for the way of escape, avoid the enemies of love and stay on the road to supernatural success.

---

[2] Noah Webster, *American Dictionary of the English Language* (New York: S. Converse, 1828).

LIMITLESS**LOVE**

Shut the Door on Strife

"Who is a wise man and endued with knowledge among you? let him show
out of a good conversation his works with meekness of wisdom. But if ye have
bitter envying and strife in your hearts, glory not, and lie not against the truth.
This wisdom descendeth not from above, but is earthly, sensual, devilish. For
where envying and strife is, there is confusion and every evil work."

James 3:13-16

As I've studied the Scriptures to find the enemies of love, I've come to believe there is
one that is more insidious and more common than any other. It is the enemy called *strife,*
which means: "vigorous or bitter conflict, discord and antagonism; to quarrel, struggle or
clash; competitions; rivalry."

According to James 3:16, where strife gets in, every other evil work will follow. Strife
opens the door to the devil and licenses him to bring confusion and evil into our lives. That's
why he's always pushing for us to argue with one another and get offended or critical of one
another. It gives him access to us!

You see, Satan doesn't want you to enjoy THE BLESSING that is yours in Christ Jesus. He
doesn't want you to be healed, happy and prosperous because, if you are, other people will
notice and want the same quality of life you have. They'll give their hearts to God because of
the goodness of God they see in your life.

To keep that from happening, the devil tries to steal THE BLESSING from you. He tries to trick
you into opening the door of your life to him by bringing you an opportunity to have conflict with
someone. He knows that the moment you step into strife, he can begin to gain mastery over you.
The devil wants control of your life, but he can't have it when you walk in love.

Don't let him have control. Make a quality decision today to shut the door on strife.
Refuse to argue with people. Refuse to fight back when people criticize or wrong you.
Determine instead to respond in love—take no account of the evil done to you. When you do
mess up and say harsh words, be quick to repent so the devil can't get a foothold in your life.

I can tell you not only from The WORD but from experience, it will be one of the best
decisions you'll ever make. It will take effort, but by God's grace you will be able to do it. It's a
small price to pay for the freedom in THE BLESSING…and you'll be forever glad you did.

Think About the Cost

"And I, brethren, could not speak unto you as unto spiritual, but as unto carnal, even as unto babes in Christ. I have fed you with milk, and not with meat: for hitherto ye were not able to bear it, neither yet now are ye able. For ye are yet carnal: for whereas there is among you envying, and strife, and divisions, are ye not carnal, and walk as men?"

1 Corinthians 3:1-3

It's bad enough that strife is one of the primary enemies of love. It's bad enough that it opens the door to confusion and every evil work. Those things alone should be enough to make us determined to resist it. But that's not all the Bible has to say about it.

In his letter to the Corinthians, the Apostle Paul gave us even more information about the damaging effects of strife. He told us that it would keep us carnal. Carnal Christians are miserable people. They know enough about God to not enjoy sin, but they aren't committed enough to stay out of it.

If you don't want to find yourself trapped in that condition (and I know you don't) then stay out of strife. Strife will inhibit your ability to digest the meat of The WORD, and without that meat, you won't be able to grow up in love. You won't be able to become a strong, victorious Christian. If you fuss and bicker with others, your spiritual growth will be stunted. You'll remain in a perpetual state of spiritual babyhood, and the devil will run over you regularly!

Remember that the next time you feel yourself getting irritated with someone about something. When you're tempted to yield to that irritation and step into strife, think about the cost. Ask yourself, *Am I willing to confine myself to the ranks of carnality over this issue? Am I willing to weaken myself spiritually and give the devil power over me?*

If you'll think of it that way, the answer will always be a swift and clear, "No!" And instead of stepping into the turbulent stream of strife, you'll choose to yield to the peaceful flow of love. You'll give a soft answer rather than harsh words to the one who irritated you. Proverbs 15:1 says, "A soft answer turneth away wrath: but grievous words stir up anger."

Every time you make the choice to walk in God's love, you'll grow up a little more into the image of Jesus. You'll leave spiritual infancy behind and take another step toward the maturity of love.

Charity Begins at Home

> "Again I tell you, if two of you on earth agree (harmonize together, make a symphony together) about whatever [anything and everything] they may ask, it will come to pass and be done for them by My Father in heaven. For wherever two or three are gathered (drawn together as My followers) in (into) My name, there I AM in the midst of them."
>
> Matthew 18:19-20, *The Amplified Bible*

There's nothing on earth more powerful than the prayers of believers who are walking together in love. Love puts them in harmony with one another. It aligns them with the will of The LORD and brings them into agreement.

The devil hates agreement between believers. Agreement opens the windows of heaven to us and closes the door on every destructive thing he can do. So he continually tries to disrupt that agreement by causing strife and division in the places where believers come together in the most powerful way: the family and the church.

Until now, you may not have realized the spiritual value of your family. But the fact is, if you have family members who are believers, your family can be a powerful force for God. So make it your goal to stay out of strife and walk in harmony with those closest to you. Keep in mind the old saying, "Charity (or love) begins at home."

Oddly enough, home is often the most difficult place to be loving. I think this is because we don't have our guard up there. We're not worried about our reputation or trying to impress anyone. At home, nothing will stop us from being selfish—except our commitment to walk in the love of God.

But don't be fooled into thinking it doesn't matter how you act at home. It matters a great deal. In fact, years ago, The LORD revealed this to me and I have never forgotten it: *If you allow Satan to stop you with strife at your front door, you'll be no threat to him anywhere else.*

So, first and foremost, practice the lifestyle of love with your brothers and sisters, your spouse and your children. See to it that your prayers prevail by being in harmony with the members of your own family. The moment you slip up and get into strife, make it right. Repent, ask their forgiveness and jump right back into your love walk.

You may have to repent quite a bit at first because you've probably developed habits that will take a while to change. But don't get discouraged with yourself when you miss it. Just keep trusting The LORD to help you. Keep acting on The WORD. Keep going and growing in love!

LIMITLESS**LOVE**

Choose Life—Not Strife

"These six things doth The LORD hate: yea, seven are an abomination unto him: a proud look, a lying tongue, and hands that shed innocent blood, an heart that deviseth wicked imaginations, feet that be swift in running to mischief, a false witness that speaketh lies, and he that soweth discord among brethren."
Proverbs 6:16-19

Once you put a stop to strife in your home, the devil will pressure you even harder to get into strife at church. He'll provoke someone to be rude to you and hurt your feelings. Or, he'll make sure you find out about something someone else has done wrong and talk you into spreading word of that wrongdoing to others.

When he presents you with that opportunity, turn him down—fast! Treat that temptation to gossip and stir up strife like you would a poisonous snake. Turn your back and run the other way because in the eyes of God, participating in strife is one of the most serious of sins.

God considers stirring up strife such a grave sin that He lists it alongside murder and lying. So stay away from it. Ask God to reveal to you if you've entered into strife, even inadvertently. He may remind you of a time you passed along gossip about someone or criticized the pastor. If He does, repent and determine that from now on, if you see your brother sin, you'll do what the Bible says to do. You'll believe God for him, pray for him and endeavor to help him instead of perpetuating the problem by talking to everyone about it.

God makes a promise to those who will do that. First John 5:16 says, "If anyone sees his brother [believer] committing a sin that does not [lead to] death (the extinguishing of life) he will pray and [God] will give him life..." (The Amplified Bible).

Think about that! You have the power either to hurt or to help the brother who has fallen into sin. You can make things worse for him by taking offense and stirring up strife...or you can make things better by loving, praying and bringing him life.

Which will you choose: the side of peace which God loves...or the side of discord which God hates? Clearly, your own life and the lives of others will be greatly affected by what you do. Your choice will make all the difference.

It's Not Your Job to Judge

"Therefore judge nothing before the time, until The LORD come, who both will bring to light the hidden things of darkness, and will make manifest the counsels of the hearts: and then shall every man have praise of God."
1 Corinthians 4:5

One of the most wonderful characteristics of love is that it always believes the best. Love doesn't criticize or judge others. Even when a great wrong has been done, love says, "I know that person's action was wrong but I cannot judge his heart. I choose to believe he did the best he could do at the time and I will treat him with the mercy I would desire to receive if I were in his shoes."

I realize sometimes that seems extremely difficult to do. But here's something that will help you. When you're tempted to step out of love and into strife by judging a fellow believer, remember what Romans 14:4 says and ask yourself, "Who art thou that judgest another man's servant? to his own master he standeth or falleth. Yea, he shall be holden up: for God is able to make him stand."

The devil will try to push you into making a decision about that person. He'll pressure you to say whether he's guilty or not guilty. But don't give in to that pressure. It's not your job to judge others. (Isn't that a relief?) In fact, according to the Bible, it's to your benefit to withhold judgment because it will save you from the judgment that's due you. Jesus said, "Judge not, that ye be not judged. For with what judgment ye judge, ye shall be judged: and with what measure ye mete, it shall be measured to you again" (Matthew 7:1-2).

If you're in a church where the pastor has done wrong and lived a wrong lifestyle, and you feel you don't want to follow him, that's fine. I don't blame you. Leave that church and go to one where there's a pastor you can trust and respect. But do it quietly. Don't sow discord in the church before you go.

You may be tempted to take it on yourself to make that pastor pay for the harm he's done to you and to others—but resist that temptation. Just love him as you leave, pray for him, and let God deal with him as He sees fit. There are strong words for believers and ministers alike who sow discord among the brethren. God hates it and it is an abomination to Him (Proverbs 6:19).

Our business is to pray for mercy rather than engage in judgment. We leave judgment to The LORD.

Most important of all, make your exit honorably and without bitterness. Let your leaving be marked by peace and love. If you do, you'll be a BLESSING wherever you go.

LIMITLESS**LOVE**

Your One Great Quest

"Eagerly pursue and seek to acquire [this] love
[make it your aim, your great quest]...."
1 Corinthian 14:1, *The Amplified Bible*

What is the No. 1 goal in your life? What things are you aiming to accomplish? What dreams do you want to achieve?

If you're a businessperson, you may be pursuing the goal of building a business so successful, you can pour millions of dollars into the work of God. If you're called to the ministry, you may be dreaming of preaching the gospel around the world.

Yet, as wonderful as those goals may be, there is something even more important you can accomplish. It is something you as a believer should "eagerly pursue and seek to acquire." It should be "your aim, your great quest."

What is this great quest? It is the goal of living a life ordered by and overflowing with the love of God.

Love is the foundation for the Christian life. Nothing works without it, and when it is in operation, success is guaranteed. When you walk in love, you put yourself in a position where God Himself can protect and promote you. When you exchange selfishness for love, when you stop seeking to be BLESSED and begin seeking ways to spread THE BLESSING, the Father Himself goes to work on your behalf. He will allow no man to harm you (1 Chronicles 16:21). No weapon that is formed against you will prosper. Even the devil himself can't damage you (1 John 5:18).

The Bible says God is love (1 John 4:8). So when you get on the side of love, you get on God's side and He gets on yours. And He is a great One to have on your side because when He is for you, no one can stand against you (Romans 8:31-34).

Love is the only commandment Jesus has given us. It is the key to God's wisdom, power and protection. If we fully understood the great return from living in God's love, we would surely make it our primary aim and our great quest. Rather than sitting around waiting for someone else to love us, we'd be competing with each other, each trying to love the other more. And without a doubt, everyone would emerge from that competition a winner!

LIMITLESS**LOVE**

A Sure Sign of Growth

"Let our lives lovingly express truth [in all things, speaking truly, dealing truly, living truly]. Enfolded in love, let us grow up in every way and in all things into Him Who is the Head, [even] Christ (the Messiah, the Anointed One)."
Ephesians 4:15, *The Amplified Bible*

Most Christians today are tired of just "playing church." We're ready to get serious about God. Discontent with carnal ways and immaturity, we want to put childish things behind us and grow up spiritually so we can be like Jesus.

Of course, we're not the first ones to have this desire. The Apostle Paul had it almost 2,000 years ago. He prayed fervently for the day when we would all "[arrive] at really mature manhood (the completeness of personality which is nothing less than the standard height of Christ's own perfection), the measure of the stature of the fullness of Christ and the completeness found in Him" (Ephesians 4:13, *The Amplified Bible*).

Paul not only prayed about that kind of spiritual maturity, he exhorted us as believers to move actively toward it. "Enfolded in love," he said, "let us grow up in every way and in all things into Him…."

That phrase, *enfolded in love,* has really come alive to me in the past few years. I've come to realize more and more that love is the single, most important key to growing up in God. If we don't grow up in love, we won't grow up at all.

That might come as a surprise to some people. They might think that love is so basic, it's something only spiritual beginners must study. They might consider things like the gifts of the Spirit—prophecy, healings and miracles, for example—as more relevant to the mature believer. But the Corinthian church proved the gifts are not marks of spiritual maturity at all. They abounded in spiritual gifts, yet the Apostle Paul referred to them as "mere infants… in Christ…still [unspiritual, having the nature] of the flesh…" (1 Corinthians 3:1, 3, *The Amplified Bible*).

Thank God, we don't have to be like that. We don't have to be perpetually stuck in spiritual infancy. We can keep growing up in Jesus every day.

What's more, we know how to measure our progress. If we want to know whether we're spiritual or not, we won't look to see what mighty gifts of the Spirit we have, we'll look at our love life. The more spiritually mature we are, the more our lives will be marked and ruled by love.

LIMITLESS**LOVE**

Let God Love Others
Through You

"But love ye your enemies, and do good, and lend, hoping for nothing
again; and your reward shall be great, and ye shall be the children of the
Highest: for he is kind unto the unthankful and to the evil."

Luke 6:35

The love of God that flows from the heart of a believer is as different from human love as day is from night. Human love is so changeable it can turn to hate when circumstances aren't right. It can behave with tender affection one moment and jealous rage the next, and be called "love" all the while.

Human love is little more than a phony, emotional counterfeit of God's love. It's dependent on whim and feelings. It says, "If you're nice to me and give me what I want, I'll love you. But if you don't, I won't."

God's love isn't like that. It's constant. It's unconditional. The chief ingredient of the God-kind of love is self-sacrifice for the benefit of the one loved. It is the type of love that will continue to love people whether or not it receives a response. Divine love is not self-seeking. It is self-giving.

God doesn't just love the lovely. He loves the unlovely, too. No matter how bad, mean or resistant someone might be, if that person will turn to Him, He'll cleanse and forgive. He'll let that person partake of the sacrifice of His Son, Jesus, so he or she can have a new life in Him.

That's the way God loves us, and that's the way He expects us to love each other. That means when someone treats us badly, we don't get huffy about it. We don't get fretful and resentful. Instead, we treat them kindly, pray for them and refuse to think about how they did us wrong.

Walking in love means we lay down our own rights and look out for the other person's rights instead. When we're tired and under pressure, we lay down our right to let people know about it by snapping at them and telling them what a hard day we've had. We set aside our own feelings and behave kindly and gently to those around us.

"That sounds pretty tough," you might say. "I'm not sure I could trust myself to do that!"

Then don't trust yourself. Trust God to do it through you! Say, "LORD, I can't love this way on my own, so I'm trusting in You today. As I step out in faith by speaking and acting in a loving way, I'll expect Your love within me to come shining through!"

Just rely on The LORD, and you'll be amazed how He can love others through you!

LIMITLESSLOVE

Our One Responsibility

"If I speak in the tongues of men and of angels, but have not love, I am only a resounding gong or a clanging cymbal. If I have the gift of prophecy and can fathom all mysteries and all knowledge, and if I have a faith that can move mountains, but have not love, I am nothing. If I give all I possess to the poor and surrender my body to the flames, but have not love, I gain nothing."
1 Corinthians 13:1-3, *New International Version*

If I have not love…I am nothing.

As far as God is concerned, love is the bottom line. Nothing counts without it. Without love, the gifts of the Spirit don't amount to anything. Without love, your faith won't work. Without love, your giving doesn't count.

In short, you and I can't go anywhere spiritually until we get our love life straight. When you think about how important love actually is, it's amazing we haven't emphasized it more. After all, love is our only law. God didn't give us a long list of rules to memorize. We don't even have ten commandments like the Israelites did. Jesus said, "This is my [one!] commandment, That ye love one another, as I have loved you" (John 15:12).

How do we keep that one commandment? By doing one, wonderfully simple thing. We do it by staying in contact with Jesus! We do it by fellowshiping with Him and obeying Him.

The more intimately we know and walk with Him, the more His love will flow through us. And the more we walk in love the more intimate our fellowship with Him becomes. It's a glorious cycle that continually lifts us higher.

Few people have captured this precious truth better than Rufus Moseley, a great man of God who passed over many years ago. The Lord spoke these words to him. *Go in love and I shall always be with you.* As Brother Moseley meditated on these words, he wrote:

The master key of the kingdom of heaven, of abiding union with Jesus had been given me. "Go in love and I shall always be with you…. Your only responsibility is the responsibility of being in union with Me…." Life in Jesus is gloriously easy and has but one responsibility, the responsibility of remaining in that union [with Him].[3]

---

[3] J. Rufus Moseley, *Manifest Victory* (Saint Paul: Macalester Park Publishing Company, 1986) p.117, 121.

LIMITLESS**LOVE**

Wash the Hindrances Away

"Wherewithal shall a young man cleanse his way? by taking heed thereto according to thy word."
Psalm 119:9

Once you understand that love, as a fruit of the spirit, abides within the reborn spirit of every Christian, you might wonder why believers so often act like we do. If we are loving by nature, why are we sometimes the meanest things on two legs?

It's because we haven't cultivated that new nature. We've simply kept yielding to fleshly habits we developed over the years. We give in to the devil's badgering, doing what our old sin-trained body wants to do instead of what the new man (or what 1 Peter 3:4 calls "the hidden man of the heart") wants to do. As a result, our fleshly nature obstructs our new nature and inhibits its expression.

How do we remove that obstruction? How do we cleanse ourselves from those old habits so the love of God can be freely expressed in our lives?

One way is by reading and meditating on The WORD of God. Ephesians 5:26 tells us we're cleansed and sanctified by the "washing of water by The WORD."

I saw one of the best illustrations of that truth in Ken's life years ago when he tried to quit smoking. Although he wasn't in the ministry yet, he was born again, loved God with all his heart and wanted to live pleasing before Him. But he had been a serious smoker for years and the habit had a strong hold on him.

He struggled for months to overcome it. Sometimes, he'd be driving down the highway and have such a desire to stop smoking that he'd throw his cigarettes out the window. Within a few miles however, his flesh would rise up and demand a cigarette and he'd go back and find the pack he'd thrown away!

All that changed, however, when he went to a meeting in Houston where he heard The WORD preached twice a day, every day for three weeks. As he was driving home from the last meeting, he realized he hadn't smoked in days. He'd been so immersed in The WORD of God, the habit that once seemed impossible to break had simply been washed away.

Want to rid yourself of old, selfish thoughts and actions that have stopped God's love from flowing through you? Spend some serious time meditating on scriptures about love. Take heed to them and let them cleanse you. If you'll apply it, the separating power of The WORD of God will go to work in you!

LIMITLESS LOVE

Be Strong and Win the Battle

*"This I say then, Walk in the Spirit,
and ye shall not fulfil the lust of the flesh."*
Galatians 5:16

When you were born again, your spirit was re-created in the image of Love Himself. Think about it. God is the greatest Lover of all time and as a partaker of His divine nature (2 Peter 1:4), you're a lover, too!

As you've already discovered, however, walking according to that loving nature is no stroll in the park. There's a struggle involved. As Galatians 5:17 says, "the desires of the flesh are against the Spirit, and the desires of the Spirit are against the flesh; for these are opposed to each other…" *(Revised Standard Version).* So when you decide to obey the desires and promptings of your reborn spirit, your untrained flesh starts to fight you.

If you want to win this battle, you have to keep your spirit strong by putting God first place in your life. You have to stay spiritually healthy by fellowshiping with Him through His WORD. The more of His WORD you put in your heart, the stronger your spirit becomes. If you'll continue to feed on The WORD, eventually it will be so powerful, it will overcome the flesh every time (Hebrews 5:14).

The opposite is also true. If you spend your time feeding on soap operas, romance novels and the evening news, your flesh will grow stronger and your spirit will weaken. And though you'll still have the inner desire to be loving and kind, the flesh will bully you into acting like the devil!

Jesus said, "If ye continue in my WORD, then are ye my disciples indeed; and ye shall know the truth, and the truth shall make you free" (John 8:31-32). Notice, Jesus said continue in The WORD. He didn't say read The WORD now and then when you feel like it. He said stay in The WORD continually because it will make you free from the bondages of the flesh, so you can walk in the spirit. Your spirit will become stronger and begin to dominate the natural desires of your flesh.

You'll still face a battle. When you're driving down the highway, for example, and someone cuts rudely in front of you, your flesh will still tempt you to become angry and shake your fist at them. But if your spirit is strong, you'll win that battle without breaking a sweat. Yielding to the love within you, you'll smile and say, "LORD, bless that person and help them get safely to where they're going today."

So, stay in The WORD and be strong. Start every day by making a decision to walk in the spirit, and then do everything you can to act on that decision all day long. It won't always be easy, but it will always be worth the effort because when you walk in the spirit, you'll live like the lover you were born again to be!

LIMITLESS**LOVE**

Healthy...Happy...and Wise

"Let nothing be done through strife or vainglory; but in lowliness of mind let each esteem other better than themselves."
Philippians 2:3

Did you know that walking in love is good for your health? That's right! Medical research has confirmed it.

Researchers discovered there are two kinds of stress. The first is the kind you experience when you're working hard to achieve something—pressing yourself to reach a goal. This kind of stress, they found, is natural and good. It doesn't hurt you.

The second kind of stress, however, has such a negative effect that it's physically dangerous. It is caused by hostility or anger toward others.

When you think of hostility, you may think of the type of anger you feel when facing some serious threat, but according to medical studies, this isn't what really causes the problem. It's the little things. It's the anger you feel when the dry cleaners ruins your favorite outfit, for example. Or when the server at the cafeteria puts gravy on your mashed potatoes after you've specifically told her not to.

In short, what researchers have discovered is what God has been telling us all along. When things like that happen, we need to immediately forgive the person responsible, release the offense and let it go. We need to resist our natural, selfish desire to give that person "a piece of my mind" and treat them kindly instead. In other words, we need to walk in love.

Imagine the benefits of living like that. What would happen to stomach ulcers and tension headaches if we never paid any attention to a suffered wrong? How much stress would we avoid if we were quick to forgive? Clearly, we weren't made to live with hostility flowing through us. We were designed to live by love.

If we'll do that, we'll not only be healthier—we'll be happier. It's impossible for a selfish person to stay happy because they're constantly stewing about someone who did them wrong...or some circumstance that didn't go their way...or how much they have to do.

When we're living selfishly, we're miserable because we're not made to live that way. God made us to think more about pleasing Him and serving others than about pleasing ourselves. And the more we do that, the harder it is for the devil to upset us.

Think about it. Living a life of love is good for our health and our happiness. Isn't God smart? Everything He instructs us to do is for our good. If we're wise, we'll obey Him and experience the best life He has to give!

LIMITLESS**LOVE**

Loose Me and Let Me Go!

"When [Jesus] thus had spoken, he cried with a loud voice, Lazarus,
come forth. And he that was dead came forth, bound hand and foot with
graveclothes: and his face was bound about with a napkin. Jesus saith unto
them, Loose him, and let him go."
John 11:43-44

In light of the overwhelming benefits of living the life of love, why do we, as believers, so often fail to do it? Usually, it's because we're still wrapped up in old, worldly habits of thinking and reacting. We continue to live from the outside instead of from the inside where God (who is Love) dwells.

We're in much the same condition Lazarus was in immediately after Jesus raised him from the dead. You probably remember the story from John 11. Jesus' friend Lazarus had been dead four days. But Jesus ordered the tomb to be opened and called his friend back from the dead.

In response to the Master's voice, Lazarus came forth from the tomb but the Bible says he was still bound up. The grave clothes were wrapped around him. Even though there was life within him, he was unable to move freely so Jesus said to those standing by, "Loose him and let him go"!

That's a good illustration of our situation. When we are first born again, our spirit man comes alive with the very life of Christ Himself. We are spiritually born of God. But the self-centered habits we acquired as spiritually dead sinners are still in place. They still have us bound. For us to be free to walk in the new life God has put within us, those deadly habits of selfishness, unforgiveness, irritation and impatience have to be removed.

How does that happen?

As we fellowship with The LORD in prayer and put His WORD in our hearts, His truth makes us free (John 8:32). Then we can say to each one of those deadly habits, "I refuse to be held down. I'm going to walk in love. I'm putting hate, unforgiveness and selfishness behind me. I'm going forward in the power and the glory of God. So loose me and let me go!"

It doesn't take weeks or months to switch over from natural to supernatural living. For a born-again follower of Jesus, all it takes is union with Him and a decision to yield to the force of love.

God has already placed His love within you. So don't keep it locked inside. Dare to do what the Bible says and put on the new man created after God (Colossians 3:10). Strip off those grave clothes and find out just how good it is to be free!

Forget Past Failures

"Hope does not disappoint, because the love of God has been poured out within our hearts through the Holy Spirit who was given to us."
Romans 5:5, *New American Standard*

Spiritually speaking, love comes naturally to every believer. No matter how selfish or wicked a person may be, when he is born again, God puts Himself and His own nature inside that person. He literally pours His love into the human heart through the Holy Spirit.

Ken and I have seen dramatic evidence of that truth firsthand. We know people who were so hardhearted before they were saved, they could kill and have no remorse. They absolutely had no conscience to bother them. Yet, after they made Jesus LORD of their lives, they became the most tender, compassionate people you could ever meet.

There is no doubt about it. God does for each of us exactly what He promised in Ezekiel 36:26: "A new heart also will I give you, and a new spirit will I put within you: and I will take away the stony heart out of your flesh, and I will give you an heart of flesh." The moment we receive Jesus as LORD and Savior, He takes out our stony heart of sin and gives us a new heart of love *(The Living Bible)!*

That's especially important for you to remember if you've stumbled recently and fallen into unloving behavior. You'll be tempted to forget what God has done in you and focus on your own failure.

But, don't do it. Stir up your faith by focusing on God's WORD instead. Remind yourself that love is your supernatural, natural disposition. It may not look like it at times. But as a believer, you walk by faith and not by sight (2 Corinthians 5:7). Therefore, simply because the Bible says so, you believe you were born to love!

The love in you isn't the kind you see on television or in the movies, either. It's the God-kind of love. It's the kind of supernatural love described in 1 Corinthians 13—the kind that loves when no one loves back. Its hallmark is unselfishness. It joyfully sacrifices itself for the benefit of the loved one.

If you haven't been yielding to that love, just repent and receive God's forgiveness. Forget past failures, step out in faith and confess what the Bible says about you.

Say, "I am a love creature. God has re-created my spirit in the image of love. He has sent His love Spirit to live in me and teach me how to love as He loves. I can live the life of love!"

Then put your faith to work. Do something loving. Say something kind. I guarantee if you'll do that, you'll quickly find rivers of divine love pouring through you!

LIMITLESS**LOVE**

The Protective Power of Love

"In righteousness shalt thou be established: thou shalt be far from oppression; for thou shalt not fear: and from terror; for it shall not come near thee. Behold, they shall surely gather together, but not by me: whosoever shall gather together against thee shall fall for thy sake…. No weapon that is formed against thee shall prosper; and every tongue that shall rise against thee in judgment thou shalt condemn. This is the heritage of the servants of The LORD, and their righteousness is of me, saith The LORD."
Isaiah 54:14-15, 17

If we fully understood the blessing that walking in love brings us, we wouldn't abandon it so easily when we encounter pressure or aggravation. If we knew, for example, that becoming fretful or resentful would cost us the divine protection God has provided for us as His children, we'd be more apt to set those unloving attitudes aside.

Walking in love puts us in a position where God can protect us. It puts us in the center of His will where no weapon formed against us can prosper. When we stop fighting for ourselves, God can fight on our behalf…and He *always* wins.

You can see that fact borne out in the life of Jesus. He always walked in love—not just when people were praising Him, but also when He was bitterly rejected and mistreated. First Peter 2:23 says, "…When he was reviled, [he] reviled not again; when he suffered, he threatened not; but committed himself to him that judgeth righteously."

As a result, no man and no demon could touch Him. When the people at Nazareth tried to throw Him off a cliff, He just walked through the midst of them. When the soldiers came to arrest Him in the garden of Gethsemane, they all fell to the ground under the power of God. If Jesus had not given Himself up, He could never have been crucified because He alone had the power to lay down His life. No one could take it from Him because He lived the life of love.

Remember that when it looks to you as if love will make you the underdog instead of the victor. At those times, when you're wrongly treated and it appears being patient and kind will be to your disadvantage, your flesh will rise up and say, "Now wait a minute! If I walk in love, people are going to run right over me."

But don't listen to your flesh. Instead, tune in to your spirit and remind yourself of how God protected Jesus. Keep living the love life just like He did, and the same power that protected Him will do the same for you!

LIMITLESS**LOVE**

Study the Manual

"This is love, that we walk according to His commandments...."
2 John 6, *New American Standard*

We hear a lot of talk about love these days. But, the truth is, few people really know what it is. For most, it's an emotional phantom that appears—then vanishes—without warning. Illusive. Undefinable. Forever sought, but rarely found.

Even Christians seem to be confused about it at times. But they don't need to be. The WORD of God reveals clearly what love truly is. It tells us, quite simply, that love is keeping the commandments of God. It is knowing and obeying His WORD.

Thank heaven, God didn't leave us wondering about love. He didn't make us struggle along with some indefinite, hazy idea about it. He made it clear and easy to define. Throughout the Bible, He gave us instructions so we could know how to love as He loves. He gave us His Manual in black and white! All we have to do is follow it, and we'll be walking in love.

This is especially important for us to know these days because as the world around us grows more sinful, people are becoming increasingly confused about love. They think doing anything that feels good is loving. They even excuse immoral lifestyles, all in the name of love.

Becoming a Christian doesn't make you an instant expert on love, either. Although the love of God was born within you the moment you made Jesus Christ The LORD of your life, initially you're a spiritual baby. It's only by feeding on The WORD of God and learning how love acts that you leave spiritual infancy behind and develop the maturity to walk in love.

Nothing—absolutely nothing—is more important than learning to love. So study the Manual God has given you. It will teach you how to make the love that's inside you show up on the outside. As you act on God's WORD, His love will be perfected in your life, and others will see Jesus in you.

LIMITLESS**LOVE**

An Open Door of Love

"A new commandment I give to you, that you love one another, even as I
have loved you, that you also love one another. By this all men will know
that you are My disciples, if you have love for one another."
John 13:34-35, *New American Standard*

Years ago, a popular song said, "What the world needs now is love, sweet love."
Remember it? Usually, secular songs are way off base, but that one was very nearly right.
All you have to do is change one word and it's perfectly scriptural.

What the world needs now is love, *God's* love.

The world is starving for the love of God. Every person in it has been created with a
desperate need for divine love. Their deepest yearning is to be treasured and cared for so
completely that all their hurts and fears just melt away.

Of course, only their Creator can care for them like that. Only He can satisfy their love-
hungry heart. But most people don't know that, so they keep looking for love in all the wrong
places. They keep reaching out and being disappointed again and again.

Where's the solution to this sad situation?

It's inside you! As a born-again believer, you are the open door into the love of God for
the people with whom you come in contact. You have the power and the privilege to love
them with His own love! By loving others the way Jesus loves you, you can demonstrate God's
love to those who are looking for it. They will be drawn to Him through you.

"I don't know," you might say. "I don't think I can really do that."

Sure, you can! As Christians, love is our commandment, and God wouldn't have given it
to us if we didn't have the ability to keep it.

What's more, the Bible says God's love is the distinguishing mark of every believer. We're
made in the image of our heavenly Father, and because He so loved the people of the world,
we can love them, too!

In fact, by the power of God within you, you can love so deeply and so well, people will
know just by watching you that you're a disciple of Jesus. They'll literally find His love in you…
and that's what they've been looking for all along.

Going Forward...
or Slipping Back?

"For every one that useth milk is unskilful in The WORD of righteousness:
for he is a babe. But strong meat belongeth to them that are
of full age, even those who by reason of use have their
senses exercised to discern both good and evil."
Hebrews 5:13-14

If you want to check up on your spiritual growth and see if you're making progress in The LORD, examine your love walk. Since our goal is to grow up into the image of Jesus, and He is Love, you can be assured that the more loving you become, the more you're maturing and becoming like Him.

"To be honest, I can't tell if I'm making progress in The LORD," you might say. "Some days I walk in love––other days I don't. It seems, at times, I take one step forward and then two steps back!"

If that's the case, what you may need to do is make what Kenneth calls a "quality decision." That's a decision about which there can be no debate and from which there is no turning back.

You are the one who has to make the decision to perfect the love of God in your life. No one else can do it for you. But if you make that decision in faith and commit yourself to strengthen your heart by feeding on God's WORD about love, you can be absolutely sure The LORD Himself will back you up all the way. He will teach you what you need to know and give you the strength in hard times to keep going and growing in love.

But I'll warn you, there *will* be some hard times. There will be times when you would rather do anything than walk in love. (It will seem as though it is taking off a pound of flesh!) There will be times when your natural senses pressure you to go ahead and get mad, to seek your own and retaliate.

That's because love is directly opposed to the senses. They have been trained to selfishly seek their own way. But love, The WORD says, does not seek its own rights or its own way. And to walk in love, you must demand that your senses––your flesh—be subject to The WORD.

Without making a quality decision, you will not be able to do that. You'll crumble and yield to the pressure of the moment, then regret it later. So, commit yourself now to live a life ruled by love. Then, when temptation comes, you'll remember your decision, and make the right choice.

You'll take another step forward instead of taking two steps back. You'll look a little more like the Master as you go on—and grow on—in love!

LIMITLESS**LOVE**

Faith Works by Love

"For in Jesus Christ neither circumcision availeth any thing, nor uncircumcision; but faith which worketh by love."
Galatians 5:6

I'm a faith person. I believe deeply in the importance and the power of faith. Yet, I'll be the first to say that faith, by itself, is not enough to make us more than conquerors. We must also have love because the Bible clearly tells us that faith works by love.

Love actually inspires faith. It gives faith a foundation to build on. You might even say love gives us reason to believe. Think about the love of God, for example. His love for us is the foundation of our faith in Him. John 3:16 says He "so loved the world, that he gave his only begotten Son," so that by believing in Him we wouldn't perish but have everlasting life.

Imagine it! God sacrificed His very own Son for us, and what prompted Him to do it was love. Actually, it's His great love that prompts Him to do everything He does for us. It's His love that provides exceeding great and precious promises that bless us both in this life and in the life to come. It's His mighty love that causes His mercy to be new toward us every morning.

Over the years, I've noticed that people who don't grasp God's love aren't able to have much faith in His WORD. They struggle and try to believe, but when push comes to shove, their faith falters and fails. Why? Because they don't have a revelation of love to back it up!

On the other hand, when we truly begin to understand and experience how full of compassion God is toward us, we can easily believe He'll keep His promises to us. When we know how much God cares, we can trust Him to do what He says. We can have faith that He'll take care of us in every situation.

In his wonderful book *Christ the Healer,* F.F. Bosworth writes, "I have seen faith rise 'mountain high' when the truth of God's present love and compassion begins to dawn upon the minds and hearts of the people. It is not what God *can* do, but what we know He *yearns* to do, that inspires faith."[4] Remember that when you find yourself struggling to trust The LORD. Spend some time in fellowship with Him, feeding on His words of love for you. Receive and act on them in your relationship with others. You'll soon see for yourself that faith truly does work by love.

---

[4] F.F Bosworth, *Christ the Healer* (Grand Rapids: Fleming Revell, 1973) p. 63.

LIMITLESS**LOVE**

Don't Let Anyone Steal Your Joy

"If ye keep my commandments, ye shall abide in my love;
even as I have kept my Father's commandments, and abide in his love.
These things have I spoken unto you, that my joy remain in you, and that
your joy might be full."
John 15:10-11

Do you want to live a truly joyful life? Then walk in love because joy and love flow together!

If you think about it, you can easily see why. In this world, we're surrounded by selfish people. They're on the highways honking and gesturing and cutting rudely in front of us. They're in the workplace, saying harsh and unkind things. Sad to say, you'll even encounter them in church, ignoring you instead of giving you a smile and a warm hello, snapping at you because you didn't do something just right.

If you don't walk in love, someone will steal your joy before lunchtime, because there is always someone out there who will be mean to you. They don't necessarily do it on purpose (any more than you and I do!), but they're human. And, apart from the influence of God, human beings are naturally selfish. They'll say something ugly to you or wrong you in some way and ruin your whole day. You can end up thinking about it and letting it eat at you until you become decreasingly joyful and increasingly upset!

Living a life of love, however, will alter that progression. Why? Because "love endures long and is patient and kind...it is not touchy or fretful or resentful; it takes no account of the evil done to it [it pays no attention to a suffered wrong]" (1 Corinthians 13:4-5, *The Amplified Bible*). Love enables you to overlook the offenses of others and let them go free. Love makes you think differently. Instead of thinking, *How dare she say such an unkind thing to me? I'll give her a piece of my mind!* love makes you think, *She must really be hurting inside to say such a mean thing to me. I wonder if there's anything I can do to encourage her or if there is any way I can help?*

I can't tell you how many times that has happened to me. There have been situations where someone mistreated me, and by the grace of God, I resisted the fleshly reaction to get angry. I just said to myself, *I'm not touchy, fretful or resentful, because I choose to yield to the love of God.* Then, instead of lashing out, I was able to look at that person right in the eye, smile and speak a blessing, instead.

As a result, no one was able to steal my joy. Because of love, I was able to go on my way and have a delightful day in The LORD!

Don't Block the Path of
THE BLESSING

"A sound heart is the life to the flesh:
but envy the rottenness of the bones."
Proverbs 14:30

If you want to find out more about what love really is, one way to do it is by finding out what love is *not*. And one thing the Scriptures clearly say is that love isn't envious of others (1 Corinthians 13:4).

If you think envy isn't a problem for you, you'd better think again. The Bible reveals that envy is a common, human condition. It was a problem for Cain in the book of Genesis, it was a problem for King Saul during the days of young David, it was a problem for the Jews in the book of Acts, and unless we guard against it, it will be a problem for us, too!

Envy can be defined simply as "a feeling of discontent and ill will because of another's advantages, possessions or success." Such feelings often sneak up on us without our notice.

We go to church rejoicing, for example, just thanking God for THE BLESSING. When we drive into the parking lot, however, we see Sister Susie getting out of her new car. Suddenly, we're not rejoicing quite as much. *Why on earth did she get a new car?* we think. *Her old car was better than the one I have now! What's more, I've been standing in faith for a new car and she hasn't….*

Watch out for thoughts like that. They're warning signs of envy. If you keep thinking them, you'll end up unhappy about another's advantage or success. You'll find yourself on the road of envy, and every step on that road is a step away from love.

Of course, just because you had an envious thought doesn't mean you have envy in your heart. Those thoughts are just invitations from the devil and the flesh. They're signals that let you know you're being tempted to go in that direction.

So be quick to recognize those envious thoughts and resist them. Give them no place in your heart or your life. Speak words of love instead. Say, "LORD, I praise You for giving my sister that new car. I rejoice that THE BLESSING is working in her life!" Then congratulate Sister Susie. Share in her excitement the way you'd want her to share in yours.

Stay in faith and keep walking in love. Refuse to let envy block the path of THE BLESSING, and before long, your new car will be in the parking lot. Then Sister Susie will be the one congratulating you!

LIMITLESS**LOVE**

No Excuse for Envy

"Let us walk honestly, as in the day; not in rioting and drunkenness,
not in chambering and wantonness, not in strife and envying.
But put ye on the Lord Jesus Christ, and make not provision for the flesh,
to fulfil the lusts thereof."
Romans 13:13-14

Although envy makes its first moves on us in subtle, seemingly insignificant ways, we should be aware from the beginning that envy in any form is a major enemy of love. What begins as a slight feeling of irritation and inferiority that comes when someone has the finances and the finesse to dress more stylishly than you, can, over time, become full-blown malice and hatred toward that person. If you keep yielding to those thoughts and feelings of aggravation, you can end up speaking slanderous words against them, defaming their character and truly injuring them—all because you didn't deal with your envy about their wardrobe!

Envy, when allowed to fester in the human heart, is a terrible thing. It becomes a demonic force and opens the door to the most ungodly, unloving behavior. Envy was behind the first murder ever committed. Cain envied Abel because the Lord found Abel's offering more acceptable than Cain's. It's hard to imagine murdering someone because they gave a better offering than you, but that's what Cain eventually did!

That, by itself, is shocking enough. But the Bible also tells us that the Jewish leaders actually handed Jesus over for crucifixion for the same reason. They did it because they envied His ministry (Mark 15:10). They envied His power and influence with the people.

Why is it important for us to know that? Because if we're not watchful, the devil will pressure us into acting the same way. He'll subtly introduce envy into our thoughts and into our emotions. He'll even use spiritual things to do it!

If we're not aware of and resistant to his devices, the devil will have us resenting a fellow believer because he operates in the gifts of healings and we don't. He'll have us opposing somebody else's ministry because they're having more success than we are. And no doubt, he'll have us covering it all with spiritual excuses.

Let's settle the fact right now that there is no excuse for envy. Let's make up our minds and hearts in advance that we'll make no room for it in our lives.

The Bible makes it plain just how serious envy can be by putting it in very wicked company. It's listed along with murder, fornication and strife (Romans 1:28-29). So when it rears its ugly head, don't take it lightly. Stomp it out before it takes you out, and protect your walk of love.

Let Your Brother Be an Inspiration to You

"…The LORD had respect unto Abel and to his offering: But unto Cain and to his offering he had not respect. And Cain was very wroth, and his countenance fell. And The LORD said unto Cain, Why art thou wroth? and why is thy countenance fallen? If thou doest well, shalt thou not be accepted? and if thou doest not well, sin lieth at the door. And unto thee shall be his desire, and thou shalt rule over him. And Cain talked with Abel his brother: and it came to pass, when they were in the field, that Cain rose up against Abel his brother, and slew him."

Genesis 4:4-8

Sometimes, you must defeat the enemy of envy by admitting that someone else is doing something better than you are. You have to swallow your pride and acknowledge that a brother is enjoying a greater blessing because he's been walking in greater obedience or greater wisdom than you have been. At those times, you may have to humble yourself and ask his help to keep from harboring envy in your heart.

If Cain had done that, his life would have had a far different ending. Just think what could have happened if he'd gone to Abel and said, "Brother, The LORD isn't receiving my offering. He says sin is at my door. You seem to be walking in a way that's more pleasing to The LORD than I am. Will you help me get back on track?" My, what heartache that would have saved—not just for Cain but his whole family!

We need that kind of love and humility in the family of God, today. There have been pastors who have labored in a small church for years who became envious of another pastor who came to town and built a bigger church in just a year or two. Envy will draw not only the pastor but the entire congregation into strife with the other church. Whole cities have been affected because of envy.

But it didn't have to happen that way. The smaller church pastor could have changed everything by humbling himself and saying, "LORD, I must be missing it somewhere. I must not be meeting the needs of the people as I should. Is there something I can learn from this new pastor that will make me a better shepherd of Your sheep?" That pastor could have ruled over the sin of envy that was at his door. He could have said, "Thank God, that man has people coming to his church! I hope he wins this whole town to Jesus. After all, that's what this is all about!"

You can do the same thing in the workplace, at church, in your family—wherever you find yourself getting envious of someone else's blessings. See if they're doing something better than you are. Look at and learn from their success. Instead of following Cain's example and envying your brother, follow love and let your brother become an inspiration to you!

LIMITLESS**LOVE**

The Benefits Are Worth the Pain

"For this is the message which you have heard from the beginning, that we should love one another; not as Cain, who was of the evil one, and slew his brother. And for what reason did he slay him? Because his deeds were evil, and his brother's were righteous.... Everyone who hates his brother is a murderer; and you know that no murderer has eternal life abiding in him. We know love by this, that He laid down His life for us; and we ought to lay down our lives for the brethren."
1 John 3:11-12, 15-16, *New American Standard*

Why is it so hard for us to resist envy and walk in love at times? Why would our flesh prefer to pay the penalty of hating our brother than to endure the pain of admitting he's grown to a place we haven't? Why are we so reluctant simply to rejoice in his success?

Because when we do, our selfish egos take a beating. Our personal ambitions have to die as we lay down our lives for our brother to walk the way of love. Think again about the case of the pastor whose small church is being outgrown by the new church in town. For that pastor to wholeheartedly support the prosperity of that up-and-coming congregation, he has to lay down his own desire to pastor the largest church in town. He has to be willing to let go of the reputation he wanted and let another person have it. And if he will walk in love instead of envy and seek The LORD, his church will also increase. Love never fails. Love doesn't take away. Love brings increase.

Or, bring things closer to home and think of it this way. To overcome envy and walk in love when your co-worker gets promoted before you do means you have to die to your own desire to be No. 1. You have to kill that selfish drive to be the person everyone else is applauding and admiring. The Bible calls that "mortifying your flesh" and says the Holy Spirit Himself will help you do it (Romans 8:13).

In the short-run, such mortification is exceedingly unpleasant to your flesh. But in the long-run, the benefits make the pain worth bearing because the process keeps the door open for THE BLESSING of God to flow freely to you. It also prevents you from falling prey to other demonic devices such as pride, hatred and strife. Those things can rob you of your inheritance as a believer and even cut your life short!

Remember that the next time envy comes knocking, and slam the door in its face. Then go boldly to the throne of grace. Ask God to help you die to that selfish need to be the center of attention and the recipient of men's acclaim. Let Him help you find such security in His love that you can genuinely rejoice when others are promoted, all the while trusting Him to bring you every blessing that belongs to you in Jesus' Name!

The Highest Kind of Wisdom

"But the wisdom that is from above is first pure, then peaceable, gentle, and easy to be entreated, full of mercy and good fruits, without partiality, and without hypocrisy."

James 3:17

Not only is strife one of the major enemies of love, it's downright dangerous.

Ken and I first had that revelation many years ago when we were reading James 3:16. We saw that strife opens the door to confusion and every evil work, so we made a definite decision never to allow it in our home or ministry. From that time on, we began to treat strife just like we'd treat a rattlesnake. We knew it was deadly, so we absolutely refused to let it in our lives.

I can tell you now, that one decision changed everything and made possible the wonderful marriage we have today.

Please understand, when I say we have a wonderful marriage, I'm not saying we never have any disagreements. At times we get crosswise with one another just like everyone else. On occasions, we irritate each other because even though we're growing in The LORD, neither of us is perfect, yet!

When that happens, however, we immediately do something about it. If one of us gets upset and speaks harshly to the other, we quickly repent and ask the other's forgiveness. Then we resolve the issue (or drop it, if necessary) and get back in harmony right away.

I'll be the first to admit, sometimes it's hard to drop an issue when you think you're right about it. But the fact is, *regardless of what issue is involved, if you're in strife—you're wrong.* Even if you're right, you're still wrong because strife itself is ungodly.

First Corinthians 13:5 says, "Love…does not insist on its own rights or its own way…" *(The Amplified Bible).* Therefore when you're walking in love, you won't demand your own way, even when you're convinced your way is right! If you love someone, you'll allow them to have their ways of doing things and their own opinions. Even though you may disagree with those ways and opinions, you'll show respect and be kind to them, anyway. You'll refuse to allow your differences to draw you into strife.

Remember that next time you're tempted to get into an argument with someone. Before you generate strife by spouting the wisdom that proves you're right and they're wrong, test it against James 3:17. Check to see if what you're about to say is pure, peace loving, courteous and gentle. If not, it's best to shut your mouth and keep it to yourself. At times like those, silence can be the highest kind of wisdom…the kind that comes from love.

Bricks, Sticks and Thorns in Your Side

"And Paul, as his manner was, went in unto them, and three sabbath days reasoned with them out of the scriptures, opening and alleging, that Christ must needs have suffered, and risen again from the dead; and that this Jesus, whom I preach unto you, is Christ. And some of them believed.... But the Jews which believed not, moved with envy, took unto them certain lewd fellows of the baser sort, and gathered a company, and set all the city on an uproar, and assaulted the house of Jason, and sought to bring them out to the people."

Acts 17:2-5

To successfully walk in love, not only must you guard your heart against the temptation to envy others, you also have to bear patiently with those who've yielded to that temptation and begun to envy you. That can be a major challenge because envious people are often the meanest, most cruel folks you'll ever meet.

If you want to see just how rough they can be, study the life of the Apostle Paul. The religious leaders who envied his success in ministry continually stirred up trouble against him. Their accusations caused him to be beaten and imprisoned. They stirred up riots and even caused him to be stoned. (Love never fails. God raised him up!) Talk about a thorn in his side! Those envious leaders brought Paul trouble everywhere he went.

When we encounter people like that, difficult as they may be, we still must love them. We must remember that they're not our real problem. The devil himself is the one who's against us, and he's simply using them to get his work done. He's used their insecurities and the lack in their own lives to make them jealous of us.

They're like the poor children someone told about who roamed the neighborhood looking for fruit trees. Because they didn't have the money to buy fruit, they threw bricks and sticks at the neighbor's trees, trying to dislodge a pear or an apple so they could get a treat for free. Obviously, those kids never threw anything at the nonbearing trees. They only attacked the ones that were producing!

Envious people are the same way. They only criticize people who are accomplishing something. They only attack if you excel. If you were mediocre, they wouldn't even bother to mention your name.

So when envious people come against you, don't take offense. Take it as a compliment! Lovingly BLESS those who persecute you, and keep doing what God has called you to do. If the bricks and sticks still cause you pain, apply the words of Jesus to remove the sting. "BLESSED are you when people insult you, persecute you and falsely say all kinds of evil against you because of me. Rejoice and be glad, because great is your reward in heaven..." (Matthew 5:11-12, *New International Version*).

In Luke's account it says to "Rejoice ye in that day, and *leap for joy*" (Luke 6:23). I've done this. It works! On hearing a report like Jesus talked about in Matthew 5:11, I got up from my desk and began to leap and jump and praise God just because Jesus said to do it. My freedom and joy was the result!

LIMITLESS**LOVE**

Take a Step Upward

"God resisteth the proud, but giveth grace unto the humble."
James 4:6

The devil is so determined to undermine your love walk that if he can't trip you up one way, he'll sneak around the back door and trip you up another way. You always have to be watching for him. You can never drop your guard!

If he can't draw you out of love with envy or strife, for instance, he'll get you to think about how well you've been doing. Since Satan is a liar, he can go to either extreme— whatever he thinks will work on you. He'll remind you of all the offenses you've overlooked lately. Before you know it, you'll be silently extolling your own virtues. *I've done so wonderfully this week. I've held my temper. I've refused to be touchy. I'm so proud of myself for walking in love!*

Do you know what will happen next?

You'll fall flat on your face. You'll do or say something so unloving it will shock you. Why? Because what the Bible says is true. "Pride goes before destruction, a haughty spirit before a fall" (Proverbs 16:18, *New International Version*).

Pride is defined as "an over-high opinion of one's self; exaggerated self-esteem or conceit, haughtiness or arrogance; self-esteem arising from one's accomplishments or possessions; an exaggerated idea of one's own dignity or importance." That's just the dictionary definition and it's bad enough. But the Bible goes even further in its description of pride by identifying it as one of the seven things that God hates. Proverbs 6:16-17 calls it an abomination to Him.

You'd think mature believers would naturally steer away from something so despised of The LORD. But actually the reverse seems to be true. Pride becomes the primary pitfall for believers who've begun to enjoy a little spiritual growth and success.

Don't let yourself fall into it. When you're tempted to think about how wonderful you are and how much progress you're making in your walk of love, think instead about the One who gave you the strength to do it. Stop considering yourself and consider Jesus, the One who loved you so much He shed His blood and paid the price for your sin. Remember how selfish you were before He redeemed you, and how selfish you would still be except for His grace.

Pride will quickly give way to humility. Haughtiness will melt into gratitude. And you'll take a step upward instead of taking a fall, as you give all the glory to Him.

LIMITLESS**LOVE**

A Life-Changing Word

"Wherefore, my beloved brethren, let every man be swift to hear,
slow to speak, slow to wrath: For the wrath of man worketh not the
righteousness of God. Wherefore lay apart all filthiness and superfluity of
naughtiness, and receive with meekness the engrafted word,
which is able to save your souls."
James 1:19-21

I haven't known many faithful, Bible-believing, church-going believers who make a habit of obvious, moral sin. Most people I know who are endeavoring to walk uprightly before God don't chronically commit adultery or live a lifestyle of lying and stealing.

But an amazing number of well-respected Christians are so touchy they get mad at the drop of a hat. They'll fuss and fret and talk to others about how someone mistreated them. Most of the time, they won't even realize it's wrong. On the contrary, they may even be self-righteous about it. "I just can't believe she'd talk to me that way," they might say. "Why, that's just gross ingratitude, after all I've done for her!"

I have a wonderful, godly friend who tells how she used to be so touchy and keep such good accounts of suffered wrongs that when she would remind her husband of things he'd said, done or neglected to do that hurt her feelings, he'd be baffled. "I don't recall doing that!" he'd say.

"Well, you did it," she'd answer, "and I can tell you when. It was on March 27, five years ago!"

That may sound strange to you, but to my friend it was normal. She came from a whole family of Christians who did that. They kept an internal record of all the wrongs done in their family for generations and they'd remind each other of them frequently. So when The LORD began to deal with her about love, she had a real job on her hands. For her, being touchy wasn't an occasional problem...it was a way of life!

Do you know what eventually changed her? The WORD of God. She wrote on index cards the phrase from 1 Corinthians 13:5, "Love...is not touchy or fretful or resentful" *(The Amplified Bible)*. Then she put those cards almost everywhere—in her kitchen, in her office at work, in her purse—and looked at them every time she had opportunity to be offended.

Often, she'd read the words out loud and apply them to herself by saying, "I'm not touchy, fretful or resentful." She testifies that before long, the warmth of God began to bubble up in her heart as she said it and she began to change.

Today, she's one of the most loving people I know. She's living proof that the engrafted WORD has the power to save the soul.

LIMITLESS**LOVE**

The Love That Just Won't Quit

"But the fruit of the Spirit is love, joy, peace, patience, kindness, goodness, faithfulness, gentleness, self-control...."
Galatians 5:22-23, *New American Standard*

Just as works of the flesh, such as envy and strife, are enemies of love, the fruit of the spirit is love's faithful friend. In fact, love is listed as the first fruit of the spirit because all the others spring from it. Love gives us reason to be patient and kind. It's the motivating power behind faithfulness, gentleness and self-control.

Actually, it's a wonderful cycle. Love becomes the foundational fruit from which the others flow. They, in turn, support love so it can finish its course.

Think about patience, for example, and you'll see what I mean. If you love someone, it's much easier to be patient with them, isn't it? Love gives you the desire to stick with them even when the going gets tough. And patience, once you put it to work, is the powerful force that enables your love to endure those hard times without getting discouraged and giving up.

Patience can be defined as "an even temper or forbearance." It's the quality that doesn't surrender to circumstances or succumb under trial. It girds you up under pressure, persecution, distress and trouble and keeps you steadfast.

"Longsuffering is love on trial, love refined and pure and selfishness conquered."[5] It endures indifference, hate or ill treatment without anger or thought of revenge. In other words, love strengthened by patience just won't quit.

You may not feel like you have that kind of patience. But if you're a child of God, you do. You've been made in His image. You've been given His nature and *The Amplified Bible* says He is "extraordinarily patient" (2 Peter 3:9).

You do, however, have to develop your ability to walk in that patience. You'll have to roll up your spiritual sleeves, so to speak, and learn to let that God-given patience flow through you.

How? First, by spending time with God in prayer and in The WORD—by meditating on His patient love and believing that very same patience is operating in you. Second, by exercising that patience at every opportunity. When the grocery store line is moving slowly, resist the temptation to get irritated, and yield to patience instead. When you're caught in a traffic jam, instead of letting your blood pressure rise, let patience arise in you. Use small situations to practice patience, and you'll find yourself much stronger when the big challenges come.

Certainly, it will take some effort, but if you want to walk in love it is definitely worth your while. Without patience, that walk will be a very short stroll. With it, however, even when life's road gets rough, you'll keep on loving, mile...after mile...after mile.

---

[5] Dr. Lester Sumrall, *The Supernatural Fruit of the Holy Spirit* (South Bend: Sumrall Publishing, reprinted 2003) p. 39.

Patience Will Soften the Fall

"I therefore, the prisoner of The LORD, beseech you that ye walk
worthy of the vocation wherewith ye are called, with all lowliness and
meekness, with longsuffering, forbearing one another in love."
Ephesians 4:1-2

One sure sign that you're not allowing patience to strengthen and support your love is when you say words like: "I've just had it with him. There's no excuse for that behavior and I'm not putting up with it a moment more."

We've all said things like that at times. Usually, we felt quite justified in doing so. We may well have been so certain we were right that we figured God Himself would agree with us and back our judgmental attitude.

The Bible, however, makes it clear He wouldn't. In every situation, it instructs us to be patient with each other and make allowances because we love one another. Galatians 6:2 says it this way. "Bear (endure, carry) one another's burdens and troublesome moral faults, and in this way fulfill and observe perfectly the law of Christ..." *(The Amplified Bible)*.

How often we are tempted not to be patient with each other's faults, but to criticize and judge them instead! How often we refuse to cut any slack for other people. When *we* stumble and sin, however, we're quick to excuse ourselves. "I didn't really mean to do that," we'll say. "I just made a mistake. It wasn't the intent of my heart." It is easy to judge others by their actions and ourselves by our good intentions!

We'll go much further in our walk of love if we'll reverse that procedure, being hardest on ourselves and most lenient with others. One thing that will help us do this is coming to grips with the spiritual truth that if we judge others harshly, we'll eventually experience that same harsh judgment being dealt to us (Matthew 7:1-2). The Bible says that what we give out to others will be given back to us again, "good measure, pressed down, and shaken together, and running over" (Luke 6:38).

It's a sobering, scriptural fact: If we are critical and short-tempered with our brothers and sisters when they fail, they will be critical and short-tempered with us. On the other hand, if we're patient and kind with the shortcomings of others, we'll reap that patience and kindness in return.

None of us is perfect yet. Whether we see them or not, we all have shortcomings that will trip us up at times and bring failure. How painful will that failure be? That depends to a great degree on how we've treated others. If we've been there for them, patiently loving and bearing with their faults, our mistakes will be softened and we'll be surrounded by kindness in our time of failure and need.

Seventy Times Seven

"Then Peter came and said to Him, 'LORD, how often shall my brother sin against me and I forgive him? Up to seven times?' Jesus said to him, 'I do not say to you, up to seven times, but up to seventy times seven.'"
Matthew 18:21-22, *New American Standard*

To patiently bear with each other's weaknesses and keep walking in love, we must develop the habit of forgiving even the most frequent offenses. We must refuse to hold grudges, even against those who treat us unkindly again...and again...and again.

Does that mean we must allow someone to continually abuse us? Most certainly not! God loves us, and He doesn't want us to put ourselves repeatedly in harm's way. At times, He will lead us to distance ourselves from someone who repeatedly mistreats us. But He will always lead us to do it in love, forgiving them as we go.

"I can't do that," you might say. "After what they've done to me, forgiving them would just be too hard."

On the contrary, failing to forgive is what will make your life hard. Unforgiveness can weaken your body and make you sick. It will embitter your mind and darken your days. If you don't forgive the wrong that's been done to you, you'll get up every morning with it on your mind. Instead of having a good day, you'll have a day of aggravation as the thoughts of that wrong cloud your steps. What's more, you'll open the door to the devil, and he'll come to steal, kill and destroy. That's what he does, you know.

So if you can't forgive, simply for the sake of the one who wronged you, do it for your own sake. Don't let that person continue to ruin your life. If they purposely mistreated you and wanted you to be miserable, the best way to thwart their plan is to stop paying attention to what they did. Undermine their efforts by forgiving, forgetting and going happily on your way.

If you feel like you can't do it, ask God to help you, and He'll quickly come to your aid. Simply go to Him by faith and say, "Father, I forgive that person once and for all. As You freely forgave all my sins in Christ Jesus, I freely forgive them."

After that, refuse to think about that wrong anymore. If the devil brings it to your mind, reconfirm your decision and say, "No, I've forgiven that person and I will not entertain those thoughts again."

When you're tempted to contemplate the damage and the hurt that was left behind, just remember that Jesus paid the price for every wrong to be made right. He has the power to restore you. And if you live in His love and forgiveness, you'll live a BLESSED and wonderful life!

LIMITLESS**LOVE**

Supernatural Power—
24 Hours a Day

"And beside this, giving all diligence, add to your faith virtue; and to virtue knowledge; and to knowledge temperance; and to temperance patience; and to patience godliness; and to godliness brotherly kindness; and to brotherly kindness charity. For if these things be in you, and abound, they make you that ye shall neither be barren nor unfruitful in the knowledge of our Lord Jesus Christ.... Wherefore the rather, brethren, give diligence to make your calling and election sure: for if ye do these things, ye shall never fall."
2 Peter 1:5-8, 10

Once we understand that the fruit of the spirit not only springs from love but upholds and supports it, we can see why the Bible so strongly exhorts us to develop that fruit in our lives. It instructs us to not just wait passively for it to grow, but to actively, aggressively pursue it.

Sometimes, however, believers are more interested in pursuing the gifts of the Spirit (such as words of wisdom, knowledge and the gifts of healings and miracles) than the fruit. That's probably because they think the gifts are more powerful. But, actually, that's not the case.

The fact is that, mighty as they are, we can have spiritual gifts operating in our lives and still fail in our walk with God. Many well-known ministers have proven it. They've prophesied and worked amazing miracles in public meetings. But, in their private lives, they've fallen into sin and shipwrecked their faith.

When you have the fruit of the spirit flowing in your life, however, you can be assured you'll never experience such a devastating fall. Why? Because the fruit continually strengthens and supplies you with supernatural power. And unlike the power of spiritual gifts, it's not available just now and then—it's in operation twenty-four hours a day, seven days a week. It's there whenever you need it, anytime of the day or night!

Contrary to popular belief, the fruit of the spirit doesn't just make us pleasant company— although people who have the fruit are delightfully pleasant! The various fruit of the spirit (love, joy, peace, faithfulness, patience, etc.) are mighty spiritual forces that enable us to overcome anything the devil can throw our way.

Each fruit of the spirit releases the power of God to make you victorious in some area of your life. And failing to walk in even one of them can make you vulnerable to the enemy's attacks.

No wonder The LORD tells us to diligently pursue the fruit of the spirit. He doesn't want us to stumble around and miss our destiny. He wants us to run our appointed course and finish it in victory. He knows that if we're strengthened by the fruit of the spirit, we shall *never* fall!

LIMITLESS**LOVE**

Look Into the Mirror

"I thank my God always, making mention of you in my prayers, because I hear of your love and of the faith which you have toward The LORD Jesus and toward all the saints; and I pray that the fellowship of your faith may become effective through the knowledge of every good thing which is in you for Christ's sake."
Philemon 4-6, *New American Standard*

When it comes to love, peace, joy or any other quality of the fruit of the spirit, we can rest assured that regardless of our own fleshly tendencies or past personality traits, we constantly have the fruit of the spirit resident within us. That's because when we made Jesus our LORD, we were born again in His image. We became partakers of His divine nature (2 Peter 1:2-4, *The Amplified Bible*).

Do you want to see what your reborn spiritual nature is actually like? Don't examine your past behavior—investigate the nature of God. Use the Bible like a mirror. Look at God's character revealed there and acknowledge by faith that His character is in you.

God is loving by nature. The Bible says, "God is love" (1 John 4:8).

God is joyful by nature. The Bible says, "in thy presence is fulness of joy" (Psalm 16:11).

God is good by nature. The Bible says that The LORD is abundant in goodness (Exodus 34:6), and good to all (Psalm 145:9).

God is peaceful by nature. The Bible calls Him "the God of peace" (Philippians 4:9).

God is patient by nature. Numbers 14:18 says, "The LORD is longsuffering [patient], and of great mercy…."

God is gentle by nature. King David said to Him, "Thy gentleness hath made me great" (Psalm 18:35).

God is faithful by nature. Psalm 119:90 says, "Thy faithfulness is unto all generations…."

God is meek by nature. Jesus—who is exactly like the Father—said, "I am meek…" (Matthew 11:29).

I don't have a scripture for it but I know God is temperate by nature. If He weren't, He'd have wiped us all out by now.

Truly, our God is wonderful…and He has put His own "wonderfulness" in us! Sometimes that's tough for us to believe, yet to walk in all that He has given us is exactly what we must do.

We can start by obeying Philemon 6 and acknowledge every good thing that is in us in Christ Jesus. We can boldly open our mouths and dare to say, "The love of God is in me. The faithfulness of God is in me. The gentleness of God is in me." As we grow confident in God's nature in us, we'll see that nature coming out and we'll grow into whom we've truly been made to be.

LIMITLESS**LOVE**

Let the Rivers Flow

"Wherefore be ye not unwise, but understanding what the will of The LORD is. And be not drunk with wine, wherein is excess; but be filled with the Spirit; speaking to yourselves in psalms and hymns and spiritual songs, singing and making melody in your heart to The LORD."
Ephesians 5:17-19

In times of pressure or trouble, it's not enough for us just to have the fruit of the spirit residing like a well of water within us, waiting for us to draw it out. We need it gushing up with the force of a fountain. We need it rushing forth like a flood to push back the devil's attack and propel us to a place of victory.

At those times, we need His Spirit within us to be, as Jesus said, like rivers of living water flowing out of our hearts (John 7:38). We must do more than just contain the Spirit of God, we must be *filled* with Him.

Although the Bible teaches we are baptized in the Holy Spirit only once, we can be filled with Him many times. In fact, the literal Greek translation of Ephesians 5:18 says, "be being filled with the Spirit," or being continually and repeatedly filled!

Such fresh fillings come when we spend time in fellowship with The LORD by reading or hearing The WORD, praying, worshiping and singing praises to Him. When we do that, the nature of God inside us is powerfully energized. The love, peace and joy residing quietly within us begins to burst forth in an overflow that pushes every hindrance out of the way!

Think about it from the negative perspective, and you'll see even more clearly what I mean. Imagine a person who hasn't been born again. He has a sinful nature within him, so he naturally and frequently sins. But when a demonic spirit moves in on him, suddenly his sinful nature is more energized. That spirit puts extra force behind the person's sinful flesh and pushes him more fully into sin.

The same thing happens to us in reverse when we actively commune with the Holy Spirit. When we're freshly filled with Him, He joins with us and becomes our helper and our strengthener. He invigorates our righteous nature and gives us a supernatural boost so that God's character not only abides but abounds in us.

Don't wait until trouble comes to get that fresh filling. Abound in advance by starting every day with a time of fellowship, worship and praise. Then when the devil comes dragging in to burden you with his load of cares, he won't even be able to get near you. The force of that river of life flowing from your innermost being will drive him back and you'll hardly even know he was there!

LIMITLESS**LOVE**

Strong in the Spirit
and Steady on Your Feet

"The steps of a good man are ordered by The LORD: and he delighteth
in his way. Though he fall, he shall not be utterly cast down:
for The LORD upholdeth him with his hand."
Psalm 37:23-24

The scripture assures us that if we continue to develop the fruit of the spirit in our lives, we'll finish our spiritual race without a fatal fall. It does not promise, however, that we won't ever stumble. On the contrary, James 3:2 states plainly that on the way to spiritual maturity, "We all stumble in many ways" *(New International Version)*.

Although we certainly don't want to stumble and act in ways that are unloving or unkind, we all do it on occasion. If we'll handle those spiritual spills wisely, however, they won't stop our progress. In fact, they won't even seriously slow us down.

God knew they were coming, and He figured them into the plan of redemption. He included our every failure and every sin—past, present and future—in Jesus' sacrifice on Calvary. Then, in His WORD, He promised that, "If we confess our sins, he is faithful and just to forgive us our sins, and to cleanse us from all unrighteousness" (1 John 1:9).

"Yes," you might say, "that gets rid of my sin, but what do I do about my failure?"

What did you do when you failed in school? They didn't kick you out of school and say, "Well, that's all for you, you can't go any further." No, they simply let you take that course again!

That's what you do when you stumble and fail in the school of the Spirit. You turn to God and find out what to do in order to get that failure straightened out. Then, you simply get up and go at it again!

As believers, we *are* in the school of the Spirit, you know. We're learning, day by day, to walk not after the flesh, but according to the new nature within us. In this wonderful school, the Father is our Principal, and He's so good, that no matter how many times we fail a course, He'll keep letting us take it over again. What's more, the Holy Spirit is our teacher, and we know that with His help, we'll eventually succeed.

Best of all, Jesus has already passed all our tests for us and given us *His* grade! That means the pressure is off. We don't have to prove ourselves or earn our right-standing with God. Because Jesus lived His life perfectly and gave us His report card, we already have straight A's!

What we must do now is learn and grow and go on with God. As we do, we'll stumble less and less. We'll become stronger in the spirit, steadier on our feet and well able to finish our race—with joy.

LIMITLESS**LOVE**

Stay Powerful and Pure

"Keep thy heart with all diligence; for out of it are the issues of life."
Proverbs 4:23

I'll never forget the first time I caught sight of what happens when we're filled with the Spirit and His rivers are flowing powerfully in our lives. I was preparing to preach in the Philippine city of Manila, looking out my hotel window at a huge fountain that was shooting water high into the air.

Suddenly, it struck me that it would be impossible to put any trash in the mouth of that fountain as long as it was overflowing. No matter how hard you tried to keep it there, the force of the water would keep pushing the trash out. Then I thought about Proverbs 4:23 and realized the same thing is true of the re-created human spirit. As long as it's overflowing with the forces of love, joy, peace, patience, kindness, goodness, faithfulness and self-control, the devil won't be able contaminate us with his ugly stuff.

The forces of spiritual life within us will push back the darkness he tries to put on us. They'll repel the evil, deceiving spirits that would try to lead us astray.

How far back it will push them depends completely on us. We can feed our hearts with just enough of The WORD and just enough fellowship with God to keep that fountain barely flowing or we can devote ourselves so fully to Him that the fountain of our hearts shoot spiritual water sky-high!

You may notice I didn't mention what will happen if we neglect our time with God altogether. I don't even want to think about that! When we ignore the things of the spirit, our inner fountain grows stagnant and still. We end up with trash in our lives that we never wanted there.

I've known wonderful believers who've found themselves in that very condition. They fell into sin, got into terrible trouble and never really knew how it happened. But I know how it happened. They simply stopped tending to their spiritual fountains. They tried to live on yesterday's revelation instead of getting something fresh from The LORD for today. As a result, they ended up in a spiritually weakened condition and Satan moved in and took advantage of them.

You don't ever have to let that happen to you. Just stay in daily fellowship with God. Tend to your spiritual life by seeking The LORD first and foremost. Then, the fountain of your heart will continually overflow with the forces of the spirit, and your life will stay powerful and pure. Remember what Jesus said: "But seek ye first the kingdom of God, and his righteousness; and all these things shall be added unto you" (Matthew 6:33).

LIMITLESS**LOVE**

Washing Away the Spots

"As Christ also loved the church, and gave himself for it; that he might sanctify and cleanse it with the washing of water by The WORD, that he might present it to himself a glorious church, not having spot, or wrinkle, or any such thing; but that it should be holy and without blemish."
Ephesians 5:25-27

Not only will the inner fountain of The WORD and the Spirit keep love flowing and growing, it will also wash away the spots and blemishes that mar your spiritual life. It will effectively remove the attitudes and actions that are inconsistent with the walk of love.

Of course, for that to happen, you can't just read your Bible religiously and ignore what it says. You must seek to hear God's voice speaking personally to you. You must make up your mind in advance that when He says something, instead of arguing, you'll agree with Him and change accordingly.

Sometimes that's not easy—especially when you think you're right. One Christian lady, for instance, was upset with her unsaved husband for years and felt totally justified about it. He didn't want to go to church, and she did. He spoke harshly to her, and she wanted him to be kind. He drank and smoked, and she wanted him to stop. As a result, she was perpetually criticizing him and stirring up strife in their home.

One day as she was reading The WORD, she came across Philippians 4:8, "...whatsoever things are true, whatsoever things are honest ...just ...pure ...lovely... whatsoever things are of good report; if there be any virtue, and if there be any praise, think on these things."

Immediately, she knew The LORD wanted her to stop focusing on the things that her husband did wrong and meditate instead on the things he did right. *Oh, no!* she thought. *If I do that, he'll never change!*

It's not your job to change him, said The LORD. *It's your job to love him.*

As this lady agreed with The WORD and asked The LORD to help her change her thoughts, she began to see the good in her husband. She focused on the fact that he was a hard worker. He was generous with his money and cared for the family's needs. Although he didn't go to church, he allowed his family to go. He even cooked dinner for them on Sundays.

Before long, things began to change. The arguments stopped, and despite the unsaved condition of the husband, peace reigned in the home. Once she let The WORD change her attitude, the wife found she could love her husband just the way he was. She discovered that even though circumstances weren't perfect, with the spots and blemishes out of the way, her life could still be a beautiful picture of love.

LIMITLESS**LOVE**

Loving the Unlovely

"Wherefore, my beloved, as ye have always obeyed, not as in my presence only, but now much more in my absence, work out your own salvation with fear and trembling. For it is God which worketh in you both to will and to do of his good pleasure."
Philippians 2:12-13

Have you ever encountered someone who seemed hard (maybe even impossible) to love? Perhaps it was someone who intentionally mistreated you. Perhaps it was someone so self-centered and insensitive that they were constantly rude and irritating.

We all deal with people like that from time to time, and they can present a real challenge to our love walk. For a while, we may be able to treat them with a kind of mechanical kindness, but it won't last long unless our hearts are truly in it. Our willpower will quickly run out because behind our smiling faces and nice words, we are inwardly cold toward those people. We have no genuine sense of love and affection for them.

When you find yourself in that situation, always remember that even though you may not be able to love the unlovely, God can. He loves them with the highest and greatest love. And He has put His own love inside you.

"I know the Bible says that," you may say. "I've heard it many times before. But it's hard to believe when I see so little evidence of it."

That may be true, but believe it anyway because it's believing that brings the evidence. The more you believe God's love is working in you, the more evidence of that love you'll see!

Actually, the fact that you even *want* to love that person is evidence that God is already working within you. Left to yourself, you wouldn't even care about loving them. But, thank heaven, God hasn't left us to ourselves. He is working in us 24 hours a day, both to will and to work for His good pleasure.

The Wuest translation puts it this way. "Wherefore, my beloved ones…carry to its ultimate conclusion [likeness to The LORD Jesus] your own salvation with a wholesome, serious caution and trembling, for God is the One who is constantly putting forth His energy in you, both in the form of your being desirous of and of your doing His good pleasure" (Philippians 2:12-13).

Just think, God is putting forth His very own energy in you! That means you can just forget about how unloving you feel toward that person and meditate on the love God has for them instead. Develop your faith in the power of His love, and you'll soon find He can love even the most unlovely people through you.

LIMITLESS**LOVE**

God Is Planning Something Good for You

"The LORD is gracious, and full of compassion; slow to anger, and of great mercy. The LORD is good to all: and his tender mercies are over all his works."
Psalm 145:8-9

We often talk about the fact that God is love. But as simple as that statement might seem to be, people still misunderstand it. That's because religion has taught them strange things about the love of God. Religion has taught that one day God might make you sick and the next day He might make you poor—all in the name of love. Some preachers have mistakenly said that God will do those things to bless you or teach you something.

But that's religious tradition and it's contrary to The WORD of God. The WORD tells us that because God loves us, He is good to us. What's more, the Bible makes it plain that He's not confused about what's good and what's not. In Deuteronomy 28, for example, where God described the BLESSING and the curse to the children of Israel, we can see that His definition of BLESSING and cursing is exactly the same as ours.

According to that passage, God says it's good when we have more than enough natural provision in our lives. He says it's good if we plant crops to reap big harvests and if we have livestock, for them to increase. He says it's good for our children to be blessed and for us to be physically healthy and whole.

On the other hand, He knows it's bad for us to be sick, poor, frightened and oppressed.

Actually, the Hebrew word *shalom* that The LORD uses so frequently to bless His people means to have wholeness in your life—spirit, soul and body. It means you have nothing missing, nothing broken. God knows that's the way things ought to be, and because of His loving nature, that's the way He wants them to be—not just for a few of His people but for every one of them.

Always remember, God's love and His BLESSING go hand in hand. You can't separate the two. That means you never have to worry about what He's going to do. You can relax, rejoice and trust Him knowing that because He truly loves you, He is planning something good for you!

LIMITLESS LOVE

The Foundation of Our Faith

"How excellent is thy lovingkindness, O God! therefore the children of men put their trust under the shadow of thy wings. They shall be abundantly satisfied with the fatness of thy house; and thou shalt make them drink of the river of thy pleasures."

Psalm 36:7-8

So inseparable is the love and the goodness of God, that in the Bible, we find a single word that joins them together. That word, *lovingkindness,* is used again and again to describe the attitude and the actions of our wonderful, heavenly Father.

I began to grasp how much The LORD wants us to know and understand His lovingkindness toward us a few years ago when the Holy Spirit spoke to my heart very clearly. *I want you to preach the goodness of God,* He said, *and fear not the reproach of men.*

As I began to search out what the Bible has to say about God's love and His goodness, I found it was a theme that ran from Genesis to Revelation. It absolutely amazed me to see how much the Scriptures talk about the goodness of God.

Why do you suppose the Bible—from front to back, Old Testament and New—would so strongly emphasize the simple truth of God's goodness and lovingkindness toward us?

Because it is the foundation of our faith in Him.

The more we know about the goodness of God's love, the more we trust Him. The more we trust Him, the easier it is for us to put our lives into His hands. And only by putting our lives into His hands can we open the way for Him to save us. bless us and work through us so His wonderful will can be done on earth as it is in heaven.

When I began teaching on the goodness of God in my healing services, I saw more miracles and healings than before. People saw from The WORD that God wasn't trying to keep healing from them. Because He loves them and wants them to be well, He was endeavoring to help them receive it. When that truth dawned on their hearts, they were able to reach out to Him by faith and be healed!

I believe that same thing can happen to all of us. The more fully we understand the lovingkindness of God, the more fully we'll be able to surrender ourselves to Him. Once we're free from the fear that He might deprive us of the good things we need, once we're really sure God has our best interests at heart, we'll no longer draw back from Him. Instead we'll trust Him to do us good. We'll have the courage and confidence we need to fully surrender our lives to Him. We'll finally be able to step out in faith and receive everything He has to give!

LIMITLESS**LOVE**

His Love Will Keep You Afloat

"And in the fourth watch of the night Jesus went unto them, walking on the sea. And when the disciples saw him walking on the sea, they were troubled, saying, It is a spirit; and they cried out for fear. But straightway Jesus spake unto them, saying, Be of good cheer; it is I; be not afraid. And Peter answered him and said, LORD, if it be thou, bid me come unto thee on the water. And he said, Come. And when Peter was come down out of the ship, he walked on the water, to go to Jesus. But when he saw the wind boisterous, he was afraid; and beginning to sink, he cried, saying, LORD, save me. And immediately Jesus stretched forth his hand, and caught him, and said unto him, O thou of little faith, wherefore didst thou doubt?"
Matthew 14:25-31

Have you ever wished you were more bold and daring in your faith? Have you ever longed to experience in your own life the kinds of supernatural adventures lived out by the heroes of the Bible?

Think of the times when you sensed the Lord calling you to do something new, to make a change in your life. Like Peter, you heard the voice of the Master calling you across the water of life to new levels in Him. You heard Him say, *Come!* You wanted to step out of your little comfort zone and walk on the water...but you didn't.

Fear stopped you. You saw the wind and the waves in the circumstances around you. You grew timid and shrank back.

If you've done that (and who hasn't?), I have good news for you. You are not doomed to a life of doubt. If you want a change, you can make a change!

You can stop being fear-full and start being faith-full simply by learning more about the love of God. You can study The WORD, and feed your heart on the truths of His goodness until your confidence grows and you know you can trust Him, not just with your eternal salvation but with every aspect of your earthly life as well.

Once your heart truly begins to grasp how much God loves you, you won't be constantly drawing back in fear. You won't be thinking, *What if He doesn't come through for me? What if He asks me to do something that will harm me in some way?*

Instead, you'll be confident in the fact that God will never hurt you. He'll never abandon you or let you down. As long as you follow Him, He'll always be there—loving you, helping you and blessing you.

You'll be bold enough to walk on water if He asks you to because you know His love will keep you afloat.

LIMITLESS**LOVE**

Courage to Slay the Giants

"The LORD is my Shepherd [to feed, guide, and shield me], I shall not lack. He makes me lie down in [fresh, tender] green pastures; He leads me beside the still and restful waters…. Surely or only goodness, mercy, and unfailing love shall follow me all the days of my life, and through the length of my days the house of The LORD [and His presence] shall be my dwelling place."
Psalm 23:1-2, 6, *The Amplified Bible*

The psalmist David is one person in the Bible who truly understood the lovingkindness of God. As a young shepherd tending his flock on the hills of Israel, he fellowshiped with God and came to know His nature. He learned that God is a loving God. He is good, kind and patient. Day by day, David discovered that God would take care of him, provide for him and deliver him from danger.

As a result, David was filled with confidence in God's love, and that confidence made him bold and daring in dangerous situations. When a lion came after the sheep of his flock, David didn't run away. He single-handedly caught that lion by the beard and killed it. When the bear came, David killed it, too.

Later, when everyone in Israel was afraid of the giant Goliath, David was the only one courageous enough to fight him. Although others warned him about the dangers, David showed no fear. He simply said, "The LORD who delivered me from the paw of the lion and from the paw of the bear, He will deliver me from the hand of this Philistine" (1 Samuel 17:37, *New American Standard*).

These words reveal that David not only knew about the love and faithfulness of God, he had seen it work in his life. He'd seen the victories God's love had gained for him and just thinking of them made him bold.

The same can be true of us today. The more we understand about the love of God and the more we see Him at work in our lives, the more victories we'll have to remember. The more victories we remember, the harder it will be for the devil to talk us into letting him run over us.

When the devil tries to convince us that he's going to defeat us this time, he won't be able to do it. We'll remember the lion and the bear in our own lives and think, *If God loved me enough to get me this far, He loves me enough to take me the rest of the way!*

Just like David, we'll stand up by faith and slay the giants that try to stop us from fulfilling God's will. With The LORD as our Shepherd, we'll face every battle without fear, confident in the fact that His goodness, mercy and unfailing love will follow us all the days of our lives.

LIMITLESS**LOVE**

When Others Let You Down

"Although my father and my mother have forsaken me, yet The LORD will take me up [adopt me as His child].... [What, what would have become of me] had I not believed that I would see The LORD's goodness in the land of the living!"
Psalm 27:10, 13, *The Amplified Bible*

Sometimes we're hindered in our ability to love others because we don't feel loved ourselves. We may have felt betrayed or rejected at a young age by those who should have loved us most. So instead of loving people as we know we ought to, we push them away to protect ourselves from being hurt again.

How do we overcome such hindrances?

By daring to believe that God's love for us is great enough to sweep away the pain of the past. His love is wide enough and deep enough and high enough to meet our every need. It will lift us up when others let us down. He will accept and cherish us when others reject us. If we will dare to trust Him regardless of our past experiences, He will supply everything we lack and bless us beyond our fondest dreams.

I can personally testify how very true this is. My life was such a mess when I first learned about God's love and goodness, I often wonder, *What would have become of me had I not believed to see the goodness of The LORD in the land of the living?*

I might not be alive right now. I certainly wouldn't be enjoying THE BLESSING like I am enjoying today. Through the years, as I have continued to trust God with my life, I've seen the evidence of His love continue to increase until it has totally overwhelmed me.

The more I've come to know the lovingkindness of The LORD, the more I've come to believe the only reason God wants us to give our lives to Him is so He can lavishly, without reserve, pour His BLESSING on us. He wants us to be so BLESSED that everywhere we look, we run into manifestations of His love.

I know it sounds too good to be true, but if you think about it, Jesus Himself seems too good to be true. The fact that God sent Him to pay the price for all our sins sounds too good to be true. But it's true, nonetheless. As Romans 8:32 says, "He that spared not his own Son, but delivered him up for us all, how shall he not with him also freely give us all things?"

If you have a history of being rejected and disappointed by others, don't let history repeat itself. Don't let your past become your future. Find out what the Bible says about God's love. If you'll dare to believe it, your world will begin to change in a wonderful way. Before long, you'll not only see His love on the pages of your Bible, you'll see it around you every day of your life.

LIMITLESS**LOVE**

Don't Buy the Lie

"As a father loves and pities his children, so The LORD loves
and pities those who fear Him...."
Psalm 103:13, *The Amplified Bible*

Ever since the Garden of Eden, the devil has been devising schemes to separate people from God. It seems to me, the one that has worked the best for him is causing people to doubt God's love. It succeeded with Adam and Eve, so he's been using it ever since.

I'm sure you know the story. God had provided a perfect place for Adam and Eve to live. He'd BLESSED them and given them everything they needed to be perfectly and abundantly prosperous. There was only one restriction. The LORD told them not to eat of the tree of the knowledge of good and evil, and He warned them that if they did, they would die.

When Satan came to tempt Eve to violate that command, do you remember what he told her? He said, "You will not certainly die.... For God knows that when you eat from it your eyes will be opened, and you will be like God..." (Genesis 3:4-5, *New International Version*). In other words, the devil said, "Hey, God lied to you. He's not protecting you from harm. He's depriving you of something wonderful. He doesn't love you as much as you think."

Eve fell for the devil's lie, but you don't have to. When he tries that line on you, tell him to jump in the lake (the lake of fire, that is!). Hold fast to your confidence in God's love, and remember that everything God tells you to do is for your own good and protection. You're His child and He wants you to obey Him because He wants you to be BLESSED.

That should be easy for you to understand. If you have children, you're the same way with them. You don't make rules for them just to restrict them and make your own life easier. You do it because you want them to stay safe, live long and be happy. You know more than they do, and you have to give them direction and guidance.

You love your children. You don't want to deprive them. In fact, it delights you to do good things for them. Most likely, you'd like to prosper enough to give your child a new car when he or she gets a driver's license. But if that child is rebellious and won't keep the rules of the road, you won't be able to give him a car because you know he'll hurt himself with it. You want your child to abide by the rules you give him not because you're seeking your own good but because you're seeking his good. You want him to obey you because that obedience will open the door for you to bless him.

God is the same way toward us. He loves us just as a father tenderly loves his children, and He wants us to be richly blessed. Don't ever let the devil convince you otherwise. Even when obeying God seems difficult to do, keep in mind your Father's love, and be assured He is endeavoring to get something wonderful to you!

LIMITLESS**LOVE**

God Never Gives Up on You

"The LORD sustains all who fall and raises up all who are bowed down. The eyes of all look to You, and You give them their food in due time. You open Your hand and satisfy the desire of every living thing. The LORD is righteous in all His ways and kind in all His deeds. The LORD is near to all who call upon Him, to all who call upon Him in truth."
Psalm 145:14-18, *New American Standard*

One of the most amazing aspects of God is how full of forgiveness He is. He truly fulfills the description in 1 Corinthians 13 which says that love is "not touchy or fretful or resentful; it takes no account of the evil done to it [it pays no attention to a suffered wrong]" (verse 5, *The Amplified Bible*). God is always forgiving. The blood of Jesus washes away every sin, and no mercy is held back when we turn to God in Jesus' Name.

"But I've failed so many times," you might say. "God has put up with a lot of trouble from me. Surely He's given up on me by now."

No, He hasn't. I know He hasn't, because "love bears up under anything and everything that comes, is ever ready to believe the best of every person, its hopes are fadeless under all circumstances, and it endures everything [without weakening]. Love never fails" (verses 7-8, *The Amplified Bible*). You and I might look at our lives and think there's no hope left for us. We might think we'll never amount to anything. But God's hopes are fadeless where we're concerned. He doesn't give up on us!

On the contrary, He says, "I will not in any way fail you nor give you up nor leave you without support. [I will] not, [I will] not, [I will] not in any degree leave you helpless nor forsake nor let [you] down (relax My hold on you)! [Assuredly not!]" (Hebrews 13:5, *The Amplified Bible*).

Granted, there may be times when we ignore God or disobey Him, and because of that, we're unable to receive from Him the help we need. At those times, it may look like He's forsaken us. But that's our fault, not His. He didn't forsake us. We forsook Him!

Even then, however, if we'll turn back to God, we'll find Him right where we left Him—waiting to love us and do us good.

Of course, the devil will try to stop us from turning to God. One of the most important things to know about the devil is that he can't tell the truth! He'll try to discourage us when we've fallen into disobedience by telling us that we're too unworthy to receive God's love anymore. But don't you believe it. Instead, remember that the Bible says if you'll call on The LORD, He will raise you back up into fellowship with Him. It guarantees that you will not be separated from Him unless you want to be. Because He is Love, He will always be there for you.

From Repentance to Rejoicing

"Oh, that men would praise...The LORD for His goodness and loving-kindness and His wonderful works to the children of men! For He satisfies the longing soul and fills the hungry soul with good. Some sat in darkness and in the shadow of death...because they had rebelled against the words of God and spurned the counsel of the Most High.... Then they cried to The LORD in their trouble, and He saved them out of their distresses. He brought them out of darkness and the shadow of death and broke apart the bonds that held them. Oh, that men would praise...The LORD for His goodness and loving-kindness and His wonderful works to the children of men!"
Psalm 107:8-11, 13-15, *The Amplified Bible*

One of the most beautiful examples of the love and forgiveness of God I've ever seen took place in the life of a young girl who attended Healing School some years ago. A car accident had left her paralyzed on one side of her body and she wanted to turn to God for help. The problem was, she'd been living in sin and rebellion. Before Healing School started, she'd even stolen some tapes from one of our tables!

Of course, she was feeling terrible about herself. Her heart was condemning her, and she didn't think God would do anything for someone as awful as she was. But during Healing School, I read the scripture that says, "The prayer of faith shall save the sick, and The LORD shall raise him up; and if he have committed sins, they shall be forgiven him" (James 5:15).

Thank God, that precious girl simply took God at His WORD that day. She received His forgiveness, and God healed her then and there.

You can do the same thing. If you disobey God, you can step right back into the place of THE BLESSING if you'll immediately repent and say, "LORD, I've sinned. I've done things I knew You didn't want me to do. I ask You to forgive me right now and cleanse me of all unrighteousness. By faith, I receive that cleansing through the blood of Jesus and right-standing with You, in His Name. I set my heart to obey You from now on. With Your help I will do what You want me to do."

How many times can you do that? As many times as you need to!

I'll tell you this, however. If you keep receiving God's forgiveness and letting Him set you back on your feet the moment you stumble, you'll disobey Him less and less. You'll be so grateful for His never-failing love that you'll walk more closely and consistently with Him. Instead of spending your time repenting, you'll spend it rejoicing and praising The LORD for His lovingkindness and His wonderful works to the children of men!

LIMITLESS**LOVE**

That's What I Call *Love*

"If you then, being evil, know how to give good gifts to your children,
how much more will your Father who is in heaven give what is good to those who ask Him!"
Matthew 7:11, *New American Standard*

The devil is constantly trying to distort the image of God. He works night and day to convince us that God doesn't love us. He lies to us and tells us that what we call love and what God calls love are two different things. He says that God's kind of love will hurt us and deprive us of the pleasures and the joys of life.

The devil will even point to the natural disasters and evil in the world and say, "If God is so loving, why do those things happen?"

But, the fact is, every bad and hurtful thing in the world can be traced back to the devil himself. He is the one who tempted Adam and Eve to sin. He is the one who brought poverty, pain and sickness into the world. He is the one who comes to steal, kill and destroy (John 10:10).

If you want to see an undistorted picture of God's love, look back to the Garden of Eden. There you can see just how much God loves people and how good He wants their lives to be. The Garden reveals God's original intent. We can see there what things were like on earth when God's will was being done and the devil had not yet had an opportunity to mess things up.

Back then, everything was totally delightful. (The very word *Eden* means "delight"![6]) Adam and Eve had the best of everything with nothing missing. According to Josephus, a Jewish historian who recorded the oral traditions that were passed down among the Jews, God said to Adam and Eve:

I had before determined about you both how you might lead a happy life without any affliction, care and vexation of soul and that all things might contribute to your enjoyment and pleasure, and should grow up by My providence of their own accord and without your own labor and painstaking.[7]

That's a wonderful picture of God's heart toward us! He wants to give us every good gift imaginable. He wants us to live happy lives without care and vexation of soul. Even when Adam and Eve rebelled against Him and condemned the whole human race to be born into sin, God's heart never changed. He immediately set in motion the plan of redemption. He began making a way for mankind to reconnect with THE BLESSING. Through Jesus, He opened the door for us to come back to the garden of His goodness.

Now that's what I call love.

---

[6] R.L. Harris, *Theological Wordbook of the Old Testament* (Chicago: Moody Press, 1999) p. 646.
[7] *The Works of Flavius Josephus,* Antiquities of the Jews, *Book 1* (Grand Rapids: AP&A Publishers) p. 26.

LIMITLESS LOVE

Hope for Your Future

> "For I know the thoughts that I think toward you, saith The LORD, thoughts of peace, and not of evil, to give you an expected end. Then shall ye call upon me, and ye shall go and pray unto me, and I will hearken unto you. And ye shall seek me, and find me, when ye shall search for me with all your heart. And I will be found of you, saith The LORD: and I will turn away your captivity…."
> Jeremiah 29:11-14

The book of Jeremiah gives us a wonderful picture of how long-suffering the love of God truly is. In Jeremiah's day, the Israelites were totally rebellious toward The LORD. They spurned Him. They talked badly about Him, yet He gave them time to repent. He sent them a prophet who warned them day and night to turn back to The LORD before their enemies took them captive. Because they didn't listen, calamity struck, and the people of Israel were taken into bondage to Babylon.

Even then, God refused to give up on them. As they went into captivity, God already had a plan in motion to gather them back to their land and bring them once again into the place of His promised BLESSING.

Think about all God went through with those disobedient people! They had turned their backs on Him for 40 years. They had rejected the God who loves, the God who only wanted to do them good. Any human being would have washed their hands of a people like that. Any one of us would have said, "OK, go ahead and perish in captivity. You're just getting what you deserve."

But God's mercy is new every morning. He still wanted good for them. He still wanted them to be free. He still wanted to lavish His love on them. Although Israel had entered into captivity by their own choice and through their own fault, instead of condemning them for it, God immediately gave them hope for their future. He promised to turn their captivity and reveal to them an "abundance of peace" (Jeremiah 33:6, *The Amplified Bible*). The Hebrew word translated "peace," *shalom*, is translated "prosperity" or "everything that makes for man's highest good." Isn't that amazing? God didn't tell them He would grudgingly forgive them and give them just barely enough to get by. He said in the time to come, He would give them an abundance of everything for their highest good.

If you're ever tempted to think you've messed things up so badly that there's no hope for your life, remember what God did for the Israelites. Just as He had a plan for them, He has a plan for you. It may take some time for it to unfold, but if you'll trust Him, He can turn your captivity and bring forth a wonderful future for you.

LIMITLESS**LOVE**

That's the Way Love Is

"Oh that they had such a heart in them, that they would fear Me
and keep all My commandments always, that it may be
well with them and with their sons forever!"
Deuteronomy 5:29, *New American Standard*

Although God's merciful attitude toward the Jews in the book of Jeremiah is amazing, it isn't unusual. God has always been that way with His people. Why? Because that's His heart. He is Love and that's simply the way Love is.

Despite the disobedience of God's people and the painful consequences they suffered because of it, His heart always longed to do good for them. When they were in trouble, He hurt for them like we hurt for our children when we see them being disobedient, getting into trouble and suffering harm because of it. He pleaded with them to obey Him because He knew if they would, they could live a free and victorious life.

That was God's heart in the old covenant, and He hasn't changed in the new covenant. You can hear it coming out through the words of Jesus as He sorrowed over the Jewish leaders' rejection of Him as the Messiah. He didn't spurn them. Instead He said, "How often would I have gathered thy children together, even as a hen gathereth her chickens under her wings, and ye would not!" (Matthew 23:37).

That's how God feels about all people. He loves all of us with that same kind of love. As John 3:16 says, "God so loved the *world*...."

That means He could say the same thing about each of us that He said about the people of Jerusalem in Jesus' day. He could say, "How often would I have met your needs and taken care of your children, how often would I have given you the desires of your heart—but you wouldn't turn and listen to Me."

Because we haven't known God's heart nor understood how good He is, there have been times in all our lives when we have felt God didn't care about us. We have had unmet needs, so we thought He had neglected us. But it has been the other way around. We have neglected Him. He has always been ready to heal our bodies. He has always been ready to supply our needs. If we have wanted something good, God has always been ready to give it. We just haven't walked closely enough with Him to reach out by faith and receive it.

As painful as that has been for us, it has been even more so for The LORD because He desires to give even more than we desire to receive. After all, He is Love...and that's the way Love is.

LIMITLESS LOVE

The Perfect Picture of Love

"Philip said to Him, 'LORD, show us the Father....'
Jesus said to him, 'Have I been so long with you, and yet you have not
come to know Me, Philip? He who has seen Me has seen the Father....'"
John 14:8-9, *New American Standard*

As wonderful as the revelations of God's love are in the Old Testament, the most perfect revelation comes to us in the New Testament through His Son, Jesus. He is the fullest expression of the Father's heart. Hebrews 1:3 calls Him "the perfect imprint and very image of [God's] nature" *(The Amplified Bible)*.

Everything Jesus said and did while He was on Earth was an expression of God (John 8:28-29). Therefore, if we want to know what God in His love desires to do for us today, all we have to do is look at the ministry of Jesus.

Acts 10:38 sums up His ministry by saying, "How God anointed Jesus of Nazareth with the Holy Ghost and with power: who went about doing good, and healing all that were oppressed of the devil...." In other words, Jesus went about doing good because that's what God's love always does...it does good things for people!

This is a simple truth but it has to be said because religious traditions have told a different story. Traditions teach God won't always do good things for you, that He's more interested in your observing man-made rules than He is in helping you. That's the way religious people were in Jesus' day, too. They got mad because He healed people on the wrong day of the week. They criticized Him for letting His disciples pick grain to eat on the Sabbath because it violated their religious rules.

But Jesus didn't care about man-made traditions. He cared about people because that's the way God is.

When He saw people were physically hungry, He didn't just turn His back and say, "Oh, they'll be OK. They ought to be fasting more, anyway." No, He said, "I have compassion on the multitude, because they...have nothing to eat" (Matthew 15:32). Then He worked a miracle in order to feed them.

When people were spiritually hungry, Jesus taught them. When people were sick and they came to Him, He healed them. Religious tradition says, "Sometimes God will heal you and sometimes He won't." But the life of Jesus contradicted that statement. He healed the sicknesses and met the needs of every person who ever reached out to Him. And He did it every time!

So when you reach out to God to meet your need, you shouldn't have a single doubt about what He'll do. You can rest assured that what Jesus did back then for others, He will do today for you!

LIMITLESS**LOVE**

God Is in the Details

"Are not two sparrows sold for a farthing? and one of them shall not fall on the ground without your Father. But the very hairs of your head are all numbered. Fear ye not therefore, ye are of more value than many sparrows."
Matthew 10:29-31

Amazing as it may seem, God loves us so much that He cares not only about the major issues in our lives but about the minor details, as well. He never for a moment forgets about us. As Psalm 115:12 says, He is ever "mindful of us"!

Isn't that a blessing? God knows right where you are at all times. You don't have to work to get His attention. He already has you on His mind.

Jesus demonstrated how thoughtful God is about the details of our lives at the wedding feast in Cana. The hosts of the wedding ran out of wine, an embarrassing situation for them, to be sure, but hardly of great, eternal significance. Yet when Jesus' mother called on Him for help, He abundantly met the need by turning the water not into ordinary wine, but into such wonderful wine that the bridegroom was commended because he kept the good wine for last (John 2:9-10)!

"That's true," you may say, "but Jesus did that because Mary asked Him. And I can tell you, I'm not nearly as perfect as Mary. I've messed some things up in a big way!"

Maybe so, but don't let that stop you from reaching out to God. He doesn't demand perfection from us before He will meet our needs. Look again at the ministry of Jesus and you can see that's true.

When the multitudes came to Him for healing, Luke 6:19 tells us that he "healed them all." Certainly among those multitudes of people there were many just like us—imperfect people who fail and make mistakes, people who by their own, natural merits don't deserve to receive anything from God. Yet Jesus healed them—every one.

That's so characteristic of Him! He never failed to give the best to those who came to Him. Jesus had such a good heart and was so willing to help that you might say He was an "easy touch."

What's more, we know He is still that way today because as Hebrews 13:8 says, He is the same "yesterday, and to day, and for ever." He is still an expression of the God who cares so much about the details of our lives that He numbers the hairs of our head. He is still the image of the God "with whom is no variableness, neither shadow of turning" (James 1:17), the God who is—and always will be—Love.

Extending the Reach of God's Love

"But thou, O LORD, art a God full of compassion, and gracious,
long suffering, and plenteous in mercy and truth."
Psalm 86:15

God's boundless love so staggers the human imagination that our natural minds often try to reason it away. *Wait a minute,* we might think, *I know God is love, but there have to be limits to that love. The evidence is all around. After all, the earth is full of people in need and the love of God certainly doesn't seem to be reaching them.*

It's true. Judging from a purely human perspective, there do seem to be limits on God's love and goodness. But the limits are on our side—not His. Sometimes, we limit our experience of God's love because we fail to listen to and obey Him. At other times, we limit the reach of His love simply by our lack of understanding and lack of faith.

Think about it for a moment. Since everything we receive from the hand of God is received by faith and trust in Him, if we're bound by fear, constantly worrying about our own well-being and doubting God's love for us, we won't be able to reach out by faith and receive from His open hand. Granted, we may not be at fault for our lack of faith if we haven't heard The WORD. But, even so, our lack of understanding can limit our ability to receive the wonderful provision that God in His love desires to give.

One friend of mine tells of a time in her life that perfectly illustrates that fact. Although she was born again at an early age, she was raised in a traditional church and had little comprehension of the love and goodness of God. After she married and had children, she and her husband went through some financially hard times.

Knowing they needed divine help, my friend would begin to pray, asking God to send them the money to meet their family's needs. Then this negative thought would short-circuit her prayers. *How dare you ask God to meet your family's needs when there are children starving in China. You should be praying for their needs—not yours!*

This cycle went on until she finally began to get some teaching and revelation about the limitless nature of God's love. Then it began to dawn on her that religious tradition and lack of knowledge had kept her from trusting God to meet her needs. In the light of that revelation, my friend realized at once how foolish she'd been. Why had she asked God to meet only the needs of the Chinese children and not her own? He is God! Certainly He has enough love and enough provision for everyone! Why couldn't she ask for both?

The answer was obvious. And from that time on, she began to open the door of God's provision by trusting Him to give it. By simple faith in God's goodness she extended the reach of His limitless love.

An Ocean of Love

"Oh how great is thy goodness, which thou hast laid up for them that fear thee;
which thou hast wrought for them that trust in thee before the sons of men!"
Psalm 31:19

Not only is God's love for us unlimited, His desire to express that love by pouring out His goodness upon us is also unlimited. Nothing delights Him more than the opportunity to give BLESSINGS to His obedient children. As Psalm 35 says, God "takes pleasure in the prosperity of His servant" (verse 27, *The Amplified Bible*).

F.F. Bosworth, in his great book *Christ the Healer*, says:

God is Infinitely Good and exists forever in a state of entire consecration to pour forth blessing upon His creatures whenever they make it possible, which all may do. Suppose the vast Pacific ocean were elevated high above us. Then conceive of its pressure into every crevice to find an outlet through which it might pour its ocean-tides over all the earth, and you have a picture of God's benevolent attitude toward us.[8]

Just imagine that! An ocean of God's goodness stored up just waiting to be poured out in our lives!

That's not just an exciting thought. That's what the Bible teaches. The Hebrew translation of Psalm 31:19 says God has "treasured up" goodness for us. That concept is confirmed in Exodus 33:18 where Moses asked God to show him His glory. In the Hebrew Bible, the comments of the sages give us insight into what actually happened there. It says that when God said to Moses, "I will make all my goodness pass before thee" (verse 19), it actually means, "The time has come to show you as much of the divine goodness as you can comprehend."

Then it says God showed Moses all the treasures of reward stored up for the righteous. That's right! According to the Jewish sages, Moses saw a large unlabeled storehouse and The LORD told him it was goodness stored up for those who would receive from His loving hand.

Yes, God in His great love has good things stored up, prepared and ready for us. He has plenty laid up to make every one of us wealthy beyond our highest dreams, free in every area of life, healed, whole, complete with our families intact. It doesn't matter what kind of need you might have in your life, it's no challenge for God to fill it. He has much, much more than enough already laid in store for you. And He desires to give it to you simply because He loves you!

If that thought staggers your mind, don't worry about it. That's just the way God is. His love is so good, it's staggering. We'll literally spend eternity receiving all He has to give!

---

[8] F.F. Bosworth, *Christ the Healer* (Grand Rapids: Fleming Revel, 1973).

An Even Better Covenant

"Praise ye The LORD. O give thanks unto The LORD; for he is good:
For his mercy endureth for ever."
Psalm 106:1

As I've studied the goodness of God's love, I've found that often the people with the best understanding of it aren't modern-day Christians, but Bible-believing Jews. The Jewish nation, from the beginning, has had a great revelation of what God's goodness truly means. In Hebrew, the very word *good* speaks of the highest and greatest of everything that is positive and desirable.

In the Jewish mind, the goodness of God and the glory of God were practically synonymous. The very word *glory* in Hebrew means "to be heavy with everything good." The Jewish people understood that it was the goodness of God's love that would deliver them, bless them and bring them victory. That's why, in battle, when they depended on the glory of God to go before them and defeat their enemies, they would proclaim, "For The LORD is good and His mercy endures forever!"

One Jewish scholar who had such understanding about the goodness of God was a man named David Baron. His commentary on the book of Zechariah contains some of the most powerful words I've ever read about God's love:

Goodness is that attribute of God whereby He loveth to communicate [or give] to all who can or will receive it, all good; yea Himself, who is the fulness and universality of good, Creator of all good, not in one way, not in one kind of goodness only, but absolutely, without beginning, without limit, without measure, save that whereby without measurement He possesseth and embraceth all excellence, all perfection, all blessedness, all good. This Good His Goodness bestoweth on all and each, according to the capacity of each to receive it, nor is there any limit to His giving, save His creatures' capacity of receiving....[9]

If Old Covenant Jews could expect God to be so loving and good to them, how much more can we as New Covenant believers be confident in God's lovingkindness toward us? After all, Hebrews 8:6 says that we have "a better covenant…established upon better promises." Our covenant is better because it includes all the promises of natural provision made by the old, plus the spiritual benefits of the new birth, including freedom from sin and the Baptism in the Holy Spirit, that comes with the new—and all of it is ours right now! Truly we can say with even more assurance than our Jewish ancestors that The LORD is good, and His mercy endures forever!

---

[9] David Baron, *Zechariah: A Commentary on His Visions and Prophecies* (Grand Rapids: Kregel Publications, 2001) p. 332-333, quote from Edward Bouverie Pusey, *The Minor Prophets: With a Commentary, Explanatory and Practical, and Introductions to the Several Books* (Oxford: J.H. & J. Parker, 1860) p. 562.

LIMITLESS**LOVE**

Living Proof of God's Love

"It is good to give thanks to The LORD, and to sing praises to Your name, O Most High; to declare Your lovingkindness in the morning and Your faithfulness by night…. The righteous man will flourish like the palm tree, he will grow like a cedar in Lebanon. Planted in the house of The LORD, they will flourish in the courts of our God. They will still yield fruit in old age; they shall be full of sap and very green, to declare that The LORD is upright…."
Psalm 92:1-2, 12-15, *New American Standard*

Do you know that God wants to pour out His love and goodness upon you, not only for your own benefit but also for the benefit of others? He wants to bless you so richly that you become a walking demonstration of His wonderful love!

The LORD has always wanted that for His people. All the way through the Scriptures, we see Him wanting to give His people such abundance and victory that it would get the attention of the heathen. He said to the Israelites in Jeremiah 33:9 that He would so openly demonstrate His love for them that they would be to Him "a name of joy, a praise and an honour before all the nations of the earth, which shall hear all the good that I do unto them."

Why does God want people to see and hear about His goodness in our lives? Because He loves them and He wants them to recognize Him as a good God and turn to Him.

I believe great numbers of people are going to be saved in the last days because God is going to show them His love in amazing ways. And I am convinced that one way it will happen is through THE BLESSING flooding the lives of believers to the point we become the living proof of God's love that all the world can see.

You may think that's a wild idea, but I have scripture for it! *The Amplified Bible* translation of Psalm 92:15 actually says that God's people are "[living memorials] to show that The LORD is upright and faithful to His promises." The word *show* means "to boldly stand out opposite, to manifest, announce, to expose, explain, praise, certify, declare, expound fully, plainly profess, rehearse, and report."

In other words, God wants our lives to so overflow with His goodness that people can look at us and see we're different. We're not worried. We're not depressed. We're prosperous when the economy is up and when it's down. Nothing seems to take us off our path. We just keep going on our way, BLESSED and full of the joy of The LORD.

God wants not only our lips, but our very lives to proclaim that He truly is love!

Days of Heaven on Earth

"Therefore shall ye lay up these my words in your heart and in your soul....
That your days may be multiplied, and the days of your children, in the
land which The LORD sware unto your fathers to give them,
as the days of heaven upon the earth."
Deuteronomy 11:18, 21

Many Christians have been taught that God wants us to lead hard, sorrowful lives here on earth. Religion has trained them to believe that He doesn't want us to have anything good until we get to heaven. But the Bible says something very different. It tells us God loves us so much, He wants us to have days of heaven right here on earth!

He has wanted that from the beginning when He gave the Garden of Eden to Adam and Eve. He designed it to be a perfect, peaceful habitation where they could get together with Him in the cool of the day and visit. We know He made it a beautiful place, too, because Genesis 2:9 says that in the Garden, "made The LORD God to grow every tree that is pleasant to the sight, and good for food."

Of course, the entrance of sin into the earth messed things up, but God's desire and heart hasn't changed. He still loves us as much as He did Adam and Eve. And according to 1 Timothy 6:17, He still "giveth us richly all things to enjoy."

The earth, even in its fallen state, proves that. You can take a ride through the mountains and see breathtakingly beautiful sights. You can go many places and see wonderful waterfalls, colorful canyons, lush forests and even starkly beautiful deserts. Psalm 19 tells us that the earthly creation is constantly speaking to us about the power and character of God. It is telling us day and night that He loves us and wants us to be richly BLESSED.

Maybe your life has been so difficult in the past, you don't think you could ever be truly happy. Maybe the devil has wrought such destruction around you that you've begun to doubt the goodness and the love of God. If so, I want to assure you today, God has not only the power but also the desire to turn your life around.

As you continue to seek Him and follow His plan for your life, "The LORD shall increase you more and more" (Psalm 115:14). Every day, as you learn to walk in fellowship with Him, more of the good things in life will come to you. And though you'll always keep looking forward to heaven and the face-to-face fellowship you'll enjoy with The LORD there, you'll enjoy many of its benefits in advance. As you learn to live more and more in the fullness of His love, you will indeed experience days of heaven upon earth!

LIMITLESS**LOVE**

Living in Your Dreams

"Who is the man who fears The LORD? He will instruct him
in the way he should choose. His soul will abide in prosperity,
and his descendants will inherit the land."
Psalm 25:12-13, *New American Standard*

One of the things I most appreciate about God's love for us is that He expresses it in very practical ways. He doesn't just give us flowery words and warm feelings while leaving us to fend for ourselves in the natural affairs of life. In His great love, He supplies all our needs (Philippians 4:19)—spirit, soul and body.

He doesn't give us just barely enough to get by, either. He blesses us so liberally that if we walk with Him long enough, we eventually find ourselves surrounded by more wonderful things than we can imagine.

One translation of Psalm 25:13 says the person who reverences The LORD shall "lodge in goodness." I can tell you from personal experience, that's a wonderful place to live! It's thrilling to dwell every day in the manifestation of the goodness of The LORD. It's almost like living in a dream.

The home Ken and I enjoy today is a testimony of that. It is literally my dream house. It is such a demonstration to me of God's love that almost every time I walk into it, I feel like shouting and dancing a little! It seems almost too good to be true. One day, just as the construction on it was being finished, I walked around it and thought, *This is so wonderful, I feel like I'm in a dream.* Suddenly, I realized that was scriptural. Psalm 126 says:

When The LORD brought back the captive ones of Zion, we were like those who dream. Then our mouth was filled with laughter and our tongue with joyful shouting; then they said among the nations, "The LORD has done great things for them." The LORD has done great things for us; we are glad (verses 1-3, *New American Standard*).

God has always loved His people so much that He wanted them to walk in their dreams. That's what He wanted for the Israelites. That's what He wants for me, and that's what He wants for you.

Granted, the place you live right now and the circumstances that surround you may not yet be what you've dreamed of, but don't let that discourage you. Just keep remembering it's not your final destination. God always has something better in store for you.

As you keep trusting and obeying Him, He'll see to it that you graduate from one good dwelling place to another until eventually you, too, will be surrounded by the practical manifestations of His love. You will be lodging in His goodness and living in your dreams.

LIMITLESS**LOVE**

A Destiny Divinely Designed for You

"For we are God's [own] handiwork (His workmanship), recreated in Christ Jesus, [born anew] that we may do those good works which God predestined (planned beforehand) for us [taking paths which He prepared ahead of time], that we should walk in them [living the good life which He prearranged and made ready for us to live]."
Ephesians 2:10, *The Amplified Bible*

Do you know God loves you so much that He made plans for your life even before you were born? He didn't wake up one day when you were about 20 years old and say, "I guess I need to figure out something for this person to do now." He didn't just leave you on your own to figure out your future.

No, God knew you and loved you before the world was ever made. Ephesians 1 says, "…[in His love] He chose us [actually picked us out for Himself as His own] in Christ before the foundation of the world…. He foreordained us (destined us, planned in love for us) to be adopted (revealed) as His own children…in accordance with the purpose of His will" (verses 4-5, *The Amplified Bible*).

Before you were born, God created a plan for you to follow—a great, victorious, abundantly prosperous plan. He designed a calling and a purpose for you. He ordained certain things for you to do and He made you in such a way that when you do those things you're created to do, you'll be happy and your life will be very good.

God loved you so much that He divinely designed you to fulfill the destiny He has planned for you. When you were born, He placed certain abilities, dreams and desires within you that would help equip you for what He wanted you to do. Even before you gave your life to Him, while you were still a sinner, they were there.

Ken is a wonderful example of that. From the time he was a small child, he wanted to fly airplanes and be a singer. That was his dream. Of course, before he was born again, he didn't use his talents and dreams exactly the way God intended. After God called him to preach, however, the real purpose behind his natural giftings became clear. The fact that he can fly an airplane has enabled us to go around the world preaching the gospel in places it would have been difficult for us to reach otherwise. His singing has also been a part of his ministry and a blessing to the Body of Christ.

Whether you know it yet or not, the same thing that is true of Ken is also true of you. God loves you and has predestined you to be BLESSED and to take that BLESSING to others. Keep seeking Him and you'll discover the good life He has planned for you!

LIMITLESS**LOVE**

God Can Work It Out

"We are assured and know that [God being a partner in their labor] all things work together and are [fitting into a plan] for good to and for those who love God and are called according to [His] design and purpose."
Romans 8:28, *The Amplified Bible*

There are times for all of us when our lives seem to have no clear plan or direction. But even then, if we love The LORD and give ourselves to Him, we can be sure He is working out His great and loving plan for us. We can rejoice over that plan even before we see it, knowing that God "is able to do exceeding abundantly above all that we ask or think, according to the power that worketh in us" (Ephesians 3:20).

I can personally testify that's the truth. When I was 19, I could not have had the slightest clue about what God wanted to do in my life. It was beyond anything I could imagine. Back then, the biggest dream I had was being an airline stewardess. Even after God began to reveal His plan to Ken and me, telling us that we were going to preach to nations, we couldn't see how it could happen. But God made it happen, nonetheless, as we followed Him by faith one step at a time.

Those two words *by faith* are very important. You have to believe God loves you and has a plan for you or you'll never be able to walk in it. You'll constantly be worrying and wavering and that will hinder you from receiving the wisdom you need from The LORD.

How can you get the faith to believe God can work out His plan for you? Just read the Bible! It will show you what a wonderful planner God actually is. You'll see that ever since Creation, He has worked on a timetable. He has had certain events scheduled and those events always take place exactly at the appointed time. The Bible proves that God never fails and He's never late.

In Genesis 15:13-14, for example, God promised to bring the Israelites out of Egypt after 400 years. Scholars tell us that God kept that timetable to the day. When the Jewish nation went into captivity in Babylon during Jeremiah's day, God had already planned their deliverance. He told them that after 70 years, He would bring them back to their own land and that's exactly what He did.

Jesus was born at the appointed time. He's coming back at the appointed time, and He won't be late. When it comes to the plan of redemption, the Almighty God is always right on time.

In light of those facts, consider this: The same good God who planned those events is the One who lovingly planned your life. Based on His track record, I believe He has the power to carry out that plan, don't you?

LIMITLESS**LOVE**

God Always Has a Plan

"If any of you lacks wisdom, let him ask of God, who gives to all
generously and without reproach, and it will be given to him."
James 1:5, *New American Standard*

God's love is so great and so full of mercy that even if you disobey Him and get off
course, He will be there to help you get back on track. He will forgive you and give you another
chance to fulfill His divine plan for you.

Even if you act like a rascal (which I strongly warn you not to do, because it will cause
you painful regret), God will receive you the moment you repent and reach out to Him. He
won't say, "Now, you just wait a minute, buddy. I think I'm going to watch you for a while and
see if you're really sincere about this before I start blessing you."

No, God knows your heart, and if it is earnestly turned toward Him, He'll immediately start
pumping His goodness back into your life. If, like the prodigal son, you will go home to the
Father, His mercy will be right there to greet you. He'll say, "Welcome home, son. Welcome
home, daughter." He'll put a robe of righteousness on your back and a family ring on your
finger, because He is so loving and good!

What's more, no matter how much trouble and hell you've gotten yourself into, God will
have a plan to get you out. He'll start moving you back into the original design He had for
your life.

One morning when we were overseas preaching, I woke up and heard these words
in my heart: God always has a plan! Isn't that wonderful? Even when to our natural minds
things seem hopeless, with God there's always hope. With God we always have a good future
ahead of us. Granted, if you've gotten yourself into trouble by disregarding His commands,
it might take some time for God to lead you completely out of it and you will have to get
some wisdom from Him to make the necessary changes. But you can be assured that when
you come to Him for His wisdom and help, He'll never upbraid you. He'll never condemn and
criticize you. He won't even talk badly to you. He'll receive you and give you what you need to
get back on the road to your divine destiny right then and there.

Once you understand just how good that destiny really is, you won't ever want to walk
away from it again. You'll stick close to The LORD because you won't want to miss a single
thing He has in store for you. You'll wholeheartedly finish the race He has set before you,
knowing that you'll hear Him say, "Well done" at the end of your journey. You'll walk in the
light of His love every step of the way.

LIMITLESS**LOVE**

God's Favorites

*"But let all those that put their trust in thee rejoice: let them
ever shout for joy, because thou defendest them: let them also
that love thy name be joyful in thee. For thou, LORD, wilt bless the
righteous; with favour wilt thou compass him as with a shield."*
Psalm 5:11-12

The Bible uses many different words to describe the love God has for us, and one of the most wonderful words is *favor*. To *favor* someone means "to take pleasure and delight in them, to enjoy doing good for them, to prefer them over others."

Did you know that as a born-again child of God, you are one of His favorites? He doesn't just tolerate you. He doesn't just put up with you. He takes pleasure and delights in you. He enjoys doing good things for you. He prefers you over the animals. He prefers you over anything else in His created universe. He even prefers you over angels! (See Hebrews 2:16.)

He doesn't just favor you now and then, or here and there, either. No, as long as you're walking in fellowship with Him, His favor surrounds you all the time…everywhere you go…24 hours a day.

You ought to wake up in the morning thinking about that. You ought not get up dreading the day, talking about all the bad things that might take place. You should cultivate the habit of saying things like, "Everywhere I go God favors me. Good things will happen to me. THE BLESSING will overtake me today, because I'm one of God's favorites!"

The more you say it, the more you'll believe it. And the more you believe it, the more of God's favor you'll be able to receive.

So even if it seems strange at first, keep talking! Talk to yourself about how much God loves and favors you. Talk to The LORD about it. (It blesses Him when you receive His love!) Talk to the devil about it when he comes to tell you God doesn't care about you and He's not going to do good things for you. The devil *will* tell you that, you know. He'll tell you that God won't heal you. He'll tell you that God doesn't want to meet your needs. He'll tell you that God doesn't love you and no one else does, either.

At times, circumstances might even make it look like he's right. But don't agree with him! Shut him up and put him in his place by speaking The WORD. Say, "Hey, Mr. Devil. You're just jealous because I'm one of God's favorites, and you're not! You're just mad because He takes such pleasure in BLESSING and prospering me!"

Before you know it, you'll be shouting and rejoicing just like the Bible says you should. The devil will flee, and you'll soon see the reality of God's favor surrounding you!

LIMITLESS**LOVE**

Freed by His Favor

"Therefore if any man is in Christ, he is a new creature;
the old things passed away; behold, new things have come. Now all these
things are from God, who reconciled us to Himself through Christ and gave us
the ministry of reconciliation, namely, that God was in Christ reconciling the
world to Himself, not counting their trespasses against them....
He made Him who knew no sin to be sin on our behalf,
that we might become the righteousness of God in Him."
2 Corinthians 5:17-19, 21, *New American Standard*

Even though the Bible plainly says we are God's favorites, some Christians have trouble believing it because they are plagued by memories of things they've done wrong. They think about mistakes they've made or sins they committed. *How could God take delight in me?* they wonder. *How could He, as a holy God, take pleasure in a sinner who's acted in the unholy ways that I have?*

He can do it because He doesn't see us as sinners anymore. The moment we trust in Jesus and make Him our LORD, God washes away our past with the blood of Jesus and replaces our sinfulness with His own righteousness. From that moment on, He considers us His very own children (which we truly are!). And because we are His beloved children, He favors us!

Years ago, Ken and I received a letter from a man whose life proved just how true that is. He had been a hardened criminal who had spent many years in prison for molesting children. But at 70 years old, while watching one of our television broadcasts, he asked Jesus to save him, and he was born again.

During the following months, he kept watching the broadcasts and reading the Bible, learning everything he could because he was so hungry for God. He wanted to give testimony of what The LORD had done for him, so he wrote the judge who had sentenced him and told him what had happened. Although he didn't ask for anything, the judge was so moved by the letter, he helped to cut short that man's prison sentence. Within just a few months, that 70-year-old inmate, who had spent more of his life inside prison than out, was finally free. Why? Because of the favor of God!

Remember that story if you're ever tempted to think you've done something so bad, you've forever lost your place as one of God's favorites. Remember, there's nothing you can do that's stronger than His love. It's so far-reaching that no matter how far we stray, the moment we call on His Name, He is there to forgive us, change us and put us back where we as His children belong—*in the midst of the favor of God.*

LIMITLESS**LOVE**

A Loving Heart and an Open Hand

"Turn unto The LORD your God: for he is gracious and merciful,
slow to anger, and of great kindness...."
Joel 2:13

Over and over again, the Scriptures tell us that God is gracious, but too often we miss the fullness of what that really means. A person who is gracious is someone who is inclined to do what you want them to do. They're disposed to show favors to those who ask them. They are, as James 3:17 says, "easy to be entreated."

My grandfather was like that. All the children in my family called him "Pop," and we dearly loved him because he so enjoyed being good to us. If we asked him for money, he'd dig into his pockets and give us whatever he had. He taught us all how to drive, and then let us take his pickup to town (even *before* we had our driver's licenses). As long as he knew it wouldn't hurt us, he let us do whatever we wanted to do.

My grandmother wasn't as much that way, so she often tried to stop him, but she didn't have much success. Despite her protests, he usually ended up giving us whatever we asked for because he couldn't help it. That was just his nature.

God is much the same way. It's not difficult to get Him to do what we want. On the contrary, He likes to say yes to us. He is disposed to show us favor!

You know how some people have hobbies like fishing or golf, and they're always looking for opportunities to do those things? You might say that God's hobby is doing good things for His children. He is continually watching for opportunities to BLESS us and give us what we want.

Ecclesiastes 3:12-13 says, "...for a man to rejoice, and to do good in his life. And also that every man should eat and drink, and enjoy the good of all his labour, it is the gift of God." God wants to give good gifts to people. It's what He loves and enjoys, so much so, that one of the Hebrew titles for God in the Old Testament is "Jehovah the Good!"

That's why we can go boldly before His throne of grace to receive what we need from Him. That's why we can go in faith, and not in fear. We don't have a heavenly Father who's hardhearted and tightfisted. We have a Father who is easily entreated, who greets us with a loving heart and an open hand. We have a Father who loves to be good to us.

LIMITLESS**LOVE**

Receive God's Bountiful Goodness

"I have trusted in thy mercy; my heart shall rejoice in thy salvation. I will sing unto The LORD, because he hath dealt bountifully with me."
Psalm 13:5-6

In the Bible, the word *mercy* and the word *love* are almost always interchangeable, because they come from the same Hebrew word. Therefore, every time God assures us that He loves us, He is also reassuring us of His mercy toward us. He's letting us know that, in spite of our mistakes and our failures, He wants to deal kindly and bountifully with us.

Most religions—even those based on Christianity—have portrayed a totally different picture of God. Long-faced, angry preachers have often represented God as mad at the whole human race and looking furiously for someone to punish. They give people the impression God is in a bad mood, so you have to be very careful around Him because you don't want to irritate Him any further. One country-western singer even wrote a song along those lines that the radio stations played some years ago. He titled it, "God's Gonna Get 'Cha (for That)!"

If those kinds of traditions have made you wary of God, you need to know that the Bible doesn't teach any of those things. It doesn't reveal a god who is out to "get us" or do us harm in any way. The Bible doesn't say anything about God being in a bad mood.

On the contrary, it says that God is gracious. He is always in a favorable mood. You don't have to worry about catching God on a bad day. He doesn't have those kinds of days. His mercy endures forever!

Of course, it's not just Christian tradition that has depicted God as angry and vindictive. The gods of the heathen religions are that way too. The difference is, that's an accurate picture of them because they're not gods at all, they're demonic spirits. People who worshiped demon gods throughout history often believed they had to hurt themselves or someone they loved in some way in order to appease the gods' anger. Although other pagan gods were not so harsh, they all needed something, offerings of fruit or gifts of some kind, to make them happy.

But our God isn't like that! He's already happy! We don't have to do penance or make sacrifices to appease Him. He provided the sacrifice for sin Himself in the person of His Son. When we receive that sacrifice in simple faith, we open the way for God to do what He always wanted. We open the way for Him to have mercy upon us, deal bountifully with us and bring "peace on earth, good will toward men!"

LIMITLESS**LOVE**

A Law Inspired by Love

"Thou shalt therefore keep the commandments, and the statutes,
and the judgments, which I command thee this day, to do them.
Wherefore it shall come to pass…that The LORD thy God shall keep unto
thee the covenant and the mercy which he sware unto thy fathers:
And he will love thee, and bless thee, and multiply thee…."
Deuteronomy 7:11-13

I didn't go to church much when I was growing up. (I tried but I just wasn't very good at it.) On the occasions I did make it to church, it seemed that all I heard were the things God said we shouldn't do. As I recall, no one said anything about God's love. So I just pictured Him as a rule-maker who didn't want me to have much fun.

I know now that I wasn't alone in that misconception. Many good, Bible-reading folks have seen the list of laws God gave in the Old Testament and assumed He gave them to people because He is harsh and demanding. But nothing could be further from the truth.

The fact is, at that time in history God was faced with a dilemma. Through man's disobedience, the devil had gained license to operate in the earth. Adam and Eve had opened the door for him to impose his will on mankind. He'd been released to kill, steal and destroy.

The entire human race had fallen under the curse of sin and God wanted to provide them with a way out. In spite of their rebellion, He still loved them and wanted to give them a way to step back under His protective wings so He could shelter, protect and provide for them once again. That's why He gave them the Law.

Old Covenant law was truly an amazing thing. It provided spiritual commands such as, "Thou shalt have no other Gods before me" that, if obeyed, would keep people from being dominated and hurt by demonic forces. Other commands such as "Thou shalt not kill" kept people from being hurt and dominated by each other.

Levitical law also provided instructions that enabled them to live safely in the physical world, which had been corrupted by sin. History reveals that the laws God gave about such things as hand washing, purification and foods often protected God's people from sicknesses and diseases that destroyed other nations. For those times when they did fall prey to sickness, God provided commands they could follow and gave them priests so they could receive their healing from Him.

Through it all, God spoke to them about the coming redemption that would be provided through the blood of Jesus. He gave them the promise of the spiritual deliverance that was to come. Why? Because even then God was, as He still is now, a good God; One who makes a way for people of every place and time to step into The BLESSING. Even then He was the God of love.

LIMITLESSLOVE

He Is Still Our Savior

"And Jesus went forth, and saw a great multitude, and was moved with compassion toward them, and he healed their sick."
Matthew 14:14

Warm feelings and sympathetic emotions are fine. We all appreciate it when we're in need and someone is warm and sympathetic toward us. But we appreciate it even more when those emotions motivate that person to actually reach out and help us!

That's why the compassion of God is so wonderful. It's not just a passive feeling. It's not just an emotion He has that makes Him feel sorry for us when we're hurting. No, the very word *compassion* as it's used in the Bible is an active word. It's a word that describes a deep and eager yearning that compels God to move on our behalf.

We see that fact clearly demonstrated in the life of Jesus. The scriptures repeatedly tell us He was "moved with compassion." Interestingly enough, the story never stops there. Invariably, when the compassion of God moved in Jesus, a need was met. Compassion compelled Him to feed hungry multitudes, heal the sick, cast out devils and even raise the dead.

That's the kind of compassion God has for you. It's the kind of compelling love that so yearned for you to be free and well and BLESSED, it moved God to send His only begotten Son to die for you. It moved Him to send Jesus to bear your sins, sicknesses and diseases, to take your punishment so you could be made whole in every way. God's compassion compelled Him to pay a staggering price so you could have righteousness for your spirit, peace for your soul and health for your body!

"I know He did that," you might say, "but He did it for the whole world—not just for me."

True, but His compassion is so personal and so strong that if you'd been the only one in the world who was willing to receive it, God would still have sent Jesus to the cross just for you.

A few years ago, Ken and I were taping a Christmas broadcast. I was thinking along these lines about the love of God and, as we gave the invitation, the Holy Spirit spoke these words to my heart: *You are not in the world without a Savior.* Obviously, that was good news for us when we were sinners needing to be born again. But, the fact is, it's still good news for us today. Jesus is still as much our Savior as He ever was. When we call on Him in faith, the compassion of God will still move through Him in our lives to heal us, deliver us and help us. Compassion is still compelling Him to meet our every need!

LIMITLESS**LOVE**

Faith Will Open the Door

"Therefore having been justified by faith, we have peace with God through
our LORD Jesus Christ, through whom also we have obtained
our introduction by faith into this grace in which we stand;
and we exult in hope of the glory of God."
Romans 5:1-2, *New American Standard*

Sometimes people doubt the love of God because of painful experiences they've had in their lives. *If God truly cares for me,* they think, *why did He allow those painful things to happen to me? Why didn't He do something to help me?*

The fact is, God earnestly desires to help us all in every time of need. In His great love, He has even made provision to do so. Yet for Him to legally get that provision to us, it is necessary for us to place ourselves (as one writer said) "where God's mercy can reach us without His having to violate the glorious principles of His moral government."

Unlike the devil, God does not attempt to impose His will—good as it is—upon any individual. He does not force it upon us or trick us into receiving it. God waits for us to give Him an open door. As Jesus said in Revelation 3:20, "Behold, I stand at the door and knock; if anyone hears My voice and opens the door, I will come in to him and will dine with him, and he with Me" *(New American Standard).*

Some folks think they've given God an open door because they whined and cried and wished He would do something to change their situation. However, that's not how the Bible says we get access to the grace and THE BLESSING of God. It says we open the door to them by faith!

What is faith? It is simply believing, speaking and acting on The WORD of God.

Actually, I think one of the reasons it is impossible to please God without faith (Hebrews 11:6) is He desires to bless us, and it takes faith for us to receive The BLESSING. When we shut them out by doubt and unbelief, God's love is frustrated. He's not able to express in our lives the great compassion and desire to do us good that constantly churns within Him. Therefore He is not pleased!

If you want to please and delight your heavenly Father, stop questioning His love for you. Step out on His WORD by faith, and put yourself in position where He can protect and provide for you without violating the governing principles He has established in His WORD. I can tell you from experience, once you do that you'll be overwhelmed with demonstrations of His love and mercy. His BLESSING will flow until you've reached the limit of your expectation.

Open the door wide and let His love flood your life!

An Eternal Demonstration of Love

"But God—so rich is He in His mercy! Because of and in order to satisfy the great and wonderful and intense love with which He loved us, even when we were dead (slain) by [our own] shortcomings and trespasses, He made us alive together in fellowship and in union with Christ.... He did this that He might clearly demonstrate through the ages to come the immeasurable (limitless, surpassing) riches of His free grace (His unmerited favor) in [His] kindness and goodness of heart toward us in Christ Jesus."
Ephesians 2:4-5, 7, *The Amplified Bible*

These verses give us a staggering glimpse into the greatness of God's love. They reveal that He saved us not only to spare us from hell, but also so He could demonstrate in our lives forever the limitless nature of His love. He did it because He wanted to eternally bless us and demonstrate His goodness to us.

Think about that! God's great desire is to pour out His lovingkindness on you! He wants to demonstrate His love in your family. He wants to demonstrate it in your church. He wants to demonstrate it in your city. He wants His goodness and love to so flood your life that it overflows onto people in the world around you. He wants them to look at you and exclaim, "Wow! God really is good! He truly is a God whose love knows no limits!"

That's the heart of God. That's why He has done all this. He longs to demonstrate His love and mercy. He yearns to express His boundless compassion.

What's more, He will always want to do that. Scripture says that for eternity, throughout the ages to come, He'll keep on demonstrating His love for us. Traditional religion taught something different. It said that God just wanted to demonstrate that love for a few years while Jesus was on the earth…or until the last of the apostles died…or until the book of Acts was finished. But, praise God, that's not what the Bible says.

It says He'll keep on demonstrating His love toward us throughout the ages to come. It says God's love will never be satisfied! God is not going to wake up one morning and say, "I'm finished pouring out My love. I'm not going to heal people anymore. I'm not going to work miracles. I'm just going to let those things pass away."

That will never happen. Every day of your life, God is going to be there desiring to demonstrate His love to you by meeting your needs and blessing you beyond your fondest dreams. Even when your natural life is over and you step into the next age, God will keep right on showing forth His love for you. Throughout eternity, He intends to make you a living demonstration of His immeasurable love.

LIMITLESS**LOVE**

The Choice That Brings Eternal Rewards

"If ye then be risen with Christ, seek those things which are above, where Christ sitteth on the right hand of God. Set your affection on things above, not on things on the earth. For ye are dead, and your life is hid with Christ in God. When Christ, who is our life, shall appear, then shall ye also appear with him in glory. Mortify therefore your members which are upon the earth...."
Colossians 3:1-5

One reason we stumble in our love walk is because we put too much importance upon the natural things of life. We get irritated and speak unkindly when someone puts a blemish on our favorite piece of furniture, for example. We lash out in anger at someone because they dented our new car.

Humanly speaking, that's understandable. But in the economy of God, it's a grave mistake. The reason is simple. The natural things of this world are temporary. A few months or a few years from now, our material possessions will all be gone. The eternal rewards for walking in love, however, will last forever.

Reward day *is* coming, you know. The Bible says, "We must all appear before the judgment seat of Christ; that every one may receive the things done in his body, according to that he hath done, whether it be good or bad" (2 Corinthians 5:10). On that day, The LORD won't be rewarding us for how beautifully we cared for our furniture. He won't be commending us for the perfect condition of our cars. Those things won't matter a bit. He'll be examining our lives to see how well we kept the one commandment He gave us. He'll be looking to see if we loved one another.

You'll walk more consistently in love if you constantly keep that in mind. You'll keep your flesh in check if you remember that the life you're living on this earth isn't your only life. It's simply your opportunity to plant seeds for your eternal life to come. And though God will give you richly all things to enjoy while you're on this earth, they are all only flawed representations of THE BLESSING to come. They're part of this fallen creation, and no matter how much time and energy you invest in them, they'll never be perfect.

So don't let natural things overcome you. Don't let them capture your affections. Keep your heart set on God and never—*ever*—treat things more lovingly than you treat people.

When you're tempted to do it, take authority over your flesh and put it in its place. Remind yourself that judgment time is coming and make the choice that will bring you eternal rewards.

Love's Hundredfold Return

"Then Peter began to say unto him, Lo, we have left all, and have followed thee. And Jesus answered and said, Verily I say unto you, There is no man that hath left house, or brethren, or sisters, or father, or mother, or wife, or children, or lands, for my sake, and the gospel's, but he shall receive an hundredfold now in this time, houses, and brethren, and sisters, and mothers, and children, and lands, with persecutions; and in the world to come eternal life."
Mark 10:28-30

Anyone who has obeyed the command of Jesus to walk in love has discovered that obedience can, at times, seem costly. Sacrifices will inevitably have to be made. There will be occasions when people will take advantage of you. There will be situations where love requires you to lay down your own rights. There will be times when, because of love, you must take some natural possession you've treasured or enjoyed and give it to another who needs it more than you.

How do you make those sacrifices without feeling bitter and resentful? How do you avoid the martyr syndrome that would cause you to constantly remind people how much you've given up for the sake of love?

You do it by joyfully trusting the promise Jesus made in Mark 10:30. You confidently expect THE BLESSING to be activated so richly, your sacrifices pale by comparison. You dare to expect the hundredfold return!

In practical terms, that means if love requires you to take the money you'd saved up for a new car and give it to a brother who has no car at all, you rejoice believing that God will provide you with the finances for an even better car than the one you were planning to buy. It means if you choose to walk in love and refuse to fight the co-worker who snatched the promotion that should have been yours, you can happily anticipate an even greater blessing and promotion to come to you directly from the hand of God.

It doesn't matter what seeming setbacks may come. It doesn't matter how much it may look like you've lost at the game of life. If you keep walking in love and believing God, He will see to it that you end up a winner. He will replace what you sacrificed for His sake with something a hundredfold better.

Instead of feeling bitter and resentful, you'll end up grateful for the opportunities you had to lay down your life for the Master. You'll find that in the end, walking in love doesn't cost—it pays with riches that last beyond this life into the life to come.

LIMITLESS**LOVE**

Take a Crash Course on Love

*"Let them shout for joy, and be glad, that favour my righteous cause:
yea, let them say continually, Let The LORD be magnified,
which hath pleasure in the prosperity of his servant. And my tongue
shall speak of thy righteousness and of thy praise all the day long."*
Psalm 35:27-28

Some people are dismayed when they find out that faith is what opens the door for God to work in their lives. They're upset when they learn that His love can only manifest to the max when they believe His WORD in their hearts and speak it out with their mouths.

I suppose that's because they're not sure they can change. They've lived so long with doubt in their hearts and unbelief on their lips, they're afraid it would take too long to turn things around.

If you've had those kinds of thoughts, let me reassure you that your fears are unfounded. You can throw the door of faith open wide and you can do it speedily by taking what I call a "crash course" in the love of God. You can throw yourself wholeheartedly into His WORD by spending extra time reading and meditating on what the Scriptures say about His goodness. You can do what Psalm 35 says and keep those verses continually in your heart and in your mouth.

When you're putting dishes in the dishwasher, you can praise Him for His lovingkindness. When you're driving to work in your car, you can shout and sing and say, "I magnify You, LORD, because You take pleasure in my prosperity. I thank You, LORD, for blessing me!"

I know you can, because that's what Ken and I did. When we found out that faith was the way to open the door to God's BLESSING, we just went for it. The first year we learned about faith, we hardly did anything except read, study and listen to tapes of The WORD. I'm not saying we ignored the responsibilities of life. We worked and took care of our family, but when we weren't occupied with those duties we gave ourselves wholly to The WORD of God.

I got so full of The WORD, it just flowed out of me. I remember one time in particular, I was outside hanging clothes on the clothesline and thinking about The WORD. The telephone rang and I was so filled with excitement and faith that when I answered the phone I said, "Hallelujah!" instead of hello.

You can do the same thing. Instead of barely cracking open the door of faith, throw it open wide. Pull it off its hinges by jumping into The WORD with both hands and feet. Take a crash course by filling your heart and your mouth with The WORD of God's love. You'll be amazed how quickly things can turn around!

LIMITLESS LOVE

The Grace That Just Won't Quit

"By grace have you been saved completely in time past,
with the present result that you are in a state of salvation
which persists through present time...."
Ephesians 2:8, *Wuest Translation*

One of the most wonderful things about God's grace, His loving favor toward us, is that it just won't quit! It persists to keep us in a constant state of salvation. So it's there for us every time we need it—and we need it all the time.

It doesn't come because we've earned it or deserved it, either. It's there simply because God loves us and He is good. Actually, that's the reason for every BLESSING God has ever given us. No one has ever deserved God's goodness except The LORD Jesus Himself.

Left on our own, the rest of us deserve nothing but judgment and punishment from God. But, thank heaven, God didn't leave us on our own. He sent Jesus to pay the price for our sin and to give us His own righteousness!

That in itself was the greatest thing grace could ever do for us—and God provided that grace when we were at our very worst. He gave it while we were still spiritually dead and living in sin. But He didn't stop there. As Romans 8:32 says, He who spared not His own Son but gave Him up to die for us will also freely give us all other things! He'll keep sending His grace and surrounding us with it for eternity. His favor and power will hover over us 24 hours a day so that all we have to do is reach out by faith and receive whatever we need.

Sometimes we think we're waiting on God, but the truth is, He is waiting on us. He has already done everything it takes for us to have all our needs met. But for His provision and grace to be activated in our lives, we must believe Him for it.

That's just the way God's system operates. Take the new birth, for example. God has provided it for every person under the sun. It's available to everyone 24 hours a day, seven days a week. A person could be alone in the deepest jungle of Africa, he could be lost and on his way to hell, but the moment he dared to believe in his heart and confess with his mouth that Jesus is his Savior, the grace of God would be there to save him. At that instant, God's power would be released in his life and he'd be born again.

Just think, that same grace is still available to us today. It persists in our lives to bring us salvation in every area—spirit, soul and body. If we'll just dare to believe and receive, all the devils in hell can't stop the goodness of God from going to work in our lives. Nothing can defeat us as long as we keep on receiving the grace that just won't quit!

LIMITLESS**LOVE**

God Is Willing and Able

"Therefore it is of faith, that it might be by grace; to the end the promise might
be sure to all the seed; not to that only which is of the law, but to that also
which is of the faith of Abraham; who is the father of us all, (as it is written,
I have made thee a father of many nations,) before him whom he believed,
even God, who quickeneth the dead, and calleth those things which be not as
though they were. Who against hope believed in hope, that he might become
the father of many nations, according to that which was spoken, So shall thy
seed be. And being not weak in faith, he considered not his own body now
dead, when he was about an hundred years old, neither yet the deadness of
Sarah's womb: He staggered not at the promise of God through unbelief;
but was strong in faith, giving glory to God; and being fully persuaded that,
what he had promised, he was able also to perform."

Romans 4:16-21

When you first begin to hear about the goodness of God and how much He loves you, every circumstance in your life may seem to deny it. You may be surrounded with such painful situations and dire problems that it looks as if God doesn't care about you at all.

That's the way it was for me. When I first read in Matthew 6 that God loved me and cared about my needs, it looked for all the world like He didn't. At the time, Ken and I were completely broke and deeply in debt. We were so poor, we couldn't even afford a refrigerator or a stove. When I cooked potatoes, I boiled them in a coffeepot!

But, even so, I didn't argue with the Bible. I didn't say, "Well, God, You need to do something to prove You love me before I'll believe it." No, I just decided to trust Him and I gave Him my life.

After I was born again, I began to hear that God not only wanted to BLESS me spiritually, but He wanted to prosper me financially. Although things had gotten better for us, prosperity still seemed worlds away. The devil would come to me and say, "You're never going to be able to afford a nice home. You'll be stuck in this dumpy shack forever." Circumstantially, it appeared he was right, but I decided to believe God anyway. I chose to trust His power and His love. I'd say, "No, Devil. God loves me and He is willing and able to give me a wonderful home." As a result, I live in my dream house today.

No matter what kind of situation you're in today, the same thing will happen to you if you'll dare to believe that God loves you. Follow the faith of Abraham and instead of considering your circumstances, choose to consider the loving promises of God. Grow strong in faith, giving praise and glory to Him for His great goodness to you. You'll find God is willing and able to make your dreams come true.

LIMITLESS**LOVE**

Become a Fruit Inspector

"And I, brethren, could not speak unto you as unto spiritual, but as unto carnal, even as unto babes in Christ.... For ye are yet carnal: for whereas there is among you envying, and strife, and divisions, are ye not carnal, and walk as men?"
1 Corinthians 3:1, 3

If you want to accurately assess how spiritual you really are, be a fruit inspector. Examine your life and see how much of the fruit of love is there. In your daily interactions at home and at work, are you gentle and kind? Are you thoughtful and courteous? Are you touchy and quick to take offense or are you patient and forgiving when others treat you wrongly?

Those things are the measure of true spirituality.

Most Christians don't seem to know that. They think if a person has visions and dreams, prophesies and has mountain-moving faith, that person must be a real man or woman of God. But that's not the case. The Bible tells us you can have every kind of spiritual gift and power there is, but if you aren't a loving person, you don't amount to anything. Even though you may be born again, you're still fleshly, carnal and immature. In other words, you may be part of God's family but you're just a baby and you don't know Him very well.

First John 4:7-8 confirms that. It says, "Beloved, let us love one another, for love is from God; and everyone who loves is born of God and knows God. The one who does not love does not know God, for God is love" *(New American Standard)*.

Someone might say, "Well, I'm a loving person. I'm really good to my friends and family so I guess I'm spiritually mature."

But the fact is, that doesn't mean too much. Jesus said even the heathen love those who love them. What's distinctive about the God-kind of love is that it loves the unlovely. God is kind and good to those who don't deserve it. He's patient with those who mess up again and again. It doesn't matter how ornery a person has been, if they'll turn to God, He'll take them in. He'll let them receive forgiveness and salvation in Jesus' Name. Instead of reminding them of their past, He'll wipe it away and BLESS them!

The more you fellowship with God and the better you get to know Him, the more you'll think and act that way. As you spend time in union and communion with Him, you'll grow up to be more like Him. You'll be able to inspect your life and find it laden with the fruit of love. Then—and only then—-will you know you've outgrown carnality and become a truly spiritual man.

LIMITLESS**LOVE**

Practice Makes Perfect

"In this the children of God are manifest, and the children of the devil: whosoever doeth not righteousness is not of God, neither he that loveth not his brother."
1 John 3:10

You might assume that since love comes naturally to your reborn human spirit, you should be able to perfectly walk in love from the moment you're born again. But if you've tried it, you know that's not true. We learn to walk spiritually much the same way we learned to walk naturally when we were toddlers. We were clumsy at first. We frequently tottered and fell. But we kept at it. We kept practicing…and practicing…and practicing until we got it right.

Why, if our spirits are already made righteous and loving, do we have to practice so diligently to act that way? Because righteous behaviors like love are foreign to our flesh. Before we gave our lives to The LORD, our flesh developed the habit of behaving in selfish, unloving ways. As a result, even when our reborn spirit indeed is willing to do right, we initially find that our flesh is weak (Matthew 26:41).

How do we overcome that weakness? By doing two things. First we must feed and strengthen our spirit by spending time with God in The WORD and in prayer. Second, we must exercise it by stepping out in faith and practicing our love walk. When we stumble and fall, instead of being discouraged, we simply repent, receive forgiveness, then get up and go at it again. We keep on practicing until we get it right.

If you think about it, that's the way we learn to do everything. We even learned to sin that way. Even though we were born into this world as sinners with a fallen nature, even though sin came naturally to us, we still had to practice to get good at it.

If you were a smoker, for example, the first time you ever smoked a cigarette you didn't like it. It made you sick. If you're like most people, you turned green and coughed. But you kept practicing until you could smoke a pack or two a day without even thinking about it.

The first drink of alcohol a person has doesn't usually taste very good to them. But if they keep practicing, they'll develop a desire—possibly even a craving—for it, and they can end up drinking it every day.

Praise God, that principle works in reverse, too! Once we're born again and quit practicing sin, we lose the taste for it. Sinful things we once enjoyed don't even appeal to us anymore. Instead, we develop a desire to walk in love. And though we may not do it well at first, as we keep practicing and practicing we can be assured we'll eventually get it right!

LIMITLESS**LOVE**

Love Is the Insulator

"For this cause I bow my knees unto the Father of our Lord Jesus Christ, of whom the whole family in heaven and earth is named, that he would grant you, according to the riches of his glory, to be strengthened with might by his Spirit in the inner man; that Christ may dwell in your hearts by faith; that ye, being rooted and grounded in love, may be able to comprehend with all saints what is the breadth, and length, and depth, and height; and to know the love of Christ, which passeth knowledge, that ye might be filled with all the fulness of God."

Ephesians 3:14-19

As sincere believers, we all long to see the presence and power of God manifest in our lives. We want to lay hands on the sick and see them recover. We want to cast out demons and let the oppressed go free. We want to move supernaturally in the gifts of the Spirit so that Jesus can BLESS others through us.

As much as it's possible this side of heaven, we want to be filled with all the fullness of God.

What's the key to walking in that kind of fullness? Ephesians 3 tells us it's knowing God's love. Not just understanding it intellectually. Not just being able to quote scriptures about it. But having our lives rooted and grounded in it. Having a heartfelt comprehension of it that comes from experiencing it for ourselves.

One reason love is so vital to operating in God's power is that it keeps us free from sin. Just read the story of Ananias and Sapphira in Acts 5 and you'll see that God's power and sin just don't mix. When He comes on the scene in fullness, sin has to go...and the person who is attached to that sin just might end up going with it!

When we walk in love, however, we're walking without sin. Love protects us from it. It's the insulator that enables God to move in power in us and through us without blowing us away. Love brings us to the place where God can manifest Himself more fully in our lives.

No wonder the Apostle Paul prayed the way he did for the Ephesian church! No wonder he continually bowed his knee before the Father of our LORD, and asked Him to strengthen them and establish them in the understanding and experience of Christ's love! He knew that more than anything else, love would enable them to be all God called them to be.

The same is true for us. And, thank God, we can pray the same prayer Paul prayed—for ourselves and for each other. No matter how much we may already know of God's love, there is always more to learn. So every day of our lives we can boldly ask for and receive an increased revelation of love. Day by day, we can increasingly be filled with more of the fullness of God.

LIMITLESS**LOVE**

Get Hungry for the Word

"How sweet are your words to my taste, sweeter than honey to my mouth!
I gain understanding from your precepts...."
Psalm 119:103-104, *New International Version*

As I've said before (and will say again many times because it can't be repeated often enough) if you want to keep growing in your ability to love, you must continue to read and meditate on The WORD of God. Unlike other books, the Bible never grows old. You never get to the point where you know what it says so well that you can put it away.

That's because God's words are alive (Hebrews 4:12). They don't just impart information to your mind, they strengthen your heart and feed your faith. Actually, The WORD of God does for your spirit what natural food does for your body. As you continue to put it in your heart, it nourishes your inner man and makes him grow.

That's why we can read the same scriptures countless times and still benefit from them. That's why we don't say, "Oh, I don't need to read what the Bible says about love anymore. I already know."

You don't get fed spiritually just by knowing what the Bible says any more than you get fed physically just by knowing what a baked potato tastes like. If you want nourishment from a baked potato, you have to put it in your mouth, chew it up and swallow it. And if you want nourishment from The WORD that will change your life, you have to put it in your eyes, ears and mouth. You have to give it opportunity to settle in your heart. If you'll do that, the very same verses of scripture will keep on changing you again...and again...and again.

As you continue to read, study and meditate on what the Bible says about love, God's words will stay alive in your heart and when you need them, they'll be there. As Proverbs 6:22 says, "When you walk, they will guide you; when you sleep, they will watch over you; when you awake, they will speak to you" *(New International Version)*.

When someone says something unkind to you and you start to take offense, the voice of your spirit will speak up inside and remind you that love "is not touchy or fretful or resentful; it takes no account of the evil done to it [it pays no attention to a suffered wrong]" (1 Corinthians 13:5, *The Amplified Bible*). Those words will give you the faith you need to access the grace you need to walk in love. They'll strengthen your spirit so that you can take authority over your fleshly desire to lash out in anger at the one who hurt you. They'll not only let you know what to do... they'll help you do it!

The more you feed on The WORD and see what it can accomplish in you, the hungrier you'll be for it. Like the psalmist, you will say, "God's WORD is sweeter than honey to me!"

When Prayers Go Unanswered, Check Your Love Life

"Little children, let us not love with word or with tongue, but in deed and truth. We shall know by this that we are of the truth, and will assure our heart before Him, in whatever our heart condemns us; for God is greater than our heart and knows all things. Beloved, if our heart does not condemn us, we have confidence before God; and whatever we ask we receive from Him, because we keep His commandments and do the things that are pleasing in His sight." 1 John 3:18-22, *New American Standard*

If you're failing to get answers to your prayers, the first thing you should do is check your love walk. Since faith works by love, it's difficult to pray in faith when you're offended at someone or behaving unkindly toward others. Your heart will condemn you and you won't have the confidence you need to believe and receive what you ask for.

At those times, it will seem almost as if the door to God's throne room is closed to you. When you try to pray, it will seem He is miles away and you'll have trouble hearing His voice.

The fact is, however, God hasn't gone anywhere. He hasn't shut you out. It's just that your unloving attitudes and actions have hindered your ability to perceive Him. Like a spiritual roadblock, they've stopped you from entering into God's presence even though as His child, that's where you belong.

To remedy the situation, simply ask The LORD to help you examine your life. Ask Him to enable you to see any areas where you haven't been walking in what He calls love.

Notice I didn't say you should look to see if you've been living according to your own definition of love. You may think you've been doing fine. You may have overlooked the fact that you gossiped about your neighbor a few days ago. (After all, you only shared her shortcomings so others could better pray for her, right?) You may have justified your criticism of the pastor. (He was wrong so he deserved it, didn't he?) You may not have noticed how harshly you spoke to your assistant at work when she made a mistake. (Hey, everyone at the office talks that way. That's what it takes to get the job done!)

God, however, is quite sensitive to those things. He doesn't excuse unloving behavior like we do. He doesn't justify it or adjust His standard of love because others do. His kind of love is unchanging. His kind of love always acts just like the Bible says it does. And when we're living by that kind of love, we do too.

Remember that the next time your prayers go unanswered or your fellowship with Him seems to be hindered. Ask Him to show you where you've failed to walk in love. You can be sure He will.

LIMITLESS**LOVE**

A Sweet-Smelling Sacrifice of Love

"Let all bitterness, and wrath, and anger, and clamour, and evil speaking, be put away from you, with all malice:
And be ye kind one to another, tenderhearted, forgiving one another, even as God for Christ's sake hath forgiven you.
Be ye therefore followers of God, as dear children; and walk in love, as Christ also hath loved us,
and hath given himself for us an offering and a sacrifice to God for a sweet-smelling savour."
Ephesians 4:31-5:2

It's easy to love and be kind to people who are loving and kind to you. The challenge comes when someone (not just a worldly stranger, but a friend or a brother in The LORD) does something ugly to you. The true test of love takes place when a person you've endeavored to BLESS criticizes you and gossips about you behind your back.

Is it possible not to become angry and bitter in those situations? Can you really be expected to be tender and kind, forgiving that one rather than treating him coldly to make him pay for his mistreatment?

Yes, it is possible, because you're a child of God. You have His nature on the inside of you. And He has proven again and again that it's His nature to forgive. What's more, through His WORD, He has clearly commanded you to imitate Him—to act as He would act in your situation—and you can always be sure that what He asks of you, He also equips and empowers you to do.

One of the best ways to tap into that power is to purposely remember how freely and graciously He has forgiven you. When you're tempted to hold a grudge or be harsh with someone who has hurt you, set the thoughts of that person aside and begin to meditate instead on the fact that in Jesus, God has forgiven not just a few but *all* the sins you've ever committed. Kneel before Him in prayer and worship Him for washing away every sinful spot and blemish, and for loving you even though you in no way earned or deserved it.

Thank Him for the assurance He gives you that if you stumble and fall in the future, His forgiveness will be there for you again. Express your gratitude to Him for His promise that if you confess your sins, He is always faithful and just to forgive you of them and cleanse you of all unrighteousness.

If you pray those things with a sincere heart, by the time you are finished, the bitterness and anger you felt toward your brother or sister will have already begun to melt away. Instead of wondering how you can possibly forgive them, you'll think, *How can I fail to forgive in light of the great debt that God has forgiven me?*

Rather than reluctantly releasing the one who did the wrong, you'll do it gladly. You'll offer your forgiveness not only as a gift to your brother but as a sweet-smelling sacrifice of love to The LORD.

LIMITLESS**LOVE**

Be Angry…and Sin Not

"Be ye angry, and sin not: let not the sun go down upon your wrath:
Neither give place to the devil."
Ephesians 4:26-27

As long as you are living in a flesh-and-blood body, you'll have to deal with feelings of irritation and anger. No matter how much you love The LORD, or how sanctified you are, if someone stomps on your toe or slaps your face (either physically or emotionally), your flesh will have a reaction. You'll probably feel angry. You may even have a natural, fleshly urge to strike back.

Those feelings in and of themselves aren't sin. They aren't an indication that you've failed spiritually. They're simply evidence that you're human and that although you're a child of God, you're still living in natural, unglorified flesh.

When those feelings come, however, you must be careful not to nurture and entertain them. You can't rehearse an irritating incident in your mind all day because if you do, you'll open the door to the devil. You'll give him an opportunity to do an evil work in you.

You can't allow yourself to fly off the handle, either, and use anger as an excuse to speak or act unlovingly. The anger itself isn't sin, but the unloving words and actions are. So determine in advance that by the grace of God, you will not let your emotions get out-of-hand.

According to the Bible, God's people aren't supposed to act like worldly people do when they get angry. We aren't supposed to give over to animosity and yell at others. We aren't supposed to give in to "road rage" and shake our fists at other drivers on the freeway.

Everyone around us may be doing it. They may get so mad in a traffic jam that they get out of the car and want to fight. People are so uptight these days that those kinds of things are happening. As we get closer to the end of the age and the pressures in the world increase, that kind of behavior will become more prevalent among lost people.

But as children of God, our behavior should be very different. It should be so different, in fact, that those around us take notice and marvel. As Philippians 2:15 says, we should be "blameless and harmless, the sons of God, without rebuke, in the midst of a crooked and perverse nation, among whom ye shine as lights in the world."

When others around us are blowing their tops, we should be keeping our cool. When the pressure mounts and our neighbors or co-workers are lashing out in anger, we can overcome the reactions of our flesh and bring a spirit of kindness and love into the situation. Although we may feel anger, we don't have to let ourselves be ruled by it. As people of God, we can be angry…and sin not. Now, more than ever, those are the kind of people the world desperately needs.

LIMITLESS**LOVE**

Love Will Find the Time

*"One thing have I asked of The LORD, that will I seek, inquire for
and [insistently] require: that I may dwell in the house of The LORD
[in His presence] all the days of my life.... You have said, Seek My face
[inquire for and require My presence as your vital need].
My heart says to You, Your face (Your presence), LORD, will I seek...."*
Psalm 27:4, 8, *The Amplified Bible*

The Bible makes many wonderful promises to those who love The LORD. Romans 8:28, for instance, promises that God will cause everything to work together for their good. (I don't know about you, but I want to make sure I qualify for that one!) First Corinthians 2:9 says God has stored up BLESSINGS for them that eye hasn't seen and ear hasn't heard. The book of James promises the crown of life (1:12), and a kingdom inheritance (2:5) to those who love The LORD.

The question all of us must answer, however, is this: *Do we truly love Him?*

"Oh, yes," someone might say. "I love Him so much I cry every time I think about Him."

That may be...but emotion alone is not evidence of love. Real love is demonstrated by action. It is proven not just by how we feel but by what we do. If we truly love God we will do two things. First of all, we will obey Him. Jesus said clearly, "If ye love me, keep my commandments" (John 14:15). And since His commandment is for us to walk in love, our devotion to Him will be demonstrated in the kindness we extend toward one another.

Secondly, we will express our love for Him by seeking Him in The WORD and in prayer. We'll spend time daily searching the Bible to find out what He wants us to do. We'll seek out His presence in seasons of quiet worship and give Him opportunity to speak to our hearts.

We have to make time for Him if He is going to do that, you know. We don't just wake up one morning automatically knowing everything God wants us to know. We learn it little by little, as we spend time with Him. We discover it day by day as we seek His face.

If we're ever tempted to think we're too busy for that, we should think again. The fact is, we all make time for the things that are most important to us. Very few of us find that we're too busy to eat or go to work. We somehow make the time.

If we truly love The LORD, we'll do the same for Him. We'll show that we love Him by giving Him first place not just in our emotions but in our daily schedules. We'll demonstrate our devotion by setting aside time for Him in our lives.

LIMITLESS**LOVE**

A Legacy That Is Worthy of The LORD

"By this all men will know that you are My disciples,
if you have love for one another."
John 13:35, *New American Standard*

What is your single greatest ambition in life?

Have you ever thought about that? If Jesus tarries and you live out your days, what legacy will you leave behind? How will you be remembered?

It seems many people in Christian circles these days are eager to be remembered as spiritual giants of faith and power. Others want to succeed financially and give great sums of money into the kingdom of God. Some relish the idea of having a reputation as a great teacher or theologian who will be quoted for years to come.

All those things are good, I suppose, but I can't help wondering what kind of impact we as believers would have on the world if we all made it our primary ambition, our life's greatest quest, to be the most loving people the world has ever known. What would happen if our single highest aim was simply to love one another?

I can tell you what would happen. The world would finally know we are truly the disciples of Jesus. They would at last see and recognize Him in us.

The world is absolutely starving for that kind of love. It's the only cure for the rejection and insecurity that plagues their lives. It's the only remedy for the depression and oppression they live with every day. Granted, they are looking for it in all the wrong places. But even so, they *are* looking for it.

Imagine what would happen if they suddenly began to see it in us!

I once read the story of a missionary in China who lived a life of such love and self-sacrifice that it softened the hardest hearts around her. Even men whose lives had been steeped in sin and cruelty, whose hearts were stubborn and scornful of the things of God, were won by the influence of this woman's kind and gentle ways. Although she was just one small woman, by the time her life was through she had reaped a great harvest of souls for The LORD. And most remarkable of all, the Chinese had nicknamed her "The One Who Loves."

Wouldn't it be wonderful if that's what the people of the world called the Church in the days to come? Wouldn't it be great if, instead of referring to us as "Right-Wingers" or "Conservatives" (fine as those titles might be), they began to refer to us as *"The Ones Who Love"*?

Truly, that would be the greatest legacy that we could ever leave…the only one that is really worthy of our LORD.

A New Kind of Selfishness

"For, 'Whoever would love life and see good days must keep their tongue
from evil and their lips from deceitful speech. They must turn from evil
and do good; they must seek peace and pursue it. For the eyes of The
LORD are on the righteous and his ears are attentive to their prayer,
but the face of The LORD is against those who do evil.'"
1 Peter 3:10-12, *New International Version*

As believers, we ought to walk in love just because God commands us to. We should do it simply because we want to be a blessing to Him and to His children. But, the fact is, even if we didn't love for The LORD'S sake, we should do it for our own sakes because when we walk in love, we enjoy our lives far more than when we don't. We're happier and we have better days when we live a life of love.

Extending love to others so enhances our own joy and well-being that one Christian writer calls it "a new kind of selfishness."

Think about the ordinary events of life for a moment and you'll quickly see why. When you're in line at the grocery store, for instance, and the clerk at the checkout counter is especially slow, if you choose to be irritable and impatient instead of loving and kind, you won't be happy. On the contrary, you'll become increasingly miserable as the minutes tick by. All your fussing and fuming won't change the situation at all. It won't make the clerk one bit faster. (I know because I've tried it!) It won't get you out of that store one second sooner. It will just rob you of your peace and joy while you're there.

So, even from a selfish perspective, which is better? To give up your happiness and get in strife with a store employee you don't even know (and who is probably doing the best job he can)…or to relax and let love rule your heart? Will you feel better when you walk out of that store knowing you snapped at the clerk and gave him a piece of your mind…or that you chose, instead, to smile and speak an encouraging word?

The answer is obvious. No one ever feels BLESSED when they step out of love. You'll never say, "Hey, I had a great day today. I got so mad and talked so ugly that it made me feel happy inside." No, that wouldn't be a great day. That would be a bummer! Once you let that anger and strife get hold of you, it would cast a shadow over everything else you did. By the time you went to bed that night, you'd probably be on edge with everybody. You'd be complaining about what a terrible day it had been.

If you really want to enjoy life and see good days, the only way to do it is to walk in love. Love not only pleases God and spreads THE BLESSING to others, it makes you happy, too. Surely, it's the best kind of selfishness there is.

Stay Connected to the Spirit

"If ye love me, keep my commandments. And I will pray the Father,
and he shall give you another Comforter, that he may abide with you
for ever; even the Spirit of truth; whom the world cannot receive,
because it seeth him not, neither knoweth him: but ye know him;
for he dwelleth with you, and shall be in you."
John 14:15-17

We'll never experience any real success in life without the help of the Holy Spirit. He's the One who communicates to us the will of God for our lives. He's the One who shows us the paths that will lead to our divine destiny. *The Amplified Bible* calls Him our Comforter, our Counselor, our Helper, our Intercessor, our Advocate, our Strengthener and our Standby. Jesus said He is the One who will teach us all things (John 14:26).

If we encounter a problem, it's the Holy Spirit who gives us wisdom so we know what to do. If we find ourselves ensnared in some kind of trouble, He reveals the truth that will make us free. When we're weak, He strengthens us. When we see what to do but can't do it on our own, He takes hold together with us and helps us.

The more attuned we are to the voice of the Holy Spirit and the more we are led by Him, the more victory we'll experience in our lives.

That's one reason we must so earnestly endeavor to continually walk in love. Love puts us in position to be controlled by the Holy Spirit.

In John 14 through 16, where Jesus gave His final instructions to His disciples before He went to the cross, we see the command of love mentioned repeatedly throughout The LORD'S teaching on the Holy Spirit. Clearly, there is a connection between the two. Since the Holy Spirit is the Spirit of love, when we step out of love, we are stepping out of His flow. We are interrupting our connection with Him.

When we disobey the command of love, He is hindered in His ministry to us.

We simply can't afford to let that happen. We need the Holy Spirit's help too much. We need Him to help us meet the needs of our families. We need Him to help us plan our schedules and deal wisely with the challenges we face every day. We need Him to constantly guide us so we can avoid the traps and snares of the devil.

That's why we must do what it takes to keep our ears open to His voice, our hearts sensitive to His leadings, and ourselves in position to be controlled by Him. That's why we must be diligent to live the life of love.

LIMITLESS**LOVE**

This BLESSING Line Is Moving!

> "Then Peter opened his mouth, and said, Of a truth I perceive that
> God is no respecter of persons: But in every nation he that feareth him,
> and worketh righteousness, is accepted with him."
> Acts 10:34-35

People who depend on this world's system for prosperity and promotion, instead of on THE BLESSING and goodness of God, perpetually fall prey to envy and strife. If they see someone else prospering more than they are, they don't rejoice—they get mad. They may even connive and scheme ways to overturn that person's success. Like hungry kids in a cafeteria line, they push and shove each other out of the way so that they can get first place.

It's really not surprising people act that way. After all, the world's system just isn't fair. It favors the rich over the poor. It rewards the beautiful and ignores the plain. Worldly promotions don't always go to the faithful. They often go to those with the best social connections or the right family name. Worldly people who don't claw and scratch their way to the top may never get there at all. So that's what they do.

They did it in Bible times and they do it today. We see in Genesis 37 that Joseph's brothers actually threw him in a well and then sold him into slavery because they envied THE BLESSING he was walking in. It made them mad that he was his father's favorite. They were jealous of the call of God on his life, so they tried to get rid of him and steal his place.

Of course, in Joseph's case those worldly tactics didn't work. Joseph kept depending on God, and despite his brother's actions to overthrow him, he just kept rising to the top. Instead of hindering his destiny, the wicked things they did actually served to help him along.

That's always the way things work in the kingdom of God. If you just keep walking in love and depending on Him, He'll see to it that you keep rising to the top. He'll take even the evil things people do to you and turn them to your good. When they throw hindrances in your path, God will turn them into stepping stones.

That's because God is no respecter of persons. He doesn't show preference to those of a certain race, nationality or family tree. THE BLESSING is for everyone who loves Him. It works to promote all those who faithfully serve Him.

As children of God, we are all standing in the same BLESSING line, so we can fully enjoy each other's successes. We can walk in love and be free of jealousy. As one friend of mine says, God's BLESSING line is like a marvelous buffet. As we watch the people ahead of us carrying plates piled high with food, we don't have to worry. We know there's more than enough. And instead of envying them, their progress makes us happy. It means the line is moving and our turn is coming soon!

LIMITLESS**LOVE**

Reason to Be Humble

"…God resisteth the proud, but giveth grace unto the humble. Submit
yourselves therefore to God. Resist the devil, and he will flee from you….
Humble yourselves in the sight of The LORD, and He shall lift you up."
James 4:6-7, 10

God delights in BLESSING us. That's what He always wants to do. But if we stop walking in love and start strutting in pride, THE BLESSING will stop working—for our own good. Rather than promoting our success, the Bible says He'll actually start resisting it, because pride works contrary to God's ways. And if He must, He will let us fail…and fail…and fail again…until we admit our own weakness and rid ourselves of pride.

Personally, I don't ever want that to happen to me. I'd rather humble myself as the scripture commands and let God lift me up, than lift myself up in pride to where I have to be brought down.

I'd rather watch over my heart day by day to be sure that I'm not being boastful or haughty. According to 1 Corinthians 13:4-5, love is simply not that way. It's not conceited. It's not arrogant. And it's not puffed up with pride.

Sometimes we jokingly say, "Hey, it's hard to be humble when you're as great as I am!" But all joking aside, God Himself is the greatest there is, yet He is exceedingly humble. He's the Creator of the universe, yet when we ask Him for help, He willingly attends to the smallest details of our lives. He is never too busy to listen. He fellowships with all who call on His Name—kings and beggars alike. He alone has reason to be proud, yet there isn't a shred of pride in Him.

If we want to enjoy His abundant BLESSING, we'll be the same way. When He begins to prosper us, we won't foolishly point to our successes and say, "Look what I've done." We'll remember that it's God who gave us the power to get wealth. He is the true reason for our success. The fact is, most of the good He has done in our lives, He has done in spite of us—not because of us. And if we're wise, we'll never let ourselves forget it.

At times you might be tempted to say, "Sure, God has prospered me…but I did the work! I studied hard. I went to school. I spent hundreds of hours practicing, planning and developing my skills. Why shouldn't I take some of the credit?"

Because God is the One who gave you the strength to work. He's the One who gave you the funds for school, the ability to study and the sense to develop the talents He gave you. You can yield to pride and take the credit, but you'll lose His BLESSING in the process. And any way you look at it, that's a very poor exchange.

LIMITLESSLOVE

The Details Make the Difference

"Finally, be ye all of one mind, having compassion one of another, love as brethren, be pitiful, be courteous: not rendering evil for evil, or railing for railing: but contrariwise blessing; knowing that ye are thereunto called, that ye should inherit a blessing."
1 Peter 3:8-9

Our idea of love and God's idea of love are often very different. We may think that as long as we don't hit anyone or steal anything major, we're walking in love. God, however, isn't satisfied with that. He wants us to be loving in our everyday interactions. He wants love to affect even the details of our lives.

That's why He tells us in 1 Corinthians 13:5 *(The Amplified Bible)* that love isn't rude or unmannerly. It doesn't act unbecomingly. That's not Emily Post talking. It's not Miss Manners giving us a suggestion we can ignore. It's God speaking to us from the Bible and requiring us to be courteous toward other people. It is God commanding us to not be rude.

Even when we're in a restaurant and the service is bad…even when a telephone solicitor calls during dinner…even when we desperately want some peace and quiet and the neighbors are partying loudly next door…we are not allowed to be rude. We can say something in those situations if necessary. We can point out the problems and make courteous requests. But in doing so, we must make sure that we do it kindly and in love.

We aren't allowed to make excuses, either. We can't say, "I know I was mean to that waitress but I was so irritated I couldn't help myself!" That kind of reasoning just won't fly. If your boss irritated you, you wouldn't act that way. You wouldn't say, "Hey, you jerk! This memo is full of errors. Get it off of my desk!"

No, irritated or not, you'd be nice to your boss. You'd be courteous because it might cost you your job to be any other way. That proves you can control your reactions.

We must put that same kind of thinking to work in the rest of our lives. We must realize that when we're discourteous to those around us, it costs us dearly. It costs us our Christian witness. (Who wants to hear about the love of God from someone who has been unkind to them?) It costs us the opportunity to brighten someone else's day. Most important of all, it costs us the privilege of pleasing The LORD.

Keep that in mind the next time some little thing goes wrong and you're tempted to be rude. Don't be deceived into thinking such small unkindesses go unnoticed by The LORD. When it comes to love, God is interested in the details because in day-to-day living, it's the details that make the difference.

LIMITLESS**LOVE**

When Your Enemies Stumble

"A righteous man falls seven times, and rises again, but the wicked stumble in time of calamity. Do not rejoice when your enemy falls, and do not let your heart be glad when he stumbles; or The LORD will see it and be displeased, and turn His anger away from him."
Proverbs 24:16-18, *New American Standard*

If we're walking in love, we will never gloat over anyone's failures—not even the failures of wicked and sinful people. We won't smile with satisfaction when we hear that the person who broke up our best friend's marriage is now going through a divorce. When corrupt politicians stumble and fall, we won't be among those who make jokes about them. Even when criminals and terrorists who have brought us or our nation serious harm finally meet their destruction, love will keep us from rejoicing.

We all need to remember that, because those things are going to happen. The Bible makes it clear that the wicked always meet a bad end. People who insist on living in sin and ignore the warnings of God will eventually be overtaken by calamity. Psalm 73 says of The LORD, "Thou didst set them [the wicked] in slippery places: thou castedst them down into destruction. How are they brought into desolation, as in a moment! they are utterly consumed with terrors" (verses 18-19).

When those terrors come, however, 1 Corinthians 13:6 says that love does not rejoice. It does not celebrate our enemies' defeat. On the contrary, it will cause us to pray for them and say, "Father, forgive them, for they know not what they do."

Isn't that what Jesus did? He had compassion on those who crucified Him. He knew they were ruled by the darkness. Even though they had willingly allowed themselves to be the instruments of evil, Jesus still forgave them.

That's just the way God is. Even when we mistreat Him, even when we talk badly about Him, if we'll repent, He'll forgive us and hold nothing against us. He'll have mercy upon us by letting us receive His Son as our Savior so we can have a whole new life.

As God's children, we're to be the same way. We're to have mercy upon the wicked until their very last breath. When we see them reaping the tragic fruit of their ways, we should ask God to grant them a spirit of repentance so that they might escape from the devil's snare. Who knows how many such requests have been uttered and answered? Who knows how many wicked men in the final seconds of life have called on the Name of The LORD and been saved because some saint of God chose the way of love and prayed?

LIMITLESS**LOVE**

A Most Costly Sin

"Therefore I tell you, whatever you ask for in prayer, believe that you
have received it, and it will be yours. And when you stand praying,
if you hold anything against anyone, forgive them, so that your
Father in heaven may forgive you your sins."
Mark 11:24-26, *New International Version*

Not only is unforgiveness a violation of love, it's one of the most costly sins we can commit. I am fully convinced that if believers understood just how deadly the consequences can be they would never, *ever* fail to quickly and freely forgive.

Unforgiveness hinders our faith and stops our prayers from being answered. It opens the door to sickness and disease while closing the door to healing. Some people have died terrible deaths, all the while calling on God for help. Yet because they continued to cling to bitterness and resentment, refusing to forgive someone who hurt them, they were unable to receive the healing they so desperately needed.

Unforgiveness consigns us to a life of guilt and condemnation because it stops us from receiving the sense of forgiveness from God that we need to be cleansed and restored. When we sin and need forgiveness from Him, our refusal to forgive another will make it seem the heavens are brass and the door to God's throne room has been closed to us.

It's no wonder that, in the sight of God, forgiveness is such serious business. He knows our whole future and standard of life depends on it. He knows that if we refuse to forgive we'll become prisoners of failure and defeat.

Of course, the devil knows that, too. So you can be sure, he'll try to deceive you. On the one hand, he'll tell you that some offense you carry is too small to cause you harm. After all, it's just a little unforgiveness. A minor grudge. In the great, big scheme of things it won't make much difference.

On the other hand, he'll convince you that the major mistreatment you suffered cannot be dismissed. It was too painful and too costly. Surely God Himself must understand that until you see justice done, you can't let it go.

But despite the devil's arguments, Jesus' words remain unmistakably clear. "If you hold anything against anyone, forgive." *Anything* and *anyone.* God has a comprehensive policy of forgiveness. Abide by it and it will protect you from much unnecessary pain and keep you in the place of answered prayer.

LIMITLESS**LOVE**

A Perfectly Safe Place to Be

"He hath chosen us in him before the foundation of the world,
that we should be holy and without blame before him in love: having
predestinated us unto the adoption of children by Jesus Christ to himself,
according to the good pleasure of his will, to the praise of the glory of
his grace, wherein he hath made us accepted in the beloved."
Ephesians 1:4-6

All fear in our lives would completely disappear if we only understood how dear and how precious we are to our heavenly Father. If we knew how He treasures us, if we comprehended how committed He is to love and protect us, our anxieties would fly out the window. Our worries would vanish. We would be the happiest, most carefree people this world has ever seen.

But most of us have been robbed of that revelation. Religion has given us the impression we're just worthless sinners saved by grace; scrubby orphans who should be content to beg at The LORD'S back door. There's a story of one little lady with that idea who would stand up to testify in church and say, "I'm just a worm in the dirt for Jesus." She said it so often that finally one man in the congregation couldn't take it anymore.

He jumped up and answered, "Yes, Granny…and one of these days the devil is going to use you for fish bait!"

That's not just funny—it's true. As long as the devil can keep us from taking our place in God's family and receiving by faith our Father's loving care, he can terrorize us day and night. He can make us live like frightened orphans, even though we've been adopted as sons of Almighty God!

Actually, we *were* orphans at one time. The Bible says before we were saved we were "without Christ, being aliens from the commonwealth of Israel, and strangers from the covenants of promise, having no hope, and without God in the world" (Ephesians 2:12). But when we called out to The LORD, He rescued us. He made us members of His own household. And that makes us especially precious to Him.

The Old Testament reveals just how fiercely protective God is of orphans who turn to Him for help. He told Israel: "If thou afflict them in any wise, and they cry at all unto me, I will surely hear their cry; and my wrath shall wax hot, and I will kill you with the sword…" (Exodus 22:23-24).

That's how protective God is toward us today. He takes it personally when anyone tries to do us harm and He comes to our defense Himself. As His adopted children, He holds us tenderly and firmly in His Mighty hand.

Even in this dangerous world, that's a perfectly safe place to be.

LIMITLESS**LOVE**

A Powerful Family of Love

"Speaking the truth in love...grow up into him in all things, which is
the head, even Christ: from whom the whole body fitly joined together
and compacted by that which every joint supplieth, according to the
effectual working in the measure of every part, maketh increase of
the body unto the edifying of itself in love."
Ephesians 4:15-16

The New Testament picture of the Church is that of a home much like heaven on earth. It's the picture of a powerful family and a heavenly Father knit together with unbreakable bonds of love.

It's a family where even the spiritual babies are safe from the storms of life. Even those not yet strong enough to fight faith's fight for themselves are fearless because they know if they need to, they can run to their family for help.

Have you ever seen a child who was awakened in the night by a clap of thunder or a flash of lightning? If that child was from a loving home, he didn't lie alone in his room shaking and trying to be brave. He ran down the hall and jumped into the bed with his mother and father, or snuggled up next to his older brother or sister. And a few minutes later, he was sound asleep, secure in the place of love.

That's how the family of God was meant to be. God never intended us to pick on and criticize one another. He never meant us to hurt each other or to be rough on those who stumble and sin. No, He told us to deal gently with even those who have fallen, to uphold the weak and comfort the discouraged. He instructed us to "bear (endure, carry) one another's burdens and troublesome moral faults, and in this way fulfill...the law of Christ" (Galatians 6:2, *The Amplified Bible*).

Imagine what will happen as we more fully obey those instructions. Think what the Church will become as we stop treating it like an institution or simply an organization, and begin to make it God's powerful family of love. We will be a family with ties so strong, that when the devil jumps on one of us, he finds he has all of us to deal with. A family that continually builds itself up instead of tearing itself down.

By the grace of God we can do it, you know. Before we in the Church are caught up to heaven, we can bring heaven right down to earth. All we have to do is take our places in God's family and start caring for each other. All we have to do is make a quality commitment to start giving our full share of love.

LIMITLESS**LOVE**

The Spirit of Adoption

"For ye have not received the spirit of bondage again to fear; but ye have received the Spirit of adoption, whereby we cry, Abba, Father. The Spirit itself beareth witness with our spirit, that we are the children of God: and if children, then heirs; heirs of God, and joint-heirs with Christ...."
Romans 8:15-17

As believers, we've been given the spirit of adoption. We're not spiritual orphans anymore. An orphan feels unloved and alone. He has no one to provide for him, no one who truly cares about his future.

An orphan continually struggles with fears and feelings of unworthiness. When prospective parents come to the orphanage, an orphan might step nervously forward in his ragged pants and worn-out shoes, trying to look his best. But inside, he's frightened. He's thinking, *No one is going to want me. I'm not good enough. I'm not handsome enough. I'm not smart enough. I have the wrong color skin....*

That's the spirit we had before we were born again. But when we made Jesus our LORD, everything changed! Suddenly we had a Father. We had Someone to love us and save us. We had Someone we could turn to when life got tough and danger threatened. At last, we could cry out, "Daddy, help me!" and be sure Someone would answer.

If you study adoption in the Hebrew culture, you'll see just how powerful the spirit of it truly is. According to Jewish law, it's illegal for an adopted child to be disinherited. He's the most secure member of the family. And no matter how many children there are, the adopted child receives all the privileges of the firstborn.

That's our position in the family of God! We have no more reason to feel insecure and no more need to fear. Through the blood of Jesus, we've been given irrevocable sonship and made joint heirs with Him. That means everything that belongs to Jesus belongs to us as well—His righteousness, His authority, His victory over sin, sickness and the devil! All our needs are met according to *His riches in glory!*

We don't have any business standing around like spiritual orphans, feeling unworthy and wondering if someone is going to help us. We've received the spirit of adoption. We ought to walk around with our heads high and grins on our faces, telling people, "My Daddy loves me! My Daddy takes care of me! My Daddy is always there for me!"

Religious folks might say, "You better watch that. It sounds like the spirit of pride to me."

No, it's not. It's just the spirit of adoption talking. It's the testimony of an orphan who has been made a son. It's the song of the redeemed!

LIMITLESS**LOVE**

He Did It Just for Me

"Giving thanks to the Father, Who has qualified and made us fit to share the portion which is the inheritance of the saints (God's holy people) in the Light."
Colossians 1:12, *The Amplified Bible*

One of the most difficult revelations for believers to grasp is the fact that they are qualified to receive THE BLESSING of God. A sense of unworthiness often dogs their steps and makes them stop short of receiving the glorious inheritance God has given them. They just don't think they deserve it.

"I could never believe I'm worthy of God's goodness," they say. "I'm nothing more than a sinner saved by grace."

That may sound humble, but the truth is, any Christian who refuses to believe they're worthy of their divine inheritance is refusing to believe the Bible. It clearly says we have been made worthy. We have been qualified and made fit to receive THE BLESSING of God. It says we are holy and beloved of God.

Granted, that's not because of anything wonderful we have done. Every person who has walked this earth with the exception of Jesus has sinned and fallen short of the glory of God. Despite our best efforts, we were so fatally flawed before we were saved that we could do nothing that was worthy of Him.

But thank God, He didn't leave us in that unworthy condition! He sent Jesus to deliver us from it. He sent Jesus to live a perfectly worthy life and then take our sins upon Himself. "He made Him who knew no sin *to be* sin on our behalf, that we might become the righteousness of God in Him" (2 Corinthians 5:21, *New American Standard*).

Every time you think of yourself, you ought to see yourself as worthy because you're in Jesus. He is wonderfully worthy…and you are *in Him!* What's more, John 17:23 says that God loves you just as much as He loves Jesus. As amazing as it may seem, God will do for you anything that He would do for Him!

Years ago, Ken was visiting with a friend of ours, a minister who had that revelation. He was one of the most joyful and loving people around. Ken once called him "an apostle of Love." Late one evening, as he and Ken walked out of a prayer meeting, they looked up at the clear night sky that was sparkling with millions of stars. "My Daddy did that just for me," he said.

In the years since, as we've come to better understand the love of God, we've realized in a deeper way just how right he was. We've come to see that in Jesus we are worthy of every good thing the Father has provided…and like our friend, we can boldly say, "He did it just for me!"

LIMITLESS**LOVE**

The Covenant Names of Love

"And it shall come to pass, that whosoever shall call on the name of
The LORD shall be saved."
Acts 2:21

We often fail to grasp the real significance of calling on the Name of The LORD, because instead of calling Him by His true Name, we simply call Him *God.* There is nothing wrong with that title, of course. It's simply an English translation of the original Hebrew word *Jehovah* that's used in the Old Testament. But it doesn't fully convey to us what the Bible intended.

In our language, the word *God* simply means "a supreme being" and though our heavenly Father is certainly supreme, He is far, far more than that. After all, the Moslems believe Allah is the supreme being. Other religions believe their gods are supreme beings. How do we know they're not worshiping the same God that we are?

We know because in the Old Testament, God didn't just call Himself by the name *Jehovah,* He identified Himself as the God of love by joining that name with His other covenant names. He called Himself *Jehovah-Shalom,* which means "the LORD is our Peace." Since the Hebrew word for *peace* carries the idea of wholeness with nothing missing and nothing broken, He identified Himself as the God who makes us whole, who restores what's missing and redeems what's broken.

He called Himself *Jehovah-Ra-ah,* which means "The LORD is my Shepherd," because He wanted us to know He would care for us and guide us. He would lead us to green pastures, beside still waters and protect us so fully that we'd never have to fear.

He called Himself *Jehovah-Jireh,* which means "The LORD will provide," so we'd never have to worry about shortage or lack. We could be sure that when we called on His Name, He'd always supply our needs.

By calling Himself *Jehovah-Nissi,* "The LORD our Banner," He let us know we'd never have to fight our battles alone. When the enemy attacks, He'll use His mighty power to fight for us and bring us victory.

He called Himself *Jehovah-Tsidkenu,* "The LORD our Righteousness," and delivered us from sin. He called Himself *Jehovah-Rapha,* "The LORD our Physician," and provided healing for all our diseases.

In all these covenant names and more, God revealed to us His true identity. He made Himself known as the Supreme Giver of Peace, the Supreme Shepherd, the Supreme Provider, Defender, Redeemer and Healer of all who would call upon His Name. No other so-called "god" in all the earth can claim such wondrous titles. No other god but the God and Father of our LORD Jesus Christ can be called the *God who is Love.*

LIMITLESS**LOVE**

Put the Devil on the Run

"Since, therefore, [these His] children share in flesh and blood [in the physical nature of human beings], He [Himself] in a similar manner partook of the same [nature], that by [going through] death He might bring to nought and make of no effect him who had the power of death—that is, the devil—and also that He might deliver and completely set free all those who through the [haunting] fear of death were held in bondage throughout the whole course of their lives."
Hebrews 2:14-15, *The Amplified Bible*

Once you know how much God loves you and what He has done for you, you won't ever have to be afraid of the devil or any of his junk again. You won't worry about sickness. You won't worry about lack. You won't be afraid that the devil is going to ring your doorbell someday and bring some kind of calamity you can't handle.

Your confidence in the love and power of God that's dwelling in you will cast out that kind of fear.

Notice, I said cast it out...not cover it up. When you really let the revelation of God's lovingkindness toward you get down in your heart, you won't have to just pretend you're not afraid. You won't have to suppress it so that instead of thinking about it in the daytime, you have nightmares all night. No, you'll just resist and it will flee from you!

"Well, I just don't know if I'm powerful enough to do that," you might say.

Are you born again? Do you have the Greater One in you? If your answer is *yes*, then you have all the power you need because "greater is he that is in you, than he that is in the world" (1 John 4:4).

It's not hard to be confident when you know you're greater than your adversary. It doesn't take tremendous courage to oppose someone who is clearly weaker than you. On Halloween, when a 4-year-old child comes to your door dressed in a spooky suit and points a plastic gun at you, do you have to overcome fear? Are you scared stiff? Do you call 911 and say, "Send help, there's a monster at my door!"?

Certainly not. You have no reason to be afraid. After all, he's smaller than you. He is weaker than you. If he gives you any trouble, you can pick him up and carry him off your property.

You can have the same attitude when you're dealing with the devil because he's been defeated. Jesus brought him to nought and made him of no effect so we wouldn't have to be afraid of him anymore!

Actually, the devil already knows that. He's just bluffing in the hope that you don't know it. So call his bluff. Resist him. He'll run because whether you know it or not, he's the one who is afraid...*of you!*

LIMITLESS**LOVE**

Love Covers a Multitude of Sins

"The end of all things is near; therefore, be of sound judgment and sober spirit for the purpose of prayer. Above all, keep fervent in your love for one another, because love covers a multitude of sins."
1 Peter 4:7-8, *New American Standard*

One of the most unloving things we as believers can do is expose and magnify each other's sins. On rare occasions when someone so stubbornly persists in a sin that he is going to hurt himself or someone else if that sin isn't brought to light, it may be necessary to go to a pastor or church leader so the person can get some help. But in every other case, love covers the sin of a brother or sister. Love magnifies and talks about the good things in people—not the bad.

People generally aren't encouraged and edified when we point out their flaws. When we criticize their behavior, even if our desire was not to be mean but to help them, they hardly ever jump up and say, "Thank you, brother, for showing me what a jerk I am! That inspires me. I believe I'll be a better person from now on!"

No, the opposite usually happens. They become disheartened and discouraged. Instead of focusing on who they are in Christ and the grace of God in them, they walk away thinking what a loser they are. And that perpetuates their weakness instead of delivering them from it.

The LORD spoke to Ken years ago not long after our son, John, had moved out of our house to live on his own. At the time, John wasn't living for The LORD, and Ken, wanting to save him from making the same mistakes he'd made when he was that age, kept talking to him about the things he was doing wrong. One day, The LORD spoke to Ken's heart and said, *You know, John thinks you think he's a bad boy.*

"Why, LORD?" Ken said. "I don't think he's a bad boy."

He thinks you do because you magnify his sin all the time.

Ken immediately made a change. He asked John to forgive him and committed himself from then on to magnify what was right about him instead of what was wrong. It made a world of difference.

If we're going to walk in love, that's what we're all going to have to do. When we see someone make a mistake, we won't make it our business to scold them for the way they're acting. We'll start praying for them. We'll believe God and make supplication and intercession on their behalf. With compassion and mercy in our hearts, we'll say, "LORD, help me pray for this brother. Multiply Your grace to him. Give him the strength he needs to get the victory!"

When we're finished praying, we won't say a word to anyone else about it. We'll cover, shield and protect that person. We'll magnify his successes instead of his failures because that's just the way love is.

LIMITLESS**LOVE**

Your Key to Success

"[Love] bears all things, believes all things, hopes all things,
endures all things. Love never fails...."
1 Corinthians 13:7-8, *New American Standard*

Love is the key to success in everything you undertake. When love motivates you, nothing can stop you. It empowers you to overcome opposition. It strengthens you to bear up under difficulties. It keeps you hoping and believing when others are growing discouraged and giving up. Love enables you to endure whatever is necessary and to patiently, faithfully pursue your goal until—at last—you achieve it!

Love can even bring you success in seemingly mundane areas of your life. Say you need to lose weight or simply get back in good physical shape. Surprisingly enough, love will enable you to do it.

Most people don't realize that. They use selfishness as a motivation. They want to get fit just so they can look good and though they start out strong, before long you can find them back on the couch watching infomercials about exercise equipment instead of in the gym working out on it. They think it's because they lack self-discipline. But the truth is, it's because their self-discipline isn't backed by love.

Those people would have an entirely different experience if they got down on their knees and asked The LORD to help them make a heart adjustment. He would awaken within them the desire to lose weight so they could better BLESS others. They'd start wanting to be strong and healthy so they could be a role model for their friends and family, an inspiration to them instead of a drain.

They'd start thinking about how much they love The LORD and how they desire to please Him. They'd be motivated to take care of their bodies so they could live longer and serve Him more effectively.

I've even seen love motivate people to stand in faith for healing even when sickness made them want to give up. They'd think of the pain and difficulty their illness or death would cause their loved ones, and they'd rise up strong in God and say, "I don't care how bad I feel, I won't let the devil steal my health. I love my family too much!"

Galatians 5:6 tells us that faith works by love. So when you take the motivation of love and add faith in God's WORD to it, you have an absolutely unbeatable combination. Faith and love together will wake you up in the morning and motivate you to put on your jogging shoes instead of your bathrobe. Faith and love will help you choose a salad instead of a sundae. They'll keep you on the fitness track until, one day, someone will look at you and say, "Hey, you look like you've lost 20 pounds! How on earth did you do it?"

You can just smile and say, "Love never fails!"

The Sweetest Thing on Earth

"Therefore as the church is subject unto Christ, so let the wives
be to their own husbands in every thing. Husbands, love your wives,
even as Christ also loved the church, and gave himself for it."
Ephesians 5:24-25

When believers get married and truly set their hearts on loving one another, they can create a situation so wonderful, it's better than anything else on earth. The only relationship that can compare with it is the one between Jesus and His Church.

Sadly enough, most Christians know hardly anything about that kind of marriage. That's why the rate of divorce in the Church is the same (or even higher) as the divorce rate in the world. Instead of focusing on how they can give to one another, believers often focus on what they can get from one other. Instead of praying for God to show them how to meet the other person's needs, they cry out to God and say, "LORD, he isn't making me happy. Make him treat me better." Or "LORD, make her stop nagging me all the time. She's driving me crazy."

I learned years ago that one of the best things I could do for our marriage was to pray for Ken and ask God to give him the best wife he could possibly have on the face of the earth. Of course, since I didn't want God to have to move me out and bring another woman in, I'd volunteer for the job myself. I'd say, "LORD, make me that kind of wife. Help me know exactly how to encourage him and BLESS him."

One day, I hadn't been as sensitive to him as he wanted me to be, and he went into another room and blurted out, "Oh, she doesn't care anything about me." I didn't hear him but The LORD did. He spoke to Ken's heart and said, *It's none of your business whether she cares for you or not. Your business is caring for her. Besides that, I love and care for you, so you just trust yourself to Me.*

Ken answered, "Yes, Sir," and he's been a better husband ever since! I've been a better wife, too. We've both learned that the more we forget about ourselves and just concentrate on BLESSING each other, the more wonderful life becomes. I can honestly say, the thought of divorce never crosses our minds.

Why should it? We have a good thing going! We not only have Jesus, we have a marriage filled with love, and that's the sweetest thing on earth!

The Ten Commandments of Love

"Know therefore that The LORD your God, He is God, the faithful
God, who keeps His covenant and His lovingkindness to a thousandth
generation with those who love Him and keep His commandments."
Deuteronomy 7:9, *New American Standard*

To best understand the message of the Bible, we must read it as a progressive revelation of God. That means each part must be interpreted in the light of the next. The letters to the churches, for example, help us understand the significance of the Gospels. And everything in the Old Testament looks different in the light of the New Testament.

That's because in the New Testament, through Jesus, God fully revealed His nature. By expressing Himself in the form of a man, He was able to communicate in a way that mankind could understand. He was finally able to demonstrate Himself as the God who is Love.

In Old Testament days, people just couldn't comprehend that. When God came down on the mountain to talk with the children of Israel and the place shook with thunder and fiery smoke, the people were frightened and ran away. They couldn't comprehend this earthshaking God as a God of love. His greatness and His power overwhelmed them. So even though He'd sworn to be faithful and merciful to them and to keep covenant with them, again and again they shrank back and said, "Moses, you talk to God for us and tell us what He says. We're afraid to talk to him. He might kill us."

It was with that mindset they received the Ten Commandments. So they interpreted them to be the demands and ultimatums from a dictator who was saying, "Do this or you will die."

In the light of the New Testament, however, we can see that wasn't God's heart at all. He wanted to BLESS those people. He wanted to make covenant with them. He was offering to be their all in all.

He was saying, "Don't have any other gods before Me. None of them will love you like I will. None of them can meet your needs like I can.

"Don't take your neighbor's stuff. I have more than enough to provide for you and him both. I'll get you everything good you could ever want. So don't steal, just come to Me.

"And don't covet your neighbor's wife. I love you and I have a girl for you who's as pretty as she is, so just look to Me and let Me bring her to you."

It is a pity God's people in Old Testament times failed to understand that. But it's an even greater pity when we fail to understand God's love today. In light of the blood of Jesus and the life He lived for us, we should forever see the Ten Commandments as the Ten Commandments *of love.*

LIMITLESS**LOVE**

Hearing the Word of Love

"Therefore I say unto you, What things soever ye desire, when ye pray, believe that ye receive them, and ye shall have them."

Mark 11:24

Our failure to comprehend the depth of God's love is one of the primary reasons we struggle to believe God will give us what we ask for in prayer. Even when we see His promises in The WORD telling us He wants us to have our bodies healed, our families BLESSED, and all our needs met, doubts often remain. We think of our own shortcomings. We think of others we've known or heard about who didn't receive what they asked for. And rather than boldly going before God's throne of grace and receiving what we need, we stand hesitantly at the door wondering if God truly desires to give it to us.

When we begin to grasp the greatness of God's love, however, that question is settled. We are confident that God will give us what we ask—not because we have in any way earned it or deserved it, but because He so fervently loves us!

Faith flourishes in the atmosphere of love. Think of a child who has gotten himself into trouble, for example. He's hurt himself doing something foolish. He knows he brought the trouble on himself by his own thoughtlessness or even disobedience, yet when he cries out to his mother for help, he has great faith that she'll come running. Why? Because she loves him. Certainly, he'll get a lecture later for acting foolishly. But the child instinctively knows that correction won't come until his mother has answered his cry and met his need. He knows her first priority is not giving him the rebuke his behavior deserves, but giving him the help her love demands.

If a child can have that kind of faith in his natural parent, how much more can we be sure that when we call out to our loving heavenly Father, He will run to our aid and answer our cry?

We're all familiar with Romans 10:17 that says, "Faith cometh by hearing, and hearing by The WORD of God." We've learned that meditating what God's WORD says about meeting a specific need helps us to have faith for that need to be met. But since the Bible says that God is Love, we can substitute the word *Love* for *God* and see another truth there: *Faith comes by hearing, and hearing by The WORD of Love!*

The more we hear about and meditate on the great love God has for us, the more we fellowship with Him and allow Him to pour out the experience of it in our hearts, the stronger our faith will become. Instead of wondering if God is going to give us what we asked, we'll leave our prayer closets believing we received when we prayed. We'll be confident He has granted our requests, not because of our great achievements but because of His great love.

LIMITLESS**LOVE**

No Reason to Doubt

"At Lystra a man was sitting who had no strength in his feet, lame from his mother's womb, who had never walked. This man was listening to Paul as he spoke, who, when he had fixed his gaze on him and had seen that he had faith to be made well, said with a loud voice, 'Stand upright on your feet.' And he leaped up and began to walk."
Acts 14:8-10, *New American Standard*

There is absolutely nothing in The WORD of God, particularly in the New Testament, that could make you doubt God's love. There isn't one incident recorded there where Jesus refused to give someone what they asked of Him. When the leper said to Him, "If you are willing you can make me whole," Jesus didn't hesitate for a moment. He said, "I am willing. Be thou made whole." When blind Bartimaeus said, "I want to receive my sight," Jesus said immediately, "Go your way. Your faith has made you whole."

Why, then, do we so often doubt God's love and His willingness to meet our needs? Usually it's because we've heard stories about people who asked God for something they needed and didn't receive it. We've heard about Sister Supersaint, the sweetest woman in the church, who asked God to heal her…and she died. Assuming that's all there is to the story, we think, *Well, if God won't answer her prayer, He certainly won't answer mine because I'm not half as good as she was.*

If you're ever tempted to think that way, first remember that God doesn't answer your prayers because *you're* good. He answers them because *He* is good. Secondly, don't assume that just because some dear saint died, God didn't send healing. I guarantee, He did. He sent healing at the same time He sent the new birth, 2,000 years ago when Jesus went to Calvary. The problem wasn't in God's sending, it was in that saint's receiving. It's none of our business what that problem was. But we know there was a problem because Jesus healed all who ever asked Him—and the Bible says He never changes.

A minister I greatly respect tells about a time he went to pray for a believer who was sick. As he was praying, his eyes were opened and he saw Jesus standing right there with them in the room. When Jesus reached out to lay His hands on the sick man's head, the man shrank back and said, "I can't receive it. I'm just too unworthy. Jesus is just so wonderful and I'm just no good. I'm not worthy."

The minister said that Jesus looked over at him with tears in His eyes and said, "You see? He won't let me heal him."

Remember that story next time someone says God didn't meet their need. Remember that God is always a lover. He is always a giver. He just needs someone to reach out to Him in faith who is willing and able to receive.

Keep the Door Open

"And, behold, there cometh one of the rulers of the synagogue, Jairus by name; and when he saw him, he fell at his feet, and besought him greatly, saying, My little daughter lieth at the point of death: I pray thee, come and lay thy hands on her, that she may be healed; and she shall live. And Jesus went with him; and much people followed him, and thronged him.... While he yet spake, there came from the ruler of the synagogue's house certain which said, Thy daughter is dead: why troublest thou the Master any further? As soon as Jesus heard the word that was spoken, he saith unto the ruler of the synagogue, Be not afraid, only believe."

Mark 5:22-24, 35-36

God is love all the time. He is good all the time. There is never a moment in our lives when God isn't longing to do for us all that we need Him to do. But it is our faith that opens the door for Him to do it. Faith is our connection to the love of God.

Fear, which is the opposite of faith, breaks that connection. Jesus could be standing right by our side, about to work miraculously to heal, deliver or bless us in some much-needed way. But if at that moment we yield to fear, we virtually shut the door in His face.

That's why Jesus said to Jairus when he received news of his daughter's death, "Don't fear! Just keep believing!" If you don't understand how spiritual things operate, you might think that was a harsh thing for Jesus to say at that moment. To your natural mind, it might seem He should have been more understanding, that it would have been more loving for Him to sympathize with Jairus and say, "I know it must be terrible to hear that your daughter is dead. You probably can't help being frightened and upset. But that's OK. I'll go and raise her up anyway."

No, Jesus couldn't do that! He understood the way spiritual things work. He knew that Jairus' faith was the crucial connection. It was his faith that would open the door for the resurrection power of God to invade that situation. Fear would have contaminated that faith. It would have hindered it and broken the connection. So Jesus said what love required Him to say. He said, "Don't be afraid. Keep believing!"

We need to let that be a lesson to us. We need to understand that to live in the full light of God's love, we must stand against fear at all times. We must treat it like a poisonous snake and drive it out of our lives. We must resist it even in the most serious situations.

If Jairus could do it, so can we. By remaining in faith and refusing to fear we can maintain our connection to God's love and power. We can keep the door of faith open so that He can be good to us all the time.

Prejudice Cannot Prevail

"And these are they likewise which are sown on stony ground; who, when they have heard The WORD, immediately receive it with gladness; and have no root in themselves, and so endure but for a time: afterward, when affliction or persecution ariseth for The WORD'S sake, immediately they are offended."
Mark 4:16-17

Once The WORD of God's love has been planted in your heart, the devil will try to use the meanness and bigotry of men to get it out. He'll send someone to make a degrading remark about your nationality or skin color. He'll send some poor, ignorant person who is prejudiced against your gender, church affiliation or family tree. If you're not alert, you'll find that prejudice getting under your skin. You'll find it pressuring you to get angry and bitter toward that person or even against the group of people that one represents.

You'll find yourself getting offended.

Someone might say, "I can't help being offended at prejudice!"

If you walk in love you can, because the Bible says love doesn't pay any attention to a suffered wrong. Love doesn't take offense.

That doesn't mean you have to agree with a bigot. It doesn't mean you can't take issue with prejudiced thoughts and speak out against them. But it does mean you can't allow yourself to get personally put out with people. You can't allow their prejudice to become an excuse for you to act or speak unkindly about them.

Actually, offense is a sign of fear. If you're offended, it's because you're afraid that person can harm you in some way. You're afraid they can rob you of safety, prosperity or promotion.

People believe that's what prejudice does. And generally speaking, they're right. But the fact is, prejudice cannot in any way harm or hinder the child of God who is standing in faith, and living in THE BLESSING. The biggest bigot in the world has never been able to stop God from promoting and prospering His people.

If prejudice could have prevailed over THE BLESSING, Joseph's social standing as a slave would have prevented him from rising to power in Egypt. Daniel's nationality would have kept him from being a ruler in Babylon. Deborah's gender would have stopped her from being a judge of Israel. Gideon's family tree would have kept him from being hailed as a mighty man of valor.

The list could go on and on. The Bible is full of examples where THE BLESSING promoted and prospered people despite the bigotry of the day. It is full of people who walked in love even in the most difficult situations. Through faith in God, they triumphed over the prejudices of men.

LIMITLESS**LOVE**

Go for the Overflow

"We have also a more sure word of prophecy; whereunto ye do well that ye take heed, as unto a light that shineth in a dark place, until the day dawn, and the day star arise in your hearts."

2 Peter 1:19

If you've had a tough time in life, if you feel especially unloved because you've suffered severe mistreatment or abuse, it may take some time for the revelation of God's love to break through the darkness of those experiences and shine brightly in your heart. There might be moments when you think you've grasped the truth of it, only to find the next moment that truth has slipped away.

If so, don't be discouraged. Just do what this scripture says and keep taking heed to The WORD of Love. Keep looking up scriptures that tell how much God loves you. Then purposely think and meditate on those verses. Talk about them with other believers. Confess them to yourself. Saturate yourself in them until your heart gets so full of the truth in them, it overflows and washes away the lies of the devil.

"But I've done that," you may say, "and so far it hasn't helped!"

That's often the way it is. In the initial stages of meditating The WORD, it may not seem to make a bit of difference. But if you keep at it hour after hour and day after day, one day you'll read a verse you've read a multitude of times before…and suddenly it will flash like lightning through your soul. Joy will rise up within you and you'll feel like saying, "I've got it! I've got it! I finally see that God truly does love me!"

The process is much like filling an empty bucket. You can pour in drop after drop of water and for a while from the outside, that bucket will look just the same. But if you keep on pouring, at some point you'll add one more drop of water and it will overflow. From that time on, if you keep adding water, it will pour out of that bucket like a waterfall. It will drench not only the bucket but everything around it!

You can do the same thing with your heart. You can just keep filling it with the gospel of love. You can keep thinking, *Yes, God loves me! His mercy and goodness constantly hover over me!* You may have to make yourself think that way for a while. You may have to make yourself talk that way. You may even feel like a phony because your old, unbelieving mind is saying, *Hey, you don't really think that's true. You don't feel loved. You feel hurt. You feel rejected.*

But you just take those kinds of thoughts captive and make your mind agree with The WORD. If you'll do that, one of these days the reality of God's love will not only fill your heart, it will shoot up out of you like a geyser and BLESS everyone around you. You'll not only believe, you'll become a living demonstration of Love!

LIMITLESS**LOVE**

A Real-Life Example of Love

"Pattern yourselves after me [follow my example], as I imitate
and follow Christ (the Messiah)."
1 Corinthians 11:1, *The Amplified Bible*

If you want to know more about walking in love toward others, follow the example of those who are most loving toward you. Pay close attention to how they talk and what they do. Let the loving way they live their lives become a pattern for you.

Noticing how others practically express God's love can inspire you and instruct you as you seek to make love a reality in your daily life. When you find your heart warmed and your spirit lifted by the sweet smile and kind words of another, you can adopt the same habit and pass that love along. When you're blessed by someone who consistently finds the best in you, rather than just enjoying the benefits of their love, you can learn from their example to look for the best in others, too.

Gloria and I have a dear friend who learned to love from her father like that. She says he was the kindest person anyone could ever know. He didn't even seem to see the faults in others. He loved everyone unconditionally with a strong yet gentle love.

Although he was not given to words of flattery, she said that every time he looked into your eyes, you could see that he appreciated you. He had a way of making you feel you were the most loved person on earth. At times, he would hear a preacher deliver a sermon full of mistakes, yet afterward when others were berating the minister, my friend's father would have something good to say. He would find some point to agree with and exclaim, "Oh, I was so blessed by that brother today!" The others around him would quickly grow quiet, sensing that his love was far superior to their doctrinal correctness.

When, at a ripe old age, this wonderful man went home to be with The LORD, his daughter said of him the greatest thing any child can say of their parent. "I just want to be more like my dad."

As her friend, I can testify she has done just that. Because she set herself to imitate the love of another, she is one of the most loving people I know. She is one who obeys the words in 1 John 3:18, "My little children, let us not love in word, neither in tongue; but in deed and in truth."

Perhaps you have no one in your life who sets such a loving example for you. Perhaps you have no flesh-and-blood father to follow. If so, draw from others what you can, and look to Jesus for the rest. Study His love life in the Scriptures, and ask Him to help you become an inspiration to those who will follow in your footsteps. Become for them what you so longed to find—a real-life example of love.

The Right Side of the Law

"For if ye forgive men their trespasses, your heavenly Father will also forgive you: But if ye forgive not men their trespasses, neither will your Father forgive your trespasses."
Matthew 6:14-15

Sometimes in reading these verses, people get the wrong idea about God. They think He's mad because they've failed to forgive someone and as a means of punishment, He is withholding His forgiveness from them. But actually, that's not the case.

God wants to forgive all of us…all the time…for everything. That's why He sent Jesus to the cross. So there's never a time when He is unwilling to forgive us.

We can put Him in a position, however, where He is *unable* to do it. And that is exactly what we do when we ourselves refuse to forgive.

Here's why. Spiritual forces are real. They are either present somewhere…or they're not. Two opposite spiritual forces can't occupy the same place at the same time. We will either have one or the other.

With that in mind, consider this. Whether you are giving it or receiving it, the spiritual fact is, forgiveness comes from God. He generates it all. So when you decide to shut off that generator and walk in unforgiveness, you are cutting it off at its source. When you make forgiveness unavailable to your brother, it instantly becomes unavailable to you.

That's a spiritual law and there are no exceptions. So the only wise thing to do is walk on the right side of that law. Walk on the side of love and by forgiving others, and keep God's forgiveness working for you.

"I've tried to forgive," you may say, "but when I see the one who wronged me, I still feel angry and upset inside. What else can I do?"

You can stick to your spiritual guns and refuse to be moved by those feelings. Love isn't based on your emotions and neither is forgiveness. It's a decision of the heart. It's a function of your spiritual will. Once you've forgiven them as an act of your will, they're forgiven whether you feel like it or not.

When you see that person on the street and your flesh reacts by tempting you to be cold or to simply ignore them, say to yourself, *Oh, no, flesh. You can't act like that. I've forgiven that person from my heart and regardless of my fleshly emotions, I intend to treat them with kindness and love.*

Then act by faith on that confession. As you do, you'll find over a period of time you'll be completely cleansed from the effects of the wrong you suffered. Those old feelings will be gone. And with the fountain of forgiveness flowing, God will not only be willing but *able* to do wonderful things for you!

LIMITLESS**LOVE**

A Small Price to Pay

"Therefore if thou bring thy gift to the altar, and there rememberest that thy brother hath ought against thee; leave there thy gift before the altar, and go thy way; first be reconciled to thy brother, and then come and offer thy gift. Agree with thine adversary quickly, whiles thou art in the way with him; lest at any time the adversary deliver thee to the judge, and the judge deliver thee to the officer, and thou be cast into prison. Verily I say unto thee, Thou shalt by no means come out thence, till thou hast paid the uttermost farthing."
Matthew 5:23-26

When you find yourself at odds with another person, don't waste a minute. Go to them and get things straight. Do whatever it takes to preserve the bond of peace between you (Ephesians 4:3).

If they won't admit they're wrong and say you're to blame for the whole problem, don't argue. Agree with them. Be spiritually big enough to take responsibility for the whole situation. Humble yourself and say, "I am at fault and I want to make it right. I love you and more than anything else I want us to be in harmony with one another again."

Most of the time, that other person will jump up and say, "No, no, no…it was my fault, too. I was wrong! Forgive me!" Then for the next few minutes, you'll have a marvelous time arguing over who gets to take the blame and you'll end up loving each other more than ever.

Even if that doesn't happen, you'll be better off because the Bible is very clear about what happens to us when we hang onto offense and strife. We pay a high price. We end up in a prison of torment that affects not only our lives but the lives of those around us.

I'll just be blunt about it. Christians who insist on staying in strife are like diseased cells in the Body of Christ. They mess up the cells that are connected to them. Take a group of Christians who love each other and are having a great time, add one person who's mad at a couple of them and before long, almost everyone will be mad at someone. That person will go from one brother to another, gossiping and spreading that spirit of offense until the whole group is spiritually sick.

Since our heavenly Father loves all of His children, He simply won't allow one of them to run around messing up the others for long. He'll shut them down in some way. He'll quarantine them spiritually until they straighten up.

If you think God won't do that in your case because you're right about the issue that's causing trouble, think again. As I've said before, if you're in strife, even if you're right—you're wrong. So whatever the problem might be between you and another, don't let it put you in prison. Let it go. Agree with your adversary quickly and be reconciled. It will cost you your pride but that's a small price to pay to stay free.

LIMITLESS**LOVE**

Don't Join Hands With the Devil

"We know that we have passed from death unto life, because we love
the brethren. He that loveth not his brother abideth in death.
Whosoever hateth his brother is a murderer: and ye know that
no murderer hath eternal life abiding in him."
1 John 3:14-15

When we think about the fact that God is Love, what usually comes to mind is how kind and gracious He is. We think about how strong He is in everything that is wonderful and good.

But sometimes we fail to consider that love, by its very nature, is totally opposed to that which is unloving. Love is a powerful enemy to all that's hateful, and all that hurts or destroys. Even though we're God's dear children, if we start violating the law of love by treating others in hateful ways, we'll soon run into a side of love we'd rather not see.

Ken tells the story about how God spoke to Him in no uncertain terms a few years ago, letting him know just how serious in His sight a refusal to walk in love can be. Apparently, someone had done something wrong. Ken hadn't let it go, and The LORD rebuked him sternly for it. *Kenneth,* He said, *you need to think about the way you've been acting toward that man. You need to realize that if you were God, he'd be in hell right now. You'd have sent him to hell by refusing to forgive him.*

That was a sobering thought for me when I heard it. It made me extra glad that God is God and we're not! But it also made me realize that when we take the side of hate and unforgiveness, we're taking the devil's side. We're joining hands with the damner of mankind and agreeing with him. We're abandoning life and stepping into death.

That's inexcusable in the sight of love. It doesn't matter what reason we have for it, either. The results are the same.

Some time ago, I saw a woman on television facing the murderer of her husband. The trial was over and she was given an opportunity to speak face to face with the man who'd been convicted of the crime. My, how that woman tore into that man! "I'll never forgive you," she said. "You have stolen my husband. You have stolen my children's father and I'll hate you till the day I die."

Later, the Holy Spirit said to me, *That woman is as guilty of murder as he is. She committed it right there in the courtroom. When she yielded to hatred, in the eyes of God she killed him.*

You might think that's a little rough, and I'm certainly not judging that dear lady, but it does drive home the point. It's a sobering reminder that love can't abide with hatred…at any time…for any reason. It's a strong incentive for us to walk continually in the light of love.

LIMITLESS**LOVE**

Almost Too Good to Be True

"Neither pray I for these alone, but for them also which shall believe on
me through their word; That they all may be one; as thou, Father, art in me,
and I in thee, that they also may be one in us: that the world may believe
that thou hast sent me. And the glory which thou gavest me I have given
them; that they may be one, even as we are one: I in them, and thou in me,
that they may be made perfect in one; and that the world may know that
thou hast sent me, and hast loved them, as thou hast loved me."
John 17:20-23

Do you want to know just how much your heavenly Father truly loves you? I can tell you in one sentence. *He loves you just as much as He loves Jesus.*

Considering the shape most of us are in and how inferior our lives are to His, that's hard to believe…but it's still true. We know it is because it came from the lips of Jesus Himself as He prayed for His disciples just before He went to the cross. It was in those last crucial moments that He spoke to the Father about us and said, "You have loved them as You have loved Me."

"Oh, no," you might say. "Jesus was talking about those first 12 disciples there. He wasn't referring to me."

Yes, He was. He said Himself that He wasn't just praying for those who were present that day. He was praying for all who would come to believe on Him through their word. That includes you and me because if you track spiritual history, you'll see that every Christian today either directly or indirectly received the gospel through the ministries of those first 12 men.

Say it out loud right now. "The Father loves me just as much as He loves Jesus!"

That's astounding when you think about it. In fact, if Jesus hadn't been the One who said it and if it hadn't been recorded in the Bible, we would never be able to believe it. It would seem too good to be true.

If you still need more evidence God has that kind of love for you, consider this: God *must* love us as much as He loves Jesus, or He would have never sent Him to die for us. If He'd loved us less, He would have spared Jesus, left us in our sins and John 3:16 would never have been written. It could have never been said, "For God so loved the world, that he gave his only begotten Son…."

It's time we accepted the full truth of that simple verse. It's time we stopped thinking God just barely puts up with us…and realize we're actually the great love of His heart. Amazing as it may seem, He loves us as much as He loves Jesus, so that's what we truly are!

A Very Personal Thing

"And Saul, yet breathing out threatenings and slaughter against the disciples of The LORD…. came near Damascus: and suddenly there shined round about him a light from heaven: And he fell to the earth, and heard a voice saying unto him, Saul, Saul, why persecutest thou me? And he said, Who art thou, LORD? And The LORD said, I am Jesus whom thou persecutest…."
Acts 9:1, 3-5

The love God has for us as His children and as members of the Body of Christ is not only as powerful as the love He has for Jesus, it is just as personal. In the mind and heart of God, we are one with Him.

That makes us extremely precious. We're not just little followers trailing along behind the Master. We're an actual part of the Master Himself. We are, in a very real way, Jesus' own Body in the earth.

Read the New Testament and you'll see that Jesus never separates Himself from His Church. He doesn't hold Himself up in some great high place while keeping us way down somewhere under His feet. He doesn't make distinctions between us as individuals, either. He doesn't consider someone who is in a visible place of ministry to be more important than someone with a less visible role. No, even if I'm the little toe of the Body of Christ, I'm still as much a part of Him as anyone else.

Actually, all of us—regardless of whether we're eyes, ears, toes or knees—are just as much a part of the Body of Christ as Jesus Himself is. We're not as vital in our function (although it's painful, you can still get along if you lose a toe, but you can't get anywhere without your head) but we're still a part of Him.

That's why He spoke so personally to Saul on the road to Damascus. Notice He didn't say, "Saul, Saul, why are you persecuting My people?" He said, "Why are you persecuting *Me?*"

It's also why He appeared to him and knocked him to the ground. Jesus didn't do that to Saul in order to save him. He never mentioned salvation to him that day. Jesus was putting a stop to the persecution of the Church. Saul just had enough sense to get saved in the process!

What Jesus did to Saul that day ought to thrill every believer because it clearly reveals how seriously protective Jesus is over each one of us who have made Him our LORD. It shows that He meant business when He said, "Inasmuch as ye have done it unto one of the least of these my brethren, ye have done it unto me" (Matthew 25:40).

So when life gets tough and the devil starts telling you that God doesn't care, remind him of what Saul learned on the road to Damascus. Remind him that God's love for you is not just powerful…it's a very *personal* thing.

LIMITLESS LOVE

The Message That Made the Glory Fall

"The trumpeters and singers were as one, to make one sound to be heard in praising and thanking The LORD; and when they lifted up their voice with the trumpets and cymbals and instruments of musick, and praised The LORD, saying, For he is good; for his mercy endureth for ever: that then the house was filled with a cloud, even the house of The LORD; so that the priests could not stand to minister by reason of the cloud: for the glory of The LORD had filled the house of God."
2 Chronicles 5:13-14

What a wonderful meeting we see described in these verses! It was the kind of meeting we all want today. The presence of The LORD was in such powerful manifestation that all the musicians and singers were working together as one. The glory of God was so thick, the priests couldn't even stand up to minister. They kept falling out on the floor!

Right in the midst of it, with the Spirit of God resting on everyone there, the people spoke out and delivered The WORD of The LORD. They preached a message straight from the heart of God.

They said, "God is good and His mercy endures forever!" If you translate more fully the Hebrew word for *mercy* there, you'll find it means "love and compassion." So what these people were actually saying was this: "God is good and He loves us forever!"

You might not think that's such a stupendous revelation but God does. Again and again in the Old Testament when He manifested Himself in that kind of awesome power and glory, that's the message He gave. *"God is good and His love endures forever!"*

That's still His message to us today. The problem is we're often so busy looking for some newer, greater revelation that we can't hear it anymore. Especially if we've been saved awhile and think we have some wisdom, we can end up hunting for meetings where someone's preaching something that hasn't been preached before. "Give me something deep," we say. "Teach me a truth that I don't know."

All the while, The LORD is saying, *OK. I'll tell you something you don't know. I love you with a love that will last forever.* Of course, we think we know that. It's a basic beginner's revelation. But if we truly believed it, we'd be living a higher quality of life than we do. Fear would have totally vanished from our lives. We'd be enjoying perfect union and communion with God 24 hours a day. Our faith would be soaring sky-high in every area of life.

The fact that we're not enjoying that kind of life tells me we still have a lot to learn about the love of God. We need to spend some more time fellowshiping with Him around the message that always caused the glory to fall. *"The LORD is good and His love endures forever!"*

From Knowing to Believing

"We are bound to thank God always for you, brethren, as it is meet, because that your faith groweth exceedingly, and the charity of every one of you all toward each other aboundeth."
2 Thessalonians 1:3

It's quite possible to know that God is Love and still be unsure about what that love will do for us. *Will God's love hold me up when I start to fall?* we might wonder. *How far will it go? Will God's love be there for me even when I've acted ugly and done the wrong things?*

As we find and meditate on the scriptural answers to those questions, our faith in God's love will grow exceedingly. We'll come to the place where we not only know, we *believe* the love God has for us.

I can personally testify just how vital that can be because many years ago when I was a young believer, my lack of faith in God's love almost cost me my life. Back then, I was smoking three packs of cigarettes a day. (That's right, God in His mercy saved me with those cigarettes in my pocket! Some people don't think God will do that. But they're badly mistaken. I'm living proof He will.)

Five minutes after I got born again, I wanted those cigarettes out of my life. It took a while for me, however, to get enough of God's WORD in me to be delivered from them. I finally did, though. During a three-week series of meetings in Houston, Texas, I got so full of The WORD, I forgot entirely about cigarettes. I didn't smoke one the whole time and when it was over I realized I was totally free!

About eight months later, though, I got out of the will of God. I stepped into a place of disobedience and the desire for cigarettes came back stronger than ever. I fought it. I begged God to help me, but I was too torn apart by condemnation to believe He'd do it. I didn't have enough faith in His love to trust it to help me in that situation. So I got hooked by that horrible habit again.

I became so discouraged and disgusted with myself, I just quit fighting sin altogether. I thought, *Well, I'm doing this…I might as well do the rest of it too.*

Before long, I'd lost the very will to live. If it hadn't been for my wife and the prayers of my parents, I might not have made it. But Gloria just wouldn't quit. She'd sit on the bed next to me and keep telling me that God loved me and He wouldn't let me go. She said it…and said it… and said it…until I was finally able to believe it.

When I did, it gave me the confidence to run (not walk, but run!) to God, repent and trust that He'd receive me. I stepped out in faith on God's love and those cigarettes got up and danced out of my life. I've never wanted them since. I've stayed free—not just by knowing that God is Love, but by *believing* that Love will always be there for me.

LIMITLESS**LOVE**

Not Looking for a License

"He hath not dealt with us after our sins; nor rewarded us according to our iniquities. For as the heaven is high above the earth, so great is his mercy toward them that fear him. As far as the east is from the west, so far hath he removed our transgressions from us."
Psalm 103:10-12

Whenever I start encouraging people to develop their faith in the love of God, in His willingness to forgive them when they sin and pick them up when they've fallen, I've noticed it upsets some folks. "Now, Brother Copeland," they say, "if you emphasize that too much, you'll just give people a license to sin."

As far as I can tell, people have been sinning without a license for years, so apparently they don't need one. Even if they did, they wouldn't want one if they truly had a revelation of God's love. I know from experience that revelation will make you fall so in love with Him, you don't want to sin anymore. You're so grateful to Him for His kindness that you avoid sin like the plague because you don't want to displease Him.

When you do make mistakes, you won't waste precious time wallowing around in them. You'll just confess them, forget them and go right on with God. If the devil tries to trip you up by messing with your emotions so you don't feel forgiven, you'll just say, "Listen, devil. Forgiveness is not a feeling. It's a fact. God says I'm forgiven, so I am. Now you'll have to excuse me because I'm going to spend some time worshiping God for His mercy that endures forever!"

Developing that kind of faith in God's love does for you what nothing else can do. It makes you bold enough to stand on God's WORD when others shrink back. When flu season comes around and everyone is saying they're afraid they're going to get it, you'll be declaring that you won't. You'll be saying, "I have a covenant with God. It says I'm healed, so the flu doesn't have any place in me!"

"I wouldn't say that if I were you," they'll warn. "What if you miss it? The devil will slap that flu on you before you know what hit you!"

"No, he won't," you'll answer. "He won't get the chance because I'll just go right to the throne room and get the mercy I need. After all, I can go there anytime I want to because God Almighty is my Abba Father. He's my Daddy, and He is totally in love with me!"

When you develop an attitude like that, you won't be messing around with sin, you'll be beating the daylights out of the author of it. Instead of looking for a way to sin, you'll have the devil looking for a way to escape from you!

Faithful to Forgive

"If we say that we have no sin, we deceive ourselves, and the truth is not in us. If we confess our sins, he is faithful and just to forgive us our sins, and to cleanse us from all unrighteousness."
1 John 1:8-9

Every one of us makes mistakes in our walk with God. No matter how committed to The LORD we may be, there are times when we miss the mark. But that doesn't have to stop us from living in victory. We can keep right on going without missing a step if we'll be quick to acknowledge our sins and repent of them.

Some believers find that difficult to do because they fail to understand the depth of the love and forgiveness of God. They fear He'll condemn them for their failures, so they're unwilling to admit them…or having acknowledged them, they refuse to let them go.

I used to make that same mistake myself, but years ago while I was preaching a series of meetings in Pensacola, Florida, The LORD was finally able to get through to me. I'd done something during those meetings that wasn't pleasing to Him. It was wrong and I knew it. I'd already confessed it to The LORD. I'd already asked Him to forgive me. But all afternoon I just kept saying, "Oh, that was so terrible. LORD, that was so awful." I couldn't even pray and prepare for the service that night because I just kept picturing in my mind what I'd done.

Finally I got ready to go to the meeting, but when I arrived I just couldn't go inside. "LORD," I said, "You'll have to get Yourself another preacher tonight because I'm not preaching after what I've done."

Suddenly, I heard the voice of God in my heart. (I'd been too busy bawling and squalling to hear it before.) He said, *Kenneth, I don't know what you're talking about. What did you do?*

"LORD, You know perfectly well what I did. I've been talking to You about it all afternoon long!"

He said, *Did you repent for it?*

"Yes, Sir."

Well, My WORD says I'm faithful and just to forgive you of your sins when you confess them—not three months later, right at that moment—and cleanse you of all unrighteousness. Unless you think I lied about that, I suggest you let that thing go and enjoy My forgiveness. Get on in there and preach. I'll be there to help you.

Right then, the revelation hit me. I saw the grace and love of My Father and it thrilled my soul. "LORD," I said, "I'm Your boy! Let's go!"

I went into the meeting that night, preached with the Anointing of God, and watched His power flow in that place. He treated me as if I'd never sinned. From that day on, I knew I'd never have to be afraid to confess my sin or waste another moment in condemnation again.

LIMITLESS**LOVE**

Something Good
Is Going to Happen

"Bless The LORD, O my soul: and all that is within me, bless his holy name.
Bless The LORD, O my soul, and forget not all his benefits: who forgiveth all thine
iniquities; who healeth all thy diseases; who redeemeth thy life from destruction;
who crowneth thee with lovingkindness and tender mercies; who satisfieth thy
mouth with good things; so that thy youth is renewed like the eagle's."
Psalm 103:1-5

"Something good is going to happen to you!"

That's what Oral Roberts used to say every week on his television broadcast. It was filled with faith when he said it, too, because that man had confidence in the love and the goodness of God.

Not everyone felt the same way he did, though. I met a preacher once who told me it made him mad when Brother Roberts said that. "Good things don't happen to everyone," he said. "What about the saint of God who prayed revival down on her town but spent her life in poverty? It would have been good for her to get some money…but that good thing never happened. So the saying isn't always true."

At the time, I knew Brother Roberts was right but I didn't know what to tell this man. When I asked The LORD about it, instead of answering me right away, He presented an additional question to me. *Did you know the same woman who prayed revival down on her town and was never BLESSED financially, could have prayed revival down on her town, never been BLESSED financially and also never received the Baptism in the Holy Ghost?*

It seemed The LORD was digging me in deeper, not helping me out.

Let me take you one step further, He said. *Did you know that same woman who was never BLESSED financially and never received the Baptism in the Holy Ghost, could also have been lying sick in bed while she prayed revival down on her town and never have gotten healed?*

Then I saw what He was saying. These things aren't rewards for our good behavior. They're the benefits of God's love made available to us when we're born again. But we receive them by faith. And faith comes by hearing The WORD of God.

Some people have heard The WORD and developed their faith to receive one benefit of God but not another. That poor woman who prayed revival down on her town probably never heard prosperity preached. She never got the revelation that God takes pleasure in the prosperity of His servant. So she served Him in poverty all her life—not because it was His will, but because she didn't know any better!

That's why you need to dig into The WORD and build your faith in the benefits of God's love. If you do, you can be sure that something good is going to happen to you!

LIMITLESS**LOVE**

People After God's Own Heart

"Be merciful and gracious to me, O LORD, for to You do I cry all the day....
For You, O LORD, are good, and ready to forgive [our trespasses, sending
them away, letting them go completely and forever]; and You are abundant
in mercy and loving-kindness to all those who call upon You."
Psalm 86:3, 5, *The Amplified Bible*

The Bible describes King David, the man who wrote these verses, as a man after God's own heart. I believe that's one of the highest compliments a person could receive. Yet there are many things in David's life we wouldn't want to copy. He made some major mistakes. If you read about his life in the Bible, you'll find he sinned against God in some flagrant and foolish ways.

Obviously, those things weren't what qualified him for that great commendation. What did qualify him, however, was the way he acted afterward. Every time David sinned, he did the same thing. He wholeheartedly repented and threw himself on the mercy of God. We can see him in the Psalms at those times, reminding The LORD of His kindness, of His tenderheartedness and His willingness to forgive.

David knew, like almost no other man in the Bible, the true heart of God. He understood that God desired mercy and not sacrifice (Matthew 9:13). And even in his darkest hours when he had most miserably failed the God he loved, he never lost sight of God's nature.

That is what made David a man after God's own heart.

Certainly at times there were unavoidable consequences of his sins. Things were set in motion that could not be stopped. But even then, David never lost heart. He never believed that God had forsaken him, nor that He had willingly afflicted him.

Even after David had committed adultery with Bathsheba, murdered her husband and watched in anguish as the baby born from that adultery died, David didn't give up on God's mercy. And despite the sadness he experienced, the light of that mercy did come shining through. For the Bible says that when he comforted Bathsheba and she conceived again, God sent a message by the prophet Nathan to tell David that the child, Solomon, should be called *Beloved of The LORD* (2 Samuel 12:25, *The Amplified Bible*).

As New Testament believers, we have less excuse for sin than David did. Even though he was anointed of God, he wasn't born again. So we can aspire to live much holier lives. But as we do, we should remember, it's not purity of life alone that makes us like our Father. It's knowing that no crime exceeds His compassion, no sin surpasses His love. It's desiring mercy more than sacrifice and giving it to others. That's what makes us people after God's own heart.

LIMITLESS**LOVE**

Talking Friend to Friend

"For it was fitting for Him, for whom are all things, and through whom are all things, in bringing many sons to glory, to perfect the author of their salvation through sufferings. For both He who sanctifies and those who are sanctified are all from one Father; for which reason He is not ashamed to call them brethren, saying, 'I WILL PROCLAIM YOUR NAME TO MY BRETHREN, IN THE MIDST OF THE CONGREGATION I WILL SING YOUR PRAISE.'"
Hebrews 2:10-12, *New American Standard*

One simple thing that will help you get a greater revelation of God's love for you is to get real with Him. If you're using Elizabethan English when you talk to Him (and you're not an Elizabethan Englishman), stop it. Speak to Him exactly like you would to anyone else you loved and respected. Be honest. Be open. And be yourself.

Don't drop your voice an octave and say, "Oh Gawwwd, what cans't I say that Thou dost not know?" Just tell Him what's on your mind. You can't fool Him, anyway. He already knows how you talk, He knows how you think, He knows what you've been doing, and He loves you in spite of it. So don't try to con Him. I was doing that some years ago, beating around the bush in prayer trying to get away from having to talk to The LORD about some foolish thing I'd done. He interrupted me and said, *Kenneth, the moment you confess a sin isn't when I find out about it. That's when you get rid of it.*

That one statement has been a basis for communication between God and me for years. It helped me realize there was no need to try to be so superspiritual when I talked to Him. As one fellow put it, "I don't have to relate to Him all 'perpendicular-like.' I can talk to Him 'horizontal,' eye to eye and heart to heart."

"Oh my, Brother Copeland, how can you say that? After all, He's God. He's above us."

I know He's God. I know He is high and lifted up. But the Bible says because I'm in Christ that I've been seated up there with Him in heavenly places. God is my Father and Jesus of Nazareth is my Brother. I call Him "LORD," He calls me "Brother," and we run together. I don't belong down under God's feet somewhere. I belong right next to Him, talking to Him as friend to Friend—not because I earned, it but because in His great love and mercy, He put me there.

What's more, I've been born again in His image. And the better I get to know Him, the more I realize He understands and appreciates me as no one else can. You'll find out the same thing when you dare to drop all your pious pretenses and get real with Him. You'll discover just how wonderfully down-to-earth the love of your heavenly Father can be.

What Moses Had…and More

"And The LORD spake unto Moses face to face,
as a man speaketh unto his friend…."
Exodus 33:11

One day, early in my Christian life, I was driving down the road thinking about this verse. I'd just read it that morning and the more I meditated on it, the more thrilled I got. Just the idea of God talking to me face to face like a friend made all the lights in my spirit come on!

But then I had this thought and all the lights went out: *God could never talk like that with me. I messed up any chance I had for that by living like an alley cat before I was born again.*

If you know anything about what the Bible says (which I didn't at the time), you've already figured out where that thought came from. It certainly didn't come from God, because it was totally unscriptural. It came from the devil.

I started to agree with him. I started to say, "Yeah, that's right. It's all over for me." But the Spirit of God stopped me.

What do you mean it's over for you? He said. *You're just getting started, and you're starting out with a closer communion with Me than Moses ever had! After all, you have everything I ever said to Moses. It's recorded in that Bible lying there on your lap. You have everything I said to Peter and John and James and Paul. You have the sermons I preached on the shores of Galilee.*

Son, I love you so much, I had everything I ever said to those men all bound up in a book and I minister it to you by My Spirit. Because you're a new creation in Christ Jesus, you have a connection with Me they never had. I not only talk to you face to face as a Friend, I talk to you heart to heart as a Father!"

When I heard that, I got so happy I had to pull the car off the road for a while so I could just sit and praise The LORD. As I worshiped Him for loving and being willing to fellowship with someone like me, it dawned on me that He has always done that.

I thought about the prophets of the Old Testament, and even the disciples in the New Testament, and realized not a single one of them could have been a member in good standing of most churches I knew. They weren't such spiritual hot rods! Most of them had messed up royally at some time in their lives. But God loved them anyway and did wonderful things through them, because they allowed Him to. They took Him at His WORD. They believed He'd do what He said He'd do.

When I pulled back onto the road that day, I was a different man. I wasn't thinking about my failures, I was thinking about my future—a future filled with the love and communion of God. I was rejoicing over the revelation that even Moses didn't have what God had given me.

LIMITLESS**LOVE**

Facts, Not Feelings

"For The WORD of God is living and active and sharper than any two-edged sword, and piercing as far as the division of soul and spirit, of both joints and marrow, and able to judge the thoughts and intentions of the heart." Hebrews 4:12, *New American Standard*

One thing you absolutely must do to successfully develop your faith in God's love is give His WORD priority over your feelings. You have to make a decision that you're going to believe God's WORD even when your emotions contradict it. You must determine in advance that God's WORD is true, and the way you feel about it doesn't count.

When circumstances in life are a mess or someone has hurt you and you start feeling like God doesn't love you, don't give in to that and start talking unbelief. Don't indulge in a session of self-pity and say, "Well, I just don't feel very loved right now. Things are so hard. I feel like if God loved me, He'd do something to help me...."

No, you take authority over your emotions and get right back in faith and stand on The WORD of God. You say, "I'm not moved by how I feel and I'm not moved by these circumstances around me. The WORD says God loves me and I believe He does. The WORD says He'll never leave nor forsake me, so I believe He is right in here with me, helping me with this mess, and together we'll get it straightened out."

Over the years, I've found this is one of the most difficult things for people to do, because most folks equate love with feelings. They think if they don't feel love, they don't have any. They think if they feel rejected and unwanted, then they are.

But I'm warning you, the devil will mess with your feelings because they aren't spiritual, they're a part of your soul. Just like the devil will put symptoms on your body so you'll believe and receive sickness, he'll also put emotional symptoms on you that make you feel unloved. If you believe those symptoms, you'll be stuck in that condition. If you stay with The WORD, however, it will divide soul from spirit. It will help you to separate spiritual truth from soulish emotions, and as you continue in that WORD, eventually your emotions will fall in line. Then you'll not only believe, you will also *feel* loved!

In the meantime, remember it's when you don't feel like God loves you that you most need to believe it. It's at those times that you need to think about facts, not feelings. The fact is, God paid the highest conceivable price to save you and make you part of His eternal family. He not only said He loved you, He proved it by sending Jesus.

"Greater love has no one than this, that one lay down his life for his friends" (John 15:13, *New American Standard*). That's a fact more powerful than any feeling you could ever have. That's the love God has for you.

LIMITLESS**LOVE**

Meditation Makes the Difference

"This book of the law shall not depart out of thy mouth; but thou shalt meditate therein day and night, that thou mayest observe to do according to all that is written therein: for then thou shalt make thy way prosperous, and then thou shalt have good success."

Joshua 1:8

Since meditating on God's love is a vital part of developing your faith in that love, you need to understand what meditation actually is. It's more than just memorization, or mentally repeating certain scriptures. When you meditate on God's WORD, you think deeply about it. You ask yourself questions that will help you apply it.

Say, for example, you're meditating Romans 8:37: "…we are more than conquerors through him that loved us." You might ask yourself, *How does that truth change my life? Since God's love for me makes me more than a conqueror, how should I be approaching the challenges I'm facing right now? Have I been expecting God's love to help me triumph over them? Have I been thinking, talking and acting like more than a conqueror?*

Fellowship with the Holy Spirit about those things. Ask Him to help you identify areas of your life where this verse needs to be applied. Let Him help you paint an inner image of yourself with such confidence in God's love for you that you are bold and triumphant in areas of your life where you've previously been fearful and defeated. Spend time seeing yourself the way God's WORD says you are—dearly loved and mightily victorious on the battlefield of life.

The word *meditate* also means "to mutter, talk or utter." So as you think about the love of God, speak it out. Say it to yourself in the form of a confession of faith. "God's love for me makes me more than a conqueror over the financial challenges in my life! Because He loves me, He meets my every need! Debt is defeated! Lack is turned back! I'm the beloved of The LORD, and those things are under my feet!"

Bring those meditations into your prayer life as well. Instead of spending all your time making petitions (although that's a perfectly scriptural thing to do), take some time just to praise God for what He's said about you in His WORD. Say, "Thank You, LORD, for loving me with such a great and mighty love. I praise You for making me more than a conqueror and giving me victory every day…."

The first few days you meditate that way you may not sense much difference in your life. But stay with it and as the weeks and months pass, you'll find that WORD you've been meditating is taking over your thinking processes. You'll realize you're talking differently. You're acting differently. You'll find like Joshua did, God's WORD is making your way prosperous and giving you good success!

LIMITLESS**LOVE**

Act Like You Believe It

"For as the body without the spirit is dead,
so faith without works is dead also."
James 2:26

If you believe God loves you, then you need to act like you believe it. Otherwise, according to this scripture, your faith is lifeless. Your unbelieving actions keep it from having any practical effect.

Think, for instance, about the person who says he believes God loves him but whenever he prays, instead of coming boldly before the throne of grace, confidently asking for what he needs, he crawls in there whining and pleading like an unworthy beggar. That person's actions short-circuit his faith. Nine times out of ten, he'll come out of that situation not having received what he asked for and wondering why.

People like that remind me of how my daughter, Kellie, acted when she was little and going through a whining phase. She'd try to ask me for something, but that whining tone of voice was almost impossible to understand. What's more, it was aggravating. Finally one day I said, "Kellie, just stop that! I love you. I am not going to hurt you, and I want to give you what you want. But if you can't talk to me without that whining, then don't talk to me at all."

As I said that, the Spirit of God spoke to me and said, *I'd appreciate it if you'd do the same.*

Of course, I was embarrassed He had to say it but I'm glad He did. In the years since I've learned it's practically impossible to do something for someone who is acting like that no matter how much you want to. Even Jesus Himself couldn't do it. He once dealt with a Syrophonecian woman who followed him around crying and begging Him to help her demon-possessed daughter. She must have had some faith or she wouldn't have been trailing after Him. But she short-circuited it by her unbelieving approach.

Finally, Jesus turned to her and basically said, "I've not been sent to help gentile dogs like you." To us, that might sound mean. But Jesus wasn't being mean. He loved that woman and wanted to provoke her so she'd cast off that whining attitude, say some words of faith, and open the door for Him to heal her daughter.

He succeeded, too! She demonstrated some spiritual backbone after that. She stood up and said, "Yes, LORD; but even the dogs feed on the crumbs which fall from their masters' table" (Matthew 15:27, *New American Standard*).

When she did, Jesus said to her the same thing He's longing to say to us, "'O woman, your faith is great; be it done for you as you wish.' And her daughter was healed at once" (verse 28, *New American Standard*).

The Only Safe Place to Be

"He that dwelleth in the secret place of the most High shall abide under the shadow of the Almighty. I will say of The LORD, He is my refuge and my fortress: my God; in him will I trust. Surely he shall deliver thee from the snare of the fowler, and from the noisome pestilence. He shall cover thee with his feathers, and under his wings shalt thou trust...."

Psalm 91:1-4

When calamity strikes, as it frequently does in these dangerous days, and the innocent lose their lives, people often question the love of God. "How could a God who is good and kind allow that to happen to people?" they ask. "Why didn't He do something to save them?"

The answer in every case is the same: *He did.*

God is not, by nature, a dominator of mankind. Although He dearly loves everyone, He will not force even those He loves to receive or respond to the help He offers. He will not force them from a course of action they have chosen, no matter how costly that course might be.

That's why God can only guarantee protection to the person who dwells in the secret place of the Most High and abides under the shadow of the Almighty. Those are the only ones who are sure to respond to His warnings. Only those who live in His secret place are certain to hear His voice and run to the refuge He provides.

One fellow minister and dear friend of mine can give personal testimony to that. Some years ago, he and a number of other people he knew were booked on a particular flight to Detroit and God spoke to Him and said, *Don't get on that airplane. Stay where you are.* Mentally, he struggled with that instruction because he had appointments to keep. He needed to be on the flight. But he knew The LORD loved him and had his best interest at heart, so he obeyed.

It was a good thing he did, too, because the plane crashed and burned just outside Detroit that day.

Several other believers he knew who were supposed to be on that flight had the same experience. In every case, God dealt with them one way or another, and let them know they shouldn't get on it. Most of them obeyed and were saved. Sadly, a couple of them didn't. My friend warned one of those people himself by telling him what The LORD had said, but that person didn't listen and he lost his life.

When I asked my friend how we can continually live in that secret place and enjoy that kind of protection, he gave me this answer: "Live every day close to God, loving Him and loving your fellow man. A step out of love is a step outside the shadow of the Almighty."

That's an answer we should take to heart in dangerous days like these, because the shadow of our loving God is the only safe place to be.

LIMITLESS**LOVE**

Sowing and Reaping in Love

"Every man according as he purposeth in his heart, so let him give; not grudgingly, or of necessity: for God loveth a cheerful giver. And God is able to make all grace abound toward you; that ye, always having all sufficiency in all things, may abound to every good work."
2 Corinthians 9:7-8

Over the years, believers have learned about the principles of sowing and reaping. We've seen in The WORD that if we'll give, it will be given to us again. If we plant a seed, we'll have a harvest.

That's a scriptural principle, but it's not a mechanical one. You can't just give away money and have it automatically come back to you multiplied again. No, the working of any spiritual principle depends entirely on the condition of the heart. You may be shocked to hear me say this but the fact is, increase doesn't come to every giver. It comes to those who give cheerfully in faith from a heart of love.

Ananias and Sapphira proved that. They gave a substantial gift to the Jerusalem church. Financially speaking, that was a big seed they were planting. But their harvest wasn't BLESSING and increase. Their harvest was a quick departure from the planet because their hearts were wrong. They weren't giving because they loved The LORD and wanted to be a BLESSING. They were giving from a motive of selfishness and pride.

Their story proves that money, in itself, isn't seed. You might say it's just the husk of a seed. It's what's inside the husk that counts. When filled with love, our financial seeds come alive. They become the means by which we release compassion.

Although it encourages us to know God will BLESS us in return and enable us to keep on giving, that's not the reason we give. If we're giving from a heart of love, we'll give tithes and offerings whether or not we ever get anything back. We'll do it because we love people. We'll do it because we want them to hear God's WORD.

Am I saying that everyone who hasn't received a harvest on their giving had a wrong motive? Certainly not. Sometimes we've given in love but then failed to receive our harvest because we didn't fully trust God's love for us. We'd start thinking, *Wow…that was a big gift I gave. It emptied my savings account. What if God doesn't BLESS me? What will I do?*

Our faith faltered because we failed to see this simple truth: If God's love *in* us won't allow our brother's need to go unmet, then surely His love *for* us cannot allow our need to go unmet!

The more I study the love of God, the more I realize it's the bottom line. When we're trusting in and operating by that love, every spiritual principle works flawlessly in our favor. When we're walking in and believing God's love, we simply can't help but be BLESSED.

LIMITLESS**LOVE**

In the Midst of the Storm

"When He got into the boat, His disciples followed Him. And behold, there
arose a great storm on the sea, so that the boat was covered with
the waves; but Jesus Himself was asleep. And they came to Him and awoke
Him, saying, 'Save us, LORD; we are perishing!' He said to them, 'Why are
you afraid, you men of little faith?' Then He got up and rebuked the
winds and the sea, and it became perfectly calm."
Matthew 8:23-26, *New American Standard*

Every one of us can identify with the disciples in this passage. At times in our lives when we're endeavoring to live by faith, we become frightened by circumstances. We let the waves of doubt overwhelm our souls and we qualify for the same loving rebuke the Master gave to that first boat full of followers.

"Why are you afraid, you men of little faith?"

Actually, that's not only a rebuke. It's a question worth answering. If you study the Greek meanings behind the phrase translated *little faith,* you'll find it can refer not only to something that is slight and small but to something of short duration. So we should ask ourselves why we so often run out of faith in the middle of the storm. *Why do we let fear cut faith short just when we need it most?*

Usually it's because our faith in God's WORD isn't fully backed by confidence in His love. We know what He said He'd do for us. He said He'd heal us, provide for us and protect us. No doubt about that. But when winds of trouble blow and the clouds of circumstance threaten, we begin to wonder if He's forgotten about us. It may seem to us He is asleep at the helm, insensitive and unresponsive to our plight.

At those times, however, we can shore up our faith. We can extend its life by reminding ourselves of God's unfailing love. When the first flash of fear arises and we catch ourselves thinking, *What if God doesn't provide for me this time? What if He doesn't heal me?* we should stop right then and say, "No, I refuse to think that way. I refuse to entertain that fear because I know My Father loves me. He loves me so much that He gave Himself for me. He loves me so much He promised He'd never for a single moment leave me or forsake me."

If at those times of crisis we'll remind ourselves of our Father's loving care, our faith will endure. If we'll consider how Jesus has proven His compassion by the great sacrifice He has already made for us, we won't grow weary and faint in our minds (Hebrews 12:3). We'll realize God has not only given us His WORD, He has given us His heart. And even in the midst of the storm, we'll know we are safe and secure in His love!

LIMITLESS**LOVE**

The Key to Freedom and Fullness of Joy

"These things I have spoken to you so that My joy may be in you, and that your joy may be made full. This is My commandment, that you love one another, just as I have loved you. Greater love has no one than this, that one lay down his life for his friends."
John 15:11-13, *New American Standard*

Of all the New Testament writers, the Apostle John had the greatest revelation of love. In his Gospel account and his letters to the Church, he makes it clear that walking with God and walking in love go hand in hand. You cannot do one without the other.

He also reveals that walking in love, even though it requires us to lay down our lives for others, is not a distressing or depressing thing. On the contrary, it is the key to fullness of joy.

The very idea of laying down your life for someone else being a joyful thing is absolutely contrary to natural, worldly ways of thinking. The world says, "If you want any happiness, you'll have to go after what you want first and foremost. You'll have to look out for yourself because no one else will do it for you." According to worldly standards, that's the normal way to live. Yet self-centered people invariably struggle with depression and oppression. They can't sleep. Their relationships are shallow and unsatisfying.

The lifestyle of love, however, is exactly the opposite. Love says, "Don't seek your own interests first, but the interests of others. Bear one another's burdens. If you want to be great, be the servant of all."

The devil will try to talk you out of that lifestyle. He'll tell you that if you put other people first, you'll never have anything yourself. He'll tell you that if you serve others, they'll walk all over you and you'll end up miserable and sad. But those are just lies.

The fact is, the more you lose sight of yourself, the happier you will be. The more you focus on BLESSING others, the more abundantly you'll be BLESSED.

A friend of mine once told me of a time in his life when he was unhappy and things just weren't going the way he had planned. He spent hours on his knees, rehashing his problems and asking God to help. Eventually, he heard the voice of The LORD say, *Son, if you'll just forget about yourself, most of your problems will evaporate.*

That's not really what he wanted to hear right then, but he took it to heart, got his mind off himself and focused instead on serving others. Recently, he said to me, "You show me someone who has matured in God, and I'll show you someone who has the ability to go lengths of time without thinking about himself. I'll show you someone who has discovered what it means to walk in freedom and fullness of joy!"

LIMITLESS**LOVE**

Creation Speaks of His Love

"...The earth is full of the goodness of The LORD."
Psalm 33:5

The Bible repeatedly declares that creation itself—God's beautiful world and everything wonderful within it—is an expression of the power and the nature of God.

Psalm 19:1 says, "The heavens declare the glory of God; and the firmament showeth his handywork."

Psalm 50:6 says, "The heavens shall declare His righteousness...."

Romans 1:19-20 says, "That which is known about God is evident within them; for God made it evident to them. For since the creation of the world His invisible attributes, His eternal power and divine nature, have been clearly seen, being understood through what has been made..." *(New American Standard)*.

Consider those statements in light of the fact that God's nature is love and you'll realize that God is constantly declaring His love for you—not only through the words of the Bible and through the witness of His Spirit in your heart, but through creation itself.

The reason the flowers are pretty is because God loves you. The reason fruit tastes good is because God loves you. The reason the sun shines is because God loves you. The reason the rain comes in the spring is because God loves you.

"But Brother Copeland," you might ask, "what about all those things in the earth that aren't good? Aren't those expressions of God as well?"

No, they're not. They're an expression of the nature of the devil who through sin has warped this earth and robbed it of its full glory. That's why Romans 8 says, "The whole creation groans and suffers the pains of childbirth together until now" (verse 22, *New American Standard)*, looking forward to the return of Jesus and the completion of His redemption plan.

Bless God, the day is coming when God's great love will drive out every damnable thing in this earth that has ever caused His children pain! The day is coming when He will deliver creation itself from decay and corruption and bring it into the glorious freedom of the children of God!

Until then, however, He will see to it that the best this old earth has to offer is made available to His children. He will continually give us all good things to enjoy. As He does, we need to receive every one of them as an expression of His compassion and tender care. We need to see in every blossom of spring, we need to hear in the voice of every bird that sings, the voice of our heavenly Father telling us of His love.

LIMITLESS LOVE

Let This Mind Be in You

> "Let this mind be in you, which was also in Christ Jesus: who, being in the form of God, thought it not robbery to be equal with God: but made himself of no reputation, and took upon him the form of a servant, and was made in the likeness of men: And being found in fashion as a man, he humbled himself, and became obedient unto death, even the death of the cross."
> Philippians 2:5-8

To walk in love as Jesus did, and as He commanded us to do, will at times require fleshly sacrifices. It will require us to lay aside our own comfort so we can comfort others. It will require us to surrender our own selfish rights and desires so we can serve someone else.

But make no mistake, such sacrifices won't leave you feeling deprived. They'll leave you so full of joy you can hardly stand it.

Sometimes folks walk around like sad-faced, self-made martyrs when they make such sacrifices. They let everyone know how much they're suffering for Jesus. But those people have missed the mark. They can't possibly be loving like Jesus loved or sacrificing like He sacrificed. If they were, they'd be experiencing joy because Hebrews 1:9 plainly tells us He was anointed with the oil of gladness!

"Yeah, but that was *Jesus!*" someone might say. "No one else can make those kinds of sacrifices and be happy."

The Apostle Paul did. For the sake of Love, he preached the gospel in places where they stoned him, put him in jail and beat him with rods. His love for God and for the saints caused him to lay down the natural pleasures of life and put up with shipwrecks, nights in the cold and days in the deep. But you didn't find Paul weeping over his suffering and deprivation. You didn't find him saying, "Poor, old me!"

Quite the opposite. He said to the Colossian Christians, "Who now rejoice in my sufferings for you…" (Colossians 1:24).

What made him rejoice? He saw how his sacrifices and sufferings benefited those he loved! He saw heathen gentiles transformed by the message he brought and become beautiful saints of God. He saw them walking in the truth and being prospered and BLESSED—spirit, soul and body. And I'm sure he would have said, as the Apostle John did, "I have no greater joy than this…" (3 John 4, *New American Standard*).

Remember this: If you're suffering in life and no one is benefiting from it, you're not suffering according to the will of God. You're not suffering for the sake of Love. You're just being cheated by the devil.

If someone is being BLESSED by it, then pull out all the stops. Forget about your own interest; lose yourself in the love of God and focus on the wonderful things He is doing for others through you. Instead of sadness, you'll have the oil of gladness, and Jesus' mind will be in you!

LIMITLESS**LOVE**

Spending a Lifetime on Love

"Let all that you do be done in love."
1 Corinthians 16:14, *New American Standard*

When we first began to work on this book, some people who heard about it were skeptical. "You're going to write a year's worth of devotions on the subject of love?" they asked. "Do you think people will want to spend a whole year thinking and studying about love?"

Yes…we can spend a year learning to walk in love. In fact, if we're wise we'll spend a lifetime on it. We'll study it and pray about it and practice it until it absolutely dominates every area of our lives.

Why? Because love is, without question, the primary emphasis of the New Testament. It is the center of true Christianity. It is the key that causes every other spiritual principle to work in our lives. As a subject, it's inexhaustible. It's as big as God Himself because God is Love.

Certainly, there are other things we must study and understand. There are other spiritual truths to learn. But as those truths come forth, we must not become so preoccupied with them that we let them take priority. We cannot afford to become so focused on faith, for example, that we let love slip. We cannot get caught concentrating on the principles of prosperity so much that we forget that compassion is the reason we must prosper. If we allow that to happen, we may speak spiritual-sounding words but we end up acting just like the world. We may be able to teach spiritual truths, but without love those truths will be nothing more than religious rhetoric.

Actually, it's impossible to overemphasize love. It's impossible to state too strongly how vital it is. After all, Jesus said that love—and only love—is the mark of a real disciple. Signs, wonders, miracles, tongues, prophecy, prosperity, even spiritual understanding are all wonderful, but wonderful as they are, the Bible says they are no sure sign a person has truly been born again. Love is the sole mark that identifies us as the genuine article. As Jesus said, "By this all men will know that you are My disciples, if you have love for one another" (John 13:35, *New American Standard*).

It will do us all well, not only during this devotional year but in every year that follows, to keep that truth in mind. It will be good for us to learn that even when we reach out to grasp other scriptural things, we should always keep one hand on love. That will help us avoid error. It will help us keep our doctrine straight and our lives in line with the true WORD of God.

While we may surround ourselves with teachings on faith or righteousness or healing, we must always keep love in the center of it all. We must keep on learning about love and growing in it until it can be said of us that everything we do is done in love.

LIMITLESS**LOVE**

The Motive Makes the Difference

"You desire but do not have, so you kill. You covet but you cannot get what you want, so you quarrel and fight. You do not have because you do not ask God. When you ask, you do not receive, because you ask with wrong motives, that you may spend what you get on your pleasures."
James 4:2-3, *New International Version*

These believers were in sad shape. They were frustrated and angered by the lack in their lives. They were jealous of those who prospered and getting in arguments with them. They'd quit praying altogether because they were tired of their prayers going unanswered.

Most of us don't identify with that group. We consider ourselves to be more mature and well-mannered than they were. We rarely have fist fights in the foyer of the church. We keep our coveting under cover. Although we might indulge in a little irritation when Brother Big Shot walks in wearing the suit we've been believing God for, killing him would be totally out of the question.

What many believers would have to admit, however, is this: As nice as we are, when we ask God for things we often fail to receive them. The reason for that failure is the same as it was for that rascally bunch James wrote—our motives have been wrong.

Many times we have prayed in selfishness instead of in love.

Selfish prayers don't carry much spiritual power. They're not backed by faith because faith can't work without love. Even when we're praying in tongues, if love for God or for others isn't the motive behind it, the Bible says those tongues are ineffectual. We might as well be banging around on a kitchen pot (1 Corinthians 13:1).

In short, when we're praying without love, we're wasting our time.

But, praise The LORD, even when we find ourselves in that position, we don't have to stay there! We can do what James tells us to do. We can humble ourselves before The LORD and admit our selfish motives. We can draw near to Him and trust Him to give "us more and more grace (power of the Holy Spirit, to meet this evil tendency and all others fully)" (James 4:6, *The Amplified Bible*).

With His help we can strip away that old selfishness and let the love of God within us come through. We can begin every prayer confessing our love for God and our desire to BLESS others, and then let the requests of our hearts begin to flow. As we do, we'll become more than just well-mannered Christians who keep their irritation under control. We'll become believers who are motivated by love. Believers who fellowship instead of fight…who rejoice over THE BLESSING working for a brother…and who *always* receive answers to their prayers.

LIMITLESS**LOVE**

For the Love of the Game

"Behold, the third time I am ready to come to you; and I will not be burdensome
to you: for I seek not yours, but you: for the children ought not to lay up for the
parents, but the parents for the children. And I will very gladly spend and be spent
for you; though the more abundantly I love you, the less I be loved."
2 Corinthians 12:14-15

The more I read the writings of the Apostle Paul, the more I see in him the love of Jesus. I believe he woke up every morning and went to sleep at night thinking about how he could BLESS the believers in the early Church. Even when he was making plans to go and see them, his mind wasn't occupied with the hardships he would suffer on the journey (and those hardships were severe). He was thinking about the impact his visit would have on them.

That's the way Jesus was. He lived every day with others on His mind. Jesus never got up in the morning and said, "What do I want to do today? How can I make Myself happy?" No, He started His day by saying, "Father, I didn't come down from heaven to do My own will but Yours. Where do You want me to go today? Who do You want Me to minister to? How do You want Me to give Myself away?"

As a result, everywhere He went burdens were removed and yokes were destroyed. People were helped and healed and delivered.

Jesus literally spent Himself on behalf of others and that's what Paul did, too. What's more, like Jesus, he did it gladly. He did it with passion and heartfelt pleasure. He did it without caring at all about what he received in return. His joy didn't come from others giving to him. It didn't even come from their grateful response to his loving care. As long as they were helped in some way by his sacrifice, he was more than happy to make it.

That kind of joy and unfettered gladness is the hallmark of real love. When it's not there, no matter how kind and giving our actions might be, wholehearted love is not behind them. Somehow selfishness or pride has gotten in and spoiled the mix.

When we abandon ourselves completely to love, we not only forget about the cost…we actually rejoice in it. We're like the snaggletoothed, scar-faced hockey player who played with such a total passion for the game that he didn't even notice the suffering. In fact, he took an odd kind of pleasure in it. He said to his opponent, "Come on, give it your best shot and I'll beat you anyway."

That's how we'll be toward the persecutions of the devil when we throw ourselves fully into the divine game of love. We'll say like Paul, "I spend myself gladly!" We'll endure the hardships and laugh. We'll make the sacrifices and smile. All for the love of the game.

LIMITLESS**LOVE**

The Perfect Expression
of Charity

"Charity suffereth long, and is kind; charity envieth not; charity vaunteth
not itself, is not puffed up, doth not behave itself unseemly, seeketh not
her own, is not easily provoked, thinketh no evil; rejoiceth not in iniquity,
but rejoiceth in the truth; beareth all things, believeth all things, hopeth all
things, endureth all things. Charity never faileth...."
1 Corinthians 13:4-8

When I study this passage of Scripture, I enjoy using the *King James Version* of the Bible because it uses the word *charity* instead of *love*. Although that translation bothers some people, *charity* is actually a very good word. In recent times it's had a bad reputation because it has come to be associated with the condescending kind of giving that some people do for the poor. In the minds of many people, giving someone charity means giving them your leftovers. It robs the receivers of their sense of worth and dignity and gives rise to the phrase, "I don't want your charity."

But when the translators originally chose that word, it carried an entirely different meaning. It represented something even deeper and more substantial than what we normally think of as love. It signified far more than an emotional feeling.

Charity was a giving love, a deep desire to help someone in need. When a person had charity, they had such a strong commitment and drive to care for another that they wanted to give the very best they had. You can get a sense of what the word meant when you realize the word *cherish* that we use today came from that same root word.

To cherish someone is to treasure them, to value them so highly you esteem them as priceless. Add to that concept a willing determination to keep on treasuring that person—no matter what they do or how they respond to you—and you have a good picture of what charity truly is.

Now, with that truth in mind, read these verses again, taking the word *charity* and putting God's Name in its place. That's a perfectly legitimate thing to do, since the scriptures themselves tell us that God is Love. He is the perfect expression of charity.

God suffers long and is kind. God envies not; and God vaunteth not Himself. God is never puffed up and He doesn't behave Himself unseemly. He seeks not His own. He's not easily provoked. God thinks no evil; rejoices not in iniquity, but rejoices in the truth. God bears all things, believes all things, hopes all things, and endures all things. God will never fail you!

LIMITLESS**LOVE**

The Ultimate Gentleman

"Love is patient; love is kind; love is not envious or boastful or arrogant or rude. It does not insist on its own way; it is not irritable or resentful; it does not rejoice in wrongdoing, but rejoices in the truth. It bears all things, believes all things, hopes all things, endures all things. Love never ends...."

1 Corinthians 13:4-8, *New Revised Standard Version*

No matter how many times we read these verses, we will always be blessed to go back to them again because they give such insight into the nature of love which is the nature of God Himself. As we've already seen, one valuable way to study them is to substitute the word *God* for the word *love,* so they not only become a description of how we should love others but how God Himself loves us.

That immediately straightens out some of our religious misconceptions. Saying that God is patient and kind, for example, dismantles the idea many people have that God is a quick-tempered tyrant sitting over them with hammer, ready to knock them in the head every time they do something wrong.

According to these verses, that is not God's nature at all. He's not irritable and quick to get mad. He bears with us, hopes in us and believes the best about us even in the worst of times. God will put up with us when no one else will. He'll stay with us to the very end.

"But what about the verses that say love isn't envious and doesn't insist on its own way?" someone might ask. "Doesn't the Bible say God is a jealous God? Doesn't it say we have to do things His way?"

Yes, but God isn't selfishly jealous like human beings are. He doesn't demand we do what He says so that He can be in control. God desires us to put Him first in our lives because He loves us and He knows that no one else can take care of us like He can. No one else can fully meet our needs. He knows that if we turn our hearts away from Him, we'll suffer pain and lack. We'll miss out on the wonderful BLESSING He has provided us.

He wants us to obey Him and do things His way for the same reason. It's not because He's a dictator who likes to call all the shots. It's because His way is the right way. His way is the way that will benefit us, prosper us and satisfy our hearts' desires.

Even so, He refuses to be rude. He won't force His way into our lives. He waits in love like the ultimate gentleman, until we invite Him in.

I'm thoroughly convinced that the more we see Him as He truly is, the more we'll do exactly that. We'll invite Him into every corner of our lives and give ourselves more completely than ever to the God who is Love.

LIMITLESS**LOVE**

The Disciples Whom Jesus Loves

"Peter, turning around, saw the disciple whom Jesus loved following them; the one who also had leaned back on His bosom at the supper and…said to Jesus, 'LORD, and what about this man?' Jesus said to him, 'If I want him to remain until I come, what is that to you? You follow Me!' Therefore this saying went out among the brethren that that disciple would not die; yet Jesus did not say to him that he would not die, but only, 'If I want him to remain until I come, what is that to you?' This is the disciple who is testifying to these things and wrote these things, and we know that his testimony is true."

John 21:20-24, *New American Standard*

The rumor that was spread among the disciples that the Apostle John would never die is especially interesting. Although it was not literally true, there was truth in it because history tells us the Romans were never able to kill him. They couldn't even stop his ministry.

At one point during the persecution of the Church, John was actually boiled in oil, yet he was miraculously delivered and came out unhurt. Finally, in desperation, the government tried to throw him away by exiling him to the desolate island of Patmos. They thought by putting him there they could keep him from having contact with anyone. They could cut off his influence.

As it turned out, they were wrong. It was on the island of Patmos that John received and wrote the book of Revelation.

What was the secret behind his astounding success? What was it that made him virtually indestructible? You can find it in John's own writings. He never referred to himself by his name. He always called himself "the disciple whom Jesus loved."

That was his confession of faith. "I am the disciple Jesus loves." He didn't say it to imply that Jesus didn't love the others. He said it to enforce the revelation in his own heart that he was personally and individually loved by the Master. He said it because he knew it was true. Yet the more he said it, the more deeply he comprehended it.

He said it…and said it…and said it…until he finally had a revelation of love that surpassed all others. As a result, He was filled with such a fullness of God that he could say with boldness and assurance, "*as he is, so are we in this world*" (1 John 4:17).

Notice, John didn't say, "As He is, so am *I*…." No, he said, "So are *we.*" That means as wonderful as he was, the Apostle John didn't have anything in God that's not available to us. The same revelation he had, we can have, too.

Whether it's dawned on us yet or not, we are also the disciples whom Jesus loves. I believe it's time we say so.

LIMITLESS**LOVE**

A Smooth and Simple Flow

"...Whatsoever ye shall ask in prayer, believing, ye shall receive."
Matthew 21:22

How amazingly simple those words are! They make believing and receiving sound like such a smooth and sure flow. They say nothing of the strain and struggle most of us have experienced as we've tried to walk by faith. They make no mention of the times when faith seems to fail and those things we need to receive stay stubbornly beyond our reach.

Why didn't Jesus warn us about those times? Why didn't He let us know just what a difficult task believing and receiving really is?

Because when we do it His way, it really isn't that hard. When our believing and receiving is born out of a life of love, the hindrances to our prayers are moved out of the way, our faith functions like it was divinely designed to, and we discover just how simple the life of faith was truly meant to be.

A friend of mine told me once of an experience that perfectly demonstrated this truth. He'd been standing in faith for some time, believing to receive specific breakthroughs in his ministry. He had struggled and strained...he'd studied The WORD...he'd confessed the victory, seemingly to no avail. One day, in the midst of it all, The LORD reminded him of a fellow minister who had mistreated him some time before.

This man had received much help and support from my friend and in return had betrayed him. "Frankly, I felt he had stabbed me in the back and twisted the knife," he said. "But I determined not to be ugly to him. I decided not to do anything to get revenge."

Yet as The LORD brought this man again to my friend's mind, he suddenly knew he hadn't fully forgiven him. He also knew what The LORD was telling him to do about it. He was telling him to take a significant financial gift to that man, hug his neck and let him know that he loved him.

That was tough for my friend to do. He didn't have any warm feelings for the man at the time. But he did it anyway. He stepped out and determined to love that fellow minister by faith regardless of his feelings. And when he did, it brought a great release.

It didn't just bring a spiritual release in his heart, either. It brought a release of those things he'd been struggling to believe God for. Suddenly, effortlessly, doors began to open to him. Long-awaited breakthroughs came. In the atmosphere of love, faith began to work just like Jesus said it would.

Believing and receiving became a smooth and simple flow.

LIMITLESS**LOVE**

Giving Your Way Into Love

"When he was gone forth into the way, there came one running, and kneeled to him, and asked him, Good Master, what shall I do that I may inherit eternal life? And Jesus said unto him…Thou knowest the commandments…. And he answered and said unto him, Master, all these have I observed from my youth. Then Jesus beholding him loved him, and said unto him, One thing thou lackest: go thy way, sell whatsoever thou hast, and give to the poor, and thou shalt have treasure in heaven: and come, take up the cross, and follow me. And he was sad at that saying, and went away grieved: for he had great possessions."
Mark 10:17-22

For years I assumed Jesus instructed the rich, young ruler to sell his possessions and give to the poor because he was deficient in that area. I figured he just needed to give financially. But eventually, I came to realize what was missing in that young man's life was love. He didn't understand God's love for him. (We know he didn't because Jesus said later that he trusted in his riches. People who know the love of God don't trust in riches, they trust in God!)

What's more, he was self-centered. He'd focused so much on his own religious perfection and natural success that he hadn't looked beyond himself and developed a love for others.

If that young man had done what Jesus told him to do, a miraculous change would have taken place in him. As he began to distribute his wealth to people in need, he would have looked into their eyes and fallen in love with them. Even though he might have started his giving with difficulty, he would have finished up with joy because of God's love flowing freely through him.

His heart would have opened to God in a brand-new way. The stinginess and selfishness that had been clogging up his spiritual arteries would have been washed away by the power of that love, and he would have begun to experience the God-kind of life he so desired.

What's more, he'd have seen the supernatural BLESSING of God begin to operate in his own life. He would have experienced the hundredfold return that comes to those who, through giving, step into the river of divine love.

That young man could have spent the rest of his days rejoicing. But because he refused to obey, he walked away sad.

Remember that the next time you sense The LORD leading you to give to someone. Realize that God isn't trying to take something away from you, He's trying to get something to you. He's giving you an opportunity to get rid of that junk in your spirit that has been robbing you of the fullness of His life. He is opening the way for you to step into His river of love—the one place you can truly rejoice!

Be a Titus Today

"Then said Jesus to them again, Peace be unto you:
as my Father hath sent me, even so send I you."
John 20:21

All believers long to know what they're called to do on this earth, and God has a specific plan for each one. But generally speaking, every one of us has been sent to do the same thing that Jesus did when He was on the earth. We are sent to be an expression of God's love to mankind.

Everywhere Jesus went, people saw God's love manifested. Every time He healed someone, every time He delivered someone or worked a miracle, people saw the love of God in action.

We are called to live our lives the same way. In fact, if we ever allow ourselves to get distracted from our primary purpose of love by the business of life—even if that business concerns the work of The LORD—we'll miss the mark. Whatever we do should be so permeated by the love of God that we should be able to say as Jesus said, "If you've seen me, you've seen the Father." In other words, if you've seen me, you've seen Love.

Someone might say, "Well, I have the love of The LORD in my heart. I just don't express it very much."

God's love in your heart doesn't do anyone any good. It's God's love flowing out of your heart through your words and actions that helps people. So step out boldly and say something encouraging to someone. Surprise someone with a warm smile and a big hug and tell them what a blessing they are. You can actually fulfill God's call on your life by doing simple things like that. You can also frustrate that call by neglecting to do them.

The reason those things are vital is because God Himself desires that people—believers and unbelievers alike—know that He loves them. He desires them to know they are precious and dear to His heart. But He doesn't communicate that love by just beaming it through the air somehow. He communicates it through people like you. So when you restrict your expression of love, you're actually restricting His expression of it. You're limiting the reach of God's love!

Paul wrote in 2 Corinthians 7 and told how God had comforted him in a time of trouble. But even Paul, as mature in The LORD as he was, didn't receive that comfort simply through supernatural means. He said he was comforted by the coming of his brother Titus. Titus actually brought Paul the love and encouragement of The LORD.

Determine today to be a Titus in someone's life. Determine to do what Jesus sent you to do—to reach out and express God's love.

When No One's Watching

"But now ye also put off all these; anger, wrath, malice, blasphemy,
filthy communication out of your mouth."
Colossians 3:8

When we make a decision to be ruled by love, one of the first things we must do is take authority over our own temper. Instead of allowing our temper to rule us, we must rule our temper.

If we find we're unable to do that, it's probably because we're inconsistent in our efforts. We try to restrain ourselves in our relationships with other people but when we're alone we turn our tempers loose. When the car won't start and we're late for work, we'll slap the dash and fill the air with angry words. When the computer won't work right we slam some desk drawers and make unsavory remarks thinking it doesn't matter because no one else can hear.

But the fact is it *does* matter, because every time we yield to anger and wrath, we are practicing those things. And the more we practice them when we are alone, the easier it is to yield to them in the presence of others. The angry habits we develop by slapping the dashboard and slamming desk drawers will inevitably rear their ugly heads when another person irritates us. And we'll find ourselves doing and saying things we will long regret.

What's more, giving in to anger and impatience even in little things grieves the Holy Spirit. We simply can't walk with Him while yielding to the flesh. The LORD spoke to me about that years ago when I was praying in the spirit, getting ready for a service. He showed me a vision of a pipeline that was so clogged hardly any water could get through it. Just a mist-like spray was coming out.

That pipe is your spirit, said The LORD. *The flow is My glory. I want to pour My glory through you.*

"What's all that junk plugging up my pipeline?" I asked.

It's made up of the little unconfessed sins of irritation and temper in your life. It's built up from all the times you shot your mouth off in anger or slammed your suitcase down on the floor because you forgot something. When you get in a big fuss with someone, you repent and make it right, He said. *But you just let that little stuff go and it has polluted the stream of the spirit that flows through you.*

I got some things right that day. I repented and cleaned out my spiritual pipeline. Since then, I've been more committed to watching over my thoughts, words and actions—not just when others are present but also when God and I are alone. I've determined to practice yielding to love all the time so when it's not just a car or a computer but the heart of another person that's at stake, I'll be well-practiced at doing the right thing. I'll be in the habit of love.

LIMITLESS**LOVE**

With God as Our Witness

"That he would grant unto us, that we being delivered out of
the hand of our enemies might serve him without fear, in holiness
and righteousness before him, all the days of our life."
Luke 1:74-75

One of the promises God fulfilled through the coming of Jesus is that we could serve God and live in His presence all the days of our lives. That's why Jesus was called *Immanuel,* which translated means "God with us"!

Developing our awareness of the fact that God is actually with us 24 hours a day, seven days a week, is one of the most powerful aids to walking in love. If we'll continually remind ourselves that He is present—witnessing everything we do, everything we say and everything we think—we'll be far more diligent in our love life and far quicker to repent when we fail.

One time when The LORD was particularly dealing with me about this, He said, *Kenneth, I want you to cultivate your awareness of the fact that I'm right there with you. I want you to talk to Me throughout the day just like I'm standing next to you. Forget the* thees *and the* thous. *Just talk straight to Me like you would any other friend you love and respect. When you do something you shouldn't or even if you entertain unloving thoughts, turn immediately to Me and say, "LORD, forgive me. I repent of that. I shouldn't have done that. I shouldn't have let those thoughts stay in my mind." If you'll do that continually, you'll become so well-developed in love that other people just can't offend you. The meanest bigot in the world could insult you and you'd just say, "Father, forgive him, he doesn't know what he's doing."*

That's what The LORD Jesus did. He walked so continually for 33 years in the presence of God that He grew to the place where even when people were killing Him, He loved and forgave them.

Most people don't realize Jesus had to grow into the fullness of that kind of love. He was born of Love but had to grow in it. Although He never did sin, He did not start out completely mature and developed in the things of God. The Bible tells us that "Jesus grew in wisdom and stature, and in favor with God and man" (Luke 2:52, *New International Version*).

It's the same way with us. We don't start out our Christian life fully developed. As we walk in the presence of The LORD, we grow up in Him. As we fellowship with Him over the details of our lives, ever aware that He is with us, we get stronger and stronger in Him. Eventually, the things that once caused us to stumble won't trip us up at all, and we'll see God's promise fulfilled in us as we, being delivered from the hand of our enemies, enjoy His presence and serve Him with love all the days of our lives.

LIMITLESS**LOVE**

The Debt of Love We Owe

"Owe no man any thing, but to love one another:
for he that loveth another hath fulfilled the law."
Romans 13:8

Because God has loved us, we owe love to every person we meet. We owe them kindness and gentleness. We owe it to them to treat them with dignity and respect, as valuable to God and to His plan in the earth.

Sadly enough, we don't always do that. At times, people act like the Christians mentioned in James 2, and give better treatment to people who wear fine clothes and expensive jewelry, than they give to those who don't have much wealth or social stature. They violate the law of love and fail to give others what they are owed. As a result, they are often robbed of THE BLESSING and favor of God.

One might pray diligently for God to help in a situation, standing on The WORD and confessing we walk in the favor of God. But carnal actions and unloving ways will thwart the answer to our own prayers. We'll reverse that favor before we receive it.

A friend of mine told me about a time he and his wife were stranded in an airport with a multitude of other people. While they were waiting in line to be booked for another flight, they prayed and agreed for God's help and favor. From the looks of the man behind the ticket counter, they knew they'd need it. His eyes were bloodshot. His hair was sticking out in every direction. He was irritable and tired.

When the lady standing in front of them was rude to him, he just shrugged his shoulders and said all the flights were booked. He didn't do anything to help.

When my friend and his wife got to the counter however, they were kind. They didn't put any pressure on the man. On the contrary, they tried to minister peace to him, treating him with consideration and respect. "We realize you're very busy," they said. "We can see this is a madhouse and you have a lot of problems on your hands…but this is our situation. Can you do anything for us?"

Amazingly enough, the ticket agent stepped around the counter and said, "Follow me." He took my friends to another area, booked them first-class seats and shook their hands. He even acknowledged that he could have helped the lady ahead of them. But because of how she acted, he didn't do it.

That's a good example of what can happen when you pay the debt of love you owe. It can open the way for God to get you where you're going. When others find themselves stranded by strife, your faith working by love will not only keep you flying…it will secure you a first-class seat!

LIMITLESS**LOVE**

Who's Getting Close to You?

"Then people brought little children to Jesus for him to place his hands
on them and pray for them. But the disciples rebuked them. Jesus said,
'Let the little children come to me, and do not hinder them,
for the kingdom of heaven belongs to such as these.'"
Matthew 19:13-14, *New International Version*

People always wanted to be around Jesus. His disciples loved to be with Him. Sinners
wanted to be with Him. Even little children wanted to be near Him.

That proves He wasn't just loving and kind when He was preaching. He was loving all the time.

If we're going to be His followers, we ought to be that way, too. We shouldn't be gentle
and kind in church on Sunday and then go to the mechanic's shop on Monday and chew the
guy out for being late with our car. We shouldn't be talking faith out of one side of our mouths
and then putting pressure on people with the other.

Some Christians do that. When they're around other believers, they'll say they trust The
LORD to bring them through. But when they step out into the world and begin dealing with
other people, they're the loudest, pushiest, most demanding folks you've ever seen.

What's worse is, they do it in the name of being bold. They'll yell at someone who isn't
giving them the service they want or getting them the results they think they deserve, then
they justify it by saying, "Well, you know, the squeaky wheel gets the grease."

That's not what the Bible says. Luke 6:31 says we should do to others as we would have
them do to us, and Galatians 5:6 says faith works by love. When we start putting pressure on
people in unloving ways, our faith shrivels up and quits working. We're no longer looking to
God or depending on Him. We're putting our dependence on flesh.

Some people even excuse unloving behavior by saying, "It's just that strong anointing
that makes me act that way."

No, being pushy isn't from being anointed. It's just rude. And when we act that way,
people won't want to be around us. Other believers won't want to be around us. Sinners won't
want to be around us. Even God won't want to be around us. (I know, because early in my
Christian life The LORD told me that even though He loved me, He didn't enjoy being around
me. My harshness and my quick temper grieved Him.)

So if you want to check up on your love walk, look around you. Are others drawn to you…
or do they steer away? Are they frightened and intimidated…or do they feel safe and secure
in your presence? One thing is sure, if you are truly walking in the love of Jesus, people will
want to be close to you.

LIMITLESS**LOVE**

Keep Yourself From Getting Calloused

*"But ye, beloved, building up yourselves on your most holy faith,
praying in the Holy Ghost, keep yourselves in the love of God,
looking for the mercy of our LORD Jesus Christ unto eternal life."*
Jude 20-21

Keep yourselves in the love of God. That's a vital instruction for us as believers. When we are first born again, we have a fresh revelation of love. We're acutely aware that God loved us enough to send Jesus to die on the cross for us. His forgiveness and His compassion toward us are foremost in our minds.

That's why as new Christians we are usually very sensitive and tenderhearted. Even though we haven't had much training, we immediately want to share the love we've received from The LORD. We're literally looking for someone to love.

Instead of keeping ourselves in that love, however, we often let it slip away. Every morning when we wake up, our flesh is there and (with some help from the devil) it's pushing us to be selfish. Every time we give in to that selfishness, we have to override the love of God inside us. We have to push it down and desensitize ourselves to it.

If we keep doing that, eventually we'll lose the kind of love we first had. By faith, we know it's still inside us because the Bible says if we're born again, we love the brethren (1 John 3:14). But we can't sense it anymore.

One friend of mine compares it to the natural process of getting calluses on your hands. He tells of a time before he went into ministry when he worked on a loading dock lifting heavy boxes all day. The men he worked with there had been loading boxes so long, their hands were completely calloused. They could actually take a pocketknife and make cuts in those calluses without feeling it, because their skin was so thick and insensitive.

After a while, my friend's hands became calloused too. They stayed that way the whole time he worked at the loading dock. But when he stopped, the calluses wore away.

That's a wonderful picture of what can happen if we'll just stop doing the things that have made our hearts insensitive. Even if we've lost the spiritual passion we had when we were first born again, we can rediscover it by laying down selfishness and beginning to act again in love. As we do, our hearts will grow tender once more and we'll find ourselves easily moved by the love of The LORD and the needs of others.

Once we've shed those spiritual calluses, we'll have a fresh sense of joy. We'll have a sensitivity and spiritual vitality that will never again fade away if we will keep ourselves in the love of God.

LIMITLESS**LOVE**

Be Aware They Are There

"Love does no harm to a neighbor.
Therefore love is the fulfillment of the law."
Romans 13:10, *New International Version*

Who is your neighbor? Your neighbor is the person who is near to you at the moment. When you're standing in line at the ballgame, your neighbor is the man standing in front of you whom you elbowed out of the way to get a better seat. When you're waiting for a parking place at the grocery store, your neighbor is the person in the car who swerved around you and took the place you'd been waiting for.

The Bible says love does no harm to those people. Love is considerate of them. Love is sensitive to them.

That sounds simple enough. But the fact is, before we can be considerate of someone and sensitive to them, we have to be aware that they're there. We have to be spiritually alert enough to notice them. To do that, we have to get our minds renewed because our culture has trained us to be so self-centered, we don't even see each other.

It's amazing. People will notice *things* before they'll notice other people. They'll admire an expensive car and never even see the person driving it. They'll appreciate buildings, clothes and jewelry, and ignore the people in them as if they're totally insignificant. But when we fall into that, we're being deceived. People are far more important than things. Never use people to get things. Use things to BLESS and show God's love to people.

The only way we can be sure not to do any harm to our neighbor is to value people enough to notice them. We must esteem others as much as we do ourselves. We must see them as being more important than things.

We should never treat someone poorly over a seat at the ballgame or a parking place. But we'll do it inadvertently if we don't renew our minds and exercise our awareness of them.

That's why walking in love requires us to cultivate our consciousness of the impact our words and actions have on the people around us. If we hurt someone's feelings because we spoke harshly to them (or didn't speak to them at all), we can't excuse ourselves by saying, "Hey, I didn't even realize I offended them," or "I was thinking about something else and didn't notice they were standing there."

That won't fly because if we're walking in love, we won't be that self-absorbed. We'll see the pain flash across that person's face when we're abrupt with them. We'll consider them more important than our own thoughts and acknowledge them when we walk by.

Love gives us a heightened awareness of others that keeps us from carelessly neglecting them. It ensures we do our neighbor no harm.

LIMITLESS**LOVE**

Developing the Gifts of the Spirit

"Covet earnestly the best gifts:
and yet show I unto you a more excellent way."
1 Corinthians 12:31

If you're hungry to develop the operations and gifts of the Holy Spirit in your life—ministering to people supernaturally through prophecy, tongues and interpretation, the word of wisdom, and other gifts the as Spirit wills—the best way to do it is by following love. When you're walking in love, you're walking in the Holy Spirit's flow. You're sensitive to Him and to the needs of others. As a result, you'll perceive things about them.

You'll pick up on the heart of God where they're concerned and you'll be more apt to receive a word of knowledge, for example, or a prophecy that will help and encourage them. You'll tap into God's power on their behalf, not because you're trying to be spiritual but because you care about that person.

One minister who operated powerfully and accurately in the spiritual gifts some years ago said that's the way she did it. When she was ministering in a service, she'd look out over the crowd and just let the love of God begin to move in her heart. As she did, she'd find herself being drawn toward one or two specific people. So she would just follow that draw of love.

Many times, she had no idea what she was going to do but would walk over to them anyway and say, "Can I minister to you?" As she would begin to pray for them or lay hands on them, almost invariably, a revelation would begin to come to her. She would flow so precisely in the word of knowledge and the word of wisdom that everyone in the place would recognize she had heard from God.

The Bible clearly states that the spiritual gifts are meant to operate through each person—not just a special few, but every believer—as the Spirit wills. But many Christians remain on the spiritual sidelines, wondering why God never uses them.

One of the biggest reasons may be that we have fallen short in our love walk. We have been so preoccupied with ourselves…what *we* need…what *we* want…what *we* have or don't have…that we are not even aware of other people. We have blocked the Holy Spirit's supernatural flow with our own selfishness.

But we can change that by getting our eyes off ourselves and onto those around us. We can say to The LORD every day, "Father, I determine to be led by love today. Draw me to people You want me to BLESS, and help me tap into the supernatural flow of the Spirit. Make me an expression of Your mighty love…and give Your gifts to others through me!"

Choose Love—It's the Only Way to Live

"I call heaven and earth to record this day against you, that I have set before you life and death, blessing and cursing: therefore choose life, that both thou and thy seed may live: that thou mayest love The LORD thy God, and that thou mayest obey his voice, and that thou mayest cleave unto him: for he is thy life, and the length of thy days...."
Deuteronomy 30:19-20

Every command God has ever given, in the Old Testament and the New, can be summed up in five simple words: *Love God and love others.* When we obey those instructions, we enjoy life and THE BLESSING. When we violate them, we open the door to death and the curse.

That's not just some mystical, unexplainable phenomenon. It's a tangible, practical fact. Scientists have recently begun to understand more about it, finding that certain human emotions and activity can create conditions in the body it was not designed to endure. Thoughts that trigger fear, bitterness and anger result in chemical reactions that affect us and cause sickness and disease.

Promiscuous sexual behaviors in today's society, for instance, have produced strains of disease that medical science has no way to cure. People may claim they are engaging in that behavior because of love, but they're not. It's born out of lust and selfishness. And the fruit of it is death.

That's why God told us to stay away from it. He knew it would kill us! Walking in sin, which is departing from the ways of love, is as dangerous as walking into a room of snakes. When we choose to live in that room, even God Himself won't keep us from being bitten.

Some people don't understand that. They want to receive healing from God while still practicing the sinful, unloving lifestyle they always have. But that won't work. God can't get healing to them because the reactions released in their bodies by sin push healing away. Even if God did get healing to them, they would soon be sick again if they didn't stop those behaviors by giving their lives to Him.

That may sound like bad news, but there's good news on the other side of it because the same system works in reverse. Just like walking outside of love will hurt people, walking in love can heal them. It will open the door for them to receive the power of God to reverse the damage disease has done to their bodies. Then it will help them maintain their health and keep their bodies running right.

By choosing love, they'll choose life and find out that's truly the only way to live.

LIMITLESS**LOVE**

The Real Thing

"Many will say to me in that day, LORD, LORD, have we not prophesied in thy name? and in thy name have cast out devils? and in thy name done many wonderful works? And then will I profess unto them, I never knew you...."
Matthew 7:22-23

As we make the commitment to walk in love, we must watch over our hearts continually to keep that love genuine. He wants our actions to be backed by genuine concern for those we are serving. He wants us to be motivated by our sincere desire to be a BLESSING to Him and to others.

"Isn't that what always motivates such actions?" you ask.

No, it's not. First Corinthians 13 tells us that it's possible to give everything we have to the poor, and burn ourselves up in service to The LORD, without doing it in love. Jesus said there would be people who prophesy, work wonders and even cast out devils in His Name without ever knowing Him. In other words, they will do those things without love. Remember, God is Love.

We can do things that look loving, perform acts of service and works of kindness. But instead of being motivated by love, we can be motivated by our desire to prove to others how great and spiritual we are.

Actually, that isn't love at all. It's another form of selfishness. It's self-centered instead of being centered around others. That kind of pseudo-love is displeasing to God.

How can we be sure we haven't slipped into it? By keeping a close check on our joy level. Jesus said in John 15:10-11 that He gave us the commandment of love so that His joy would remain in us and our joy would be full. So we can be sure if we're not experiencing joy, we're not walking in genuine love.

Instead of being happy in our service to others and the sacrifices that service might require, we'll have a heaviness about it. Inwardly, we'll sigh and think, *I guess I have to do this because it's the right thing. I'm not looking forward to it, but it's my duty so I'll do it.*

Frankly, no one wants that kind of "love." God doesn't want it, and neither does any one else. So if you ever catch yourself thinking that way, make a change. Get in the presence of The LORD. Worship and fellowship with Him until the genuine spirit of love comes alive in you again. Don't settle for superficial substitutes. When it comes to love, make sure you have the real love that comes only from Him.

LIMITLESS**LOVE**

The Discipline of Love

"For whom The LORD loveth he chasteneth, and scourgeth every son whom he receiveth. If ye endure chastening, God dealeth with you as with sons; for what son is he whom the father chasteneth not? But if ye be without chastisement, whereof all are partakers, then are ye bastards, and not sons. Furthermore we have had fathers of our flesh which corrected us, and we gave them reverence: shall we not much rather be in subjection unto the Father of spirits, and live? For they verily for a few days chastened us after their own pleasure; but he for our profit, that we might be partakers of his holiness. Now no chastening for the present seemeth to be joyous, but grievous: nevertheless afterward it yieldeth the peaceable fruit of righteousness unto them which are exercised thereby."

Hebrews 12:6-11

Many people make the mistake of thinking that someone who loves them will always make them feel good. They equate love with warm emotions and flattering words.

I've heard about mothers who've fallen into that misconception and said things like, "I love my child too much to discipline him. It hurts me to see him cry, so I don't do it."

The mother who talks like that doesn't really love her child. She loves herself. If she truly loved her child, she would endure her own emotional discomfort to do what was is best for him. She would suffer through the tears and even be willing for that child not to like her for a while. She would be more concerned about his training and long-term success in life than about her need for his love and approval.

The same is true among friends. A real friend who truly loves you will be willing to say things to you that bring correction and truth. They'll be honest with you even if it upsets you, because they care more about your spiritual growth and well-being than about their own need for your friendship.

That's why we shouldn't be surprised when God, through His written WORD, His servants, or by the voice of the Holy Spirit in our hearts, says things to us that initially cause us discomfort. We shouldn't be shocked when He corrects or rebukes us. He isn't a selfish God. He truly loves us. He's a good Father and a good Friend. So He is willing to speak to us in ways that cause emotional discomfort and stir up our souls if He knows it is necessary for our ultimate good.

Keep that in mind next time The LORD chastises you and you feel the sharp pang of fleshly embarrassment that often follows such correction. Instead of rebuking the devil and thinking your loving Father would never say something so unpleasant to you, give that correction some consideration. Let the Holy Spirit show you how it can help you. And thank God for loving you enough to tell you the truth!

LIMITLESS**LOVE**

Our Greatest Protection

"They answered him, Jesus of Nazareth. Jesus saith unto them, I am he.
And Judas also, which betrayed him, stood with them. As soon then as
he had said unto them, I am he, they went backward, and fell to the
ground. Then asked he them again, Whom seek ye? And they said, Jesus
of Nazareth. Jesus answered, I have told you that I am he: if therefore ye
seek me, let these go their way: that the saying might be fulfilled, which he
spake, Of them which thou gavest me have I lost none."
John 18:5-9

Initially, when I read some of the scriptural descriptions of love, I wasn't especially excited about acting on them. When I thought about turning the other cheek, for instance, or taking no account of a suffered wrong, I wanted to say, "LORD, do You know what people will do to me if act like that? They'll make a rug out of me!"

I didn't understand that acting in love puts the power of God to work on my behalf. I didn't realize that if I made the decision to love, supernatural deliverance would operate for me in the unseen realm.

When Jesus told us to turn the other cheek, He wasn't saying we should invite people to slug us. He was encouraging us to move out into the realm of love where our protection never fails. One day as I meditated on that truth, He said to me, *If you'll walk in this long enough, when you turn the other cheek, people won't be able to slap it. The power of God will hold them back.*

If you want scriptural evidence of this, study what happened when the Roman soldiers came to seize Jesus before the crucifixion. Even at that difficult and painful time, Jesus had love on His mind. He concerned Himself with the safety of His disciples. As a result, that whole band of rough, tough Roman soldiers was unable to apprehend this one, gentle, unarmed man. All Jesus had to do was say, "I am he," and they all fell flat on the ground.

That wasn't the first time such a thing had happened in Jesus' life. There was a time in Nazareth when a mob tried to throw Him off a cliff, but Luke 4:30 says He just passed through them and went His way.

The fact is, no one could do anything to harm Jesus. He had to lay His life down. He had to purposely receive death to fulfill the plan of God, because the delivering power of love that constantly surrounded Him made it impossible for Him to be killed any other way.

Love will work for us the same way if we will walk in it like He did. It's a spiritual principle. When we put love to work on our behalf, the devil has no defense against it. He can't come up with any weapon that will bring us down. The power of love is our greatest protection.

LIMITLESS**LOVE**

Don't Drop Your Defense

"We know that whosoever is born of God sinneth not; but he that is begotten of God keepeth himself, and that wicked one toucheth him not."
1 John 5:18

The more I study love and see how it worked in the life of Jesus and the lives of people like the Apostle John, the more convinced I am that the force of love creates an impenetrable barrier against evil. When we walk in love, it creates a supernatural defense that keeps the devil from doing us any permanent damage or real harm.

One of the best descriptions of that divine defense system (apart from the insights given in the Bible itself) can be found in the writings of John G. Lake. He was a powerful minister who had a vision from The LORD many years ago that helped him grasp the protective power of love. In the vision, he saw millions of demons, organized as a modern army. They would charge with great ferocity toward a group of believers. Recounting the vision, he wrote:

> After a little while I observed there operated a restraining influence that constituted a barrier through which they could not force themselves. With all the ingenuity of humans at war, this multitude of demons seemed to endeavor to break the barrier or go further, but were utterly restrained. In amazement I said to the angel, "What does it mean?" He said to me, "Such is the care of God for those that strive in unselfishness for His best."[10]

That is a wonderful picture of the power of love and it's absolutely scriptural. The Bible says when we don't sin, when we keep ourselves in the love of God, the wicked one can't touch us. That doesn't mean we can't ever miss it or make a mistake. Certainly we're going to make mistakes sometimes, but love covers that.

When we do sin and knowingly step out of love, we can get ourselves right back in it by quickly repenting and receiving cleansing from all unrighteousness. If we'll do that, we can walk in love's protection every moment of every day.

If we don't…we won't. That's a sobering statement but it's true. When we get out of love and stay there, we remove our defense. We lower our barrier of protection and become vulnerable to the enemy's assaults. That's how the devil has gotten access into the lives of so many Christians. They have dropped their defenses and he is able to touch them because they failed to walk in love.

Don't ever let that happen to you. Don't ever let a disagreement or someone's mistreatment of you draw you out of love and into strife. Keep yourself in the love of God and stay out of danger. Keep love's impenetrable barrier in place over your life.

---

[10] *John G. Lake, His Life, His Sermons, His Boldness of Faith* (Fort Worth, Kenneth Copeland Publications, 1994) p.140.

LIMITLESS LOVE

For Love's Sake, Slow Down

"Wherefore, my beloved brethren, let every man be swift to hear, slow to speak, slow to wrath: For the wrath of man worketh not the righteousness of God."
James 1:19-20

Most of us have developed the habit of doing exactly the opposite of what these verses tell us to do. We've trained ourselves through practice to be slow to hear, quick to speak, and quick to get angry. But to successfully live a life of love, we'll have to turn that around.

We must learn to stop and really listen to people—especially when they're talking to us about a difficult subject or telling us something we don't want to hear. Our natural, human tendency is to react and start shooting off our mouths before we've gotten the whole story. We jump up and make a judgment before hearing people out and giving some thought to what they're saying. As a result, we end up saying hurtful things we later regret.

The Bible compares words to arrows. When we get in a hurry and start shooting them thoughtlessly in every direction, we often end up wounding people around us. When we're finished, they're hurt and we're saying, "Oh, I'm sorry. I wasn't aiming at you. I was just shooting off my mouth." Our apology may be nice, but it doesn't undo the damage.

What's more, Proverbs 18:13 says a man who answers a matter before he hears and understands it, it is folly and shame to him. So, it's not only loving, but wise and will save future embarrassment if we'll just take some time before we give our opinion about things.

When something rubs us the wrong way, the best thing is for us to bite our lips for a while, and give God time to talk to us. We need to give God time to work on our souls and make adjustments in our thinking until it lines up with His.

That's not easy to do, first of all, because it's foreign to the nature of our flesh. Our flesh just doesn't like to be restrained. Secondly, the devil will usually be there trying to pressure and rush us. "You'd better do something about this, now!" he'll say. "Don't wait another minute. Just give them a piece of your mind." He wants to keep us from giving God time to deal with us. He wants to push us out of love and into sin.

When you sense the devil pressuring you like that, rebel against him. Be stubbornly determined not to rush into reacting. Instead, just calm down and say to yourself, "I'm not going to get upset about this thing. I'll wait and listen awhile. I'm not going to respond until I get love's perspective on it."

If you'll do that, you'll save yourself tremendous trouble and serious embarrassment. And you'll develop some wise habits that will help you keep your love life in line.

LIMITLESS**LOVE**

Break the Cycle of Doubt

"We walk by faith, not by sight."
2 Corinthians 5:7, *New American Standard*

Many people find out about God's love for them and then let the revelation of it slip away. They lose their grip on it because of what they feel and what they see. On Sunday, they're shouting and singing about how God loves them and will take care of their every need…but on Monday when the bill collector calls, they're crying and wringing their hands, saying, "I just don't know what's going to happen to me!"

If you find yourself caught in that cycle of believing God's love for you one day and doubting it the next, there's something you can do to help break the cycle, once and for all. I've done it many times myself when I've needed to make significant changes in my life. Get the elements of Communion. Take the time to sit down at the table with them, and go through the scriptures that deal with the problem you're facing. Write down all the verses, for example, that particularly speak to you about God's love.

Then go before The LORD and settle that truth once and for all in your heart. Pray about it. Say, "Father, You've told me through Your WORD that You love me. You've promised that You'll never leave me nor forsake me. You've given me Your WORD that if I'll just put You first place in my life, everything else I need will be added to me. Today, I am making the commitment to believe and trust in Your love for me. From now on I will walk by faith and not by sight. From here on out, I will refuse to doubt Your love, no matter what I feel or see. I will continue to believe, speak and act as if You love me, protect me and provide for me in every area of life. In Jesus' Name."

Then, take Communion over that commitment. Mark your thinking with the Communion elements that represent the covenant of love God has with you. Let them remind you that His love for you is so great that He sent Jesus to be the sacrifice for you. Let the sign of His body and His blood be an unforgettable symbol to you that God's love for you has been forever established in the broken body and shed blood of Jesus.

The next time you run into some circumstance that makes it look like God doesn't love you or that He isn't taking care of you, instead of just flying apart and spouting unbelief in every direction, remember that commitment you made before The LORD. Think about those Communion elements and how the very body and blood of Jesus testify of God's love for you.

When you do, faith will rise up within you and instead of letting the revelation of God's love slip away, you'll stand steadfast in it. Instead of rejoicing in God's love on Sunday and wringing your hands on Monday, you'll be shouting and singing every day of the week!

LIMITLESS**LOVE**

The Love That Sets Others Free

"And they arrived at the country of the Gadarenes, which is over against Galilee. And
when he went forth to land, there met him out of the city a certain man, which had
devils long time, and ware no clothes, neither abode in any house, but in the tombs.
When he saw Jesus, he cried out, and fell down before him, and with a loud voice
said, What have I to do with thee, Jesus, thou Son of God most high? I beseech thee,
torment me not. (For he had commanded the unclean spirit to come out of the man. For
oftentimes it had caught him: and he was kept bound with chains and in fetters; and he
brake the bands, and was driven of the devil into the wilderness)."

Luke 8:26-29

When we walk in fear and focus on self-preservation, instead of walking in love and
trusting God to protect us, we are not only robbed of the joy of *our* salvation, we're robbed of
the joy of ministering that salvation to others. How many times have we drawn back in fear
and failed to tell someone about Jesus because we were intimidated by them? How many
times have we been so focused on taking care of ourselves during a time of danger or crisis
that we missed the opportunity to care for someone else?

I often think when I read about Jesus' dealings with the demon-possessed man of
the Gadarenes, that most Christians would have run from him in fear. When they saw that
dangerous madman charging at them, they wouldn't have been concerned about *his*
deliverance, but about their own!

Personally, I'm convinced that madman wasn't running toward Jesus to worship Him. He
intended to kill Him, but couldn't because Jesus walked perfectly in the love and protection
of God. As a result, the man went home delivered from a legion of demons and telling others
about the love and power of God.

There may not be many believers who walk in that kind of love these days—but there
are some. I heard about one of them some years ago while visiting with a fellow who was in
prison. It seems he had broken into the home of an elderly woman and was in the process
of stealing her stuff when she walked in and caught him. Instead of screaming and fainting
like he expected her to, she sat him down and read the Bible to him. He said, "You know, that
old girl sat right there and talked me into giving myself up. I don't know why she had so much
power over me. But I do know this, if I hadn't come to prison, I would never have met Jesus. I
would never have been born again."

Just think, the power of love not only protected that dear lady and stopped a robbery, it
got the robber saved. If she can walk in that kind of love, so can the rest of us! And the more
we do, the more we'll see people set free.

LIMITLESSLOVE

Handle With Humility and Love

"Command those who are rich in this present world not to be arrogant nor to put their hope in wealth, which is so uncertain, but to put their hope in God, who richly provides us with everything for our enjoyment."
1 Timothy 6:17, *New International Version*

If you know anything about Gloria and me, you know we believe it's God's will for His people to prosper. We believe He takes pleasure in the prosperity of His servants.

Through the years, as we have trusted and obeyed Him, He has BLESSED us beyond our wildest dreams. But whenever people seem to be impressed with those blessings, we are quick to let them know that those things have come to us simply because of the goodness of The LORD. We try to make sure everyone understands that we're nothing special in ourselves. We're just ordinary believers who found out God loves us and wants to BLESS us. So we trusted that, obeyed Him...and He did!

We also want people to know that they're just as precious to The LORD as we are. And as they continue to walk with Him and develop their faith, they can walk in THE BLESSING the same as we do!

That's important for us all to remember as we prosper. It's vital that we wear our prosperity not pridefully, but humbly and in love. We must realize that others may be intimidated by THE BLESSING we've been given. They may feel they're somehow less important than we are. We're all just learning to receive and walk in His love.

To behave any other way is simply immature. It brings us down to the level of two Bible school students I once heard about from a fellow minister. One of them was bragging to the other about his new car, his new clothes and all the other material blessings he'd gotten recently. As he went on and on about how much he had, the second student couldn't stand it anymore. "Oh, big deal!" he snapped. "All this natural stuff is going to burn up anyway. So when we get to heaven, your pile of ashes will just be bigger than mine."

Actually, that fellow had a point. Even though God gives us good things on this earth to enjoy, the only way they'll have any lasting value is if we'll use them to BLESS and encourage someone else. The only way they'll ultimately amount to anything more than ashes is if we handle them humbly and with love.

LIMITLESS**LOVE**

All for the Sake of Love

"The Pharisees also with the Sadducees came, and tempting desired him that he would show them a sign from heaven. He answered and said unto them…. A wicked and adulterous generation seeketh after a sign; and there shall no sign be given unto it, but the sign of the prophet Jonas. And he left them, and departed."
Matthew 16:1-2, 4

It's often been said that Jesus healed people and worked miracles during His ministry as a sign of His divinity. It's been said that He used His power to prove He was the Son of God. But that's not true. Jesus flatly refused to give such signs. When asked to do so, He said no.

Why, then, did Jesus do the wonderful things He did?

Because He loved people. Jesus always used His power to demonstrate God's love. He operated that way because that's how the Father Himself operates. God *has* power…but He *is* Love. And He only uses His power on behalf of that love.

Every work of power God has ever done has been an expression of His love. Creation itself is a manifestation of His love. (That's why the earth is beautiful instead of drab and ugly.) He stopped the sun in its course one time, lengthening a day, to give His people time to win a battle. Why? Because He loved them! Throughout history, He has healed the sick, raised the dead, provided food for the hungry and worked miracles for those in desperate situations—all because of love.

I can say from personal experience, every true miracle or healing I've ever seen has been unmistakably marked by the love of God. I remember one man in particular who came to Healing School some years ago. An older man, he'd spent his life doing bad things and had reaped the results in his body. He was suffering with a terminal, debilitating disease and was in serious pain.

Most people would have looked at him and said, "Well, he's lived a wicked life. He's just getting what he deserves." The man himself even thought that. Although he wasn't a Christian, in desperation he decided to reach out to God anyway and at least ask for His help.

You know what happened? God healed him!

God is good. He's full of mercy. He's full of compassion. He is good to all who call upon Him. He has always made a way for His people to be well through Him. Psalm 145:8-9 says: "The LORD is gracious [disposed to show favors], and full of compassion; slow to anger and of *great mercy*. The LORD is good to all: and his tender mercies are over *all* his works."

God's mercy hovers over us and overshadows us…all because of His love!

LIMITLESS**LOVE**

Just Because You Love Him

"Jesus said unto him, Thou shalt love The LORD thy God with all thy heart, and with all thy soul, and with all thy mind. This is the first and great commandment."
Matthew 22:37-38

There's no doubt about it, when we serve The LORD we are BLESSED. When we obey Him and keep His WORD, we enjoy greater joy and success in our lives than we could ever experience any other way.

Even so, however, that's not the reason we serve Him. That's not our motivation for obeying Him and believing His WORD. We do all those things—and do them gladly—just because we love Him. Because He laid down His life for us, we willingly give Him our all.

We should all have the attitude of the outlaw biker I heard about years ago. He came to a friend of mine when he was still a sinner and said, "I understand you pray for the sick and my son has cancer. Will you pray for him?"

My friend agreed and when he prayed, The LORD healed that little boy. Shortly thereafter, the biker came back and said, "I'm here to give my life to God. He healed my boy, and anyone who would do that for me, I want to serve for the rest of my life."

You and I might not have had the same experience that biker had, but we're in the same position, nonetheless. As born-again children of God, every one of us has been saved from a spiritual cancer that had doomed us to hell. We've been delivered out of the kingdom of darkness and brought into light. We've been loosed from the bondage of death and given God's free gift of eternal life.

What's more, not one of us earned it. Not one of us deserved it. We all received our deliverance just like that biker did—not on our own merits, but in total dependence on the mercy and love of God.

In light of what He has done for us, we owe Him our service. We owe Him our lives and our love.

We ought not be saying, "OK, LORD, I'll do what You're telling me to do because I believe I'll be BLESSED if I do. But I'm warning You, if THE BLESSING doesn't come, I'm not doing it anymore."

No! If we'll just meditate on what God has already done for us, and let the truth of the sacrifice He's already made for us dawn in our hearts, we'll be so in love with Him, we'll jump at every opportunity to serve Him. We'll want to obey Him. We'll say as Psalm 40:8 says, "I delight to do thy will, O my God...."

Of course, THE BLESSING will follow, as it always does, and because we walk by faith, we'll expect it. But as much as we enjoy it, we'll get far more pleasure simply from serving Jesus. We'll do everything we do for Him just because of love.

Turbocharge Your Faith

"For he hath said, I will never leave thee, nor forsake thee. So that we may boldly
say, The LORD is my helper, and I will not fear what man shall do unto me."
Hebrews 13:5-6

In the past, there have been far too many faith failures in the Body of Christ—not just among people who are backslidden or carnal, but among people who know The WORD and pray, people who are seeking to obey The LORD. For a long time those failures puzzled me. But the more I study what the Bible says about love, the more certain I become that we can track those faith failures back to a lack of revelation of love.

How often we have attacked poverty, disease or some other devilish thing that threatened us by simply using the scriptures that promise us deliverance from those things! How often we've majored on faith in God's *power* to save us from them without being fully grounded in the knowledge of His *love!*

As a result, our faith didn't function like it was supposed to. It didn't work properly because faith works by love.

"But I know God loves me," someone might argue, "and my faith still stopped short!"

Maybe you know it with your head, but is your heart rooted in that love? Do you have an abiding confidence in it that cannot be shaken?

One way to find out is to check yourself for fear. If you have any fear, it's a sign that you're deficient in the area of love. The Bible says perfect love casts out all fear. So when you detect a trace of fear, don't just try to stamp it out. Cast it out with a greater revelation of love.

Say, for example, you were faced with sickness in your body. Certainly you would need to have faith in God's healing power and promises. But that faith should be established on the revelation that God loves you so much, He wants you well. He loves you so dearly, He paid the price for all your sicknesses. He loves you so much, He put all your sins on Jesus when He went to the cross so that you could receive righteousness as a free gift. He loves you so much, He is not only willing but eager to perform His WORD on your behalf.

That kind of revelation of God's love will put a turbocharge on your faith. It will give you a boldness and calm confidence that absolutely defies the power of that sickness to hurt you. It will enable you to look it square in the eye and say, "Sickness, I am not afraid of you. You've already lost this battle because Almighty God loves me. With Him on my side, what can you do to me? Nothing!"

That kind of boldness isn't something you "put on." It's something that rises up within you when you begin to understand just how much God cares for you. It comes when you truly know you are loved.

Faults, Failures and All

"But God demonstrates His own love toward us, in that while we were yet sinners, Christ died for us. Much more then, having now been justified by His blood, we shall be saved from the wrath of God through Him."
Romans 5:8-9, *New American Standard*

Even though the truth of our right-standing with God through the blood of Jesus is the foundation of the gospel, many believers have a difficult time fully embracing it. Even though the Bible tells them to come boldly before the throne of grace, they find themselves standing outside the throne-room door feeling too unworthy to go in.

They know they have a legal, scriptural right to go to God in Jesus' Name because of what He did for them, but to them it seems almost presumptuous to use that right. *After all, they think, I'm not like Jesus. I have faults and failures. I've fallen short of what I ought to be. Why should I expect God to receive me as though I'm righteous? Why should I expect Him to forget all those failures just because I come to Him in Jesus' Name?*

You can expect God to do those things for you because He loves you.

The whole plan of redemption is based on His love. God didn't send Jesus to the cross just to satisfy the legal requirements of the divine justice system. He didn't do it just because His righteous nature required payment of the price for sin. He did it because He loves you.

He loves you so much, He didn't want anything separating you from Him ever again.

The more clearly you see that, the more you'll realize that God isn't annoyed when you take advantage of that right-standing with Him. When in simple faith, you come running to Him, He doesn't shake His head and say, *What are you doing in here? You messed up big-time yesterday. Don't think you can just ask for forgiveness and expect Me to forget what you did!*

No, He is thrilled to receive you in Jesus' Name. His blood has taken care of those sins. He delights in forgiving and cleansing you. So go into His presence boldly knowing that your Father loves you. Dare to act like you belong there, because that's exactly what He wants you to do!

LIMITLESS**LOVE**

Open the Door to Miracles

"Jesus said, 'Remove the stone.' Martha, the sister of the deceased, said to Him, 'LORD, by this time there will be a stench, for he has been dead four days.' Jesus said to her, 'Did I not say to you that if you believe, you will see the glory of God?'… When He had said these things, He cried out with a loud voice, 'Lazarus, come forth.' The man who had died came forth, bound hand and foot with wrappings; and his face was wrapped around with a cloth. Jesus said to them, 'Unbind him, and let him go.'"

John 11:39-40, 43-44, *New American Standard*

Love is the key to the miracle-working power of God. If you think about it, you can see why. First of all, faith works by love and it takes faith to step out into the area of miracles. Secondly, it takes boldness to operate in that realm because working miracles involves doing the unusual. It involves doing things normal people just won't do.

God cannot use the timid or the fearful to manifest His miracle-working power. He must have someone who is bold. And since love is the force that casts out fear, He must have someone who walks in love.

Jesus demonstrated that kind of boldness and love when He raised Lazarus from the dead. He loved Lazarus and his sisters so much that He wept with them. Yet He was so confident in God's love for Him that when He prayed at Lazarus' tomb, He said, "Father, I know that You have heard me."

The power of that love flowing to Him and through Him gave Him the boldness to say, "Remove the stone!"

That made other people nervous. "LORD, he's been dead awhile now. He's going to smell!"

Jesus had no fear about that. He didn't have His fingers crossed, hoping this thing was going to turn out. He didn't call Lazarus out of that tomb with a whisper that would keep him from being embarrassed if nothing happened. He had boldness born of the love of God and of faith in Him. So he said with a loud voice, "Lazarus, come forth!"

No doubt, some of the folks standing around were wishing He'd be a little quieter. They were probably thinking, *Couldn't we send all these people away before You try this, LORD? Couldn't we do this privately just in case it doesn't turn out like You expect?*

Such thoughts never occurred to Jesus, however. He had no fear of failure. He had full confidence that what He had asked, God would do.

The more we walk in the love of God, the more that same kind of boldness will rise up in us. We'll become so confident in what God will do, doubt will melt and run off us like snow in the Texas sunshine.

That's when we'll take the key of love and boldly open the door to the kind of power that makes dead men rise and walk. That's when we'll step into the miracle-working power of God.

LIMITLESS**LOVE**

The Great Commission of Love

"And he said unto them, Go ye into all the world, and preach the gospel to every creature. He that believeth and is baptized shall be saved; but he that believeth not shall be damned. And these signs shall follow them that believe; In my name shall they cast out devils; they shall speak with new tongues; they shall take up serpents; and if they drink any deadly thing, it shall not hurt them; they shall lay hands on the sick, and they shall recover."
Mark 16:15-18

Why do so few believers fulfill the Great Commission? Why do so many who love The LORD and sincerely desire to please Him draw back from obeying this all-important command?

In most cases, they're stopped by fear. They're reluctant to share the gospel with someone for fear of rejection. They're hesitant to lay hands on the sick for fear they won't get healed, and terrified to deal with a demon because they'll look foolish if they can't cast it out.

Some believers so desire to do what's right and serve The LORD, they try to push themselves past the fear by sheer determination. But that's not really the solution. Eventually, they get tired of the battle, give in to the fear and go back into their shell.

What, then, *is* the answer?

Setting our sights on the commandment of love. Asking The LORD to help us increase and abound in love toward people (Philippians 1:9). But that's not enough. Faith in prayer calls for faith in action. We begin by confessing love. "I love The LORD God with all my heart, all my soul and all my might. I love my neighbor as myself!" Then, we can forget about ourselves and reach out to them. Instead of trying to force ourselves into the role of the bold witness of faith and power, we then can just let God love people through us.

We can let love open our eyes to their hurts and their needs. And when we see them, we can simply look to God and say, "LORD, show me what to do for this person. Show me what to say to BLESS them and share Your love with them."

When we open our hearts to love that way, we open the door for God to move through us in power. We'll forget about being embarrassed and stop worrying about being rejected. We'll quit focusing on how we look to others and focus instead on meeting their needs. When that happens, the gifts of the Spirit can begin to flow through us. God can use us to speak His words, minister His deliverance and transmit His healing power. He can use us to convey His love.

That experience is so thrilling that, once we have it, we'll not only be willing to share the good news of Jesus wherever we go…we'll jump at every opportunity. We'll find our greatest joy in obeying the Great Commission of Love.

LIMITLESS**LOVE**

Overcoming Evil With Good

"Dearly beloved, avenge not yourselves, but rather give place unto wrath: for it is written, Vengeance is mine; I will repay, saith The LORD. Therefore if thine enemy hunger, feed him; if he thirst, give him drink: for in so doing thou shalt heap coals of fire on his head. Be not overcome of evil, but overcome evil with good."
Romans 12:19-21

Love can overcome evil in a way that nothing else ever will. It can renew the mind of a person who has been brainwashed with the lies of the devil. It can dissolve hatred, destroy prejudice and bring tears of repentance to eyes so blinded by deception they simply cannot see.

I not only know that from the Scriptures, I've seen it work in my own family, and I can tell you, it's an awesome thing.

Love changed the life of my grandfather when he was 70 years old.

Although he was a first-rate farmer and rancher, a sharp-minded Cherokee Indian man who knew how to make a good living farming the land, he was uneducated and mostly raised himself in the wilds of West Texas. He couldn't study things out, like the Bible, on his own. So, to a great extent, he was subject to the prejudices and opinions of others. Back then, the people around him believed and taught that the black man was made to be an animal of burden. They told him black people had no souls, so you could treat them any way you wanted to and it didn't really matter.

As untrained as he was, my grandfather couldn't believe all of that. He knew God, and he knew somehow it just wasn't right to mistreat someone God created—no matter what color they were. But because of ignorance, that devilish idea that black people were different still influenced his mind.

At 70, he got cancer and ended up in a hospital, little more than skin and bones. The nurse who cared for him was a black woman, and every day she would lift him from his bed and tend to him as lovingly as a mother would her baby. "That's all right, sweetheart," she'd say to him. "You just relax. I'm taking care of you."

One day when she was holding him, the whole pack of lies he'd been told was just swept away by her love. With tears running down his face he cried out, "How could someone this full of love be without a soul? It ain't so! It just ain't so!"

The love in that woman broke through the racial lies he'd been told all his life. It broke through man-made traditions. It demolished the deception of evil and replaced it with God's truth.

Just so you know, that's not the end of the story. The hospital sent my grandfather home to die, but he didn't. My mother sat by his bedside, loving and praying for him until he was completely healed. When all was said and done, love restored his body and his soul. Love triumphed and overcame evil with good.

LIMITLESS**LOVE**

Speaking the Truth in Love

"The wise in heart shall be called prudent:
and the sweetness of the lips increaseth learning."
Proverbs 16:21

Sometimes when believers begin to find out what The WORD of God says and gain some spiritual discernment, they become harsh and abrasive to others. If they see someone else making a mistake, they're quick to point it out and correct that person. They speak scriptural truth, yes, but instead of being BLESSED by that truth, those who receive it end up feeling hurt or condemned.

It can be tempting just to shrug off others' hurt feelings and say, "Well, it's just my job to tell people the truth. They can do with it what they want." But that's not what the Bible says for us to do. It doesn't just instruct us to tell people the truth. It says we should speak the truth *in love* (Ephesians 4:15).

How we approach something determines, to a great degree, how well people can receive it. Words that BLESS and are full of kindness and genuine concern for the well-being of another, enhance that person's ability to learn from them. On the other hand, words that are accurate but cold and uncaring rarely help anyone.

It's love that makes the truth receivable.

Even the gospel message, as powerful as it is, will often be rejected by people who would otherwise want it, when it is preached without a spirit of love. We can preach salvation with a tone of judgment, and an attitude that we're "holier than thou," and actually rob people of the ability to receive it. But if we'll speak to them about it in love, their defenses will start to fall. When they hear not only our words but the compassion behind them, their hearts will open up and they'll want to hear what we have to say. They'll want to accept and embrace it instead of pushing it away.

So before we jump out and just start telling people everything we see and all the truth we know, we need to check our hearts. We need to ask, "Why am I saying these things? Am I just trying to show how much I know? Am I trying to be the big-shot teacher and corrector? Or am I genuinely and deeply concerned about this person?"

If we truly desire to speak from a motivation of love, the majority of the time we'll clothe our words with gentleness and kindness. We'll emphasize the goodness of God and His love for that person, rather than magnifying what they've done wrong.

After all, the Bible says it's the goodness of God that leads to repentance (Romans 2:4). It's His love in our hearts and on our lips that will inspire and encourage others to change.

LIMITLESS**LOVE**

No Sympathy...Just Love

*"You are from God, little children, and have overcome them;
because greater is He who is in you than he who is in the world."*
1 John 4:4, *New American Standard*

As believers, we're to love people who are hurting. We are to love those in need.

Notice I said *love* them—not *sympathize* with them. Love and sympathy are totally different things. They're not even kin to one another. Sympathy is a sense of pity that comes from the human mind and emotions. Sympathy virtually says, "Oh, I feel so sorry for you. I wish there was something I could do for you." Sympathy seems outwardly sweet, but it has no true power to help. Sympathy just agrees with the hopelessness of the situation.

Love, however, grabs the hand of faith, goes to God and says, "LORD, what do You want me to do here? You're the greater One and You're inside me, so let's apply Your power and change this situation."

I'll never forget the first time I stepped into that revelation of love. It was back in the days when I was working as a pilot for Brother Oral Roberts. I'd flown him to a meeting for the first time, and I was assigned to help with the ministry to the sick.

I was absolutely overwhelmed when I walked into the auditorium that day. There were several thousand people there and almost all of them were sick. Many were terminally ill. The atmosphere was thick with the fear and oppression of pain and disease.

I took one look at that place, turned around and walked out. It scared me so bad, I decided right then I was going home. When my feet hit the sidewalk outside, however, The LORD stopped me cold. He literally stuck my feet to the pavement. "What do You want?" I asked.

I want to know where you think you're going, He said.

"You know perfectly well where I'm going, LORD. I'm going home. It's terrible in there, and I don't have anything to offer those people."

With a force that almost knocked me down, He answered, *I know you don't, Kenneth—BUT I DO! That's why I baptized you in the Holy Ghost. I did it so you could take My power and deliver it to people who need it. I did it so you could destroy the works of the devil in the lives of people just like those!*

Suddenly, the scripture rose up in my heart, "Greater is He that is in you..." and I realized I didn't have to settle for sympathizing with people. I had the power of God to actually love them. I had within me the power that could change their condition.

I turned right back around and marched into that place with a boldness I'd never had before. I went in there and saw the sick healed. I saw the oppressed delivered. I saw miracles happen. I saw what the power of love can do.

LIMITLESS**LOVE**

Love Gives the Answer of The LORD

"The plans of the heart belong to man, but the answer of the tongue is from The LORD."
Proverbs 16:1, *New American Standard*

The more we develop in love and in the knowledge of The WORD, the more we desire to give answers to people who are struggling, especially when they are reaching out to us for help. We must be cautious, however, that the answer we give them isn't just the latest formula from a CD we heard or a book we read.

We shouldn't just spout off the first thing that comes to our minds. If we're really going to help people, we need to love them enough to search our hearts for the words they specifically need to hear. We need to take the time to give them an answer that is from The LORD.

Sometimes that's tough to do, because pride and human nature will pressure us to come up with something brilliant—in a hurry. We'll be tempted to make it appear that we immediately have all the answers.

But if we're truly walking in love, we'll resist that temptation. We'll be humble enough to say, "I wish I had an answer for you, but I don't really know what to tell you right now. So let's get quiet here for a few minutes. Let's seek The LORD and see what He has to say."

Then we can take the time to turn inward and find the Holy Spirit's leading. We can receive from Him the wisdom He promised to give to those who ask. That specific wisdom can make all the difference.

A fellow minister once told me of an elderly woman he went to visit in the early days of his healing ministry. She had been diagnosed with cancer and was in the hospital, dying. At first this minister just jumped in and started teaching her about healing. He told her she was redeemed from the curse of sickness. He told her that by the stripes of Jesus she was healed. But those truths didn't seem to help this woman at all.

The minister loved her enough to keep trying, though, so he kept coming to see her, searching his heart for the wisdom of God. Finally, one day he was reading Psalm 91 to her, and when he reached the verse that said, "With long life will I satisfy him," the little lady perked up, so he read it again. "…With long life will I satisfy him."

Suddenly, this minister realized he'd discovered the key. "Sister," he said, "are you satisfied with your life and your service to God? Do you think you've done everything He wants you to do? I don't think so! We younger people need your wisdom. We need you to help us."

Sure enough, that dear woman's eyes filled with tears and she said, "I want to do that! I want to help young people!" Within a few days, she was out of the hospital and in church testifying about her healing. She got the help she needed because someone loved her enough to search out the words she needed to hear. Someone cared enough give her the answer of The LORD.

LIMITLESS**LOVE**

God Gives the Reward

"But love ye your enemies, and do good, and lend, hoping for nothing
again; and your reward shall be great, and ye shall be the children
of the Highest: for he is kind unto the unthankful and to the evil.
Be ye therefore merciful, as your Father also is merciful."
Luke 6:35-36

Have you ever known someone so touchy and easily offended, you simply didn't know how to deal with them? Have you ever encountered someone who refused to like you, no matter how hard you tried?

If you haven't…you will. (There are plenty of them to go around!) When you do, there's only one scriptural course of action to take. You must take the path of love.

"Oh, no!" you might say. "Don't tell me that! If I do something loving for this person, they won't respond well. They'll just reject me or criticize me again. It's too hard to love them. I can't do it!"

Yes, you can! If you're born again, you have the ability to love like God loves. The Bible says He is good to the unthankful and the evil, so you can be good to them too.

To successfully do that, however, you must follow the instructions Jesus gives us and truly expect nothing in return.

What Jesus asks us to do is to love people for one reason, and one reason only: because we want to please our heavenly Father. We are to love others not because they've earned it or deserved it. We are to love them not because they bless us and make us feel good. We are to love them because God loves them, and we are ambassadors for Him.

Although that kind of love may not always bring a swift and sweet response, it can change people's lives. I'll never forget one particular time when Gloria expressed that kind of love for me. I'd been irritable and hard to deal with that day. Nothing she did or said seemed to please me. Finally, I was trying to have a fuss with her (it was hard because she wouldn't participate) and I barked off some harsh words.

Instead of barking back, she looked up at me with tears in her eyes and said, "I am going to find some way to be a BLESSING to you."

When she said that, the spirit of love behind it—which is truly the Spirit of God—hit my heart and absolutely turned my life around. I haven't been the same since. Hopefully, I've been more rewarding to live with. But even if I haven't, Gloria would still have been richly BLESSED. Because when someone loves like that, it's God Himself who gives the reward.

LIMITLESS**LOVE**

Rebel Against the Devil and Enjoy the Good of the Land

"If ye be willing and obedient, ye shall eat the good of the land: But if ye refuse and rebel, ye shall be devoured with the sword: for the mouth of The LORD hath spoken it."
Isaiah 1:19-20

As believers, we need to settle this fact in our hearts: Walking in love is not a suggestion The LORD has given us. It's not a nice thing to do or just a good idea. Walking in love is the New Testament commandment.

When we walk in obedience to that command with a willing heart, we open the door to THE BLESSING of God. We open the door to supernatural prosperity. We open the door to health and healing. We open the door to peace and well-being in every area of our lives.

The reverse is also true. When we disobey the command of love and yield to things like bitterness, irritation, unforgiveness and selfishness, we throw open the door to the devil. We give him an open invitation to come in with his sword of destruction and cut up our lives.

That's why the devil fights us so hard over the issue of love. That's why the moment we begin to study about love and commit ourselves to walk in it, the devil will try to see to it that someone challenges us. He'll try to make sure that someone does something to thoroughly offend us. He knows that if we truly begin to live our lives according to love, we'll get out of his reach. So he tries to pull us back into a life of strife.

Once, when I was preaching a series of meetings about the love of God in a church in south Texas, the devil pulled that kind of stunt and got the song director in a fuss with someone in the church—right in the middle of the meeting! Believe it or not, the guy got so mad, he threw a songbook while I was preaching about love!

"LORD," I said, "what on earth is going on here?"

The LORD said, *Love is so powerful, it casts the devil and all his works right out of people's lives. So he's doing his best to throw a fit on his way out, hoping you'll back off a little and let him back in.*

When the devil does that to you, don't fall for it. Don't back off your love walk one bit. Just keep on being willing and obedient. Instead of getting mad at the person who offended you, get mad at the devil and rebel against him. Determine, *I'm going to be more loving still. I'll be kinder than I've ever been to that person. I'll not only forgive them, I'll give them a hug. I'll send them a card. I'll buy them a gift!*

Keep right on obeying the command of love and demolish the plan of Satan. Make him sit and watch while you enjoy the good of the land!

LIMITLESS**LOVE**

Inferior to None

"Thou didst form my inward parts: Thou didst cover me in my mother's womb.
I will give thanks unto thee; for I am fearfully and wonderfully made: Wonderful are thy
works; and that my soul knoweth right well. My frame was not hidden from thee, when
I was made in secret, and curiously wrought in the lowest parts of the earth. Thine eyes
did see mine unformed substance; and in thy book they were all written, even the days
that were ordained for me, when as yet there was none of them. How precious also are
thy thoughts unto me, O God! How great is the sum of them! If I should count them,
they are more in number than the sand: When I awake, I am still with thee."
Psalm 139:13-18, *American Standard Version*

One of the greatest problems people face these days is the feeling of inferiority. Psychiatrists' offices are full of people trying to overcome a sense of worthlessness and insignificance.

Feelings of inferiority rob people of the joy of life. They keep us from reaching out and developing relationships. They keep us from achieving the things we're destined to do. They even keep us from enjoying the blessing of God. They cause us to shrink back, thinking we're unworthy to receive anything from God.

What is the cure for such feelings of inferiority? A greater revelation of the love of God. He has clearly shown us in His WORD how precious and valuable He thinks we are. (And if the Almighty God of the universe thinks we're valuable, what does it matter what anyone else thinks?) He understands us completely. He knows us so intimately that He knows what we're going to say before we say it. And knowing us that well, He says we are "fearfully and wonderfully made"!

God considers us to be so important that before we were born, He planned all our days and wrote them in His Book. His thoughts of us are as numerous as the sands of the sea. We must really be worth something if God Himself can't get us off His mind!

What's most important is this: When He saw we would need to be rescued from sin and death, He sent His own Son—His most precious, perfect, beloved Son—to die for us.

I once saw a cartoon of a little boy kneeling at his bedside praying. Apparently someone had treated him as if he weren't important. He was battling feelings of inferiority. But this little fellow knew how to win the fight. He lifted his face to The LORD and said, "God didn't die for a nobody."

That's the truth. The simple fact that Jesus laid down His life for us makes us somebody... somebody precious...somebody important...and somebody divinely loved. The price He paid has established with God, our Father, our eternal value. In His eyes we are inferior to none. In Him, we are valuable and precious.

LIMITLESS**LOVE**

Taking the Test of Love

"Examine yourselves to see whether you are in the faith; test yourselves. Do you not realize that Christ Jesus is in you...?"
2 Corinthians 13:5, *New International Version*

The principles of love are good, powerful principles and they work for anyone who will put them to work. But the fact is, no one can really use them the way God intended until he makes Jesus The LORD of his life. That's because the only person who can truly keep the law of love is Jesus Christ Himself. And the only way we can love like He loves is by allowing His love to flow through us.

So, the first thing we must do is establish our relationship with Him. We must be sure we have believed on Him as the Son of God who came to earth, lived a perfect life, went to the Cross to die for our sins, and was raised again and seated at God's right hand. We must be sure we have renounced the devil and all his works and received Jesus as our LORD and Savior.

Many people do that, thank The LORD they are saved and then never examine themselves again. But that's a mistake. The Apostle Paul wrote to Christians—people who knew they'd made Jesus their LORD—and said, "Examine yourselves to see whether you're in the faith; test yourselves."

Certainly, Paul didn't mean they should doubt their salvation. What did he mean? He meant we should regularly check our lives to see how we're doing. Are we walking in the salvation we've received...or are we sitting on the sidelines doing nothing? Are we living our lives in such a way that Jesus can be seen in us?

To answer those questions, we must check up on our love walk. Since love is God's nature and our sole commandment, and since Jesus said we'd be known as His disciples by our love, we should test ourselves regularly to see how we're measuring up to the standard of love presented in 1 Corinthians 13.

One way you can do that is by confessing verses 4-8 out loud, substituting the word *I* for the word *love*, and saying: "I endure long and I am patient and kind. I am never envious, nor do I boil over with jealousy. I am not boastful or vainglorious and I do not display myself haughtily. I am not conceited (arrogant and inflated with pride). I am not rude or unmannerly and I do not act unbecomingly. I do not insist on my own rights or my own way, for I am not self-seeking. I am not touchy or fretful or resentful. I take no account of the evil done to me (I pay no attention to a suffered wrong). I do not rejoice at injustice or unrighteousness, but I rejoice when right and truth prevail. I bear up under anything and everything that comes. I am ever ready to believe the best of every person. My hopes are fadeless under all circumstances, and I endure everything [without weakening]. I never fail [because God's love in me never fades out or becomes obsolete or comes to an end]" *(The Amplified Bible)*.

If you're falling short in your love walk, you'll immediately notice it as you make the confession, so you can repent and receive God's forgiveness. What's more, as you continue speaking those words, you can use them to release your faith. You can visualize yourself acting in love. The more you rehearse that confession and see yourself that way, the easier it will be for you to behave accordingly. The easier it will be for you to pass with flying colors when you take the test of love.

LIMITLESS**LOVE**

Bacon, Eggs, and the Economy of Love

"Do not love the world nor the things in the world. If anyone loves the world, the love of the Father is not in him. For all that is in the world, the lust of the flesh and the lust of the eyes and the boastful pride of life, is not from the Father, but is from the world. The world is passing away, and also its lusts; but the one who does the will of God lives forever."
1 John 2:15-17, *New American Standard*

I once heard a story about a chicken and a pig going to a church prayer breakfast. They had asked the chicken to provide the eggs and the pig to provide the bacon. The pig said, "Miss Chicken, you're certainly involved, but I'm committed!"

When it comes to walking in love, we must be both involved and committed. We must be like the pig, willing to give ourselves and lay down our very lives for the sake of others. But we must also be like the chicken, holding loosely the things God has given us so that we can gladly part with them when the need arises.

Some believers stumble over the second part, because they've fallen in love with material things. They've gotten so attached to them, it hurts to let them go. So even if they obey The LORD and give when He tells them to, it's difficult for them to do it cheerfully.

That's why we need to keep money and material possessions in perspective. We need to remember that they are most valuable when they are used to express God's love. When you get right down to it, that's all this material world was ever meant to be—an expression of God's love for people. So, when we take the material things He has given us and give them to others in love, we keep those things in their proper place. We perpetuate the fulfillment of their original purpose.

What's more, we keep the cycle going. God gives to us…we give to others…then He gives to us again, "good measure, pressed down, and shaken together, and running over…" (Luke 6:38).

That keeps us out of the world's economic system and in the economy of the kingdom of God. The world's system is based on selfishness and says, "If I get something I must keep it." God's system is based on love and the words of Ephesians 4:28: "…let him labour, working with his hands the thing which is good, that he may have to give to him that needeth."

In God's economy, we use things to love people. We never use people because of the love of things. And when we see a need in the life of another, we're willing not only to get involved but to be committed and gladly give whatever love demands.

LIMITLESS**LOVE**

Anointed of Love

"The Spirit of The LORD is upon me, because he hath anointed
me to preach the gospel to the poor; he hath sent me to heal the brokenhearted,
to preach deliverance to the captives, and recovering of sight to the blind, to set at
liberty them that are bruised, to preach the acceptable year of The LORD."
Luke 4:18-19

Do you realize it was the Spirit of Love who anointed Jesus? Since Jesus is the Anointed of God, and God is Love, we can confidently say that Jesus is the Anointed of Love. It was Love who bestowed upon Him the supernatural power that annihilates the works of the devil. It was Love who anointed Him to go "about doing good, and healing all that were oppressed of the devil" (Acts 10:38).

Isaiah 10:27 gives us a further description of what that anointing can do. It says, "And it shall come to pass in that day, that his (the oppressor's) burden shall be taken away from off thy shoulder, and his yoke from off thy neck, and the yoke shall be destroyed because of the anointing."

Imagine, if you will, someone bent over with a large weight or pack on his back, which is too heavy to allow him to straighten up. He also has a yoke around his neck with a chain attached. This person does not have any means of getting the steel collar off his neck, nor can he get the weight off his back. It is a terrible thing.

Then comes Jesus! The One Anointed of Love! He removes the burden from the person's back and helps him stand up straight again. He removes that awful yoke from his neck. But that's not all. Love is not satisfied until He has destroyed—not just broken, but totally, completely destroyed—that yoke!

That was true during Jesus' earthly ministry, and it's still true today! If you've received Jesus as your Savior, you can be sure the Anointing of Love that's on Him is at work in your life. You can receive it by faith, and boldly throw off every burden the devil has tried to lay on you. You can confidently believe that the power of God is working now to crush every yoke the devil has used to hinder and oppress you.

Why? Because God loves you and that's what He sent the anointing to do.

What's more, He loves others too. So He has put the anointing on you to continue the ministry of Jesus. The word *Christian* actually means "Belonging to the Anointed One" or "Little Anointed One." So, if you say you're a Christian—dare to act like one. Dare to believe that you can bring to others that burden-removing, yoke-destroying power. Dare to believe you are Anointed of Love!

The Master Key of the Kingdom

"I will give you the keys of the kingdom of heaven; whatever
you bind on earth will be bound in heaven, and
whatever you loose on earth will be loosed in heaven."
Matthew 16:19, *New International Version*

As members of the Church of The LORD Jesus Christ, you and I have been given the keys of the kingdom of heaven. We've been given The WORD of God and the wisdom of the Holy Spirit to help us find the specific key that will open the door to God's supernatural power in every situation.

No doubt, there are many such keys. But there is one master key that applies to them all. It is the key the Master Himself used in every situation. It is the key that constantly connected Him to the wisdom and power of God.

I like to say it this way: The Master's key is the master key to the Kingdom.

What is it? It is the key of love.

I first caught a glimpse of this when I was meditating on Ephesians 3:19 one day, translating the word *Christ* into its English meaning, "the Anointed One and His Anointing." When you make that translation, the verse becomes a prayer that we may "know the love of the Anointed One and His Anointing, which passeth knowledge," that we might be filled with all the fullness of God.

As I pondered that verse, I thought, *I know God loves me. I believe He does because He says so in His WORD. But what does it mean to know the love of His Anointing?*

It didn't make sense until one day a light came on in my heart. Suddenly, I realized that verse is talking about the anointing to love! It's telling us that we have Jesus' Anointing to love operating inside us. When strife and trouble come through other people to draw us off course, and when situations threaten our lives, we have the same anointing Jesus had to respond to those things in love.

If we just make the quality decision to obey the commandment in 1 John 3:23 by believing on Jesus and loving one another, we can step out in that anointing. We can live in the power of His supernatural love. We don't have to rely on our own puny ability. We can draw on His ability—and He has ample ability to love in every situation.

When we step out in that love, every other spiritual force is made available to us. And as Ephesians 3:19-20 says, we are "filled up to all the fullness of God.... who is able to do far more abundantly beyond all that we ask or think, according to the power that works within us" *(New American Standard)!*

Thank God for the master key of love!

LIMITLESS**LOVE**

The Divine Mark of Excellence

"But now He has obtained a more excellent ministry, by as much as He is also the mediator of a better covenant, which has been enacted on better promises."
Hebrews 8:6, *New American Standard*

Every committed Christian wholeheartedly aspires to excellence of life and excellence of ministry. We can't help it. We've been given the nature of God. We've been born again in the image of Jesus. And Jesus was the Man of Excellence. Everything He did on this earth was excellent, and His Anointing for excellence is available to you and me.

Why haven't we walked in it more than we have?

Primarily because we've been bound by a worldly definition of excellence. We've thought to be excellent meant to be top-notch and highly polished in the external affairs of life. We've equated it with being exceptionally skilled in our vocations, and superbly organized and efficient in our endeavors at church, work and home.

Those things are fine, but they are not the mark of God's kind of excellence. His excellence is inspired by and finds its foremost expression through love. Psalm 36:7 says, "How excellent is thy lovingkindness, O God!"

Anything that is not an expression of God's love falls far short of excellence—no matter how naturally efficient and polished it may seem. A job performed with great skill is shoddy in the sight of God if it isn't done in love. A ministry that's efficiently planned, beautifully marketed, and expertly administered is a failure in God's eyes if it isn't run by love.

That's why the first decision we must make if we're to partake of the excellence of Jesus is the decision never to compromise our walk of love. We must begin by declaring boldly, "I am a child of God, therefore I am a child of Love. God's love has been shed abroad in my heart by the Holy Ghost. He has commanded me to walk in that love. Therefore, from this day forward, that's what I will do."

Once we take that stand, we begin to do those things that love demands—things like giving, bridling our tongue, acting kindly toward others (regardless of how they act toward us), and keeping our thoughts in line with God's love. When we miss it, we refuse to justify ourselves. Instead, we are brutally honest with ourselves before God. (I didn't say condemning, I said honest.) When we're wrong, we repent and change. We immediately make adjustments and get ourselves back in line with the law of love.

As we do that, we'll find ourselves coming up to a higher level in every area of life. We will indeed be more highly skilled and efficiently organized. We'll be top-notch in our service to The LORD and to others. We'll be the best because we want to love the most…and that will make all the difference.

LIMITLESS**LOVE**

Watch Your Big Mouth

*"I exhort therefore, that, first of all, supplications, prayers,
intercessions, and giving of thanks, be made for all men; for kings,
and for all that are in authority; that we may lead a quiet and peaceable life
in all godliness and honesty. For this is good and acceptable in the
sight of God our Saviour; who will have all men to be saved, and
to come unto the knowledge of the truth."*
1 Timothy 2:1-4

One of our first priorities as New Testament believers is to pray for the leaders of the nations. Why? Because those leaders have under their authority multitudes of men and women who need to hear the gospel. Their decisions can open the door to that gospel so that many can be saved...or they can close the door and keep people in spiritual darkness.

The love of God within us should absolutely compel us to pray for those leaders. It should keep us continually on our knees, asking God to turn their hearts toward righteousness. It should inspire us to hold them before Him in Jesus' Name.

When believers pray that way, miracles happen. We saw an example of that in 1991 during the Gulf War. At that time, believers rose up and flooded heaven with a tidal wave of prayer. The Church opened her "Big Mouth" of faith and power, and one of the greatest miracles we've ever seen in our nation took place.

The fourth largest and one of the best-equipped armies in the world was defeated by the most unheard-of, overwhelming odds in the history of warfare. They suffered more than 150,000 casualties. Our side suffered fewer than 400. Was it because our Air Force and Army were so well-trained and equipped? That was certainly part of it, but the main element of victory was heaven's involvement.

We know that's true, because a short time after the great victory in the Gulf, our same well-trained army was sent into Somalia. However, when they went into harm's way there, they went on the wings of criticism, strife and bickering instead of prayer. We opened our big mouths all right, but only to gripe because we didn't approve of the mission. We didn't approve of the president or his administration. As a result, our same well-trained and equipped army suffered tragic losses and was eventually driven out by a ragtag bunch of outlaws and drug dealers.

As believers committed to the life of love, we must never let that happen again. We must keep our leaders lifted in prayer and ensure they make righteous decisions where our nation is concerned. Then, we must back them—not with criticism—but with our continued prayers. We must open our big mouths before the throne of grace and keep them covered with love.

LIMITLESS**LOVE**

Don't Just Sit There...Do Something

"But someone may well say, 'You have faith and I have works; show me your faith without the works, and I will show you my faith by my works.' You believe that God is one. You do well; the demons also believe, and shudder. But are you willing to recognize, you foolish fellow, that faith without works is useless?"
James 2:18-20, *New American Standard*

Do you believe God loves you? Do you really, truly believe it?

There's only one way to know for sure. Look at your life and see if you are acting on that love.

Something you genuinely believe, you'll act on. For instance, if someone were to come into a crowded room and say, "The building is on fire!" everyone who believed it would immediately get out. Those who did not believe it would say things like, "I don't smell any smoke. Do you smell any smoke?" They'd just sit there, waiting for their physical senses to tell them if what was said was true.

Now let's add another element to this illustration. Let's say the person who came in and said "The building is on fire!" was a fireman. Now with that added to it, it would really be foolish not to act on his word because he knows what he's talking about.

That's the position you and I are in today. God—who definitely knows what He is talking about—has said that He loves us. Most of us have mentally agreed. If someone asks us, we tell them, "Oh yes, I know God loves me." But most of us haven't done much about it. We're still just sitting there, waiting for further evidence of that truth.

That evidence won't come until we get up and do something! Why? Because just knowing God loves us isn't enough. It's acting on that knowledge that brings results!

"What should I do?" you ask.

First of all, open your mouth and say something. Start talking about how much God loves you. Instead of saying, "Gee, I hope this situation turns out all right," say, "Praise God, I have confidence this situation is going to turn out all right, because my Father loves me and perfects that which concerns me" (Psalm 138:8). Use every opportunity to confess your faith in God's love for you.

Second, start acting on God's WORD. When you read, for example, that as a believer you can lay hands on the sick and they'll recover, don't shrink back in fear. Don't sit around wondering what will happen if you lay hands on someone and they don't get well. Get up and get after it, believing God loves you enough to back you up. The minute you do that, God's love will suddenly become more than a religious concept to you...it will become a reality. That's when you'll begin to see what the power of love can do.

LIMITLESS**LOVE**

Continual Conversations With God

"Pray without ceasing."
1 Thessalonians 5:17

The best way I know to grow in the revelation of God's love is to spend time fellowshiping with Him—not just when you're on your knees or when you're in church, but throughout the day. During the normal activities of your life, make it a point to talk with God. Pray without ceasing. Become God-is-right-here-inside-me-and-with-me-minded. Walk with Him all the time.

Certainly, there are times when formal prayers of supplication, petition and intercession must be prayed, but don't limit your conversations with God to that. All prayer is not just asking for things or changing things. Those kinds of prayer are important, but developing a real and loving friendship with your heavenly Father is vital to a full and healthy life of faith.

Think about it. Most of the things that you and I have had to pray to change or overcome in our lives would most likely have been avoided had we been in closer fellowship with our loving, heavenly Father—following His lead, or as Ephesians 2:10 says, walking in the good ways He has prepared for us.

We can walk in those ways if we'll develop a base of fellowshiping with God all the time—not in some spooky, unrealistic way, but the way it really is…a Father and a growing, learning, eager child…asking questions, sharing secrets…never afraid to make mistakes and try again…knowing at all times the overshadowing, hovering-over, loving Father and faithful Friend is ever so close…never condemning…never accusing…always honoring the blood and the Name of Jesus on our behalf.

Wouldn't you love to have that kind of relationship with God?

You can! WORD-based prayers prayed in love and faith are the keys to it.

Jesus said in Luke 18:1, "Men ought always to pray, and not to faint." So take Him at His WORD. Pray and never quit. Pray and never cave in. Talk to The LORD continually. Talk to Him like He is your Father. Talk to Him like He is your very best Friend!

He is, you know. He'll stay with you when no one else will. He loves you like no one else can. He's the smartest, wisest, most powerful Friend you've ever had or ever will have.

Take your place, and become His best friend. Every day that you do, you'll get a deeper revelation of just how much He loves you.

LIMITLESS LOVE

Keeping Our Priorities Straight

"See then that ye walk circumspectly, not as fools, but as wise, redeeming the time, because the days are evil."
Ephesians 5:15-16

One of the greatest benefits of living a life ruled by love is that it helps us keep our priorities straight. When we're head-over-heels in love with Jesus, we never lose sight of the fact that He is coming soon. We live every day in great expectancy, looking forward to His appearing.

Love for Him, and love for the people of this world for whom He shed His blood, compels us to live our lives in such a way that we gather up all the souls for Him we possibly can. Our No. 1 priority is to help our LORD fill this ship of salvation before it sails.

Politics is not the most important thing. Finances are not the most important thing. Education is not the most important thing.

All those things have their place, but when our hearts are filled with the love of God, nothing is as important as being obedient to Him. We are constantly attentive and quick to follow His leadership, because we know that being right where He says to be and doing what He says to do will result in the maximum harvest of precious souls before the terrible time of Tribulation comes on the earth.

Being obedient in our everyday lives gives the Spirit of God opportunity to influence people for Jesus, even when you and I don't realize it. When we allow love, joy peace, faith and all the character qualities of the Holy Spirit to dominate our lives, it affects the people we meet, whether or not God leads us to say or do something directly. Our smiles and kind words in a difficult situation may prepare someone for another person to come along later and lead them to Jesus.

It is the love of God flowing through individual believers on the street, in one-on-one ministry to the lost, that will win the greatest multitude of people in these last days. Thank God for full-time evangelists! Thank God for full-time pastors and teachers! They're wonderful, but the Bible says their job is to train the saints for the work of the ministry. Ultimately, it's Jesus working through the members of His Body who will bring in the last, great end time harvest!

But to do it, we'll have to keep our priorities straight. We'll have to keep our eyes focused on Jesus. We'll have to keep our ears tuned to His voice, and we'll have to keep our hearts full of His love.

If we do, we'll redeem these evil days and buy up every opportunity He gives us to win souls for Him. And when He comes we'll hear Him say, "Well done, good and faithful servant!"

LIMITLESS**LOVE**

Entering the Joy of The LORD

> "'If you abide in Me, and My words abide in you, ask whatever you wish, and it will be done for you. My Father is glorified by this, that you bear much fruit, and so prove to be My disciples. Just as the Father has loved Me, I have also loved you; abide in My love…. These things I have spoken to you so that My joy may be in you, and that your joy may be made full.'"
> John 15:7-9, 11, *New American Standard*

The joy of life! What a wonderful ring that phrase has to it!

Ever since the day man committed high treason in the Garden of Eden, people have searched for it. And ever since the Holy Spirit was poured out on the Day of Pentecost, the joy of The LORD has been available to anyone who would receive it. Jesus said that He wanted us to have it—and have it to the full.

What must we do to get it? We must love The LORD with all our hearts, minds and strength. We must put Him first place in our lives.

That's what Jesus meant when He said, "Abide in Me." He didn't mean we should just run to Him when our plans don't work out. We're to stay with Him and in Him all the time. We're to put Him first place in our lives every moment of every day. When His plans are first and become our plans, then they work out and bring great joy to our lives. His plans are always for our success.

Remember this: What He did on the Cross was about us. What we do here on earth is about Him.

Practically speaking, we abide in Jesus and put Him first place by making His WORD our final authority. We believe what His WORD says because He said it, and we act on it…now. When we do that, we experience great joy because the joy of life comes from doing what is right. And when we believe and act on The WORD we are doing right—every time!

"Well, I believe that, Brother Copeland, but sometimes it's difficult to know just how to apply The WORD to specific situations in my life."

I know it is. That's why Jesus asked the Father to send us the Holy Spirit. He's been given to us to be our helper, guide, teacher and counselor. He lives inside us, and when we look to Him, He sees to it that we receive the wisdom of God for our lives.

Once He does make God's will known to us, we are obligated to obey it. We must put His counsel first place and act on it just as we'd act on the written WORD. If we want to continue abiding in Jesus, we must love Him so much that we do what He tells us to do in The WORD and by His Spirit—every time, all the time—without compromise and without complaint.

When we do, we'll discover the true joy of living. We'll enter in to the joy of The LORD!

LIMITLESS**LOVE**

"I Will"

"When Jesus came down from the mountain, large crowds followed Him. And a leper came to Him and bowed down before Him, and said, 'LORD, if You are willing, You can make me clean.' Jesus stretched out His hand and touched him, saying, 'I am willing; be cleansed.' And immediately his leprosy was cleansed."
Matthew 8:1-3, *New American Standard*

I will. Those are two of the most revealing words Jesus ever said.

They are the words that resound in every believer who has ears to hear His voice. They are the words that drive out our doubts and banish our fears. They are the words that answer everyone who dares to come before the throne of grace and say, "LORD, will You meet my need?"

I will! I will! I will!

That is the answer the Father of Love always gives to those who ask for His good gifts. It is the answer that inspires faith. Once the leper heard it, it was easy for him to receive from Jesus' ministry. It was easy for him to believe once he understood it was God's will for him to be made whole.

"But aren't there times when God says, 'No'?" you ask. "Aren't there times when I have to say, 'Not my will, but Yours be done?'"

The only time you might ask this would be when your requests are out of line with The WORD and the promises of God, or when, in immaturity, you ask for something that would ultimately hurt instead of help you.

One of the dictionary definitions of the word *will* sheds light on that kind of situation. It says *to will* is "to reason with respect to the value or importance of things, judge which is to be preferred and then choose the most valuable." God always knows the value and true importance of all things, and He has judged which is to be preferred. His decisions are recorded in His written WORD. Through that WORD He has provided us a perfect description of His loving will.

On the other hand, we don't always in our natural selves have the ability to know what is truly valuable. That's why people make a lot of wrong decisions and do things that bring disastrous results. As Proverbs 14:12 says, "There is a way which seemeth right unto a man, but the end thereof are the ways of death."

Keep that in mind when you start to pray. Don't let your own human desires and understanding determine what you ask for. Go to The WORD first and find out what it promises. Look and see what your heavenly Father has lovingly written there for you.

When you find it, approach Him boldly and joyfully make your request, knowing even before you ask Him if He'll do it for you, His answer is...

I will.

LIMITLESS**LOVE**

Good Will Toward Men

"And there were in the same country shepherds abiding in the field, keeping watch over their flock by night. And, lo, the angel of The LORD came upon them, and the glory of The LORD shone round about them: and they were sore afraid. And the angel said unto them, Fear not: for, behold, I bring you good tidings of great joy, which shall be to all people. For unto you is born this day in the city of David a Saviour, which is Christ The LORD. And this shall be a sign unto you; ye shall find the babe wrapped in swaddling clothes, lying in a manger. And suddenly there was with the angel a multitude of the heavenly host praising God, and saying, Glory to God in the highest, and on earth peace, good will toward men."
Luke 2:8-14

This isn't just a part of the Christmas story. It's not just some sweet idea from the inside of a greeting card. It is one of the most powerful announcements ever sent from heaven. It established forever the good will of God toward men.

Notice the angel didn't say God has good will toward men, sometimes...but at other times it's not so good. He didn't say, "Well, God wants to BLESS you today, but He might not tomorrow. You just never know what God is going to do."

No! A thousand times no!

God is always Love, and His will for us is always good. He sent Jesus to the earth to take our sin and punishment so we could step into that good will. He came so we "might have life, and...have it more abundantly" (John 10:10). Every day. All day. Forever.

"If that's the case," someone might say, "why do so many bad things happen to people?"

As much as He desires to BLESS us, God will not force anyone to choose His will. He will not make them receive Him or His way of doing things. Those who will choose Him and submit to His good will end up BLESSED. Those who won't...don't.

Their refusal to receive God's will, however, doesn't change it one bit. God's will is always solid as a rock. It's never *yes* one day and then maybe *no* tomorrow. God's will toward us is good.

As 2 Corinthians 1:20 says, "All the promises of God in him are yea, and in him Amen...." So don't let the devil make you doubt for a second that God has wonderful plans for you. Settle it forever in your heart and mind that He is always working for your good. Then shout like the angels, "Glory to God in the highest! Peace on earth! Good will toward men!"

LIMITLESS**LOVE**

Make Your Father's Dream
Come True

"And I said, 'Who are You, LORD?' And The LORD said, 'I am Jesus whom you are persecuting. But get up and stand on your feet; for this purpose I have appeared to you, to appoint you a minister and a witness not only to the things which you have seen, but also to the things in which I will appear to you; rescuing you from the Jewish people and from the Gentiles, to whom I am sending you, to open their eyes so that they may turn from darkness to light and from the dominion of Satan to God, that they may receive forgiveness of sins and an inheritance among those who have been sanctified by faith in Me.' So, King Agrippa, I did not prove disobedient to the heavenly vision."

Acts 26:15-19, *New American Standard*

In this passage, where the Apostle Paul described his conversion experience to King Agrippa, we see a most amazing fact. God has a dream for mankind. He has a heavenly vision that can only be fulfilled through people like you and me. What is God's vision for us?

He described it to Paul in three parts: First, that our spiritual eyes be opened. Second, that we turn from darkness to light, from the power of Satan to the power of God. Third, that we receive our divine inheritance.

Many Christians have fulfilled the first and second parts of God's heavenly vision. They're born again and living holy lives. But they haven't taken hold of their full inheritance in Him. They haven't received THE BLESSING and the power to live supernatural lives right here on earth as witnesses to the world of God's love and grace.

That is the inheritance laid up for us in Jesus. It includes all the provision necessary for us to be made whole in every area of our lives—spirit, soul and body. It gives us the power to be filled with all the fullness of God.

Our Father will not be totally pleased until we receive that inheritance. So, let's rise up in faith and do it! Not because we want to be some kind of spiritual superheroes. Not just because we want to enjoy full and wonderful lives. Let's do it because we love our God. Let's do it because we want to see His heavenly vision fulfilled!

Let's change our reason for receiving, right now. Let's stop trying to receive our healing and our deliverance just because we're hurting and have great needs. Let's stop reaching for our divine destiny just so we'll feel happy and satisfied with our lives. Let's do it to please our heavenly Father and help Jesus carry out His vision.

When the devil tries to rob us of our divine inheritance, let's say, "I rebuke you, Satan, in the Name of Jesus. Flee from me. I'm a joint heir with Jesus. Get your hands off my life, now!"

Rise up in love for the Father and make His dream come true.

Stake Your Claim

"And now, brethren, I commend you to God, and to The WORD of his grace, which is able to build you up, and to give you an inheritance among all them which are sanctified."

Acts 20:32

God loves you so much, He paid the ultimate price not only for your deliverance from sin and death but for the fullness of your inheritance in Him. The LORD Jesus bore stripes on His back so you could be healed. He became poor so you could be rich. He suffered the ultimate punishment so you could have peace and complete wholeness—spirit, soul and body.

Jesus shed His precious blood to ratify the eternal will and covenant of God that provides these things for us. And the best way we can show our love and appreciation to Him for it is to receive that inheritance, and lay claim to it by faith.

In recent times, the word *claim* has fallen into disrepute in some circles. People have actually criticized faith folks by calling us "the name it and claim it crowd." But the fact is, it's absolutely unloving and ungrateful for us to know what our Father has laid up for us, to know the price He paid for it, and to be too lazy or faithless to claim it.

What does it mean for us to claim our inheritance? Imagine yourself at a large conference table and a judge has passed out legal papers of a will and said, "Your father has left you an inheritance. The property and assets stated in these documents now belong to you." The first thing you would do is read what the document said had been willed and granted to you. The next thing you would do is make arrangements to take possession of everything that's yours—immediately!

But let's say after you read the papers, someone came into the room and said, "I'm taking over all the land and buildings that belonged to your father. I'm going to live on that property that's been left to you." What would you do? Would you just sit there and say, "Well, I guess it just wasn't my father's will for me to have it."

No! You would stand to your feet and claim what belongs to you. You would wave your father's will in that man's face and shout, "No, you don't, you thief! That land belongs to me. I have the legal documents to prove it. So, stay off my property!"

Do you think you would be dishonoring your father if you did that? Do you think you would be acting arrogantly and presumptuously to demand what he'd provided for you? Certainly not! You would be carrying out your father's will. You would be upholding his word and honoring his name.

We do the same thing when we claim what God has promised us in His WORD. When we declare it's ours, by faith, and refuse to let the devil talk us out of it, we bring glory to our Father. By claiming our covenant promises, we see to it that He gets exactly what He paid for—the joy of seeing His children enjoying their full inheritance in Jesus' Name.

LIMITLESS**LOVE**

Take Your Place at the Table

"The Spirit itself beareth witness with our spirit, that we are the children of
God: And if children, then heirs; heirs of God, and joint-heirs with Christ;
if so be that we suffer with him, that we may be also glorified together."
Romans 8:16-17

Joint heirs with Jesus. What a powerful phrase! If you're ever tempted to doubt how great God's love is for you, if you're ever inclined to wonder if you have a special place in His heart, remember this: He has made you a joint heir with Christ.

You're not a sub-heir. You don't have a place with God that's inferior to the place that Jesus holds. When you received Jesus as Savior and LORD, you not only received Him, you received His right-standing with God and all that God has given Him.

How much does that include? Everything! Hebrews 1:2 says He has been appointed heir of *all things!*

"I know," someone might say, "but Romans 8:17 says we'll have to suffer to receive it. We'll have to let the devil beat us up awhile with poverty or sickness and disease so we can give some glory to The LORD, won't we?"

No! It doesn't bring any glory to Jesus, or to us, to let the devil put back on us the very things we've been redeemed from. It doesn't honor God for us to put up with sickness or poverty any more than it honors Him for us to put up with sin.

The suffering we experience is spiritual—not physical. It comes from the pressure that's involved in standing for what's ours in faith and patience, even when things look hopeless. It comes from standing and resisting everything Jesus bore for us on the cross. He bore our sins—so we resist sin. He bore our sickness—so we resist sickness. He bore our poverty—so we resist lack.

Some people think we'll have to wait until we get to heaven to enjoy our joint heirship with Jesus. They think we'll have to wait until after we die to partake of the feast Psalm 23 says has been provided for us. But that's not the case at all. That Psalm says God has prepared a table for us in the presence of our enemies, so that can't be a heavenly feast. We don't have any enemies in heaven.

We are supposed to be eating at that table *now,* in this life. Everything on it belongs to us. And our Father expects us to fight the good fight of faith for it. He expects us to pull up our chair, push the devil out of the way and say, "Father, pass me the bread!"

If you don't think you have a right to do that, think again. Your Father loves you so much He has made you a joint heir with Christ. You've been given His place at the table. And everything He has belongs to you, in His great Name!

LIMITLESS**LOVE**

Sweet Satisfaction

"Jesus saith unto them, My meat is to do the will of him
that sent me, and to finish his work."
John 4:34

One of the best indications that you love The LORD with all your heart is the pleasure you get from doing His will. When you're fully in love with Him, you get more joy from carrying out His plans than you do from carrying out your own. Doing the will of The LORD satisfies you as absolutely nothing else can.

Over the years, Gloria and I have learned to stay in communion with God and be quick to make corrections that keep us lined up as closely as possible to His perfect will. We don't want anything less than that for our ministry or for our personal lives. We learned many years ago that if we would seek God for His will and plan, then do it with all our heart, His BLESSING and Anointing would be there. That's so much better than figuring out some plan I think might work and then trying to get God to BLESS it.

How do you find the will of God for your life? Study and meditate The WORD of God until it begins to unfold and you get clear in your inner man what The LORD is directing you to do. Once you grasp it with your heart, you can be sure your mind will soon catch up.

I heard the great soul winner and apostle to the nations, T.L. Osborn, say that he discovered God's will for him by reading and meditating on Mark 16:15-20, where Jesus said, "Go ye into all the world, and preach the gospel to every creature." Brother Osborn said he read that and prayed over it until he knew what to do about it.

That scripture is a great place to start because it's the will of God for the whole Body of Christ. All of us have our part in that plan, one way or another.

Of course, all of this takes time. Time spent in The WORD. Time spent in prayer. Time spent fellowshiping with your heavenly Father. But if you truly love The LORD, you'll be willing to take that time.

Once you do, you'll find out it was time well-spent. You'll realize that God loves you and desires for you to be in His perfect will even more than you do. Why? Because that's where your success in life is. That's where your divine deliverance is. That's where things work right. That's just the best place all the way around.

So don't ever be afraid of God's will for you. It's not a place of terrible suffering or lack. God knows you. He knows what you can do and what He can do through you. What others might think is the worst place in the world will seem like heaven on earth when it's where God wants you to be. It will offer the sweet satisfaction that comes only from pleasing your heavenly Father. It will give you the gratification granted to those who love Him enough to do His wonderful will.

LIMITLESS**LOVE**

Discovering the Secrets of God's Love

"For one who speaks in a tongue does not speak to men but to God;
for no one understands, but in his spirit he speaks mysteries."
1 Corinthians 14:2, *New American Standard*

God's love for us is so far beyond all that we can ask or think, it is, for the most part, a mystery to us. It is so wonderful, our natural minds alone just can't conceive it. *The Amplified Bible* says, "the love of Christ…far surpasses mere knowledge…" (Ephesians 3:19). It tells us we need the strength and power of God just to grasp it!

First Corinthians 2:9 says much the same thing about THE BLESSING God has given us: "But as it is written, Eye hath not seen, nor ear heard, neither have entered into the heart of man, the things which God hath prepared for them that love him."

We'd be in a mess if that thought stopped there. We'd be doomed to walk around without a revelation of God's love and provision. But, it doesn't stop there! Verse 10 goes on to say, "But God hath revealed them unto us by his Spirit: for the Spirit searcheth all things, yea, the deep things of God."

If we'll go beyond our natural thinking and get into the realm of the spirit, God will expand our comprehension. He'll give us deeper and deeper revelations of how much He loves us. He'll show us great and mighty things He has laid up for us that we have never known.

How do we get into that spiritual realm?

One of the best ways I know is by praying in other tongues. When we pray in tongues, we pray out those mysteries. We draw them from the depths of our spirits and get in position where the Holy Spirit can give us the interpretation so we can understand them.

"Oh, Brother Copeland," you might say, "I could never do that."

Yes you can, because the Bible clearly teaches that when you speak in tongues, pray that you may interpret (1 Corinthians 14:13). And whatever God tells you to do, He gives you the ability to do. So get started!

While you're at it, you'll also be increasing your spiritual strength so that you can take hold of the powerful revelations God wants to give you. You'll be doing what Jude 20 says, "…building up yourselves on your most holy faith, praying in the Holy Ghost."

God isn't trying to keep these things hidden from us. He doesn't want the fullness of His BLESSING to remain a mystery. He wants us to be continually discovering more about it.

Give Him opportunity to do it. Spend time praying in tongues. Get over in the spirit so He can tell you the secrets of His love.

LIMITLESS**LOVE**

Forever Springtime

"But I see another law in my members, warring against the law of my mind,
and bringing me into captivity to the law of sin which is in my members.
O wretched man that I am! who shall deliver me from the body of this death?
I thank God through Jesus Christ our LORD.... There is therefore now no
condemnation to them which are in Christ Jesus, who walk not after the
flesh, but after the Spirit. For the law of the Spirit of life in Christ Jesus
hath made me free from the law of sin and death."

Romans 7:23-8:2

Being in bondage to sin and the flesh is a dark and desolate place to be. It's like living continually in the dead of winter. The nights are long and the days are short and full of storms. It makes us want to cry out like Paul did, "O wretched man that I am! Who shall deliver me from the body of this death?"

That would be a sad and lonely cry if there were no answer to it. But thank God, there is!

The answer is in Jesus. In Him we find springtime! When we step out of sin and into the spirit of His love, everything around us begins to show signs of new life. His power and forgiveness set us free from all the wickedness and evil in the world. We are filled with His wonderful warmth and light.

Amazingly, that life was there all the time. It was there just like the life of spring is present in the barren trees of winter. It is just waiting for its due season so it can come forth.

Because God loves us, He is always there. Even in those wintry times, when we stumble and fall into sin, or when we let the devil deceive us and draw us into darkness again.

Even then, God is there. He will never leave us nor forsake us. He is inside us waiting for His due season. Waiting for us to release our faith. Waiting and listening for words of repentance to come from our hearts and lips that He can support with His power.

No amount of death and darkness can drive Him away. No amount of sin can overcome His love.

The very moment we begin to repent and act on His forgiveness, it's springtime again. His love begins to bud in our lives. The more we act on it, the more it grows. His mercy pops out all over the place in bright, clean colors like new flowers in a garden. The sweet fragrance of the Spirit tells us everything is OK. The blood of Jesus has kicked sin and death out. Life is flowing once more. It's springtime.

Thank God, the law of the spirit of life in Christ Jesus has made us free from the law of sin and death. Winter is over forever. It can always be springtime in our lives!

LIMITLESS**LOVE**

Vessels of Glory

"I do not ask on behalf of these alone, but for those also who believe in Me through their word; that they may all be one; even as You, Father, are in Me, and I in You, that they also may be in Us, so that the world may believe that You sent Me. The glory which You have given Me I have given to them, that they may be one, just as We are one."

John 17:20-22, *New American Standard*

Every once in a while I hear someone say, "God will never share His glory with any man." They usually say it in a deeply religious tone of voice. And if you don't know better, you'd think it was not only very spiritual but absolutely true.

The problem is, it contradicts the Bible.

Difficult as it is for our minds to comprehend, God loves us so much that in Jesus, He has given us His glory. We can't take credit for it, of course. We didn't do anything to earn it or deserve it. It's part of our divine inheritance. It's a gift to us from our LORD Jesus Christ—The LORD of glory and The LORD of love.

When God's glory is in manifestation, great and unusual things happen. Overwhelming life comes on the scene and changes things suddenly. Romans 6:4 says that Jesus was raised from the dead by the glory of the Father. Ephesians 1:19-20 says that same glory power is at work in and for us who believe.

The Hebrew word translated *glory* means "the heaviness of God—His heaviness with everything good, the heaviness of His splendor and majesty." In His goodness, splendor and majesty is the hiding place of His power. In Luke 2, it was the glory of The LORD that shone round about the angel who announced the birth of Jesus. It's the glory that made the face of Jesus shine on the mount of transfiguration.

It's the glory of The LORD that blinded the Apostle Paul on the road to Damascus. It's the glory of God that Stephen saw when the Jews began stoning him. Revelation 15:8 says it's the glory that fills God's heavenly temple!

Our natural mind staggers at that. It says, "What could that glory possibly have to do with a nobody like me? I can't even understand it!"

Yes, you can! You can not only understand it, you are a container of it. Second Corinthians 4:6-7 says that "God, who commanded the light to shine out of darkness, hath shined in our hearts, to give the light of the knowledge of the glory of God in the face of Jesus Christ. But we have this treasure in earthen vessels, that the excellency of the power may be of God, and not of us."

Remember that next time you hear someone say God will never share His glory. Give a shout of praise for the amazing God of love and grace who chose to put His glory in you.

LIMITLESS**LOVE**

Receive Your Inheritance of Love

"BLESSED be the God and Father of our LORD Jesus Christ, who hath
BLESSED us with all spiritual BLESSINGS in heavenly places in Christ:
according as he hath chosen us in him before the foundation of the world,
that we should be holy and without blame before him in love: Having
predestinated us unto the adoption of children by Jesus Christ to himself.... In
whom also we have obtained an inheritance, being predestinated according to
the purpose of him who worketh all things after the counsel of his own will."
Ephesians 1:3-5, 11

A few years ago, someone told me of a college student who found her name in a special list of people published in a local newspaper. She was heir to a sizable sum of money and didn't know it. You can imagine how surprised she was.

Up to the time she found out about it, the only thing that kept her from using that money to meet her needs was her ignorance of its existence. The one who left it to her wanted her to have it. That's obvious. The bank wanted her to have it. They had it in an account with her name on it. But, she could not withdraw from an account she was not aware belonged to her.

Every one of us as born-again children of God has just such an account. It's an account that contains all things that pertain to life and godliness (2 Peter 1:3). As joint heirs with Jesus we've been given an inheritance that outshines the sun. It is so vast that no earthly human mind can even come close to grasping what belongs to us.

It's already ours. Now! We don't inherit it after we die. We inherited it when Jesus died. But we've had the same problem that young college student had. Most of us don't know we have inherited anything. Others have heard of it, but don't know it's ours now—right here on this earth where we need it. Then there are those who have heard about it, but don't really believe it belongs to them. If that college student had not believed and received her money, it would have done her no good whatsoever. Her benefactor would have left it to her in vain if she had refused to act on the knowledge she received about her inheritance.

Don't let lack of knowledge or unbelief rob you of your inheritance. Dig into The WORD and find out more about what belongs to you in Jesus.

After all, your heavenly Father wants you to have it. He so loved you that He sent Jesus to save you and secure that inheritance for you. He made you part of His family. He made you His blood kin so that you could inherit all that He has.

He opened a heavenly account and put your name on it. So reach out with the hand of faith and start receiving your inheritance of love!

The Mercy That Makes You a King

"Incline your ear, and come unto me: hear, and your soul shall live; and I will make an everlasting covenant with you, even the sure mercies of David."

Isaiah 55:3

God, in His great love, has promised each of us who come to Him that He will give us the sure mercies of David. What are the sure mercies of David? They are the mercies bestowed on us by God that make us great in spite of our sin and failure.

Second Samuel 7:8 says that God took David from the sheepfold, "from following the sheep, to be ruler over my people, over Israel." God took David from nothing and made him a king! That's what God does for everyone who receives Jesus as LORD and Savior. He lifts us out of the ash heap of sin and sets us with princes, even the princes of His people (Ps. 113:7-8). He takes us out of darkness and makes us lights to the world. He delivers us from the curse and makes us like Abraham—a BLESSING to the families of the earth (Genesis 12:3).

You might think your life is such a mess, God couldn't do that for you. But He can. What's more, you can be confident that He will because He said Himself that His mercies are *sure!* The word *sure* is a powerful word. The dictionary says it means "free from doubt; certain; confident; and positive." It also means "to be trusted; safe; reliable; never missing, slipping or failing; unerring and firm."

You don't have to sit around wondering if God is going to pour out His mercies on you. You don't have to waste your time wishing He would enable you to do something great in the kingdom of God. You can be sure He will because His WORD to you is sure!

Then, you can open the door for those mercies to flood your life by doing what David did. He took the words God spoke to him, put them in his own mouth and lifted them up in praises to The LORD. That's the way David walked in the power and covenant of God.

Abraham did the same thing. Romans 4:20-21 says, "He did not waver through unbelief regarding the promise of God, but was strengthened in his faith and gave glory to God, being fully persuaded that God had power to do what he had promised" *(New International Version).*

Don't wait until the storms of life hit and then try to put this truth to work. Do it all day, every day. Fill your mouth with the blood-sworn promises of God and praise them back to Him. Then when the devil shows up and tries to steal them from you, he'll be stopped cold by the wall of faith and praise that surrounds you. He'll stand helplessly by as the sure mercies of David lift you out of nothingness and make you a king.

LIMITLESS**LOVE**

BLESSED to Be a BLESSING

"Jesus said to them again, 'Peace be with you;
as the Father has sent Me, I also send you.'"
John 20:21, *New American Standard*

There's a reason why we, as believers, need to receive all THE BLESSING God has promised us. There's a reason why we should fight the good fight of faith and receive the fullness of the victory Jesus bought for us—spirit, soul and body. It's not just so that we can have our bills paid and our bodies healed. It's not just so that we can enjoy our lives and watch television in comfort. No, the reason is far greater than that.

We ought to do it because we love The LORD Jesus. We ought to do it because He sent us to represent Him to the world just as He was sent to represent the Father to the world. We ought to do it because He's given us a purpose and a calling, and we want to fulfill it.

Many Christians seem to have the idea that Jesus is going to do things in the earth apart from His Church. They seem to think that even without us, He can minister to people and carry out the Great Commission. But that's not the picture the New Testament presents. It says that we are the Body of Christ in the earth. Although Jesus is the Head, the works that He does now in the earth, He does through us!

Our bodies are necessary to Jesus. They are the temples of His Holy Spirit. We need strong, healthy bodies to do what He needs done. Our minds are important to Jesus. We need minds that are free from the oppression of the devil. We need minds that are keen, filled with the wisdom of God so that we can effectively serve the Master. Our finances are important to Jesus. We need to prosper enough to have money to do what Jesus has called us to on the earth.

Do you remember how Jesus healed and delivered the madman of Gadara? Jesus set that man free from a legion of demons. He clothed him and put him in his right mind. But, that's not the end of the story. Before Jesus left that man he said to him, "Go home to thy friends, and tell them how great things The LORD hath done for thee…" (Mark 5:19).

Jesus set that man free to fulfill a purpose and a calling. He does the same thing for you and me.

That's why it's selfish for us to be satisfied with less than God intends us to have. That's why it's selfish for us to let the devil defeat us in any area of our lives. Jesus needs you and me to prosper and be in health even as our soul prospers. If we're sick, broken-down and always hurting, we won't be able to carry out the mission He has given us. Jesus needs us to be spiritually, physically and financially able to complete the works He started.

He needs us to be BLESSED so that we can be a BLESSING. And if we truly love Him, that's exactly what we'll do.

Behold, the Dreamer Cometh

"...And Joseph went after his brethren, and found them in Dothan. And when they saw him afar off, even before he came near unto them, they conspired against him to slay him. And they said one to another, Behold, this dreamer cometh."

Genesis 37:17-19

The Old Testament story of Joseph is the story of a son who was dearly loved by his father. It's the story of young man who had a God-given dream and dared to believe it. It's the story of those who, having no dreams of their own, tried to steal and kill their brother's dream. But they failed because Joseph just kept trusting God, through the most trying circumstances, until he finally saw his dream come true.

That's not only Joseph's story. As a dearly loved child of God, it's meant to be your story too. You have a destiny and a God-given dream. The question is: Will you dare to believe and keep on believing until you see that dream come true?

Years ago, Gloria was presented with that very question as she read a book by Brother Oral Roberts. In it, he challenged believers to write their dreams and confirm them with the written WORD of God. He urged Christians to take a stand of faith and refuse to let anyone talk them out of it. So that's just what Gloria did. She wrote down the dreams God had given her for ministry, for our family and for the house she had always wanted.

Since then, all those dreams have come true. But, one of the most interesting to watch has been that house. There have been many times through the years when it looked like there was no way for Gloria's dream house to ever become a reality. But Gloria paid no attention to those negative circumstances. She just kept collecting magazines, pictures and articles that helped her envision and plan for her house.

Even more important, she kept collecting scriptural promises. She found house scriptures, land scriptures, tree scriptures and furniture scriptures. She had God's WORD for every detail of that house. Each one of those scriptures strengthened her faith. Finally, the day came when her faith became the evidence of her dream (Hebrews 11:1). The house was built. We stepped over the threshold and stood in Gloria's dream.

God loves you just as much as He loves Gloria. He longs to fulfill your dreams. But He can only do it if you'll dare to believe. So start taking steps of faith today. Write down the dreams God has given you and the scriptural promises that support them. Cultivate the habit of reading your promises and your dream list. Then see yourself with them. Speak as if you're already standing in them. Not someday—now!

Others may scoff at you and try to discourage you. Circumstances may seem solidly against you. But don't let those things stop you. Be like Joseph. Just keep trusting God in spite of it all. Live in such a way that when people see you they say, "Behold, the dreamer is coming!" Keep believing until you see your dreams come true.

You Know the Right Answer

"Humble yourselves therefore under the mighty hand of God, that he may exalt you in due time: casting all your care upon him; for he careth for you. Be sober, be vigilant; because your adversary the devil, as a roaring lion, walketh about, seeking whom he may devour: whom resist stedfast in the faith...."
1 Peter 5:6-9

I once heard a story about a lion who was roaming around the jungle, flaunting his power. Every time he'd encounter another animal, he'd let out a roar and demand they answer the question, "Who is the king of the beasts?" One after another, they would wilt before him in fear—the zebra, the antelope, the monkey, the flamingo—they all told him what he wanted to hear. "You are, Lion! You are surely the king of the beasts."

Toward the end of the day, he encountered an elephant. "Tell me, Elephant," the lion roared. "Who do you say is the king of the beasts?" Without saying a word, the elephant reached over and wrapped his trunk around the lion's neck. He picked him up, swung him in the air a few times, then slung him across a mudhole and stuck him headfirst in the bank like a dart.

The old lion struggled free of the mud, shook his head and looked back at the elephant. Well, you don't have to be so rude," he said, "just because you don't know the right answer!"

Remember that story next time the devil comes roaring at *you*. Remember he isn't king in your life. The LORD Jesus Christ is your King. And He is the King of all kings! He has done to the devil everything necessary to defeat and humiliate him. The Bible says He "disarmed the powers and authorities, he made a public spectacle of them, triumphing over them by the cross" (Colossians 2:15, *New International Version*). Jesus has destroyed and brought to nothing him who had the power of death, that is, the devil (Hebrews 2:14).

When you made Jesus The LORD of your life, He became your blood-covenant Brother. He gave you His own power and authority. In essence, He said to you, *Don't worry about a thing, little brother. Cast all your care over on Me. I care for you. I love you. So when the devil comes after you, resist him and I'll back you. He'll flee from you just like He flees from Me because we're in this together. And since I've already defeated him, he is under your feet!*

Once you understand the covenant of love you have in Jesus, you won't run in terror from the devil. You'll just take The WORD of God and the Name of Jesus, wrap them around his neck and sling him out of your way. When he asks you who the king is, you'll put him on the run because you're a covenant child and you know the right answer.

LIMITLESS**LOVE**

Don't Let Trouble Trouble You

"...I will sing aloud of thy mercy in the morning: for thou hast been my
defence and refuge in the day of my trouble. Unto thee, O my strength,
will I sing: for God is my defence, and the God of my mercy."
Psalm 59:16-17

Every once in a while, I hear someone accuse faith preachers of telling people that if they'll just believe God, they'll never have any more trouble. Personally, I've never heard anyone preach that, and I can't imagine anyone being naive enough to believe it. As long as we're living in this world, the devil is going to be trying to mess up our lives. Jesus made that clear when He said, "In this world you will have trouble. But take heart! I have overcome the world" (John 16:33, *New International Version*).

Where then, do people get the idea that those of us who preach faith claim to have trouble-free lives? I think it's because of our attitude. It's because when we're truly trusting God with a revelation of how powerful He is and how greatly He loves us, we aren't troubled by the trouble that comes our way. We don't cry and sweat over it because we truly believe that Jesus has overcome it. We trust Him to defend us. We understand our covenant of love with Him, so we expect Him to use all His mighty power to protect us and see us through to victory.

When I think of the fiercely protective love God has for us and the boldness it inspires, I always think of a story I heard another minister tell about a time he encountered a group of elephants on a game preserve during a visit to Africa. He and the guide who was with him moved closer to get a better look at the animals, when suddenly a huge bull elephant stepped out in front of them, threw his trunk in the air and trumpeted a warning. He let them know if they came one step closer, he'd mash them like a grape.

A split second later, they understood why. Standing right behind that big bull elephant was a baby elephant, and they realized the father had sensed they were a threat to that baby. Needless to say, they wasted no time beating a hasty retreat.

You know as well as I do, that baby elephant was oblivious to that whole interaction. He wasn't worried. He wasn't upset. Are you kidding? Why should he be disturbed when he has a giant of a father on his side? Why should he waste a moment in anxiety when the one who is committed to protecting him can annihilate any enemy that comes his way?

He didn't have a care. He'd cast them all over on his father, and he could just enjoy watching his father take care of business on his behalf. That's the way we ought to be. After all, Almighty God is our Father. The LORD Jesus is our covenant Brother. They've promised never to leave us or forsake us. They love us with a fiercely protective love.

With them on our side, why should we let trouble trouble us?

LIMITLESS**LOVE**

The God of All Ages

"Even the youths shall faint and be weary, and the young men shall utterly
fall: But they that wait upon The LORD shall renew their strength;
they shall mount up with wings as eagles; they shall run, and not be weary;
and they shall walk, and not faint."
Isaiah 40:30-31

These days, many people are concerned about what's going to happen to them in their later years. Naturally speaking, there are no real assurances. Investments can't offer guaranteed returns. Medicare is uncertain. Corporations often find ways to avoid paying retirement. Selfishness and strife are so rampant in families that some aren't even sure they'll be loved and valued by their relatives when they grow old.

If you're a child of God, however, I want you to know you have nothing to worry about. He loves and treasures you at every age. He never forgets you. He never sets you on the shelf. In fact, if you're willing to receive it by faith, instead of retiring you, He'll refire you! He'll renew your strength so that you're stronger and more alive than people half your age. Psalm 103 says He'll satisfy your mouth with good things so that your youth is renewed like the eagle's.

I know from experience God will do that for you. There was a time in my life and ministry when I was so tired, I wanted to die. I went out in the country, got alone with The LORD and said, "I've come to the end of myself. I don't have anything left. I'm either going to leave here with my ministry renewed, or they'll have to carry me out in a box."

Needless to say, I never needed the box. The LORD spoke to me and said, *This is the beginning of the second half of your life.* When I came out of that place, I was stronger in every way—spirit, soul and body—than I'd been when I was 25 years old.

God renewed my youth like the eagle's, and He'll do the same thing for you. He'll make your golden years the best and the brightest of your life. He'll make you a living demonstration to the youngsters all around you that the God of the ages is the God of *all* ages. In the end, He'll have *them* envying *you!*

LIMITLESS**LOVE**

Blood-Covenant Love

"And he said unto him, I am The LORD that brought thee out of Ur of the Chaldees, to give thee this land to inherit it. And he said, LORD God, whereby shall I know that I shall inherit it? And he said unto him, Take me an heifer of three years old, and a she goat of three years old, and a ram of three years old, and a turtledove, and a young pigeon. And he took unto him all these, and divided them in the midst, and laid each piece one against another…. And it came to pass, that, when the sun went down, and it was dark, behold a smoking furnace, and a burning lamp that passed between those pieces. In the same day The LORD made a covenant with Abram…."
Genesis 15:7-10, 17-18

When God wanted Abraham to know how much He loved him, when He set about to prove how fully committed He was to keeping His promises to him, He did it with a covenant of blood. Sadly enough, our civilized cultures don't know much about such covenants. We've replaced them with contracts printed on paper and signed with ink—contracts full of promises made to be broken.

In Abraham's day, it wasn't that way. In his culture, as in other covenant-based cultures before and since, when two people or two families came together in a blood covenant, it was a solemn, unbreakable commitment. When the covenant animal was slain and cut in two, the covenant partners would walk back and forth in the path of blood that had been created and make promises to one another.

They would swear to be forever loyal to each other. They would say, in essence, "Everything I have and everything I am, from this day forward, belongs to you just as much as it belongs to me. I'll fight every enemy that comes against you. As long as I have the ability to help you, you'll never be in need. I'll lay down my very life for you if necessary. As long as I live, you'll never be alone again."

To further ratify that covenant, they would make cuts in their hands and mingle their blood together. They would treat the scar so it would become a prominent mark in their flesh that would never fade away. It became a permanent reminder of their covenant of blood.

That's the closest thing on earth to the covenant of love God has made with us. It's not just a contract of paper and ink. It's a solemn commitment between the Father and Jesus and it was ratified in Jesus' very blood. The scars on His resurrected body—the holes in His hands and feet—are eternal marks of the oath God made to all of us who are in Jesus, that He has joined Himself to us for eternity.

He will love us forever with blood-covenant love.

LIMITLESS**LOVE**

LORD, This One Is for You

"When the Son of man shall come in his glory, and all the holy angels with him, then shall he sit upon the throne of his glory: And before him shall be gathered all nations: and he shall separate them one from another, as a shepherd divideth his sheep from the goats: And he shall set the sheep on his right hand, but the goats on the left. Then shall the King say unto them on his right hand, Come, ye blessed of my Father, inherit the kingdom prepared for you from the foundation of the world: For I was an hungered, and ye gave me meat: I was thirsty, and ye gave me drink: I was a stranger, and ye took me in: naked, and ye clothed me: I was sick, and ye visited me: I was in prison, and ye came unto me. Then shall the righteous answer him, saying, LORD, when saw we thee an hungered, and fed thee? or thirsty, and gave thee drink? When saw we thee a stranger, and took thee in? or naked, and clothed thee? Or when saw we thee sick, or in prison, and came unto thee? And the King shall answer and say unto them, Verily I say unto you, Inasmuch as ye have done it unto one of the least of these my brethren, ye have done it unto me."

Matthew 25:31-40

There's one thing each one of us must get straight if we want to receive commendation from Jesus on the day of eternal rewards. We must realize that we can't serve Jesus while ignoring our brothers and sisters in Christ. We can't serve the Head at the expense of the Body.

Some people have pushed for spiritual promotion in the Church and actually stepped on other people—hurt them and pushed them out of the way—to do it. If anyone complains, they say, "Hey, I'm just doing what God called me to do. I'm here to serve Jesus—not to serve you."

They're not serving Jesus! It's impossible to serve the Head while kicking the Body in the knees. Jesus Himself made that clear when He said, "As ye have done it unto one of the least of these my brethren, ye have done it unto me."

The fact is, if we desire to minister to the Head of the Church, the primary way we can do it is by ministering to the Body. Once we understand that, we'll not only be willing to serve one another, we'll be thrilled to do it!

Think about it for a moment. Wouldn't it be wonderful if you could express your love to Jesus this week by buying Him a new suit of clothes? Wouldn't it be delightful to BLESS Him with a home-cooked meal? Wouldn't it be great to encourage Him by throwing your arms around Him and telling Him how much you love and appreciate Him? Wouldn't it be fun to mow His lawn?

"Jesus doesn't need any of those things!" you might say. "He doesn't need a new suit or a home-cooked meal. He doesn't need someone to encourage Him or mow His lawn."

The brethren do. And if they need those things, He needs them too. So go ahead! Have the time of your life BLESSING The LORD. Start searching for ways to serve the brothers and sisters around you. Then, with every work of love and every act of kindness you find to do, lift your eyes to heaven and say, "Here, LORD. This one is for You."

LIMITLESS**LOVE**

Like Living Stones

"To whom coming, as unto a living stone, disallowed indeed of men,
but chosen of God, and precious, ye also, as lively stones, are built up
a spiritual house, an holy priesthood, to offer up spiritual sacrifices,
acceptable to God by Jesus Christ."
1 Peter 2:4-5

One major reason that we, as members of the Body of Christ, must learn to walk in love is because God Himself is putting us together. He is positioning us right next to one another to build Himself a dwelling place, just like a rock mason picks stones and positions them together in a certain way to build the strongest possible wall.

I know a little about that, because one of Gloria's brothers used to be a rock mason. He built the fireplace in our prayer cabin and I spent some time watching him do it. As I did, I realized that laying rock is very different from laying brick. Bricks are all the same shape and size. When someone is laying brick, they can pick up any brick and put it just about anywhere in the wall, and it will work. It will fit smoothly with the other bricks because they're all just alike.

Stones are an entirely different story. Every one of them is different. Some are big and beautiful. Some are small and strange. They have sharp, uneven edges, and the rock mason picks each one individually and places it in exactly the right spot. When Gloria's brother built our fireplace, he chose one funny-looking L-shaped stone and put it right in the middle. There were some strong, massive rocks around it, but they left a gap that only that one little stone could fill.

That's a perfect picture of how God builds the Body of Christ. He takes each one of us and puts us next to someone else who is entirely different from us. He positions us beside people with jagged edges that irritate our flesh. He connects us with people we would never ordinarily choose to be connected with.

Why? Because His ways are higher than our ways. He sees a bigger picture than we see. He knows our weaknesses and strengths, so He puts us together in such a way the strengths of one can shore up the weaknesses of another. He arranges us so that my rough edges can sharpen you, and your smooth strength can even out my rough edges.

Of course, humanly speaking, that's a recipe for disaster. It's an obvious opportunity for us to get in conflict and strife. That's why we have to walk in the *agape* kind of love. We must *choose* to love—not because it's easy or because we feel like it, but because we're committed to The LORD and we're committed to each other.

When we do that, love becomes the divine mortar that holds us all together. It transforms us from a tottering stack of loose rocks and into one solid, stone wall. Love joins us perfectly together and makes us a holy habitation for The LORD.

LIMITLESS**LOVE**

You Can't Go It Alone

"…Holding fast to the head, from whom the entire body, being supplied and held together by the joints and ligaments, grows with a growth which is from God."
Colossians 2:19, *New American Standard*

All of us who have been saved for a few years and tried to grow up in The LORD have, at times, gotten stuck. We've found no matter what we do, it seems we've grown as far as we can grow. *Why can't I get over this hurdle in my life?* we'll wonder. *Why can't I walk in a greater degree of prosperity or divine health than I do now? I know what the Bible says, but I'm just not seeing the fullness of it in my life.*

Once, when I asked those questions, The LORD reminded me of Ephesians 4:15-16. It says that we, as believers, grow up into the image of Jesus as whole Body of Christ is joined and knit together by what every joint supplies. As every one of us does our share, growth comes because we are building each other up in love.

That means our spiritual maturity isn't just going to come from simply sitting home alone reading the Bible and listening to CDs (as important and helpful as that is). It isn't going to come just because we sit by ourselves praying in tongues for hours (edifying as that can be). The fullness of our growth and development in Jesus is going to come to us through one another!

Something mighty and supernatural happens when believers get together that just can't happen when we're alone. That's why I like to tape television broadcasts in a meeting full of people so much better than in a television studio with just a crew and a camera. I've found the hunger other believers have for The WORD of God draws things out of my spirit that would never otherwise come forth. When I preach to people like that, they pull such revelation out of me that I learn as much while I'm preaching as they do!

On the other hand, I've found there are ministers who have revelation that I just can't get on my own. I might spend all day trying to figure out what some end time prophecy means, for example, and end up as confused as I was when I started. But I can go hear a man like Hilton Sutton who has God-given insight on those things and suddenly that same passage will become absolutely clear to me. *Why couldn't I see that before?* I'll wonder.

I couldn't see it because I wasn't designed to see it without Brother Sutton's help. I wasn't given all the spiritual equipment necessary to grow up on my own. Neither were you. That's why we need each other.

The more I love and draw on the supply of God in you…and the more you love and draw on the supply of God in me…the more we'll both start to look like Jesus. The more we get together in love, the faster we'll be able to grow up in all things into Him!

Chosen by God

"For we know, brothers and sisters loved by God, that he has chosen you."
1 Thessalonians 1:4, *New International Version*

It is a wonderful thing to be chosen.

Every kid who has ever stood in a line during gym class, waiting for the best athletes in the class to pick kids for their teams, knows just how great it is to be chosen. Every budding young actor or musician who has tried out for the school play or the band knows what it's like to stand at the bulletin board, anxiously scanning the names on the list posted there to see if they were chosen.

And most of us, at one time or another, experienced the shame and pain that came when some vital selection was being made and despite our waving hand and loud plea—"Pick me! Pick me!"—we didn't make the cut. Most of us know what it's like to feel worthless and rejected as we watch others take the place we longed to have. We know what it's like to wish we were somehow a little better and a little more worthy so that "someday, someone would choose me."

That's why the greatest message we'll ever hear is the message of the gospel. It's the good news every one of us has been waiting for: *Someone has chosen me!*

Not just someone…but Almighty God Himself. The Eternal Creator, the Most Excellent, Most Awesome, Most High God picked us before the foundation of the world. He looked down through the ages and saw us at our very worst. He saw us fallen from glory and darkened with sin. Yet, He loved us and said, "I choose that one."

No man asked God to do that. No man asked Jesus to go to the cross. Mankind didn't understand redemption's plan. It was a mystery hidden in God. It was God Himself who desired to save us. He was the One who asked Jesus to shed His blood so we could be brought out of darkness and into the light of His eternal family.

Let the enormity of that soak into your thinking. God chose you. He chose you before you knew Him. He chose you before you were righteous. He chose you before you accepted Jesus Christ as LORD.

Remember that next time you're tempted to wave your hand in the air and say, "LORD, please choose to heal me! Choose me for THE BLESSING! Choose me for prosperity!" Remember that He made His choice before the foundation of the world. He picked you to be born again. He picked you to be well. He picked you to be prosperous. He picked you to be a conqueror in every area of life.

So stop pleading and start rejoicing. Give a shout of praise and say, "Thank God, He has chosen me!"

LIMITLESS**LOVE**

Our El Shaddai

"Now when Abram was ninety-nine years old, The LORD appeared
to Abram and said to him, 'I am God Almighty; walk before Me,
and be blameless. I will establish My covenant between Me and you,
and I will multiply you exceedingly.'"
Genesis 17:1-2, *New American Standard*

Every time God introduces Himself by a particular name in the Bible, He is always revealing another dimension of His love. Sometimes, we as non-Hebrew-speaking people, miss the revelation He is giving because we fail to fully translate God's names.

When He said to Abram, for example, "I am Almighty God," what He actually said in the Hebrew was "I am El Shaddai." Although *El Shaddai* is "the Almighty One" or "the Supreme Being," the root word from which *Shaddai* is derived literally refers to a woman nursing a baby. It can actually be translated "the breasty one."

My, what a marvelous description of God! On one hand, it points to the inexhaustible and bountiful supply He has for us. It reveals that He is the ultimate Provider. He has more than enough of everything we will ever need.

On the other hand, this name reveals that God not only has a full supply, He is yearning to give it. As one commentary says, "The title 'Shaddai' really indicates the fulness and riches of God's grace, and would remind the Hebrew reader that from God cometh every good and perfect gift,—that He is never weary of pouring forth His mercies upon His people, and that He is more ready to give than they are to receive…"[11]

Just as a mother who is full of milk for her baby longs and even needs to nurse that child, our God is so full of compassion that He searches throughout the earth for someone to receive it. It is only in the giving of His supply that He finds full satisfaction and release!

That's an amazing revelation in itself. But even more staggering is this: Abram isn't the one who went to God and asked Him to be his divine Provider. Abram didn't know enough about God to ask Him for anything! God was the initiator. God was the One who came to him and said, "Here I am, Abram. I have come to be your BLESSER. I have come to be your Multiplier. I've come to pour out on you My inexhaustible supply."

As children of Abraham (Galatians 3:7), God has said the same thing to us. He has, by His Holy Spirit, and His written WORD, spoken to us as surely as He spoke to Abram. He has come to be our El Shaddai, and in His love and bountiful provision, we are richly BLESSED!

---

[11] Girdlestone, R. B. *Synonyms of the Old Testament : Their bearing on Christian doctrine* (Oak Harbor, WA: Logos Research Systems Inc., 1998) p. 32.

Don't Leave THE BLESSING Sitting on the Shelf

"And these are they which are sown on good ground; such as hear The WORD, and receive it, and bring forth fruit, some thirtyfold, some sixty, and some an hundred."
Mark 4:20

Some years ago, right after I'd finished recording a new album, The LORD spoke to my heart and told me to offer the recording free to all my Partners. *You even pay the postage on it,* He said. *Don't charge them a dime. I want to use that music to BLESS them in a special way.*

I knew it would be expensive, but I love The LORD and I love my Partners, so I bought enough to send a copy of that record to everyone on our mailing list. Then, I wrote a letter, included a card they could return along with a postpaid envelope, and told them just to send that card back to me if they'd like to receive the record. I'd send it to them free.

Much to my amazement, only a small percentage responded! So I went back The LORD about it. "What happened here?" I said.

The same thing happened to you that happens to Me all the time, He answered. *I provide THE BLESSING for My people. I offer THE BLESSING as a free gift. But most don't respond. I'm ready to give, but they won't receive.*

That's the truth! I thought. Most people aren't receiving THE BLESSING of God's love for the same four reasons my Partners didn't receive the record I offered them.

No. 1, they didn't want it. I can understand that in the case of my music…but it astounds me to think people have that attitude toward THE BLESSING of God. They do, though. I've heard people say things like, "Oh, I don't need to speak in tongues. I don't have any use for that. I don't need to prosper financially." Imagine, God loving us enough to give people gifts, and they don't even appreciate them enough to receive them!

The second reason people miss out on THE BLESSING of God is they don't know they're available. Just like some of my Partners didn't read the letter and find out I had a gift for them, some of God's children don't bother to read The WORD and find out all He has provided for them. So even though His gifts to them have already been paid for by the blood of Jesus, they're left unused, sitting on a heavenly shelf!

Third, there were the people who read the letter, but didn't believe it. They doubted either my ability or my willingness to do what I promised.

Finally, there were the folks who read it, believed it, but just didn't act on it. They got distracted with other things and ended up missing out.

When it comes to receiving THE BLESSING of God, don't let yourself miss it for any of those four reasons. Don't leave it sitting on the shelf. Find out what He has provided for you, believe and receive.

Enjoy *all* the good gifts God has lovingly laid in store for you!

LIMITLESS**LOVE**

THE BLESSING of Giving

"I have showed you all things, how that so labouring ye ought to support
the weak, and to remember the words of The LORD Jesus, how he said,
It is more BLESSED to give than to receive."
Acts 20:35

Most people quote this verse without having any idea what it really means. "Yes, brother," they say in their most pious tone of voice, "it is more BLESSED to give than to receive."

Why? Have you ever asked that question? What is it that's so much better about giving than receiving?

I'll tell you. It's when you're giving that you begin to understand something about the heart of God. It's when you're giving with a cheerful attitude and a true desire to BLESS someone that you get a glimpse into the mind of your heavenly Father. The more you give, the more you realize how much joy there is in it. You start finding out how much fun it is to be like Him. You become more aware that He is in you and that His nature springs to life when you start to express it.

What's more, as you experience the delight of BLESSING others, you get a firsthand look at how much The LORD delights in BLESSING you. As a result, your faith is strengthened. That's why giving puts receiving into motion. Receiving doesn't put giving into motion. Once you give, your revelation of God's love increases and you're better able to receive. Then, because you've caught on to the thrill of giving, your receiving just becomes a way for you to give more!

If you get on that road and stay on it, you'll act more like God every day. You'll want to meet every need you see. My mother was like that, not so much in the realm of finances but in the area of prayer. She had a revelation of the power of prayer and started praying for others at an early age. She was at the throne of God day and night, obtaining BLESSING or help for someone who needed it. She lived to pray for people, and got greater joy from it than you can imagine.

In the process, she learned more about God than most folks will ever know. She was so close to Him, she could get Him to do just about anything for her. I remember once, The LORD guaranteed I wouldn't fail in ministry. When I asked Him why, He simply said, *Because I have your mother in My face!*

Mama was like that even in her very last days on earth. Just before she died, she got so weak that the doctor ordered her not to pray for anyone else. Her body was just worn out, and he wanted her to reserve her strength. But even so, she was praying for people who were in the hospital with her right up to the very end.

At a time when you would expect her to be asking for prayer from others, she was still getting a thrill out of giving it away. No doubt, she entered heaven shouting, "Hallelujah!" and looking for someone to pray for, because she'd discovered it's more BLESSED to give than receive!

LIMITLESS**LOVE**

All Things to All Men

"Until we all attain to the unity of the faith, and of the knowledge of the
Son of God, to a mature man, to the measure of the stature which belongs
to the fullness of Christ. As a result, we are no longer to be children, tossed
here and there by waves and carried about by every wind of doctrine...."
Ephesians 4:13-14, *New American Standard*

The more we grow up in love, the less we'll allow winds of doctrine to blow us apart. We'll settle down securely on the basic truths the Bible teaches and we won't run away from people just because they don't agree with us. We'll stop saying things like, "I can't fellowship with the people in that church. Our doctrinal differences are just too great." Instead, we'll go visit them to receive the insights God has given them that are good, and to share with them what God has given us.

To do anything less than that is childish.

"I don't know about that, Brother Copeland," someone might say. "We sure don't want to start associating with everyone. Some of those groups don't even believe in Jesus."

I know they don't. That's why we need to reach out to them! Obviously, we can't fellowship with them closely like we do our brothers and sisters in The LORD, but we can't win them to Him by staying totally away from them, either. We can't tell them Jesus loves them if we won't have anything to do with them. That's why we haven't been able to reach people like the Muslims and New Age folks. We've hidden from them. We've been afraid that if we get around them, their ungodly beliefs will rub off on us and taint us.

That could happen if we're so immature and ignorant of the Bible that we don't know why we believe what we believe. But we shouldn't be that immature. We ought to get so strong in faith and in The WORD that we don't have to perpetually protect ourselves from everyone else. What's more, we need to grow up in love so that we care enough about them to risk their rejection, and tell them about Jesus.

That's the attitude the Apostle Paul had. He didn't run away from people who were different from him. He sought them out and said, "I have made myself a slave to everyone, to win as many as possible. To the Jews I became like a Jew, to win the Jews.... To those not having the law I became like one not having the law (though I am not free from God's law but am under Christ's law), so as to win those not having the law.... I have become all things to all people so that by all possible means I might save some" (1 Corinthians 9:19-22, *New International Version*).

Love doesn't run and hide. Love reaches out. Love inspires us to become all things to all men, so that we can bring as many as possible into the kingdom of God.

LIMITLESS**LOVE**

Don't Miss the Greater Blessing

"(Love)…does not seek its own…."
1 Corinthians 13:5, *New American Standard*

When we start loving each other enough that we're willing to set aside our own interests so that someone else can be BLESSED, we step into the place where God can really move in our midst. We throw open the door so He can pour out His abundant goodness, not only on the people we love, but on us, too!

We also put ourselves in position to receive. Instead of being so tightfisted and holding on to our own selfish desires with an iron grip, we open our hands to share with others—and, in the process, we find we are finally free to take what our Father has been trying to give!

I saw a marvelous example of how that can happen when, years ago, a pastor confided to me how much he'd struggled over what to do about a convention I was holding in his town. He wanted to support the meeting but he was worried because one of the other speakers at the convention also had a church in that area. "I was afraid the people in my church might hear that fellow and think he was a better preacher than I was," he said. "They might decide to join his church, and I'd lose half my people."

But, thank God, love prevailed in this pastor's heart. He prayed about it and realized the people in his church didn't belong to him, they belonged to God. And if the other pastor was that much better than he was, they all ought to go to his church. They should go wherever they'd be most BLESSED.

The next Sunday, that pastor stood in his pulpit and encouraged all his church members to attend the convention. He didn't just tell them to come to my services, either. He especially urged them to attend the services the other pastor would be preaching. Sure enough, the people turned out in numbers to hear him.

Did his church suffer as a result? Absolutely not! In fact, the next Sunday he had the biggest attendance he'd ever had. In the following weeks, his congregation continued to grow until he'd increased by about 40 percent!

Another interesting fact is this: Before long, The LORD led the other pastor to close down his church and focus more on his traveling ministry. So, some of the folks from the travelling minister's church ended up going to that other pastor's church.

See what he would have missed had he yielded to selfishness instead of love? He would have deprived his people of THE BLESSING they received from the convention meetings *and* lost out on the growth God wanted to give to his church! By trying to hang on to what he had, he would have missed the greater BLESSING that always comes when we dare to walk in love.

LIMITLESS**LOVE**

A Place at the King's Table

"David asked, 'Is there anyone still left of the house of Saul
to whom I can show kindness for Jonathan's sake?'"
2 Samuel 9:1, *New International Version*

The love of God is so superior to natural love, it's almost impossible to describe. There is one Old Testament story, however, that provides a striking picture. It's the account of King David and his love for his covenant friend, Jonathan. The Bible tells us that David and Jonathan were so committed to each other, so willing to lay down their lives for one another, their very souls were knit together in love.

If you've read about it, however, you know their fellowship was cut off by the jealousy and cruelty of King Saul, Jonathan's father. Saul drove David from his household—despite his brave and loyal service—and persecuted him for years. The Scriptures abound with accounts of Saul's attempts to murder David and discredit his name. Eventually, Saul became so obsessed with killing David that it cost him the throne of Israel...and it cost his son Jonathan's life.

You might think the terrible treatment David received at the hand of Jonathan's father would have diminished his commitment to Jonathan, or that the years of cruelty would have tempered the fervency of his love. But, they didn't.

On the contrary, David's desire to express his loyalty to Jonathan, his yearning to serve and give to him continued to consume David. Eventually, after David became king, he could contain it no longer. "Isn't there *anyone* left of Saul's house," he cried, "to whom I can show mercy for Jonathan's sake?"

As it turns out, there was. Jonathan had a crippled son named Mephibosheth, who lived in a pitiful place called LoDebar. No doubt, he'd been hiding there thinking David might try to find him and kill him in retribution for all the grief his grandfather had caused David. But David wasn't looking for someone to punish, he was looking for someone on whom he could pour out his love.

So, he sent a royal company down to LoDebar to bring Mephibosheth to the palace and give him a place in the king's court and at the king's table for the rest of his life. David even commanded that he be given all the wealth of his grandfather's household. Why? Because Mephibosheth was the heir of David's covenant friend, Jonathan. Despite Mephibosheth's weakness, despite his natural limitations, David loved him for Jonathan's sake. He loved him like a son.

Sound familiar? Sure it does. It is the picture of the love God has for every one of us who are heirs of Christ Jesus. Despite our weaknesses and limitations, we are forever unconditionally loved for Jesus' sake. Through Him, we've been given a place at the king's table. We have become God's beloved sons.

LIMITLESS**LOVE**

The God Who Will Provide

"By faith Abraham, when he was tried, offered up Isaac: and he that had received the promises offered up his only begotten son, of whom it was said, That in Isaac shall thy seed be called: accounting that God was able to raise him up, even from the dead; from whence also he received him in a figure."
Hebrews 11:17-19

If you don't understand covenant, you'll never be able to grasp how a God of love could ask an old man like Abraham to sacrifice his only son. It will seem like an absolutely horrible, hardhearted thing to do. You'll imagine Abraham weeping and distraught at the thought of losing Isaac, his heart torn with grief because of God's command.

Nothing could be further from the truth. God had made covenant with Abraham, a covenant ratified by blood. One of God's covenant promises was that Abraham's seed would come through Isaac, and Abraham so fully believed that, he was convinced there was no way God could let that boy die. If He did, He'd have to raise him from the dead, because the promise had been made. The covenant had been cut. God had shown Abraham the stars of heaven and said, "So shall thy seed be" (Genesis 15:5).

Abraham was so certain of the outcome that just before he bound Isaac to lay him on the altar, and Isaac asked, "Dad, where is the sacrifice?" Abraham confidently answered, "God will provide" (Genesis 22:8).

In that phrase, we find the real reason God asked Abraham to sacrifice his son. It was because God Himself wanted to provide such a sacrifice for all mankind. He wanted it recorded in the eternal laws of heaven that He was bound by honor to do so…and that's exactly what Abraham's willingness to give Isaac accomplished.

I believe if we could have looked into heaven that day, we might have seen God saying to Jesus, *All right, Son. Abraham did it. As My covenant brother, he offered his only son up for Me. Can I now do any less for him?*

The God of all love was longing to send His only Son to the earth as a sacrifice to pay the price for all sin. He wanted to exchange the life of Jesus for the lives of all of us who through faith would be called the sons of Abraham. That was His redemption plan. But since man had been given dominion on the earth, it was man who had to open the door for Him to do it. And that is what he was asking of Abraham.

It wasn't some cruel test God was giving to Abraham and Isaac on that mountain of sacrifice. It was God extending His loving hand to bring forth a plan that would offer mercy to all men. It was God reaching out to a world desperately in need of a Redeemer and becoming the God Who Will Provide.

The Devil's Worst Nightmare

"Finally, my brethren, be strong in The LORD, and in the power of his might. Put on the whole armour of God, that ye may be able to stand against the wiles of the devil."
Ephesians 6:10-11

Most people don't realize it, but these verses point powerfully to the blood-covenant ceremony. They hearken back to the times when men who wanted to cut covenant, killed an animal, stood in its blood, and made promises to one another. They'd swear by that blood, for example, to use every weapon and source of power at their disposal to protect one another.

In essence, they would say to one another, "You are no longer limited by your own might because we are now joined together. My strength is your strength. My might is your might." Then, as a demonstration of that oath, they'd exchange their armor and weapons.

That's the image that should come to mind when we read about standing and putting on the armor of God. We should think about the covenant of love God has made with us in the blood of Jesus. We should picture ourselves standing in that precious blood and receiving the weapons of Almighty God, while our Covenant Brother, The LORD Jesus Christ, says to us, "All power and authority in heaven and earth has been given to Me. Therefore you go…and I'll back you with it. Anyone who gives you trouble will have to deal with Me. So be strong in Me and in the power of My might!"

When we start thinking like that, the devil will flee from us. He'll back off and say, "I'm sorry I bothered you. I really didn't mean it. Just put that sword up and I'll leave, I promise."

There's only one thing that scares the devil more than a believer who understands the power and privileges of his covenant with God. It's a believer who understands that his brothers and sisters in The LORD were standing in that blood with him when the covenant was made. It's a Christian who knows that just as this covenant of love has made us one with Jesus, it's made us one with each other.

The believer with that revelation can't turn against his brother in Christ any more than he could turn against The LORD Jesus Himself. He can't criticize that brother and call him an enemy once they've stood in the covenant blood together. He can't do it! It doesn't make any difference what that brother looks like, or what his background, culture or denomination is. The blood of the Lamb is between them, and that overcomes everything else!

Just the thought of such a holy alliance makes the devil tremble. It's his worst nightmare. And as we move into a greater revelation of our covenant of love, it's a nightmare that is sure to come true!

LIMITLESS**LOVE**

It's Time to Grow Up

"For everyone who partakes only of milk is not accustomed to The WORD of righteousness, for he is an infant. But solid food is for the mature, who because of practice have their senses trained to discern good and evil."
Hebrews 5:13-14, *New American Standard*

The reason so many Christians are living with unmet needs is because they simply don't know how to walk in their covenant of redemption. It's not because God doesn't love them, nor is it because He hasn't made provision for them. It's because they haven't learned enough about The WORD to partake of it. Many of them have been saved for years, but they've stayed in spiritual infancy. They're unskilled in The WORD of righteousness.

You could put a baby in a house totally filled with provision, and it wouldn't do him any good, would it? You could stock the refrigerator with all kinds of food and load the closets with blankets and clothes. You could stack enough money around the house to buy him everything he'd ever need, but as long as he remained a baby, he wouldn't be able to use a bit of it.

That's exactly the situation many Christians are in right now. They're surrounded by the provision of God. The Bible says He has already given them everything that pertains to life and godliness. But they're lying on the floor, crying and throwing a fit. "God, I just don't understand!" they wail. "Why don't You take care of me? Why don't You supply my needs? Don't You love me, LORD?"

Certainly, He loves us! That's why He planned our lives before the foundation of the world and set aside everything we'd ever need to be abundantly BLESSED. But, He also expects us to grow up. He is not willing to treat us like babies forever. He requires us to stand on our spiritual feet, get out our Bibles, and find out what He has provided. He expects us to start receiving those things by faith.

"Get out my Bible?" someone might say.

Yes, your Bible! It's a copy of God's covenant with you. It spells out His promises and reveals everything He has given you. If you'll read it, you'll see there is no such thing as a covenant child of God with an unmet need. There are only covenant children who lack The WORD skills to take advantage of all that's been provided.

Remember that the next time you catch yourself thinking God isn't taking care of you. Stop immediately and say, "No, that's a lie of the devil. God has already supplied all my needs according to His riches in glory." Then, get your Bible and find out how to lay hold of that provision by faith. Leave babyhood behind. Grow up and enjoy the benefits of your covenant with God.

LIMITLESS**LOVE**

The Greatest Servant of All

"Whatever you ask in My name, that will I do, so that the Father may be glorified in the Son. If you ask Me anything in My name, I will do it."
John 14:13-14, *New American Standard*

So often, during times of prayer and fellowship with The LORD, our hearts are overwhelmed with the desire to serve Him. Again and again as we fall more deeply in love with Him, we find ourselves longing to do His will. "LORD, I'll do whatever You ask," we say. "All I want to do is be a BLESSING to You!"

It's easy to understand why we feel that way. After all, He is Almighty God. He is the One who loves us with a never-failing love. He is our Redeemer. He is the perfect, omnipotent, marvelous LORD!

What's difficult for us to comprehend is this: Despite our weaknesses and failures, despite the frailty of our flesh, He feels the same way about us. His heart is full of the desire to serve us. He is saying to us, *Just ask Me for something, son. Just ask Me for something, daughter. I want to be a BLESSING to you!*

The very thought of that is offensive to the religious mind. It refuses to entertain the idea that Almighty God would ever put Himself in the position of serving us. But the fact is, that is exactly what He has done. Jesus demonstrated that clearly just before He went to the cross by taking off His robe, donning a servant's towel and washing the feet of His astonished disciples. Philippians 2:7 says that to accomplish our redemption, Jesus "stripped Himself [of all privileges and rightful dignity], so as to assume the guise of a servant..." *(The Amplified Bible).*

"Yes, but that was Jesus," someone might argue, "not the Almighty Father God."

Jesus Himself said, "The Son can do nothing of himself, but what he seeth the Father do..." (John 5:19).

The LORD drove that point home to me one day when He said to me, *Kenneth, won't you do anything I ask you to do?*

"LORD, You know I will," I answered. "All You have to do is let me know what You want, and I'll do it. I'm on call to You, twenty-four hours a day."

I am the same way, He said. *I will do anything you ask Me to do. Don't you remember My WORD says that whatever you ask Me in Jesus' Name, I'll give to you? I'm covenanted to you. I am more committed to you than you are to Me. I gave My Son and shed His blood for you. How could I desire to withhold from you anything else?*

That's the kind of covenant love God has for us, and we need to start believing it. We need to realize that our desire to serve our LORD is just a pale reflection of His desire to serve us. Our Master is truly the greatest Servant of all.

LIMITLESS**LOVE**

Signed, Sealed and Delivered

"But ye are come unto mount Sion, and unto the city of the living God, the heavenly Jerusalem, and to an innumerable company of angels, to the general assembly and church of the firstborn, which are written in heaven, and to God the Judge of all, and to the spirits of just men made perfect, and to Jesus the mediator of the new covenant, and to the blood of sprinkling, that speaketh better things…."
Hebrews 12:22-24

When a believer understands God's love and walks in the covenant of redemption that love has provided for him, he talks differently than other people. He doesn't spend his time talking about the natural circumstances and problems around him. He spends his time talking about what his covenant provides.

He walks around saying things like, "Yes, thank God, I'm healed. God said it in His WORD. I believe it, and that settles it."

"How can you say that?" someone might ask him. "You're walking around with a limp. Everyone can see you're not healed!"

I'll tell you how he can say it. He can say it because he is more covenant-minded than he is circumstance-minded. God's WORD is more real in his heart than what he can see, hear or feel in the natural realm. His mind is anchored in his covenant with God.

While other people are thinking about their symptoms or their difficult situations, this believer is thinking about what God has said to him. He is thinking about the blood of Jesus that was shed to ratify that WORD in his life. He is thinking about the angels that are sent as ministering servants to help carry out that WORD on his behalf. He is thinking about all the other covenant men and women who went before him, trusted God's WORD and saw it come to pass in their lives—men of faith like Abraham "who patiently endured, [and]…obtained the promise" (Hebrews 6:15).

When a person like that says, "Thank God, I'm healed!" or "This is the victory that overcomes the world, even my faith!" he's not speaking out of his own ego. He's not self-confident. He is God-confident. He's speaking out of faith in his Covenant Partner's mighty love for him. He's so secure in that love that he calls those things which do not exist as though they did (Romans 4:17) without even flinching.

He's not saying those things trying to make them happen. He is saying them because he is so established in God's love, power and faithfulness, as far as he is concerned, they have already happened. He doesn't have to see them to believe it. He knows that because he believes he will surely see THE BLESSING the Father has promised. It's been signed, sealed and delivered by the covenant of love.

LIMITLESS**LOVE**

To Your Children's Children

"But the mercy of The LORD is from everlasting to everlasting upon them that fear him, and his righteousness unto children's children."
Psalm 103:17

The covenant love of God is so strong and far-reaching that it not only covers you, it extends to your children and your grandchildren. Of course, they'll one day make Jesus their LORD and enter that covenant for themselves, but until then, God will look after them for your sake. He'll protect them and BLESS them, just because they're yours.

I not only know that because the Bible says so, I've seen it work in my family. I found out by watching some of my relatives, that even the most rebellious can't outrun the angels of God when their mother or father is standing on their covenant with Him.

The best example is my cousin, Larry. His mother and mine were prayer partners for years, and they prayed us into the kingdom of God. We both tried for years to go to hell, but Mama and Aunt Barbara just wouldn't let us. They knew the love of God and they knew The WORD, so they just stayed on their knees and held fast to their faith until we gave up and got saved.

Larry's case was particularly interesting because even while he was doing all kinds of dope and other crazy stuff, the Spirit of God would be so hot on his trail it would scare his buddies. They finally told him, "Man, we're not doing any more drugs with you. Every time you get stoned, you start preaching!" (Actually, I was the same way. I won several people to The LORD before I ever got born again myself.)

The experts finally told my aunt that even if Larry did stop doing drugs, he'd be a mental vegetable because of the damage already done to his brain. But the experts didn't figure in the love of God. They didn't know He was watching over that boy for Aunt Barbara's sake. They didn't know that her covenant covered her son.

But, thank God, she did. So, she just kept calling him BLESSED. The devil tried to curse him, but as the heathen prophet Balaam found out, you can't curse those God has BLESSED (Numbers 23:8). The LORD stayed after Larry until he got saved and baptized in the Holy Spirit. He restored Larry's mind so fully that he was able to go back to college and graduate with a degree in physical therapy, which, apart from a medical degree, is one of the toughest to get.

Eventually, he started preaching and pastoring a church. He's good at it, too. I like to say, "Larry, if you're a mental vegetable, you're one of the preaching-est carrots I've ever seen!" We can both laugh about that now, because we know we are living demonstrations of just how far the love of God can reach. We are walking proof that His covenant extends to His children's children.

LIMITLESS**LOVE**

Take Love to Work

"Servants, obey in all things your masters according to the flesh; not with eyeservice, as menpleasers; but in singleness of heart, fearing God; and whatsoever ye do, do it heartily, as to The LORD, and not unto men; knowing that of The LORD ye shall receive the reward of the inheritance: for ye serve The LORD Christ."

Colossians 3:22-24

The Church could win greater numbers of people to The LORD if believers would take the love of God with them into the workplace. People are turned off to the gospel by Christians who carry their Bibles to the office while they're cheating their employer out of a full day's work. It's a sad thing when a believer professes his faith to his fellow employees, and then comes in late morning after morning, uses company time to do personal business, spends business hours chatting with co-workers, and then tops it all off by talking ugly about his boss!

A Christian who behaves like that would give more glory to The LORD by leaving his Bible at home and keeping his mouth shut until he learns to demonstrate the love and integrity of God with his life, and not just his lips. I know that's a strong statement, but it's true. I have firsthand knowledge of one Jewish man, in particular, who wouldn't give the gospel the time of day for years because of the shabby work habits of those he knew who called themselves Christians. He finally did get saved, but he did it in spite of them, not because of them.

On the other hand, believers who do walk in love on the job shine like stars in a dark night. They preach without saying a word! It gets people's attention when someone works diligently and keeps a good attitude. It's an outstanding thing when an employee gives 110 percent on the job—not only when the boss is looking, but when he isn't.

Generally speaking, the business world these days is one of the most brutal places you can find. It's considered normal for employees to undercut and betray each other in an effort to get ahead. Criticism of supervisors and those in authority is commonplace.

But as believers, the love of God compels us to act differently. It demands that we serve our employers with the same devotion and excellence with which we serve Jesus Himself. God's love will cause us to get to work a little early and come back from lunch on time. It will inspire us to speak kindly and respectfully of bosses and supervisors—focusing on their strengths instead of their weaknesses.

When we walk in love in the workplace, we'll forget about pushing for our own success and search out ways to contribute to the success of others, while trusting The LORD to bring us our reward. It *will* come, too. It will come not only in the form of pay raises and promotions, but in the form of souls won to The LORD. And that is the greatest reward of all.

LIMITLESS**LOVE**

Putting the Flies to Flight

"'But you will chase your enemies and they will fall before you by the sword; five of you will chase a hundred, and a hundred of you will chase ten thousand, and your enemies will fall before you by the sword. So I will turn toward you and make you fruitful and multiply you, and I will confirm My covenant with you.'"
Leviticus 26:7-9, *New American Standard*

Until now, most Christians have focused primarily on their own spiritual growth. We've realized we are responsible for developing our own faith and using it to overcome our flesh and defeat the devil in our lives. That's been a good and necessary revelation. But, the more we grow up in love, the more we'll realize that God's plan on the earth can't be carried out by us individually. It can only be accomplished when we come together as a Body.

Individually, we may be able to deal with the devils that come against us in our own personal affairs. We can resist and overcome the pesky little devils of sickness and discouragement that attack us and our households. But those aren't the only devils out there. There are myriads of others continually working to pester, irritate and hinder the progress of the Church. There are so many of them, Jesus compared them to flies by calling Satan *Beelzebub,* which means "lord of the flies."

No one of us individually can deal with all of them at once, but when we start walking together in love, the Bible says our spiritual power and effectiveness increases exponentially. Suddenly, the principal God set forth in Leviticus goes into operation, and we're not just driving out the little, personal devils that have dogged our steps, but we're driving out multiplied thousands of them who have restrained the plan of God in the earth!

That's what happened in the book of Acts. It says those early believers were of one heart and one soul (Acts 4:32). They walked in such love, they were totally unified, and as a result, the Church exploded with growth. Signs and wonders were daily occurrences. People dragged the sick out into the streets to get healed as Peter passed by. The Church took Jerusalem by storm, and there was nothing the devil could do to stop it.

Can that happen again? Absolutely! It can and it will. The more we get together in love, the more power we'll see. When we commit ourselves to each other, just like we've committed ourselves to The LORD, refusing to be critical of one another and constantly looking for opportunities to give to each other and build each other up, we'll trample the devil under our feet at every turn. The Church of The LORD Jesus Christ will put the lord of the flies to flight!

LIMITLESS**LOVE**

The Sword That Sets You Free

"Some became fools through their rebellious ways and suffered affliction because of their iniquities. They loathed all food and drew near the gates of death. Then they cried to The LORD in their trouble, and he saved them from their distress. He sent out His WORD and healed them; he rescued them from the grave."

Psalm 107:17-20, *New International Version*

God's written WORD is an expression of His love for you. The reason you can hold a Bible in your hand, and read the promises and provisions of God, is because He loves you so much He made it possible for you to have it.

Sometimes we forget the tremendous price that was paid to get that WORD to us. I'm not just talking about the $30 you spent for it at the bookstore. I'm talking about the men and women who laid down their lives, spending years translating and recording it. Those people literally shed their blood to get the Bible in print.

Those men and women were energized by the grace of God and inspired by His Spirit. God compelled them to do what they did because He loves you. He wants you to be free from every bondage of the devil, and the truth of The WORD is what makes you free.

I'll never forget a vision The LORD gave me in the early years of my ministry. I was praying in a little church in south Texas where I'd gone to preach some meetings. I suddenly saw with the eyes of my spirit a dragon come through the front door of that church. It was so big, it filled the entire church. It had blazing eyes and fire that blasted out of its mouth, burning my clothes and knocking me on my back.

In the vision, Jesus was standing beside me and He was clearly displeased with that dragon (and the fact that I was on my back in front of it). *Why doesn't Jesus do something about this?* I thought. *Why doesn't He use that sword He has in His hand and kill this beast?*

About that time, Jesus held the sword out to me. I didn't want to take it but I knew I would be in trouble if I didn't, so I put my hand on the sword. Amazingly, it lifted me up off the ground and I felt power shoot up through my arm and into my body. Suddenly, I wasn't afraid of that big lizard anymore. I thrust the sword toward him and the minute it touched him, it split him wide open. When it did, I realized he was full of people! They had been swallowed up by that dragon's devices, and the sword of the Spirit had set them free.

Remember that the next time you pick up your Bible. Don't treat it like it's just a good book. Use it like the sword of the Spirit, a gift from love, straight from the Father, that has been sent to set you free.

LIMITLESS**LOVE**

Defeated by the Army of Love

"Above all, taking the shield of faith, wherewith ye shall be able to quench all the fiery darts of the wicked. And take the helmet of salvation, and the sword of the Spirit, which is The WORD of God: praying always with all prayer and supplication in the Spirit, and watching thereunto with all perseverance and supplication for all saints."
Ephesians 6:16-18

The spiritual armor Paul describes in Ephesians 6 is intended to equip us for prayer. He instructs us to put on the belt of truth, the breastplate of righteousness, the shoes of the gospel, and the helmet of salvation, lifting up the shield of faith and the sword of the Spirit—*praying always...for all the saints!*

Many Christians have overlooked that last phrase. They've eagerly donned their spiritual armor and taken up their weapons. But they've done it to win their own, personal victories, instead of doing it to win the victory for a brother.

Although there's nothing wrong with praying for ourselves, we shouldn't stop there. We ought to be praying for each other's healing, praying for each other's deliverance, praying for each other's prosperity. When we do that, we set up a spiritual situation against which Satan has no defense. Jesus said that if two of us agree as touching anything they shall ask, it shall be done for them by our Father in heaven (Matthew 18:19). By praying for each other, we put that spiritual law into motion and are guaranteed results!

God never meant for us to use our shield of faith only for our own protection. He meant for us to hook our shields together for the common good. The Roman shields in Paul's day had hooks on the sides. Each was bigger than a man and pointed at the bottom. When soldiers faced a serious attack, they would drive their shields into the ground and hook them together to form a solid wall of protection.

That's what we, as believers, are supposed to do in prayer. We're to link our shields of faith together and commit ourselves to fight for one another. We're to go into battle like covenant brothers and say, "I'll stand here as long as I have to and use every weapon God has given me to keep the devil off you. We're born of the same Spirit, bought with the same blood. I'll fight more fiercely for you in prayer than I'd fight for myself, because I love you the same way God loves me."

When we use the weapons of our warfare with that attitude, the devil will be hard-pressed to put anything over on any of us. We'll be watching over each other all the time. No matter where in the Church the devil goes, he'll find someone praying and swinging the sword of the Spirit at him. He'll find a solid wall of faith that he can't go over and he can't get through. He'll be totally defeated by the army of love.

LIMITLESS**LOVE**

The Will of the King

"The entrance of thy words giveth light; it giveth understanding unto the simple. I opened my mouth, and panted: for I longed for thy commandments. Look thou upon me, and be merciful unto me, as thou usest to do unto those that love thy name. Order my steps in thy WORD...."
Psalm 119:130-133

It's tragic how little of the Father's BLESSING is received by His children. In His love, He has provided all things richly for us to enjoy. He has paid for them with His own blood. He has laid them in store for us to draw upon whenever we desire to do so. He has given us detailed descriptions of them in His WORD so that we can reach out and take them with the hand of faith.

Yet time and again, He has been robbed of the delight of seeing us partake of those provisions. No doubt, His loving Father's heart has grieved as He has watched us needlessly suffer lack—simply because we have not read and believed His promises. We have not fully taken Him at His WORD.

Years ago, I heard a story about a woman who served many years ago as the handmaiden to the queen of England. She had begun her service as a young girl and lived most of her life in the palace. She never learned to read or write, so when the queen died and she was released from the royal service, she was left destitute—an old woman with no hope of gainful employment.

For years, the lady lived in poverty in a shanty by the river. One day, a preacher came to visit who had heard of her glorious past. "Is it true that you spent your life in the service of the queen?" he asked.

"Oh, yes!" she answered, beaming with pride. "I served her ladyship for many years. I have the proof hanging here on my wall."

Intrigued by this wonderful piece of history, the preacher walked over to examine the document which had been framed and given a place of honor in the tiny home. As he read the words written there, he was dismayed to find it was the will of the queen of England, which commanded that in honor of her handmaiden's faithful service, she be richly provided with a home, servants, clothing and food for the rest of her life. The document was signed and sealed by the queen herself.

Although the dear old lady had honored and cherished the will for years, she had never read it and understood what it promised her. Therefore, she had never been able to take the queen at her word and receive what her majesty had provided.

Don't let that sad story ever be told about you. Determine to find out what your Almighty King has so richly provided. Give His WORD—which is His will for you—an honored place, not just in your home but in your heart. Let the entrance of His WORD give you light, so you can believe and receive all of the bountiful BLESSING of The LORD!

LIMITLESS**LOVE**

In the Arms of Jesus

"...If we love one another, God abides in us, and His love is perfected in us."
1 John 4:12, *New American Standard*

Remember the old saying, "Practice makes perfect"? When it comes to love, that's absolutely the truth. The way to perfect God's love in you is by practicing that love on others.

Don't just practice it on the easy ones—those who are kind and gracious to you. (The Bible says even sinners can do that.) Determine to love those who irritate you and act ugly toward you. Purposely love those who are most challenging to you.

Don't sit around waiting for some kind of supernatural, warm, fuzzy feeling to make you do it. Just step out in faith and love them by an act of your will. One way to begin is by asking God to help you see that person the way He sees them. If it's someone who has really been ugly to you, that may be difficult. In fact, it may irritate you a little that God loves them at all. Let's be honest. At times, all of us, in our fleshly selfishness, looked at someone who was acting badly and thought, *How could God love that idiot?*

When I was a little boy, I overheard my mother talking to a man of faith about someone like that. "I just wonder how in the world God is going to deal with that person," she said.

"Mercifully," he answered. "With great mercy."

Even as a young boy, I knew what that man was really saying: "God will deal with them mercifully, just like He did with you...just like He did with me. If it weren't for His mercy, none of us would have survived. So we'd be wise to extend that same mercy to each other."

That's the attitude to have when you're asking God to help you see someone like He sees them. Cultivate that attitude by remembering how many times God has been gracious to you when you acted badly. Think about the price Jesus paid to save you while you were yet a sinner. Then, in that frame of mind, begin to pray for the one who has been difficult to love.

Sometimes, I get the process started by picturing them in my mind, and then visualizing Jesus coming right up behind them and taking them in His arms. I see them totally engulfed in Him. I think *Yes, Lord, that's the way You treated me. You loved me when I didn't deserve it. Help me do for them what You did for me. Just let Your mercy and compassion for them find expression through me.*

You may think right now that you can't do that, but I guarantee if you'll step out in faith, you'll find you can. You'll find that the more you believe the love God has for you, and the more you practice it on others, the more it is perfected in you.

LIMITLESS**LOVE**

In the Image of Love

*"But we all, with open face beholding as in a glass the glory of The LORD,
are changed into the same image from glory to glory,
even as by the Spirit of The LORD."*
2 Corinthians 3:18

As born-again children of God, you and I ought to be growing up into the image of Jesus. With every day that passes, we should be walking, talking, thinking and acting more like Him. Instead of crying in fear about the storms of life that come against us, we ought to be learning how to take authority over them. We should be saying, as Jesus did, "Peace! Be still!"

Some folks think it's practically blasphemous for us to imagine we could ever be like The LORD. But, the New Testament plainly states that is our destiny. Jesus Himself said, "He that believeth on me, the works that I do shall he do also; and greater works than these shall he do; because I go unto my Father" (John 14:12).

The Apostle Paul wrote that we are "...predestined to become conformed to the image of His Son, so that He would be the firstborn among many brethren" (Romans 8:29, *New American Standard)* and to "grow up into him in all things, which is the head, even Christ" (Ephesians 4:15).

The Apostle John said it this way, "...as he is, so are we in this world" (1 John 4:17).

As amazing as those scriptures are, every believer knows instinctively they're true. Our spirits instantly bear witness that we've been born again to be just like Jesus. God wants to do the same things through us that He did through Him!

Some of us have stepped into that on occasion. We've had moments when we experienced the life and power of God flowing unhindered through us. But we haven't yet lived in that place on a day-to-day basis. Why haven't we? What is it that we've been missing?

The fullness of God's love.

Love is the key to it all. Since Jesus is the embodiment of love, to be conformed to His image means to be conformed to the image of Love. So the more we behold Him in our hearts and realize we are born of that love, the more fully Jesus will be revealed in us.

Some time ago, The LORD said to me that we need to develop, to a much higher degree, our revelation that God is Love and His love is in us to be used. *As you develop and exercise that love,* He said, *it will not only fill you up, it will flush the fear out of your soul. Once fear is flushed out, you'll begin to step out in faith and live in a way the world cannot explain. They'll begin to wonder, "Who is this that even stops and stills the storms?"* They'll see in us the Person of Jesus. They'll see in us the image of Love.

LIMITLESS**LOVE**

According to Your Faith

"According to your faith be it unto you."
Matthew 9:29

Faith works by love. We've acknowledged that fact many times. But did you know that love cannot work without faith?

It's true. I could love you with all my heart. I could love you so much that I would buy you a house, put a new car in the driveway, and give you the keys to both of them—but if you didn't trust my love, those things would do you no good. When I tried to give you the keys, you'd just refuse them and say, "No, you can't fool me. I know you haven't bought me a car, and I certainly don't believe you bought me a house. So, just keep those silly keys because I'm not falling for that lie."

Ridiculous? No, that's reality. In fact, there was an actual case much like that some years ago in Chicago. A man who had been living in terrible poverty, just barely getting by with the help of some government welfare programs, was contacted by someone and informed he had been named heir to a multimillion-dollar fortune.

Just imagine. Here's a fellow who has been living on the street, hungry, suffering from the heat and cold. You'd think he'd jump for joy at the news, thrilled at even the possibility someone had provided for him.

But he wasn't. Instead, he refused to believe the messenger. "Ain't nobody ever given me nothin'," he said. "And ain't nobody ever going to give me nothin'. You get out of here and leave me alone."

As the story goes, the mayor of the city himself was finally recruited to help convince this man to receive his inheritance. So, he drove up in his limousine in front of the dumpy place where this man was living. The man clearly realized this was the mayor. But he still didn't believe. "No…" he said again. "Nobody's ever given nothin' to me, and they aren't going to start now. So just get back in your fancy car and go on."

The mayor had to order the man to come with him. He told him he was tired of the state having to pay for his food when he had a million dollars in the bank. So, he took the man to the bank, fussing and kicking all the way.

Sadly enough, many Christians are like that. They have a heavenly Father who loves them so much He has provided everything they'll ever need. They have an inheritance so rich, it's literally inexhaustible, but they haven't developed enough faith in God's love to receive it. "LORD," they say, "I'm not asking for very much. Just enough for me and my family to get by."

So, in spite of the riches God longs to give, He is obligated to parcel out that pitiful provision His child has asked for as He says, *According to your faith, be it unto you.*

LIMITLESS**LOVE**

Dare to Walk Worthy

"For this cause we also, since the day we heard it, do not cease to pray for you, and to desire that ye might be filled with the knowledge of his will in all wisdom and spiritual understanding; that ye might walk worthy of The LORD unto all pleasing, being fruitful in every good work, and increasing in the knowledge of God."

Colossians 1:9-10

Religion has cultivated an attitude in many Christians that chokes off their revelation of God's love for them. It has taught them they are unworthy to be called His sons. So instead of going boldly to the throne of grace and enjoying fellowship with their Father, they are continually cowering outside, whining about how unworthy they are.

For the most part, their intention is honorable. They desire to be humble before The LORD. They want to give Him all the glory for what He's done for them and take none of it for themselves. But their approach is unscriptural. Rather than honoring The LORD, they are dishonoring Him by refusing to receive the gift He has given them.

Even though as sinners we were all unworthy of salvation, once we made Jesus our LORD, His blood made us worthy. He became sin so that we could be made the righteousness of God. When we received Him as Savior, He gave us authority to become the children of God.

Do you know what that means? It means when you belittle yourself, you are belittling what He did in you. When you tell Him how unworthy you are, you are telling Him that the blood of Jesus wasn't enough to sanctify you. It wasn't enough to make you worthy.

You are, in essence, refusing to take the rightful place in God's family He paid so dearly to give you. That grieves His heart. Think about it and you can see why. How would you like it if you adopted some little, bedraggled child, loved him like your own flesh and blood, and yet he always refused to look you in the eye? How would you like it if you gave him the best of everything, but he wouldn't receive it because he felt unworthy?

It would probably bring you to tears. *Here I am spending all this money on this child,* you'd think, *just because I love him. Here I am trying to give him a wonderful life, and all he can talk about is this unworthy business!*

Don't treat your heavenly Father that way. Don't frustrate His love. Receive your love position as a born-again child in God's family. That's the honor of all honors to Him. Instead of telling Him how unworthy you are, tell Him how worthy of praise He is. Every time you approach Him, do it with your head up and joy in your heart. Dare to take your place as a son who has been made worthy of his Father's love. Dare to walk worthy of The LORD, fully pleasing Him.

LIMITLESS**LOVE**

Keep Your Focus on Jesus

*"But now in Christ Jesus you who formerly were far off
have been brought near by the blood of Christ."*
Ephesians 2:13, *New American Standard*

Sometimes, as believers begin to mature in the things of God and live holy lives, that first passionate love they had for The LORD begins to wane. Have you ever noticed that? In the first months of their Christian life, they may have wept with gratitude every time they prayed. They often overflowed with worship as they told The LORD how much they loved Him, and how they appreciate the cleansing that came to them through His precious blood.

But as time passes, something changes. They still love The LORD. They still pray and worship Him. But somehow, He doesn't seem as near to them or dear to them as He did during those first wonderful days.

Why is that?

Often, the reason is very simple. In the early days of their walk with The LORD, those believers put all their confidence in the blood of Jesus. They had no good works to rely on. They had to put all their trust in the Savior and simply draw near to God through faith in Him.

As they grew, however, without even realizing it, they allowed their focus to shift. They became more aware of their own spiritual successes or failures than they were of Jesus. They began to draw near to The LORD, thinking they were acceptable to Him because they'd behaved well or unacceptable because they'd behaved badly. Unconsciously, they fell from their place of grace to a place of works. They lost the affection they once had for God because they started trying to earn rather than receive as a gift their fellowship with Him.

Don't let that happen to you. No matter how mightily The LORD works in your life…no matter how many wonderful things He enables you to do…never, ever bring those things with you into the throne room of God. Never base your confidence on them.

Instead, keep your focus on Jesus. Remember, it is always and *only* His blood that brings you near to God. Whether you've acted wonderfully—or miserably—it is still your faith in Him, and Him alone, that secures your place with the Father. It is through Jesus only that you have access by faith into the grace wherein you stand (Romans 5:2).

If you'll keep those truths ever fresh in your mind, you'll never lose that first love you had for the One who paid it all for you. You'll never cease to be grateful for the sacrifice of your Savior and for the blood that brought you near.

LIMITLESS**LOVE**

Settled by the Blood

"Then the soldiers of the governor took Jesus into the Praetorium and gathered the whole Roman cohort around Him. They stripped Him and put a scarlet robe on Him. And after twisting together a crown of thorns, they put it on His head, and a reed in His right hand; and they knelt down before Him and mocked Him, saying, 'Hail, King of the Jews!' They spat on Him, and took the reed and began to beat Him on the head. After they had mocked Him, they took the scarlet robe off Him and put His own garments back on Him, and led Him away to crucify Him."
Matthew 27:27-31, *New American Standard*

As believers, we have a covenant that has been ratified in the blood of Jesus Himself. Every provision recorded in God's WORD, every promise God has made to us in the Bible, has been established forever in His precious blood. As God's covenant sacrifice for us, Jesus became the guarantee of our divine blessing. His blood ended all debate, and forever settled the fact that God loves us and has promised to provide for us everything that pertains to life and godliness.

Once you truly grasp that, it will practically sound like profanity when you hear someone say, "Well, I just don't know if it's God's will to heal me. I'm not sure He's going to provide for my needs." They might as well be saying, "I don't really think the blood of Jesus meant that much. After all, God is sovereign. He might just decide to break His promises and ignore that blood."

You won't even be able to think such a thing, much less say it. Your heart will be anchored, your mind will be firmly established, your whole being will be settled in faith. Every time you think of God's WORD, you'll remember the blood and you'll be fully assured that God will do for you what He has promised.

To get to that point, however, you have to meditate on what happened at the Cross. Saturate yourself in it until you're standing out there at Calvary's mountain. Meditate on it until you can smell the old dungeon where He was whipped and you can see the flesh ripped from His body as the stripes for your healing are laid on His back.

Let the Holy Spirit help you hear the ring of the hammer driving the nails into His body and see the blood pouring from His wounds as the laughter and mockery of ignorant and sinful men foul the air. Look at Him hanging on that cross and remember Galatians 3:13-14. "Christ hath redeemed us from the curse of the law, being made a curse for us: for it is written, Cursed is every one that hangeth on a tree: that the blessing of Abraham might come on the Gentiles through Jesus Christ; that we might receive the promise of the Spirit through faith."

Let the blood of the everlasting covenant do within you what it was divinely designed to do. Let it settle forever every question you might have about God's love. Let it drive out every doubt and leave you fully persuaded that He will forever keep His WORD to you.

LIMITLESS**LOVE**

Now *That's* Good News

"For I am not ashamed of the gospel of Christ: for it is the power of God unto salvation to every one that believeth; to the Jew first, and also to the Greek. For therein is the righteousness of God revealed from faith to faith: as it is written, The just shall live by faith."

Romans 1:16-17

Over the years, religion has watered down our idea of the gospel. It's given us the idea that the gospel is little more than a sweet Sunday school lesson. It's reduced the gospel to a set of rules and regulations that we have to obey to keep God from being mad at us.

But the *gospel* means the "good news." The Bible says the gospel is the power of God—but there is very little good news and very little power in things like rules and regulations.

One day, I was thinking about the covenant God made with Abraham in the Old Testament. I was meditating on the day that God cut that covenant in the blood of animals and swore to Abraham to bless him and to be his God. Suddenly, I heard this question in my heart. *If you'd have asked Abraham that night what the gospel was, what do you think he would have said?*

Instantly, I knew the answer. He'd say, "I'll tell you what the good news is, brother. Almighty God made a decision to enter covenant with me! He's promised to provide for me. He's promised to BLESS me. He's promised to protect me. He said anybody who cursed me would be cursed. So don't mess with me, or you'll end up with God Himself opposing you. I have it made forever!"

"But that was Abraham," someone might say. "I don't have a covenant with God like He did."

You do if you're born again. But your covenant is established in more sacred blood. It's ratified in the blood of Jesus. And the Bible says that through Him, THE BLESSING of Abraham has come on you!

What is THE BLESSING? You'll find it in Genesis 12 where God says to Abraham, "'And I will make you a great nation, and I will bless you, and make your name great; and so you shall be a blessing; and I will bless those who bless you, and the one who curses you I will curse. And in you, all the families of the earth will be blessed'" (verses 2-3, *New American Standard*).

No wonder the Bible tells us to pray for those who persecute us! We have a covenant of love with Almighty God. He is on our side, and anyone who comes against us runs up against Him. That's why no weapon formed against us will prosper, and every tongue that rises against us will be condemned (Isaiah 54:17). It's our covenant heritage!

Oh, that's good news, my friend! That's the power of God working on our behalf! That is the gospel of love!

LIMITLESS**LOVE**

Remember the Covenant

*"And The LORD thy God will circumcise thine heart, and the heart
of thy seed, to love The LORD thy God with all thine heart, and with
all thy soul, that thou mayest live."*
Deuteronomy 30:6

When we think about the covenant we have with God through Jesus, we are immediately reminded of THE BLESSING it provides for us. We remember (as we should) the marks of that covenant on the body of Jesus. The scars on His head from the crown of thorns, the stripes on His back, the nail prints in His hands and the hole in His side—those marks will forever signify God's promise to give His all to us as His covenant people.

We must also remember, however, that we bear the mark of the covenant, as well. Like the circumcision of the Old Covenant saints, ours is not a mark that can readily be seen. Our sign of the covenant is borne in our spirits. It is the circumcision of the heart.

When I say we should remember that, I don't mean simply that we shouldn't forget it or that we should occasionally bring it to mind. The word *remember* is a covenant word. It means "to be continually conscious of the one you are in covenant with." God remembers His covenant with us by keeping us perpetually on His mind and in His heart. He remembers us by constantly making Himself and all His resources available to us. In the same way, as His covenant people, we are supposed to be in total, absolute remembrance of God, twenty-four hours a day, every day of our lives.

We are to remember that we are committed to love Him. We are to be more concerned with meeting His needs than we are about Him meeting our needs. We should get our minds on what we can do for Him and how we can minister to His Body.

We ought to be more driven by our desire to BLESS Him than we are by our desire to receive His BLESSING. We should forget about our own will and become totally consumed by His. As we continue to grow in our covenant love for Him, we'll find ourselves neglecting to pray about our own needs, because we're too busy praying for the needs of others God has put on our hearts. Yet we'll never lack anything, because while we're taking care of God's business, He is taking care of ours.

Only when we start loving The LORD like that will we really discover what covenant is all about. That's when we'll remember countless times a day, that all we are and all we have belongs to God as our Covenant Partner. We'll be driven by the love within us to be His servants, His champions on the earth…to be whatever He needs us to be.

Only then will we discover what it really means to live.

LIMITLESS**LOVE**

When Love Gets Angry

"And The LORD said unto Moses, Go, get thee down; for thy people, which thou broughtest out of the land of Egypt, have corrupted themselves: They have turned aside quickly out of the way which I commanded them: they have made them a molten calf, and have worshipped it, and have sacrificed thereunto.... Now therefore let me alone, that my wrath may wax hot against them, and that I may consume them: and I will make of thee a great nation. And Moses besought The LORD his God, and said, LORD, why doth thy wrath wax hot against thy people, which thou hast brought forth out of the land of Egypt with great power, and with a mighty hand?... Turn from thy fierce wrath, and repent of this evil against thy people. Remember Abraham, Isaac, and Israel, thy servants, to whom thou swarest by thine own self, and saidst unto them, I will multiply your seed as the stars of heaven, and all this land that I have spoken of will I give unto your seed, and they shall inherit it for ever. And The LORD repented of the evil which he thought to do unto his people."
Exodus 32:7-8, 10-14

Don't think that just because you walk in love, you won't ever be angry. God Himself becomes angry at evil and injustice. He feels about those things just like we do. The difference between our anger and His is that, first of all, His anger is a whole lot bigger than ours, but He doesn't sin with His anger like we do. He never loses His temper. As we grow in love and the other fruit of the spirit (such as temperance) we won't lose ours, either. As Ephesians 4:26 says, we will be angry, and sin not.

God's loving nature also causes Him to be easily entreated (James 3:17). He is willing to turn from His anger, even though He is right and just in having it. He is willing to let go of His wrath and forgive simply because His covenant friend asks Him to. In this case, for instance, God's love for Moses caused Him to have mercy on the Israelites even though they didn't deserve mercy and weren't asking for it at the time.

In so doing, He set the example for us. He revealed how we should treat those who move us not only to fleshly anger but to righteous indignation. We must love like He loves and be willing to turn from our anger even when it is justified. We must be merciful simply because our covenant Friend The LORD Jesus Christ has requested it.

He said, "...forgive, if you have anything against anyone" (Mark 11:25, *New American Standard*). Although the people who have done the wrong may not deserve mercy, although they may not even be repentant, because we love the Master, we will yield to His request. We will turn from our anger and do what He has asked us to do.

LIMITLESS LOVE

Keep on Serving

"And whoever wishes to be first among you shall be your slave;
just as the Son of Man did not come to be served, but to serve,
and to give His life a ransom for many."
Matthew 20:27-28, *New American Standard*

Have you ever found yourself irritated with someone who didn't appreciate your kindness to them? Have you ever caught yourself saying, "I just can't believe they treated me so badly! After all I've done for them, they owe me more than that!"

The next time you're tempted to take that attitude, remember this: The moment you step into the martyr mentality, you are stepping out of love. You are using the good things you did for that person as a kind of emotional manipulation. Instead of being content simply to BLESS them, you are demanding something in return.

"Doesn't everyone do that?" someone might say.

Jesus didn't. When He came to the earth, He didn't come here trying to talk people into believing in Him so that He could get something from them. He came totally, absolutely, unreservedly to give of Himself so that whosoever would believe on Him wouldn't perish but have everlasting life.

He sacrificed Himself in love for the world, even though there was no guarantee that anyone would receive Him. And, the fact is, most people didn't. When He went to the cross, no one appreciated or understood what He was doing. It was a mystery hidden in God. People laughed at Him and scorned Him, but He didn't take offense. He didn't say, "Can you believe this? I'm pouring out my blood for them, and they don't even appreciate it!" No, He prayed, "Father, forgiven them for they don't know what they do."

Even after He was raised from the dead, the majority of His followers didn't receive Him. The Bible says He appeared to about 500 people after He was raised from the dead (1 Corinthians 15:6). He told all of them, "You go to Jerusalem and wait for the promise of the Holy Spirit." Yet, only 120 were in the upper room on the Day of Pentecost. You'd think every one of them would have been there after seeing Him raised from the dead, but they weren't. Clearly, even though they saw with their own eyes what He had done for them, they didn't respond as they should have.

But, Jesus never let people's ingratitude affect Him. We have no record that He ever mentioned it. He just kept on doing what the love of God within Him compelled Him to do. He kept on giving, serving and pouring out His life.

As His disciples, that's what we'll do, too.

LIMITLESS**LOVE**

Designed by Love

"For when Moses had spoken every precept to all the people according to the law, he took the blood of calves and of goats, with water, and scarlet wool, and hyssop, and sprinkled both the book, and all the people, Saying, This is the blood of the testament which God hath enjoined unto you."
Hebrews 9:19-20

Sometimes people read the Old Testament and miss the amazing demonstration of God's love that's revealed there. They look at the Mosaic law and the animal sacrifices it required, and say in ignorance, "What kind of God sets up a system like that?"

A God who loves people! Even though mankind had yielded to the devil and become a fallen race, God loved the people of that day. Even though they were spiritually dead and had no way to be regenerated, God still wanted to meet their needs. He was so consumed with love for them, that even knowing they could not truly love Him in return, He wanted to make a covenant with them so He could BLESS them.

The problem was, they couldn't keep their end of the covenant. They were so spiritually degenerate, they'd break it before bedtime the first day—and He knew it. The penalty for a broken covenant was death, and He wanted to help them, not hurt them. He had to find another way.

So He brought in the Old Covenant priesthood. He appointed a certain group of people to represent Him and in essence said, *Listen, my covenant brothers and sisters, I know you're going to mess things up. I know you're going to break our agreement and sin. So when you do, instead of killing you for it, we're going to kill an animal instead. We're going to let that animal be your substitute. That way, I'll be able to satisfy the demands of justice without hurting you. We can stay in covenant with each other, and I can BLESS you in spite of your sin.*

God didn't do that because He was insensitive to the death of the animal. If God had His way, there wouldn't ever have been any death in the earth at all. Adam is the one who opened the door to it. Once sin and death were in the earth, something had to be done to shelter man from the curse of it. That's why God instituted the Old Testament laws and priesthood—to protect the people He loved from the full effects of their own sin and to establish a covenant of BLESSING with them, in spite of their fallen condition.

It was a temporary solution, only a type and shadow of the wonderful Priesthood of our LORD Jesus Christ who would come and pay the penalty for sin and cleanse us from it, forever. Even so, it was clearly devised by the biggest heart of compassion ever known. It was designed by the God of love.

LIMITLESS**LOVE**

The Perfect Picture of Love

"And one of the scribes came, and having heard them reasoning together, and perceiving that he had answered them well, asked him, Which is the first commandment of all? And Jesus answered him, The first of all the commandments is, Hear, O Israel; The LORD our God is one LORD: And thou shalt love The LORD thy God with all thy heart, and with all thy soul, and with all thy mind, and with all thy strength: this is the first commandment."
Mark 12:28-30

The greatest picture of covenant love ever seen on the earth was the relationship between The LORD Jesus and His heavenly Father. They loved each other with an absolute, unwavering love. The Father exalted Jesus and said, "This is my beloved Son.... Hear ye him" (Matthew 17:5). Jesus exalted the Father and said, "I do nothing of myself; but as my Father hath taught me, I speak these things" (John 8:28).

Through love, they were in perfect union with each other.

Sometimes, we take that for granted because we focus on the fact that Jesus was the Son of God. But He was also the Son of Man. Jesus was as much flesh and blood during his earthly life as you and I. He got tired, hungry and thirsty just like other men. He experienced pressure and temptation.

Yet, Jesus always obeyed the Father. He didn't sin one time. He didn't break His covenant with God once. Why? Because He was so in love with His Father that He couldn't bear to break their union. He was so committed to the Father and the Father to Him, that as they walked together, you couldn't tell where one stopped and the other started. They were fused together by love.

That's why Jesus agonized so greatly in the Garden of Gethsemane. That's why He sweat drops of blood. He wasn't upset over the physical pain and death he would experience on the Cross. He was grieving over the thought of being separated from His Father. It caused Him so much sorrow, the very prospect of it almost killed Him.

Actually, it was the love Jesus had for the Father, the same love that produced the life and union they had together, which demanded that union be broken. It was love that drove Him to the Cross to pour out His life's blood. It was love that compelled Him to take into His pure, sinless spirit, all the horror of fallen mankind. It was love that took Him into hell to suffer the penalty for our sin.

Jesus loved the Father so much that He wanted to give back to Him the world God so dearly loved. The Father loved Jesus so much that once redemption had been accomplished, He gave Him the Name that is above every name and crowned Him LORD of all. That is true covenant love.

LIMITLESS**LOVE**

In You, I See Jesus

"For the love of Christ constraineth us; because we thus judge, that if one died for all, then were all dead: and that he died for all, that they which live should not henceforth live unto themselves, but unto him which died for them, and rose again. Wherefore henceforth know we no man after the flesh...."
2 Corinthians 5:14-16

The command to love your neighbor as you love yourself is a wonderful command. It's more than most people even try to do. But as members of the Body of Christ, we have an even higher call. We're called to live for Jesus by living for each other. We're called to love our brothers and sisters in The LORD just like we love The LORD Himself.

"Brother Copeland," you might say, "surely you aren't telling me I ought to treat you like I'd treat Jesus!"

Yes, I am. And, I ought to be treating you the same way. After all, we are one Body. We are one spirit with Him. The Bible says when one suffers, we all suffer. When one is honored, we are all honored. We're joined together in a supernatural union.

Think about it for a moment. Jesus is in me, and I am in Jesus. Jesus is in you, and you are in Him. That must mean we're all mixed up together. I can't separate you from Jesus. I can't treat Him one way and treat you another because whatever I do to you, I'm doing to Him. And whatever you do to me, you're doing to Him.

When we understand that, we'll be like the Apostle Paul and stop looking at each other after the flesh. We'll stop thinking that just because we live in different packages of skin, we're separate from each other. We'll realize that we are truly one in Jesus. We are each part of Him.

That means when I see you, I see Jesus. So I ought to love you as if you are Jesus. I ought to care for you with the *agape* kind of love that's only interested in what I can do for you, not in what you can do for me. After all, if I'm going to treat you like Jesus, I'm going to treat you like you've already done everything for me that you could possibly do. I'm going to treat you like you died for me. I'm going to treat you as if you're the reason I'm going to heaven.

I'll be looking for ways to BLESS you. I'll be searching for opportunities to care for you. Nothing you do will affect my love for you. Natural facts won't have any bearing on it. I won't care about your skin color. I won't care about your denominational background. When I look at you, I'll see Jesus. I'll see the One who loved me and gave Himself for me.

When I look at you, I'll see the One I love.

LIMITLESS**LOVE**

Do It God's Way

"You have heard that it was said, 'Eye for eye, and tooth for tooth.'
But I tell you, do not resist an evil person. If someone strikes you on the
right cheek, turn to him the other cheek also. And if anyone wants to sue
you and take your shirt, hand over your coat as well. If anyone forces you
to go one mile, go with them two miles. Give to the one who asks you,
and do not turn away from the one who wants to borrow from you."
Matthew 5:38-42, *New International Version*

Most of us absolutely choke at the thought of responding in love to those who mistreat us. We want to argue with The LORD about it because it seems to us that just wouldn't work. From our limited, human perspective, it appears that if we don't slap the other guy back, if we don't get a lawyer and file a countersuit against the person who's trying to take advantage of us, we'll be beaten up, broke and defeated.

So, instead of walking in love and doing things God's way, we insist on doing things our way, instead—as if we know better than He does what is the wisest thing to do. As a result, we sin and miss the mark. We rob ourselves of THE BLESSING our obedience to Him would bring.

I made that same mistake when I was a kid and my dad was trying to teach me to play baseball. He'd give me the bat, position my hands on it just right, then step back to throw me a pitch. But as soon as he did, I'd reposition my hands so I could hold the bat my way—which was the wrong way.

"Kenneth," he'd say, "you'll never be able to hit anything holding the bat like that. You have to hold it like this." After correcting my grip, he'd step back to pitch and I'd change my hold again.

"It doesn't work for me to do it your way," I protested. "I have to do it my way."

Dad would go ahead and pitch the ball and of course, despite my best efforts I'd miss it. Looking back, it's ridiculous that I thought I knew more about baseball than my father. I was only about four years old, and he was a grown man. What's more, he was practically a professional-quality baseball player. He wanted to give me the benefit of his wisdom. He wanted to set me up so that I could knock the ball clean out of the park, but he couldn't do it as long as I wouldn't trust him and do what he said.

Our heavenly Father is the same way. When He tells us to respond in love, even to those who act like our enemies, He is trying to set us up for victory. He positioning us to receive THE BLESSING that comes when we walk in love, so we can knock the devil clean out of the park!

The Only Reasonable Thing to Do

"Now faith is the substance of things hoped for,
the evidence of things not seen."
Hebrews 11:1

The more you realize just how much God loves you, the more you'll fall in love with Him. You'll become consumed with the desire to BLESS Him. You'll so appreciate all He's given you, you'll start looking for ways to give back to Him.

Even then, God will keep on outgiving you. There will be times when you're worshiping Him and telling Him how much you love Him and want to serve Him—and He'll interrupt you right in the middle of it to tell you about something He wants to do for you. *Do you remember what I said about My people living in goodly houses?* He might say. *Well, I want you to know I have a good house for you. It's far better than the one you have now, and I want you to have it.*

When you're in the atmosphere of love, it's not hard to have faith for promises like that. It's not hard to believe God's WORD. You don't have to struggle and strain. You can just rejoice and say, "Thank You, LORD! I appreciate that. I'll start boxing things up today, so we'll be ready when moving time comes!"

Some people think that kind of faith is strange or extreme. But the fact is, it's perfectly reasonable between those who love and trust each other. That's true even in the natural world.

Say, for example, you had an older brother who always loved you and looked after you as you were growing up. You and he had always been there for each other, through thick and thin. You always made sacrifices for each other. You always kept your word to each other.

Let's say that brother eventually became a multimillionaire. One day, he calls you and says, "Hey, I just want you to know I bought the house across town you've been admiring. I knew you liked it, and I thought it would be fun to buy it for you. I'll sign the papers on it tomorrow and have the realtor come by and give you the keys."

How would you respond? You'd shout and jump and tell your friends. You'd act like a person who just got a new house!

"How do you know you have that house?" someone might ask. "Have you seen the papers yet? Do you have the keys in your hand? Maybe it's not really your brother's will to give you that house. How can you be sure?"

"I'll tell you how I can be sure," you'd say. "I can be sure because my brother and I love each other. He's never yet lied to me. So if I have his word on it, that house is as good as mine!"

That's how simple it can be to believe and receive the promises of God. In the atmosphere of love, it's the only reasonable thing to do.

LIMITLESS**LOVE**

To Tell the Truth

"...[The devil] was a murderer from the beginning, and does not stand in the truth, because there is no truth in him. Whenever he speaks a lie, he speaks from his own nature; for he is a liar, and the father of lies."
John 8:44, *New American Standard*

Walking in love means more than just being nice and sweet to people. It means telling them the truth with their best interests at heart. It means refusing to lie to them.

Through the years, it has amazed me to see how many times Christian people lie. "Sorry, I missed your meeting the other night, Brother Copeland," they'll say. "I sure wanted to be there. I just couldn't make it." Sometimes, just by the spirit, I'll know they aren't telling the truth. They never intended to come to the meeting. They wanted to stay home and watch television. That didn't really bother me. But, their lying about it did. I wished they'd have respected me enough to tell me the truth.

If we're going to be people of love, we need to get lying in perspective. We need to realize that the devil himself is the father of it. The very first time we see him in the Bible, he's lying to Adam and Eve. He's telling them that God's WORD isn't true, and then giving some advice that he says will bless them.

It didn't, of course, because he's a deceiver. He'll promise you everything to get what you have, and then he won't give you anything in return. He is the father of the counterfeit covenant. He's the originator of the word that can't be trusted.

As Christians, we should refuse to have anything to do with that. We should hate lying so badly that we get every trace of it out of our lives. Instead of being the worst people in the world to do business with (that's the way it's been in times past), Christians ought to be the *best* people to do business with.

Our word should hold up when no one else's does. Christian people shouldn't be content to make business agreements with a handshake. They ought to insist on writing things down, making contracts and giving everyone a copy. They ought to do it, not because they need a written document to force them to keep their word, but because they are so watchful and eager to do everything they promised, they want it in black and white to make sure they don't forget it.

Instead of looking for ways to get out of keeping our word, we should be like God—absolutely determined to keep it to the last jot and tittle. Our God is the Father of love, not the father of lies. So let's get rid of the lies, and be like Him. In matters great and small, let's tell the truth.

Before You Take Aim

"Live in harmony with one another; do not be haughty (snobbish, high-minded, exclusive), but readily adjust yourself to [people, things] and give yourselves to humble tasks. Never overestimate yourself or be wise in your own conceits."
Romans 12:16, *The Amplified Bible*

Humility is one of the marks of a person who has matured in love. It's characteristic of the believer God can trust with real power. That's why you'll often find that people who walk in true spiritual authority are slow to criticize others. They may have much scriptural wisdom and knowledge, yet they'll never use it to put down a brother or sister in The LORD.

Even if they see someone behaving badly and can prove by the Bible that person is wrong, they refuse to pass judgment. They're humble enough to realize there are probably aspects of that person's situation they don't understand. And they're loving enough to make adjustments in their own attitudes in order to give the erring brother the time and space to grow.

People who are immature, however, are just the opposite. They're quick to point out the faults of others. They'll use scriptural truth to blast away at the sin in someone else's life, and never stop to think about the damage they have done in the process. It will never occur to them that their arrogant attitude grieves the Holy Spirit even more than the shortcomings of the brother they attempted to correct.

People who act like that (and we all do at times) remind me of the way my son, John, was when he first learned to shoot a gun as a young boy. He was a good shot, and he had no difficulty hitting his target. But I never let him out of my sight when we went hunting together, because he still lacked wisdom.

One time, for example, we were out together and he spotted a huge, ugly spider crawling up the side of a barn. He wanted to kill it, so he lifted his shotgun and took aim.

"Don't do that!" I said as I grabbed his gun. "You'll blow a major hole in the side of that barn!"

"Oh," he said sheepishly. "I hadn't thought about the barn."

That's the way you and I are when we first begin to learn about the things of God. We have all our spiritual equipment. We have the faith of God in us and the capacity to use it. We have the Anointing of the Holy Spirit and the capacity to use it. We have The WORD of God and the authority to use it. But before God can fully turn up the power in us, we have to grow up and mature in love.

We have to be wise enough to put up with a spider for a while for the sake of the barn... and humble enough to check with our Father before we take aim, because there might just be a few things we still don't know.

LIMITLESS**LOVE**

Don't Judge Another Man's Servant

"Who are you to judge someone else's servant? To their own master, servants stand
or fall. And they will stand, for The LORD is able to make them stand."
Romans 14:4, *New International Version*

Years ago, The LORD spoke to my heart and asked me a question I'll never forget: *Do you know what one of the greatest problems I have with the Body of Christ is?*

"No, Sir," I answered. "I don't."

It's your dogged determination to correct one another, He said.

I realized immediately how true that is. I thought about all the disputes and debates that have taken place over minor doctrinal issues, and ended up bringing division to the Church. I thought about all the ugly, unloving things I'd heard believers and ministers say about one another, all in the name of scriptural correctness.

Through the years, I've seen some people spend more time studying The WORD in an effort to prove someone else wrong, than they'd spend studying it to get the wisdom and grace to correct their own faults and failures. That's not what The LORD intended for us to do. He never planned for us to use The WORD to destroy someone else with it.

It doesn't matter what we think our fellow servants are in error over, God didn't call us to judge them. He called us to walk in love and be an example to them. He called us to "consider one another to provoke unto love and to good works" (Hebrews 10:24). He called us to say things that edify and "minister grace unto the hearers" (Ephesians 4:29).

Obviously, if our friend and fellow believer is stepping into sin and yielding to immoral behavior, we can't ignore that. We'll need to lovingly reach out to help him and say, "Hey, brother, you don't want to get into that. It will hurt you. It will rob you of THE BLESSING of God. Let me give you a hand and help you out of that trap."

But the fact is, most of the time what we end up getting onto each other about are questionable issues, things that are a matter of opinion. That's why the Bible tells us not to get involved in disputes over doubtful things (Romans 14:1). They don't make that much difference! They draw us out of the love walk and into legalistic arguments that hurt instead of help the Body of Christ.

Remember this: None of us is absolutely correct about every spiritual issue. Even if we were correct in everything we know, in the overall scope of things, we don't know much. So, our own ignorance makes us incorrect in some situations. What's more, the Bible doesn't require us to be technically correct about everything. It requires us as stewards to be faithful (1 Corinthians 4:2). It requires us to walk in love.

LIMITLESS**LOVE**

Born to Love

"Seeing ye have purified your souls in obeying the truth through the Spirit unto unfeigned love of the brethren, see that ye love one another with a pure heart fervently: Being born again, not of corruptible seed, but of incorruptible, by The WORD of God, which liveth and abideth for ever."
1 Peter 1:22-23

One thing that robs us of the divine energy it takes to love one another is our refusal to leave our past behind. It seems we insist on dragging it around with us everywhere we go. "Oh, LORD," we say, "I just don't know how I can love people the way I ought to. I've been so selfish all my life. I have such a history of being thoughtless and unkind. God, forgive me but that's the way I've always been."

We need to realize that's not how God sees us. He sees us only in the light of redemption. He's never known you any other way except cleansed by the blood of Jesus and robed in His righteousness. When you come crawling into the throne room telling Him what a bad person you were 25 years ago, He doesn't know who you're talking about. He's forgotten your iniquities. He's removed them as far as the east is from the west.

As far as He is concerned, the day you were born again was the day you were born! One friend of mine found that out personally when she asked The LORD to give her a new clothes dryer for her birthday. She was surprised when her natural birthday came and went with no sign of her new dryer. Late one night a few months later, however, someone called her and said, "Please forgive me for calling so late, but The LORD instructed me to give you my clothes dryer, and He said I had to do it before midnight, tonight!" Sure enough, when my friend checked the calendar, she realized it was the date she had been born again!

Wouldn't it be silly to pick up a little baby who's just a few days old and say, "My, isn't he precious? Isn't he beautiful? It's too bad he has such a terrible past."

Past? What past? That baby doesn't have any past! He was only born a few days ago. He's a new creature!

The same is true for you. When you were born again, you became a new creation. The Bible says old things passed away and all things became new! You exchanged your life for Jesus' life. You exchanged your past for His past. You exchanged your nature for His nature.

When you consider your past in that light, you'll boldly say, "Yes, LORD, I can love people the way You want me to. Love comes naturally to me because I have Your nature. In You, I have a history of kindness and compassion. Through the blood of Jesus and The WORD of God, I was born to love!"

LIMITLESS**LOVE**

The Greatest Sinner of All

> "And it came to pass, as Jesus sat at meat in the house, behold, many publicans
> and sinners came and sat down with him and his disciples. And when the
> Pharisees saw it, they said unto his disciples, Why eateth your Master with
> publicans and sinners? But when Jesus heard that, he said unto them,
> They that be whole need not a physician, but they that are sick. But go ye and
> learn what that meaneth, I will have mercy, and not sacrifice: for I am not come
> to call the righteous, but sinners to repentance."
> Matthew 9:10-13

In Jesus' day, the most unloving group of people on earth was the Pharisees. Jesus rebuked them more sternly than anyone else. He warned His disciples not to be like them. "For they bind heavy burdens and grievous to be borne, and lay them on men's shoulders; but they themselves will not move them with one of their fingers" (Matthew 23:4).

Those words reveal what Jesus considered to be so wrong with this group of people. It was the fact that they had no mercy for sinners.

As far as a Pharisee was concerned, a sinner was the most rotten thing that existed on the face of the earth. If he brushed up against a sinner in the marketplace, he would go straight home, take a bath and wash his clothes. What's more, he was self-righteous about it, because he assumed God hated sinners just as much as he did.

When Jesus taught that heaven would rejoice over one sinner who repented, it totally upset their traditions. They were repulsed by the concept of such mercy. Why? Primarily because they thought they didn't need it. They mistakenly believed their religious works had earned them a place of right-standing with God. They didn't realize it was the mercy of God that was keeping them alive. They didn't realize that they were chief of all sinners.

The first Pharisee we have record of who received that revelation was the Apostle Paul. He called himself the chief of sinners (1 Timothy 1:15) because in the days before he was born again, he had no mercy. He genuinely thought Christians were wrong, so he had them imprisoned and killed. He had no mercy on them.

In the sight of God, a person who has no mercy is the greatest sinner of all. Therefore, as born-again children of God, that is the one fault we must guard most carefully against. We must never allow ourselves to fall into the trap of the Pharisees. We must never despise someone because they've fallen prey to sin.

On the contrary, we must forever remember that we have all sinned and fallen short of the glory of God. We must remember that God loves us in spite of—not because of—ourselves. And the mercy we have received from Him we must always be ready to give.

LIMITLESS**LOVE**

The Mercy That Never Stops

"O give thanks unto The LORD; for he is good: for his mercy endureth for ever. O give thanks unto the God of gods: for his mercy endureth for ever."
Psalm 136:1-2

The Old Testament word used to refer to the *agape,* God-kind of love is the word *mercy.* Because God is merciful, He is good to those of us who don't deserve that goodness. Because God is merciful, He gives us THE BLESSING, and more favor than we could ever deserve. God's mercy caused Him to intervene and take upon Himself through Jesus the punishment for sin…and then give to us the righteous rewards that only He Himself is worthy of.

Mercy is a quality that is uniquely God. Just as God is Love, God is Mercy. There is no mercy outside of God. He is the source of all mercy. So any mercy we receive, we actually receive from Him. Mercy is always and forever the gift of God.

Actually, mercy is such an unchangeable part of God's nature that the original Hebrew text of these verses in Psalm 136 simply says, "Oh give thanks unto The LORD, for He is good! His mercy forever." The word *endureth* isn't even there. It was added by the translators in an attempt to magnify the fact that God's mercy never comes to an end. For God's mercy to cease God Himself would have to cease, for He is goodness and mercy forever.

Practically speaking, that means God never stops extending His goodness to you in every area of your life. He doesn't just have mercy on you spiritually, forgive you of sin and then say, "OK now, that's as much as you're going to get from Me. I've delivered you from sin and I'll get you to heaven, but you'll just have to put up with that sickness in your body. After all, you brought it on yourself by your own stupidity. So I'm not going to heal you of it."

For God to say something like that, His mercy would have to stop! It would have to cease operating. And according to the Bible, that's impossible. God's mercy endures forever!

What's more, Psalm 145 says He is full of mercy and compassion. If God stopped after delivering you from 60 or 70 percent of your afflictions, that would mean He was just 60 or 70 percent mercy, wouldn't it? But that's impossible because the Bible assures us He is 100 percent mercy, 100 percent of the time!

The only thing that can hinder God's mercy in your life is your own failure to receive it. So get out of His way! By simple faith and trust in Him, throw open the door to God's mercy in every area of your life. Like the psalmist, you too will soon be shouting, "The LORD is good, and His mercy endures forever!"

LIMITLESS**LOVE**

The Reason for It All

"And Jesus went about all the cities and villages, teaching in their synagogues, and preaching the gospel of the kingdom, and healing every sickness and every disease among the people. But when he saw the multitudes, he was moved with compassion on them, because they fainted, and were scattered abroad, as sheep having no shepherd. Then saith he unto his disciples, The harvest truly is plenteous, but the labourers are few; pray ye therefore The LORD of the harvest, that he will send forth labourers into his harvest. And when he had called unto him his twelve disciples, he gave them power against unclean spirits, to cast them out, and to heal all manner of sickness and all manner of disease."
Matthew 9:35-10:1

A lot of Christians want to walk in the power and Anointing of Jesus. Almost all of us want to do the works that He did. But sometimes we lose sight of the purpose behind those works. We forget the anointing didn't come on Jesus so that He could have a big ministry. It wasn't given to Him so He could impress folks and prove that He was the Son of God.

God anointed Jesus so He could demonstrate God's love to people. He clothed Jesus with power so that He could bring mercy, healing and deliverance to those in need. The love of God was the reason for the anointing. It was compassion that brought it forth.

Compassion is the drive inspired by mercy. It's an awesome force. Compassion will cause a father to storm into a raging inferno to save the life of his child. Compassion will make a person so gut-wrenchingly determined to protect, assist or provide for someone, that he refuses to allow anything to get in the way.

When compassion moves, it draws from God every gift of the Spirit necessary to meet the need at hand. It explodes into action, takes hold of the power of God, and releases His Anointing to relieve suffering and bring deliverance to people who desperately need it.

Compassion was the force moving in Jesus when He saw the multitudes and realized He couldn't minister to all of them by Himself. It was compassion that caused Him to call His disciples and give them power over unclean spirits and to heal all kinds of disease. He didn't do that so He could gain more notoriety or expand the size of His organization. He didn't do it so the disciples could feel good about themselves and develop a reputation as men of faith and power. He did it because He so desperately desired to meet the needs of the people. He did it because He was driven by love.

The same is true today. That's why the more we are moved by God's love, the more we will move in His power and Anointing. Love is the reason for it all.

LIMITLESS**LOVE**

The Love That Prevails

"He sent and had John beheaded in the prison. And his head was brought
on a platter and given to the girl, and she brought it to her mother. And his
disciples came and took away the body and buried it; and they went and
reported to Jesus. Now when Jesus heard about John, He withdrew from
there in a boat to a secluded place by Himself; and when the people heard
of this, they followed Him on foot from the cities. And when He went ashore,
He saw a large crowd, and felt compassion for them and healed their sick."
Matthew 14:10-14, *New American Standard*

One reason we, as believers, fall short when it comes to walking in love is that we fail
to realize just how great the love of God residing within us actually is. We measure it by the
wrong standard. When we get short-tempered with others because we've had a bad day, we'll
say to ourselves, "See there! I don't have much love!" Then we end up feeling condemned and
discouraged. We judge our inward capacity by our outward behavior, and we put more faith in
our fleshly weaknesses than we do in The WORD of God.

It's time we turned that around. It's time we stopped believing our experiences and
started believing what the Bible says. It says we've been made partakers of the divine nature.
It says the very same love that God bestowed on Jesus, He has put within us (John 17:26)!

Just how powerful is that love? Look at the life of Jesus, and you will see. Even at times
when He was dealing with personal pain and difficult circumstances, Jesus put His own feelings
aside and ministered to others. He lost sight of Himself because of His compassion for them.

Jesus' response to the death of John the Baptist reveals that clearly. No doubt, that
was a painful time for Jesus. John was his cousin, a member of his own family. He was the
only man on the face of the earth at that time who actually knew Jesus' true identity. Under
any circumstances, his death would have been a great loss. But he didn't die under just any
circumstances. He was killed for a disgusting reason, and in the most despicable way.

Initially, Jesus did what most of us would want to do. He withdrew to an isolated place. He
wanted some time to deal with what had happened. He sought some time alone.

But when the people followed Him and found Him, He didn't send them away. His love
for them prevailed over His personal pain. Compassion rose up within Him like a tidal wave,
swept away all self-interest, and moved Him to minister to the people.

Do you want to know what kind of love is within you? Don't look at your pitiful past. Look
at powerful love of your LORD. Look at how that love prevailed even in times of personal pain.
That's the kind of love that abides in you.

Stronger Than Death

"And it came to pass the day after, that he went into a city called Nain; and many of his disciples went with him, and much people. Now when he came nigh to the gate of the city, behold, there was a dead man carried out, the only son of his mother, and she was a widow: and much people of the city was with her. And when The LORD saw her, he had compassion on her, and said unto her, Weep not. And he came and touched the bier: and they that bare him stood still. And he said, Young man, I say unto thee, Arise. And he that was dead sat up, and began to speak. And he delivered him to his mother."

Luke 7:11-15

The compassion of Almighty God is the strongest force in the universe. It is literally stronger than death. Compassion reaches out with the very resurrection power of God and answers the cry of a person's heart. Compassion shoves aside the fact that they have no faith for THE BLESSING themselves, and gets it to them anyway.

Compassion drove Jesus to sail through a storm and go to the place of the tombs, where a demon-possessed man was crying out and cutting himself with stones. Compassion empowered Him to deliver that man even though he was incapable of asking for that deliverance.

Compassion moved Jesus to take the little woman caught in adultery out of the hands of her accusers, and stand there by her side for everyone to see, until every person left and only the two of them were standing there. In compassion, He forgave her, even though she was expecting condemnation. Compassion delivered her, even though she was expecting to be stoned to death.

When the widow of Nain was weeping behind the coffin of her only son, compassion moved Jesus to walk over to it, raise that boy from the dead and give him back to his mother. She wasn't asking for God's help. She probably didn't even know He *could* help her. But Jesus couldn't bear to let that situation go. That crying momma touched His heart. Her pain hit Him so hard that He barged into that funeral, totally uninvited, and put a stop to it. He jerked that boy back from death and then took his momma by the arm and said, "Now, don't cry anymore."

Where is that kind of compassion now, when the world needs it most? It's still here. It's in you. It's in me. It's in every believer on the face of the earth.

First John 4:17 says that as Jesus is, so are we in this world. Let's dare to believe it and let His compassion move again through us.

LIMITLESS**LOVE**

A Divine Generator of Love

"But as many as received Him [Jesus], to them He gave the right to become children of God, even to those who believe in His name, who were born, not of blood nor of the will of the flesh nor of the will of man, but of God." John 1:12-13, *New American Standard*

Sometimes believers find it hard to believe that the same love that flows through Jesus is flowing through them. "That's not possible!" they say. "At best, all I could ever have is a pale imitation of His love."

They think they're being humble when they say that, but in reality, the very idea that we could come up with even a pale imitation of God's love is actually quite arrogant. Nothing that we could conjure up in our own, human strength could ever be compared to the love of God. If we have any real love in our lives at all, it comes from Him. It is Jesus' very own love.

Think about the new birth, and you'll understand why that's true. When we made Jesus The LORD of our lives, God raised us from spiritual death by giving us His own life. Old things passed away, and God made us new by putting Himself inside us. That process is sometimes called *regeneration.*

I like that word because it so accurately describes what happened to us. When we were born again, we were joined to God Himself, and He became our generator. His light and His life began to flow through us.

That doesn't mean we're equal with Him. It doesn't mean we are the Sovereign God. It means we're connected to Him. His very life, love and power are in us. We're not the originators of them, but they're in us nonetheless.

Think about the electrical outlet on your wall, and you'll see what I mean. That outlet has power in it, doesn't it? The power doesn't originate there. It originates across town at the power plant, but the power generated by that plant—the very same power, not an imitation of it—is present in the outlet. How much power is there? However much you need. If you keep using it, it will keep flowing. You won't run out of power unless that plant runs out of power (or your connection to it is broken). You'll have all that you need to do what you want to do.

With that illustration, it's easy to see that when we hook up by faith to Jesus, we hook up to all He is. We suddenly have the capacity not just to love *like* He loves but to love *with His love!* We can have as much of it as we believe for, and as much as we need. As long as we keep drawing on it, that love will keep flowing through us!

LIMITLESS**LOVE**

Jesus Will Finish the Work

"Wherefore seeing we also are compassed about with so great a cloud of witnesses, let us lay aside every weight, and the sin which doth so easily beset us, and let us run with patience the race that is set before us, looking unto Jesus the author and finisher of our faith…."
Hebrews 12:1-2

Faith works by love. That's an important scriptural truth. But, did you know that the reverse is also true? Love works by faith. The more we hook up with Jesus by faith, putting trust and confidence in who He is within us, the more fully we'll walk in love.

Fellowshiping with Jesus every day, just walking and talking with Him, will increase the flow of His love in our lives. Why is that? It's because He is the Author and the *Finisher* of our faith (Hebrews 12:2.). The word *finisher* refers to someone who brings something to perfection or to completion. In carpentry, for example, the logger who cuts a tree down might begin a woodworking project. But, the finisher is the craftsman skilled enough to develop that wood and bring it to completion. He's the man who knows, for example, how to turn that rough piece of wood into a fine and beautiful piano.

Spiritually, Jesus is both our Author and our Finisher. He started this work of faith and love within us, and He will bring it to completion. The more time we spend in communion with Him—not just during special times of private prayer, but all day long during the normal affairs of life—the more He can develop us in Him.

He can bring us to the place where we're not only like Him on the inside, we're walking and talking like Him on the outside.

"Oh, Brother Copeland," someone might say, "surely you're not implying we could ever be like Jesus."

No, I'm not implying it. I'm saying it plainly. We were born again in His image and as we walk with Him and let Him teach, train and help us grow up, we begin to look and act just like Him.

Years ago, I was told about someone who was upset with a preacher who had become a friend of mine. They said, "That fellow is ruined now. He's started hanging around with that Copeland fellow, and they're both running around acting like a little Jesus!"

Actually, I was BLESSED by those comments, because that's my goal—to be like Jesus. To think, live and love like Him.

Jesus Himself told us to love one another just as He loves us (John 13:34). If He said that, it means we have the capacity to do it. We might not look like we do right now—especially if we're just beginning our life with Him. We might look as rough as a log that's just been dragged out of the forest. But if we'll just keep walking by faith with Jesus and stick close to Him, He'll finish the work He began in us. He'll turn us into a finely tuned instrument of His love.

Just Like Your Dad

"...Be a worthy steward and a good minister of Christ Jesus,
ever nourishing your own self on the truths of the faith and of the
good [Christian] instruction which you have closely followed....
Train yourself toward godliness (piety), [keeping yourself spiritually fit]."
1 Timothy 4:6-7, *The Amplified Bible*

When you were born again, you became a child of God. That's a fact you probably take for granted. But have you ever stopped to think about what that actually means?

A child is born in the image of his parents. If he is born healthy and whole, even at birth, he has all the physical parts his parents have. When my son, John, was just a tiny boy, I could stand him up beside me and you could see that we were basically alike. He had all the same muscles and organs that I had. He had every bone in his body that I had in mine. Nothing was missing. He had my skin color and my eyes. You could look at him and see where he came from. You could see that he was my son.

Of course, he was smaller than I was. He had a lot of growing up to do. I was a big man and he was a little man. But in many ways you could already see how he was going to turn out. You could see what he was going to be, just by looking at me.

The same thing could be said spiritually about you and your heavenly Father. You are born of Him. You have within you all the elements He has within Him. You could even say this: Because He is Love, you are Love. You're not as well-developed in it as He is. You're not as mature or strong, but if you'll just keep growing up, and allowing Him to teach and train you, you'll end up loving just like He does, because you were born again with His capacity for love. You're born to be just like your Dad.

Remind yourself of that next time you feel weak or wobbly in your love walk. Instead of condemning yourself and getting discouraged over your inadequacy, look away from yourself and look to Jesus. Fill the eyes of your heart with Him, and rejoice that what He already is, you are ultimately destined to be.

Then, focus your energy on growing up in Him. How? By doing the same things for your spirit that you do to help your body grow. Feed yourself! Nourish your heart on the truths of the faith. Spend time reading and meditating on The WORD of God. Then make sure you get plenty of exercise. Build your spiritual strength by stepping out on what you're learning. Practice love. Exercise it at every opportunity, and you will surely grow!

A Life-Changing Revelation

"May you be rooted deep in love and founded securely on love, that you may have the power and be strong to apprehend and grasp with all the saints [God's devoted people, the experience of that love] what is the breadth and length and height and depth [of it]."

Ephesians 3:17-18, *The Amplified Bible*

There are some scriptural prayers you can pray that will help you grow stronger in love. One of them is this prayer recorded by the Apostle Paul in Ephesians 3. You'd do well to pray it for yourself as often as the Holy Spirit brings it to mind.

"But why should I pray about love?" you might ask. "I thought the Bible said I already have the love of God shed abroad in my heart!"

You do, but that doesn't mean you're operating in it in fullness. It doesn't mean it is automatically going to flow abundantly out of you. Even though God's love abides within you, you may not be rooted and founded securely on it. You may not have much comprehension of its depth and its power.

Those things come by revelation of the Holy Spirit. He can so illuminate the love of God in your heart that you begin to see and experience it as you never have before. Ephesians 3:19 says He can make you know that love in a way that surpasses mental understanding.

It refers to something discovered through personal encounter and living contact. It refers to the kind of intimate relationship that makes two people one.

When we begin to have that kind of revelation of the love of God, it will change everything about our lives. Love won't be just an action we take anymore; it will be the very fabric of our hearts and lives. We'll become one not just with God but with each other or, as Paul put it, with all the saints. Our hearts will be knit together in Christ Jesus.

I won't care what denomination you are from, and you won't care what denomination I am from. The bond of love between us will make that irrelevant. The same love that makes us committed to Jesus and willing to lay down our lives for Him will make us committed and willing to lay down our lives for each other.

Suddenly, biblical concepts like prosperity won't mean to us what they used to mean. Prosperity, for example, won't mean having enough to meet our own needs. It will mean having enough to meet each other's needs. That's the kind of grace and Holy Ghost revelation of love that came to the early Church, and caused them to sell their belongings and give so that none would be in lack. If we'll pray and keep growing in love, it is a revelation that will surely come to us again.

LIMITLESS**LOVE**

LORD, Don't You Love Me Anymore?

"My brethren, count it all joy when ye fall into divers temptations; knowing this, that the trying of your faith worketh patience. But let patience have her perfect work, that ye may be perfect and entire, wanting nothing."
James 1:2-4

Do you ever feel like things came more easily when you first became a believer? Does it ever seem as if God was more attentive to you back then? If so, you shouldn't be surprised. Most of us who have been walking with The LORD for a few years have found that to be true.

In the early days of our Christian walk, if we got sick, we could go the pastor, ask for prayer and we'd be instantly healed. We could beg God for help when we ran out of money and, without standing on one single scripture, The LORD would swoop in and take care of our need.

But as we grew a little, things began to change. What used to come instantly and easily takes a little longer and requires more spiritual effort. It sometimes seems as if God doesn't care as much about our needs. "LORD?" we want to ask, "don't You love me anymore?"

Certainly He loves us! He loves us so much that He is making us grow up. He's allowing us to stretch and strengthen our spiritual muscles. He is requiring us to stand on The WORD and develop in our faith. He loves us too much to pamper and protect us all our lives from every difficulty and every challenge. He is committed to help us grow up, to become perfect and complete, lacking nothing.

Think about what happens in the life of a child, naturally speaking, and you'll quickly see what I mean. When a baby is first born, his mother and father do everything for that child. They require nothing from him. When the baby makes a noise, Momma's foot hits the floor and she comes running to meet his need. When the baby cries for help—whether the danger is real or imagined—Daddy picks him up instantly and says, "Don't worry. Daddy won't let anyone hurt you."

But come back to that house in 15 years and you'll find a very different picture. If that child is lying on the couch watching television, and cries out to his mother to get him a drink, she won't even move. She'll just answer, "Get up and get it yourself, if you're thirsty, son." Will she say that because she doesn't care? No, she'll say it because she *does* care. She'll say it because she knows its time for that boy to grow up!

Let that be a comfort to you next time you have to stand in faith a while to receive something from God. Let it encourage you next time you face a challenge, and instead of lifting you out of it, God requires you to walk through to victory by His strength, but on your own spiritual feet. Remember that doesn't mean He loves you less. It means He loves you enough to help you grow into all He has made you to be.

LIMITLESS**LOVE**

As for Me...

"Now when Abram was ninety-nine years old, The LORD appeared to Abram and said to him, 'I am God Almighty; walk before Me, and be blameless. I will establish My covenant between Me and you, and I will multiply you exceedingly.' Abram fell on his face, and God talked with him, saying, 'As for Me, behold, My covenant is with you....'"
Genesis 17:1-4, *New American Standard*

The blood-covenant commitment God made to Abraham is the best Old Testament picture we have of the true *agape* kind of love. There we see God, by an act of His will, making a blood-sworn oath to Abraham to BLESS him, care for him and be all he needed Him to be.

God didn't wait to see if Abraham was going to love Him in return before He made the commitment. He didn't say, "If I keep having warm feelings toward you, Abraham, I'll keep acting in love toward you. But if you aggravate Me and take Me for granted, I'm walking out on you."

No, God made His choice to love and commit Himself to Abraham, regardless of what Abraham chose to do. Abraham could either receive His love or reject it. He could take God up on His commitment or turn away. But on God's part, the decision was already made. He said, *As for Me, behold, My covenant is with you.*

God loves us the very same way. He determined to love us before we ever decided whether or not we would respond to His love. He sent Jesus to the cross as the most precious blood-covenant sacrifice ever made…while we were yet sinners. He didn't wait to see what we would do. He went ahead and made the commitment to love. He said, *As for Me, behold, My covenant is with you.*

Now that we've received His love, He expects us to love each other the same way. In fact, He commands us to do it. He commands us to make the same decision He did. He desires that we commit ourselves to others in the Body of Christ regardless of how they respond to us, to love them when they appreciate it and when they don't. He expects us to honor the covenant blood of Jesus with the same unconditional love for others that He has given us. He expects us to say to them, "No matter how you act, no matter what you do, as for me, I'm in covenant with you."

How do you walk in that kind of love? You do it by making a decision. You do it by an act of your will. Of course, you don't love by your own will or your own strength. You simply use your will to open the door to God's love that abides within you. When you make the decision and open the door, His own mighty covenant love comes pouring through.

LIMITLESS**LOVE**

Debate...or Deliverance?

"And he was teaching in one of the synagogues on the sabbath. And, behold, there was a woman which had a spirit of infirmity eighteen years, and was bowed together, and could in no wise lift up herself. And when Jesus saw her, he called her to him, and said unto her, Woman, thou art loosed from thine infirmity. And he laid his hands on her: and immediately she was made straight, and glorified God. And the ruler of the synagogue answered with indignation, because that Jesus had healed on the sabbath day, and said unto the people, There are six days in which men ought to work: in them therefore come and be healed, and not on the sabbath day."

Luke 13:10-14

Love is more interested in meeting someone's need than in analyzing the theology behind it. Love is more interested in helping to solve someone's problem than in figuring out who is to blame for it.

I've heard great spiritual debates about whether a demon can oppress the spirit of a Christian or just his soul and body. There have been untold hours spent discussing that question, while believers suffering demonic torment went without help.

When a believer is bound by a devil, who cares where it is? It could be in his pocket for all that matters! What counts is getting that brother delivered. What matters is getting him free.

Maybe you're not theologically inclined to debate over demons. But we all fall prey to the Pharisee mentality in our own way. How often have you found yourself with another believer discussing what's wrong with Sister So-and-So? How often have you been involved in conversations where critical things were said about other people in the church?

"Well, that woman needs to pay more attention to her children! Have you seen how she dresses them? She doesn't even comb their hair before they come to church! Of course I'm not saying that to be critical, you understand. It's just that I care about those kids."

The fact is, if we really care about those children, we'll be reaching out in kindness to that mother instead of talking about her. We'll be praying for her and going to visit her to see how we can lend a hand. We'll be digging into our own pocket and buying those children some new clothes if they need them. Instead of being so upset over that mother's failure to live up to our religious standards, we'll be lifting her up...encouraging her...and honoring her (in spite of her shortcomings) as a child of the Most High God.

We'll do whatever it takes to loose her from her difficulties and let her go. That's what love always does.

LIMITLESS**LOVE**

Reawaken the Compassion Within

"But whoso hath this world's good, and seeth his brother have need, and shutteth up his bowels of compassion from him, how dwelleth the love of God in him? My little children, let us not love in word, neither in tongue; but in deed and in truth."
1 John 3:17-18

When a believer is unloving and indifferent to the needs of people around him, it's because sometime in his life he shut the door of his heart, and refused to release the compassion of God. He may have been afraid that if he reached out to someone in love the way he wanted to, he would be hurt or rejected. He may have shut the door because he was afraid those he gave to would take advantage of his compassion, and deplete his resources by asking him to give again and again.

All of us have dealt with those fears at one time or another. If we keep walking with God and reading The WORD, however, we eventually learn those fears are unfounded. After all, God promised that if we gave it would be given to us again—good measure, pressed down and shaken together. He promised if we'd just keep loving and giving and putting His kingdom first, everything else we needed would be added to us, as well!

The problem for many of us is that by the time we learn those things, we've kept God's love locked up within us for so long we can hardly even sense it's there. The mercy flow of God, once so strong we had to work to resist it, doesn't stir our hearts anymore.

If you ever find yourself in that condition, one of the best ways to reawaken the compassion of God within you is by giving to someone in need. If you aren't in the habit of doing that, the idea may not excite you much at first. Your inactivity in that area may have caused you to grow so spiritually cold and insensitive, you may not even be aware of those in need around you. You may have to make a determined effort to seek them out.

I can assure you, however, that once you do it, something wonderful will start to happen inside you. As you step out in love through an act of giving, you'll sense a deep, inner yearning beginning to rise within you. You'll find you have reawakened the compassion of God that was lying dormant in your heart.

You'll immediately want to give again. When you do give, your desire to do it again will increase even more. After you've acted on that desire a few times, you will be amazed at the drive you have to give. The river of God's compassion will not only abide, it will *abound* in you. The more you yield to it, the more forcefully it will flow. I can tell you from experience, it will bring you such joy that you'll never shut the door on it again!

Watch Out for the Foxes

"Take us the foxes, the little foxes, that spoil the vines...."
Song of Solomon 2:15

When we talk about walking in love, all too often we think about doing it in only major, world-changing ways. We think about what we can do to help the poor in our city...or what we can do to be more loving toward the people at church. But real love starts at home, and it is expressed in small, seemingly insignificant ways.

Real love, for example, will make Mom throw away that old, faded, ugly bathrobe with the holes in it that she's been wearing to breakfast every morning for the past 10 years. It may be her personal favorite. She may think it's the most comfortable thing around. But love will cause her to think about how that dumpy robe is affecting everyone else. Love will make her realize they're praying she'll make a dishrag out of it, and show up one day in something clean and new. Love will make her want to be a BLESSING—even first thing in the morning—to her husband and her children.

Real love will wake up Dad to the fact that his family would appreciate it if he'd put on something other than that old undershirt with the hole in it on Saturday. Even though it is his day off, love will make him want to dress as though the people at home matter as much as the people at the office. Sure, he can be casual and relaxed, but love will help him do it in a way that shows his family a little respect.

When it's time to wake up the kids for school, love will convince Mom and Dad to come up with a kinder, more gentle way to do it than by just sticking their head in the door and shouting, "Get up!" Love will keep them from starting in on the children first thing in the morning with criticism and correction. Love will find a way to help them start out feeling good about themselves and their day.

Love will smooth over little troubles and mistakes and, by adding words of kindness and understanding, will keep them from turning into major traumas. When someone knocks over a glass of milk, love won't act as if it's a federal offense. When someone loses their lunch money, love won't make the offender feel like a loser for life.

Instead of letting the little foxes of selfishness and irritation spoil the family vine, love will cover and protect it. Love will take every opportunity to nurture and cultivate those who are nearest and dearest. Love will make home a safe and peaceful refuge for every member of the family. Love will make home a heavenly place to be.

LIMITLESS**LOVE**

The Conquering Lambs of Love

"Who shall separate us from the love of Christ? shall tribulation,
or distress, or persecution, or famine, or nakedness, or peril, or sword?
As it is written, For thy sake we are killed all the day long; we are
accounted as sheep for the slaughter. Nay, in all these things
we are more than conquerors through him that loved us."
Romans 8:35-37

There are times when it will seem to your natural mind that if you walk in love, others will take advantage of you. It will seem that loving those who hate and mistreat you will make you a victim. But walking in the love of God will never make you a victim. It will make you a victor every single time.

One of the best modern-day examples I've ever seen of a man who walks in the power of love is my good friend, Johnny Johnson. A black man who was raised in the midst of racial prejudice in the Deep South, Johnny's father taught him when he was just a child to be merciful toward the children who mistreated him. "Their brains overheat in the sunshine because of their white skin, Johnny," he said. "They don't have black skin to protect them like you do, so you need to be kind to them and help them."

Johnny took his dad at his word and treated his persecutors with such kindness that he won them over and became one of the most popular boys in his school. By the time he realized that his father's words weren't literally true, he'd already learned the lesson behind them. Love overcame hostility. Love was beyond defeat.

When Johnny Johnson joined the U.S. Marine Corps, that understanding carried him to unprecedented success...and it kept him gracious once he achieved it. He tells of a time after he became Secretary of the Navy when a white admiral failed to recognize him, even after Johnny introduced himself by name. The admiral simply couldn't believe a black man could hold that post.

Instead of taking offense and making that man's life miserable (which he could have easily done), Johnny overlooked it and treated him with such respect and love that within days, the admiral was on his knees asking Johnny's forgiveness. Of course, Johnny forgave him and led him to The LORD right there.

Some people would have said that for a black man to allow a white man of lesser rank to get away with such disrespect was weakness. Some would have said it made Johnny the victim of prejudice. But in the end, because Johnny Johnson walked in love, he wasn't the victim of anything. He was a victor who overcame the evil of prejudice with love. While others accounted him as a sheep for the slaughter, he followed the footsteps of his Master and become a conquering lamb of love.

LIMITLESS**LOVE**

God's Fail-Safe Plan

"Because thou hast made The LORD, which is my refuge, even the most High, thy habitation; there shall no evil befall thee, neither shall any plague come nigh thy dwelling. For he shall give his angels charge over thee, to keep thee in all thy ways. They shall bear thee up in their hands, lest thou dash thy foot against a stone. Thou shalt tread upon the lion and adder: the young lion and the dragon shalt thou trample under feet. Because he hath set his love upon me, therefore will I deliver him: I will set him on high, because he hath known my name. He shall call upon me, and I will answer him: I will be with him in trouble; I will deliver him, and honour him. With long life will I satisfy him, and show him my salvation."
Psalm 91:9-16

We often think of Psalm 91 as the description of divine protection guaranteed to those who live by faith in God. But it is also a description of the safeguards provided for those who walk in love. Since God is Love, the person who dwells in God is one who dwells in love. He is a man who has set his love upon God and who walks in love toward his brothers (1 John 5:1).

God promises the person who abides in love an absolutely fail-safe plan of protection. I first learned about fail-safe technology through my training as a pilot. One particular jet airplane I was type-rated to fly, for example, had a fail-safe mechanism built into its fuel system. It was designed in such a way that if the valve that directed the fuel to various parts of the engine were to fail, it would fail open. It would never fail shut. The system guaranteed you wouldn't find yourself in that airplane at 40,000 feet with the fuel to your engines cut off.

It didn't guarantee the valve would never fail. But it did ensure that failure would not be fatal. Even if something went wrong, you would still be protected.

That's what walking in the love of God will do for us. It will protect us from our own failures and mistakes. It will provide perfect protection for us, even though we ourselves aren't yet perfected.

When we find ourselves in situations where we don't know what to do, if we'll follow the path of love, we'll be all right. When danger threatens all around and circumstances overwhelm us, if we'll just trust the love of God for us and walk in love toward others, we can rest assured that everything will turn out all right.

When we walk in love, we walk with angels at our side and the devil under our feet. Even when the world is shaking around us and every natural guarantee is giving way, love will be a refuge that never fails.

When THE BLESSING Overtakes You

"Now it shall be, if you diligently obey The LORD your God, being careful to do all His commandments which I command you today, The LORD your God will set you high above all the nations of the earth. All these blessings will come upon you and overtake you if you obey The LORD your God."
Deuteronomy 28:1-2, *New American Standard*

When we keep God's commandment of love, we don't have to run after THE BLESSING. THE BLESSING will run after us! While we're busy seeking God—finding out what He wants us to do…who He wants us to pray for and encourage…where He wants us to give of ourselves and our resources—THE BLESSING will literally come upon us and overtake us.

I can tell you from experience, letting THE BLESSING overtake you is the best way to increase. It's better than the increase you struggle and strive for, because THE BLESSING God sends on you is far beyond anything you'd ever dream up for yourself.

Gloria and I began to understand the magnitude of that fact years ago when The LORD began BLESSING us with some outstanding automobiles. We hadn't been using our faith for expensive cars. I was driving a perfectly good pickup truck at the time and enjoying it. But during one of our meetings, a fellow walked up to me and handed me the keys to a brand-new Mercedes-Benz. I appreciated it, but I couldn't figure out how I ended up with it. I hadn't prayed for it. I never made one confession about it. Yet there it was.

If that weren't enough, when we got home from those same meetings, there was another one sitting in my driveway. Suddenly, my cars were worth more than my house! It so surprised me that I talked to The LORD about it. "What's going on here?" I asked.

He reminded me of all the vehicles I had given away. (When Gloria and I figured it up, we realized we'd given away something like 17 cars, seven trucks and seven airplanes at that time.) He said, *You obeyed My command. You did what I asked you to do in the area of giving and My BLESSING overtook you. So enjoy it!*

I hadn't been counting up those vehicles as I gave them away. I hadn't been in God's face saying, "Now, I've sown all these cars and trucks as seeds, so You'd better see to it that I get a harvest." No, I never even gave that a thought. I just expected Him to meet my needs according to His riches in glory.

I figured how He chose to do it was His business—not mine. My business is loving people. My business is sharing The WORD, taking care of the Body of Christ and winning souls to Jesus. If I tend to that business, I will always walk in THE BLESSING.

LIMITLESS**LOVE**

Get Some Satisfaction

"God is love…. Whosoever is born of God doth not commit sin; for his seed remaineth in him: and he cannot sin, because he is born of God."
1 John 4:8, 3:9

When we live the life of love, we live a sin-free life. Not because we're incapable of sin, but because love drives out all desire for it. Sin is selfish. It gratifies no one but us, and it always hurts someone. Even sins that no other human being knows about grieve the Holy Spirit. So every kind of sin violates the heart of love.

People who try to keep religious commandments just to be right always end up in sin. They end up doing the very thing they're trying not to do. That's because they're still caught in the cycle of selfishness, and in that cycle, sin provides the only satisfaction they can get.

When we're walking in love, however, we get no thrill out of self-gratification. We find no satisfaction there. Love gets gratification from giving. The more you walk in love the more addicted you become to doing good for others. You actually get hooked on BLESSING them!

First Corinthians 16:15 tells of a group of believers who walked in love so much they actually "addicted themselves to the ministry of the saints"! I understand that. The most gratifying moments of my life have been when the compassion of God was flowing through me in the strongest degree.

I remember one meeting when the Holy Spirit moved on me to minister to people with AIDS. The love of God was so strong in my heart, it wasn't enough for me just to pray for them. I ended up putting my arms around each one and hugging them—even though several of them didn't look very huggable! Later we heard from one who called to ask for a tape of the service and to tell us he was totally healed.

I think of times when the compassion of God hit me as it did the day I stood by the bedside of a delirious woman whose eyes were blinded and whose legs were full of gangrene because of diabetes. The love of God roared through me like a freight train and before I knew what I was doing, I was shouting at that disease, commanding it to go in the Name of Jesus. As I stood there, I watched her legs begin to turn from deadly black to healthy pink. I had the privilege of witnessing her blinded eyes once again begin to see.

I'd rather have five minutes operating in the compassion and Anointing of God than be the wealthiest man in the world. And, I wouldn't give up a second of it for some stupid sin. It isn't worth it. After all, what does sin have to offer? If you're born of God, walking in love provides the only real satisfaction there is.

LIMITLESS**LOVE**

Be Totally Carefree!

"Be anxious for nothing, but in everything by prayer and supplication
with thanksgiving let your requests be made known to God. And the
peace of God, which surpasses all comprehension, will guard your
hearts and your minds in Christ Jesus."
Philippians 4:6-7, *New American Standard*

Once you begin to walk in love—trusting God's love for you and giving that love to others—you'll have the most wonderfully peaceful life you can imagine. You'll be totally free from fear and worry. When a care comes to your mind, you can roll it over on The LORD, knowing that He cares for you.

That's the way you and I were divinely designed to live. Our minds weren't created to deal with the pressure of figuring out how to protect ourselves from every possible situation. Our bodies weren't designed to handle the stress caused by anger, frustration and fear. Those things will kill us. We break down under the strain of them because we weren't made to live that way.

We were made to live in an atmosphere of love. But, staying in that atmosphere takes practice. We have to practice casting our cares on The LORD, and then we must discipline ourselves to keep from going back and picking them up again. We have to take authority over our minds and refuse to touch those cares with our thought lives anymore.

I heard a story about one strong man of faith who was faced with a handful of bills he had no money to pay. He'd already committed the matter to The LORD, so when someone picked up those bills, waved them in his face, and asked what he was going to do about them, he didn't even flinch. He just picked them up, threw them in the air and said, "I've already rolled that care over on The LORD." Then he walked off.

The man was a minister who spent his life loving and serving people. He had faith in God's love, so he acted on that faith. Sure enough, a few hours later those bills were paid.

Some might say that's irresponsible, but it's not. Walking in love and trusting God is the most responsible thing you can do.

"Yeah, but Brother Copeland," you might say, "don't we have to be sure we're doing the right thing in the situation?"

Love *is* the right thing. If you're walking in it, you will make the wisest possible decisions. You'll bring the power of God to bear on the situation. And, by trusting God's love, you'll keep the door of faith open for Him to work.

Why walk the floor and worry, when you can walk in love and be carefree? Once you do it, you'll see it's the most wonderful way to live!

Put Fear on the Run

"And it shall be, when ye are come nigh unto the battle, that the priest shall approach and speak unto the people, and shall say unto them, Hear, O Israel, ye approach this day unto battle against your enemies: let not your hearts faint, fear not, and do not tremble, neither be ye terrified because of them; For The LORD your God is he that goeth with you, to fight for you against your enemies, to save you."
Deuteronomy 20:2-4

The Bible clearly tells us that perfect love casts out all fear. But, even when you're walking in love, fear won't necessarily go without a fight. Just as we have to resist everything else the devil would try to force on us, fear has to be vigorously resisted. When it rears its head, we must refuse it and cast it out of our lives.

If you study the Greek phrase translated *cast out* you'll find it carries the idea of powerful movement, of "throwing" or "propelling,"[12] Love doesn't just show fear the door, it throws fear out on its ear!

Why does love cause us to treat fear like that? Because fear flies in the face of the God we love. Fear calls Him a liar and says, "God isn't going to protect you in this situation. You can't trust Him to care for you."

What would you do if someone came into your house, and said those kinds of things about your husband or your wife? How would you respond to such insults? If you had any courage, you'd throw them out of your house!

That's what we have to do with fear. We throw it out of our lives. We stop using fear to express ourselves. We stop talking about it like it's a normal thing. Instead, we rebuke it. We stand against it with The WORD of God. And we absolutely refuse to act on it.

When she was a young child, Lyndsey, one of my granddaughters, contracted a deadly kind of meningitis. By the time my daughter, Kellie, got her to the hospital, Lyndsey was already delirious and slipping into unconsciousness. The doctors told Kellie that several children had recently died at that hospital from that same disease, and that Lyndsey most likely would die, too. If she lived, they said, she would most certainly suffer brain damage, hearing loss and various other terrible effects.

Every parent knows the kind of fear that attacks at times like that. It comes with a vengeance to rob us of our faith and steal our victory. But Kellie loved Lyndsey too much to give in to it. She was not about to trade the faith she needed to stand on The WORD for her daughter's life, to indulge in a few minutes of fear.

Instead of crying, wringing her hands, saying, "Dear heavens, Lyndsey's going to die. What are we going to do?" Kellie stood up right in the midst of that mess and declared, "I WILL NOT FEAR!"

When she did, the power of God backed up her decision, and she, along with our family and friends, fought the good fight of faith and won. As a result, Lyndsey is alive and well today. Love won the victory and put fear on the run!

---

[12] *Theological Dictionary of the New Testament.* 1964-c1976. Vols. 5-9 edited by Gerhard Friedrich. Vol. 10, compiled by Ronald Pitkin, G. Kittel, G. W. Bromiley & G. Friedrich, Ed. (Grand Rapids, MI: Eerdmans), Vol. 1, p. 526.

A Revival the Devil Can't Stop

"For by one Spirit are we all baptized into one body, whether we be Jews or Gentiles, whether we be bond or free; and have been all made to drink into one Spirit. For the body is not one member, but many.... But now hath God set the members every one of them in the body, as it hath pleased him."
1 Corinthians 12:13-14, 18

You might think it would take some terrible, carnal sin to push believers out of love with each other. You'd think the devil would have to get them to steal from each other or lie to each other to get them out of love and into strife. But that's not usually the case. Usually, the devil succeeds in dividing us over seemingly spiritual things.

He'll convince us to break fellowship with someone, for example, just because they left the church we go to and joined up with a church across town. Even though they were trying to follow the leading of The LORD, all too often we get upset about it, decide they are wrong and get into strife with them. Even if they *are* wrong (and it's arrogant to presume we know better than they do what The LORD is leading them to do), we're doubly wrong if we take offense and stop treating them with love. We play right into the devil's hands.

It's time we stopped that kind of thing. Instead of giving the cold shoulder to someone who left our church and went to another, we ought to call them on Sunday afternoon and say, "Hey, what did you learn at your church today? Did you have a wonderful service?"

We ought to keep sharing with each other and letting the expansion enhance our love for one another, instead of diminishing it. We should go out to dinner together, invite the pastors of both churches and just have a great time in The LORD, loving and learning from each other!

That might sound strange to you, but God is increasing the love in the Body of Christ. We're coming to the place where we'll let God be God and allow Him to set each member in the Body according to His will, instead of demanding He do it according to our will. We're coming to the place where we love each other too much to let those kinds of things separate us.

As we do, we're going to give the devil more trouble than he's ever had before. He's going to be totally unable to stop us, because He has no defense against the power of love. Love conquers him every time. Love never fails.

When we start walking in love and refuse to be drawn out of it, we'll start a revival that he can't stop. We'll loose the move of God that will sweep this earth and then sweep the Church out of here and into the Rapture. We'll love each other right into the marriage supper of the Lamb!

LIMITLESS**LOVE**

Like No One Else Can

"To all in Rome who are loved by God and called to be saints: Grace and peace to you from God our Father and from The LORD Jesus Christ."
Romans 1:7, *New International Version-84*

Have you ever been discouraged by your own failures? Have you ever tripped over your inadequacies and shortcomings so many times, you are sick of yourself? That's when you need to stop and think about how much God loves you. You need to close your eyes and say, "I am a dearly beloved child of God."

Your mind might argue with you. It might interrupt your meditations and say, *How can you even think that, you ugly thing! You are always making messes He has to clean up. You are forever pestering Him to give you something. Why would God ever love a mess like you?*

I can tell you why He loves you—because He is your Father. He has within Him the kind of love for you only a father or a mother has. He has an inner drive to meet your needs. He sees in you His very own image and delights so much in who you are that He is willing and eager to do whatever it takes to help you grow up.

Think about the love of a natural parent, and you can easily understand that. The Bible says we get the similitude of our parenthood from God, and everyone knows there's just something about a newborn baby that makes his parents love him. They may not have even wanted to have a baby nine months before, but when they take that little fellow in their arms, they fall in love with him. Suddenly, all the pain, all the money it's going to cost them to raise him, all the sleepless nights they'll have to endure, seem like nothing in comparison to the worth of this dearly beloved child.

In the days to come, they'll comfort him countless times when he cries. They'll change myriads of diapers, wash piles of extra laundry because the baby spits up on *everyone's* clothes. But, all that will be wiped out when those tiny hands reach out for them. Their hearts will melt with love and they'll say, "Isn't he beautiful?! Isn't he the most precious baby you've ever seen?!"

That's the kind of love your heavenly Father has for you. The reason your heart reaches out to Him and says, "Abba! Father!" is because His heart reached out to you first and said, "Beloved child of My heart! I loved you so much I sent Jesus. I love you so much I'll never forsake you. I'll be with you always—even to the end of the world."

Sometimes, it's hard to receive that kind of love when you've failed or fallen. But that's when you need it most. That's when you need to run to the One who loves you like no one else can.

Only God Could Think of That!

"For my thoughts are not your thoughts, neither are your ways my ways, saith The LORD. For as the heavens are higher than the earth, so are my ways higher than your ways, and my thoughts than your thoughts."
Isaiah 55:8-9

God's ways of love are so much higher than our ways that on our own, we'd never think of them. We have to tune our hearts to His voice and listen to what He has to say. We can only walk in love by doing what He tells us to do.

Once, I was out mowing my lawn. The LORD told me that when I was finished, He wanted me to mow my neighbor's. Initially, I wasn't too excited about that, first of all, because mowing the lawn is not something I like to do. If Gloria would let me, I'd pour cement all over the yard and paint it green, so I'd never have to mow again.

Secondly, I wasn't sure my neighbor would appreciate my mowing his lawn. I didn't even know him. He might think I was insulting him and acting like he didn't do a good job mowing it himself. Try as I might, however, I couldn't talk The LORD out of the idea. (That's always pointless. You might as well do what He tells you to do without murmuring and disputing because He never changes. After you've finished whining, He'll still be there telling you to do what He originally told you to do.) So I obeyed Him and started mowing.

As I stepped onto my neighbor's lawn, The LORD said, *Now as you walk around this property, I want you to do like I told Abraham to do and claim the ground everywhere you walk. Claim it for Jesus.* I would have never thought of that on my own, but I jumped on it quickly. I actually had a good time praying and mowing that afternoon.

As it turned out, the neighbors weren't even home. They were out of town, and the grass grew back before they got back, so they never even knew what I did. But a few weeks later, a little blond lady knocked on our door and started witnessing to us with such excitement I thought she was going to come apart. "Oh, I have to tell you about Jesus!" she said. "He loves you! He'll save you!"

Do you know who it was? The lady who lived next door! It turned out that a week or two after I mowed that lawn, the whole family went to a lay-witness retreat and got born again! Our families got acquainted, got to loving one another and not long afterward, she came over again and asked if our children could help her start a Bible study for the neighborhood kids. They got kids from all over the neighborhood saved…on the ground that was claimed for Jesus while I was mowing their lawn. Who but God could ever have thought of that?

Plant the Seed

*"And He said to them, Be careful what you are hearing.
The measure [of thought and study] you give [to the truth you hear]
will be the measure [of virtue and knowledge] that comes back to you—
and more [besides] will be given to you who hear."*
Mark 4:24, *The Amplified Bible*

A deep and full revelation of how much God loves you is, without question, the most valuable BLESSING you could ever receive. It will affect every area of your life—everything you think, everything you feel and everything you do. A full revelation of God's love will make you absolutely fearless. It will cause your faith to soar sky-high. It will free you to walk in the power and Anointing of God like nothing else ever could.

"Yes, but, Brother Copeland," you might say, "I just don't have that revelation. I want it. I've asked God for it. I know I desperately need it. But God just hasn't given it to me."

Yes He has. He has given it to you in His WORD. You might say He has put it there in seed form. If you take that seed, plant it in your heart, as Jesus taught in Mark 4, meditate on it and pray over it, it will grow. If you'll spend time fellowshiping with The LORD over what the Bible says about His love for you, and let Him help you pull out those lying weeds the devil has planted that keep choking off that WORD, those seeds will flower and bloom into a revelation that will fill your heart and life with their fragrance.

Some people think they're too busy to spend that kind of time with The LORD and His WORD, so they don't do it. Then, when they're hurt and in trouble, they say, "God, help me with this right now!"

They're like the young farmer whose father helped him get started by giving him a piece of land, a crop-load of cotton seed, and all the tools he needed to cultivate the land. Instead of planting the seed, that foolish young man spent his time doing other things. When his money ran out, he went back to his father in a panic. "Dad! I'm totally broke. I need a cotton crop and I need it today!"

What's that father going to do? He can't produce a cotton crop for that boy overnight. He might be able to give him some money to get by for a little while, but that son will never really prosper until he takes what his father provided and does what he knows to do.

That's the way it is with the revelation of God's love. It doesn't come to us just because we want it. It doesn't come to us just because we beg God for it. It comes to us because we honor His WORD enough to work it deeply into our hearts. It comes to us because we treasure it enough to give thought and study to it. Its power is released in the soil of our hearts as we put it first place in our lives.

LIMITLESS**LOVE**

A Grand Finale of Love

"And they stoned Stephen, calling upon God, and saying, LORD Jesus, receive my spirit. And he kneeled down, and cried with a loud voice, LORD, lay not this sin to their charge. And when he had said this, he fell asleep."
Acts 7:59-60

We all want to be found walking in love in the pivotal moments of our lives. We want to be victorious in love at the important times when the pressure is on and everyone is watching. We want to be like Stephen and, in the historic hour when we find ourselves in the greatest battle of our lives, we want to finish it in a blaze of glory. We don't want our words at that moment of persecution to be, "You jerks! Why are you doing this to me? I hope someone stones you someday so you find out what it feels like!"

Those words would have made a pathetic ending for Acts 7. But thank God, Stephen didn't say them. He was prepared for that crucial hour of pain and pressure. He was full of the Holy Spirit, full of grace and full of the love of God. He didn't have time to stop and wonder, *Now what was it Jesus said when He was being crucified?* He didn't have time to think at all. People were throwing rocks at his head!

No, at that moment Stephen spoke from the fullness of his heart. He spoke in love and said, "Lay not this sin to their charge."

Do you know why he said that? Because he was a man who habitually walked in love. He spent his days serving people, waiting on tables, passing out food at the church. He served people naturally and supernaturally. He stayed so filled with the Holy Spirit and faith that he worked great wonders and miracles among the people.

Sometimes, we over-spiritualize men like Stephen, and we don't realize they had to walk out the love of God in everyday life just as we do. Stephen wasn't floating around on a puffy cloud, working wonders while people applauded. He was probably working in the "mess hall" with his sleeves rolled up, handing people biscuits and praying for their healing while they ate them. He probably had to get up early and stay up late to get everyone taken care of. Any way you look at it, that's the mark of a man who walks in love.

It's no wonder that when the rocks started to fly, he was ready. When the pressure was on and all heaven and hell were watching, Stephen responded with the compassion of Jesus and left a legacy that's lasted for thousands of years. He saw the heavens open, and caught up by the glory of God, he slipped from the hands of his persecutors into the arms of the Master in a grand finale of love.

Not Just for Me and Mine

"Confess your faults one to another,
and pray one for another, that ye may be healed...."
James 5:16

As we learn the principles of faith, we sometimes slip into a selfish mindset and begin to think only of ourselves. Instead of learning to pray for each other's healing, we focus our faith only on our own. We use our faith to increase our own income. We study Psalm 91 so we can believe for our own protection and the protection of our families.

But in doing so, we miss the point. As fellow believers, we're in covenant with one another. We're called to be as committed to seeing each other's needs met as we are our own. As Philippians 2:4 says, "Do not merely look out for your own personal interests, but also for the interests of others" *(New American Standard)*.

That's what being the Church is all about! It's about covenant living. It's about my family praying and believing God for your family, while yours prays and believes God for mine. It's about all of us coming together, finding out who has a need and taking care of it!

A church is a group of people so in love with Jesus and with each other that they're looking for ways to BLESS each other. They're learning to use their faith to help each other and build each other up.

Actually, since faith works by love, if we don't do that, we'll never really learn to walk by faith. If the only things we ever use faith for is our own deliverance, our own healing and our own success, we'll never really get off the ground! God didn't give us His WORD and His promises just to use "on me and mine that we may shine." He gave them to us so we could serve Him by serving one another.

Once we start doing that, believing for our own needs will be as easy as falling off a log. Our faith will be so powerfully backed up by love and our fellowship with God and each other, that we can just lean back into it and receive whatever we need!

Just give it a try, and you'll see what I mean. If you've been frustrated in your faith, if it hasn't been producing what you've been believing for, forget about yourself for a while. Go find another believer who has a need bigger than yours, and start believing God to help you meet his need instead. Don't just do it mechanically. Put your heart into it. Let the love of God flow out of you for that brother. Pray for him. Give to him with passion. Get in there with him and help him shoulder his load. Let God show you what faith working by love can really do.

LIMITLESS**LOVE**

How Much Are You Worth?

"Ye were not redeemed with corruptible things, as silver and gold, from your vain conversation received by tradition from your fathers; but with the precious blood of Christ, as of a lamb without blemish and without spot."
1 Peter 1:18-19

Have you ever found yourself struggling for a sense of self-worth? Everyone has. People work long hours and sacrifice their families to gain the approval of an employer and feel valuable at the office. They get in debt buying clothes, cars and houses, hoping those things will somehow make them feel more important. They even push for visible positions of honor and respect in the Church because they want to know they're valuable in the kingdom of God.

The problem is…those things never bring the comfort we're looking for. Once we get them, we live in constant fear of losing them. We are in bondage to them, knowing that their loss will prove what we've always feared—that we're really not worth very much.

Instead of offering comfort, traditional religion made our fears even worse. It taught us we were nothing. Just unspiritual worms God chose to take pity on. Just old sinners saved by grace.

Of course, you already know better than that. You know that by trusting in Jesus and making Him your LORD, you've been made the righteousness of God. But have you ever let His sacrifice settle the nagging question of your self-worth?

It does settle it, you know. Once you realize that God sent Jesus to pay the price to save you, you never again have to wonder how valuable you are. You don't have to look at your performance, your possessions, or even your position in your local church to see how much you're worth.

All you have to do is look at the Cross. All you have to do is ask yourself, "How precious was the blood of Jesus that was shed there? How precious was the spotless Lamb of God who laid down His life for me?"

When you answer those questions, you will forever answer the question of your own value. You are worth as much to God as Jesus is because God gave Him in exchange for you.

"How could that be?" you might ask. "I know my own failures! I know my own faults! I'm not worthy to be valued at such a price!"

No, you aren't. Neither am I. But, God, because of His great love with which He loved us, paid it for us anyway. The Sovereign God who establishes all truth and all value, declared us to be as precious as Jesus. In the blood of His Firstborn, He forever established our worth.

A Lesson From Madison Avenue

"I beseech you therefore, brethren, by the mercies of God, that ye present your bodies a living sacrifice, holy, acceptable unto God, which is your reasonable service. And be not conformed to this world: but be ye transformed by the renewing of your mind, that ye may prove what is that good, and acceptable, and perfect, will of God."
Romans 12:1-2

Sometimes, we get the idea that dealing with our flesh is harder than it really is. Because it has run our lives so long, we have the impression it's really strong and powerful. But it's not. It just yields to the influences that surround it. It conforms to what it is consistently exposed to.

Madison Avenue has proven that. If you give an advertising agency a big enough budget and enough time, they can so flood the eyes and ears of the public with something that, before long, people everywhere are conforming to it. Put enough pictures of models wearing bell-bottom jeans in magazines for example, put bell-bottom jeans on television shows and on billboards...and before long, people who swore they would never wear them will be walking around town in bell-bottom jeans!

Why? Because that's the way human flesh is. It's made to conform to the influences that surround it. Some of those influences come from the inside, some from the outside. Some pull it one way...and some another way. But the strongest, most consistent influences always win. Once you understand that principle, you can put it to work in your favor. You can let it help you in your quest to be fully conformed to the image of Jesus, and live the life of love.

Because the Holy Spirit dwells within you, you already have the influence of God working on your flesh from the inside. What you have to do next is get that same influence working on it from the outside. How can you do that? The same way Madison Avenue does it—by renewing your mind through constant exposure to Jesus. Spend time in The WORD and continually fellowship with Him. Fill your mind with His thoughts instead of the world's thoughts. (That's what the Scriptures are, you know. They are God's own thoughts!) Replace the image you have of yourself with the image the Bible gives you of Jesus.

Then, go out and start acting like Him. Let His nature flow from your heart. Instead of fighting you, your flesh will progressively conform to who you are inside, and you'll become the loving person your heart desires to be!

Let God Be True

"For what if some did not believe? shall their unbelief make the faith of God without effect? God forbid: yea, let God be true, but every man a liar...."
Romans 3:3-4

It's amazing how many believers claim they love The LORD, lift their hands and cry big tears of devotion when they're in church, then walk out the door and treat Him like He's a liar. Of course, they don't realize that's what they're doing, but they are doing it just the same.

We'd notice it more quickly if we did that to another human being. Say, for example, you needed someone to pick you up from the airport, and your best friend promised you he'd do it. Assuming that friend was a person of his word and had always been faithful to do what he told you, you'd believe what he said, wouldn't you? Not to believe it would be unloving and dishonorable. It would be a slap in his face for you to keep asking other people to pick you up. They wouldn't think much of your friend if they heard you saying, "Well, he told me he'd pick me up, but would you be there too, just in case he doesn't come? I'm just not sure I can count on him."

We'd never do that kind of thing to a faithful friend, but believers do that to God all the time. They receive His promises through His WORD—something so serious to Him, He guaranteed it in the blood of His own Son—then talk and act as if The WORD is not true. They treat God like a liar who cannot be trusted. I know that sounds harsh, but it's true, and we need to realize it.

Some years ago, during a series of meetings I was preaching, I attended a kind of reception some people had put together for the ministers who were attending. When I walked into the room, a fellow grabbed my hand. "Brother Copeland, I need you to pray with me," he said. "My sister is sick and not expected to live. I want you to agree with me that God will intervene and turn that situation around."

"Absolutely!" I said. We caught hands and agreed together on the words of Jesus in Matthew 18:19 that whenever two agree on anything they ask in His Name, it will be done for them. We prayed and thanked God for the answer. Later, I saw that fellow grab another preacher and say, "Brother, my sister is in bad shape. We think she's going to die...." He must have prayed with a dozen people that evening, but never once did he actually believe The WORD of God.

We need to get real about our love for God, and stop doing things like that. We need to honor Him enough to believe what He tells us, and act as if it's true. Given the fact that He shed His own blood to guarantee His promises, I'd say that's the kind of love He is due.

LIMITLESS**LOVE**

Think on These Things

"Finally, brethren, whatsoever things are true, whatsoever things are honest, whatsoever things are just, whatsoever things are pure, whatsoever things are lovely, whatsoever things are of good report; if there be any virtue, and if there be any praise, think on these things."
Philippians 4:8

Proverbs 23:7 says that as a man thinks in his heart, so is he. That means if you're going to live a life of love, you will have to think loving thoughts about people—even those you don't particularly like.

"But Brother Copeland, I just can't do that!" you might say. "I know some people who are downright mean. I think they're awful, and I can't help not liking them!"

Yes, you can. We all have 100 percent control over what we think. We can choose to think unloving, negative thoughts about someone, or we can choose to think loving, positive thoughts about them. God makes it very clear that He expects us to choose to think those things that are loving and good.

Frankly, most of us have to retrain our minds in order to do that. We've spent years habitually focusing on what's wrong with people, instead of what's right with them. Someone might have been kind to us our entire lives, and we hardly give it a thought. But let that person say something ugly just once, and (unless we stop ourselves) we'll fuss and fume about that one statement for days, weeks and sometimes years. We'll think about that one ugly comment until it overshadows every nice thing that person ever said or did.

Negative thoughts will always come to you. The devil will see to that. But, you can refuse to entertain them. You can resist them, and replace them with something better. As one minister said, "You can't stop the birds from flying over your head, but you can keep them from building a nest in your hair!"

One way to stop unloving thoughts from getting a grip on your mind is by saying something loving out loud. It's impossible for you to think one thing and say another at the same time. If you want to prove it, start counting from one to 10 in your mind, and try saying your name at the same time. You can't do it. Your mind has to stop counting and refocus when you stop to say your name.

Turn your thoughts in the right direction by saying something about that person that's positive and true. If you can't think of anything else, just remind yourself that person is so precious, Jesus died to save him. Say out loud, "My Jesus loves that person, and I love him, too!"

LIMITLESS LOVE

No Fish in Your Bathtub

"For I would that ye knew what great conflict I have for you, and for them at Laodicea, and for as many as have not seen my face in the flesh; that their hearts might be comforted, being knit together in love, and unto all riches of the full assurance of understanding, to the acknowledgement of the mystery of God, and of the Father, and of Christ; in whom are hid all the treasures of wisdom and knowledge."
Colossians 2:1-3

We may as well be honest. There are some people who are, naturally speaking, practically impossible to love. There are people who will take your expressions of kindness and throw them right back in your face. They will take offense even when there is no offense to be taken.

You say, "Good morning, you look very nice today!"

They answer, "I'm sure that's a surprise to you, since I can't afford to buy the kind of clothes you do."

Those kinds of people will not only trip you up in your love walk, but practically drive you crazy if you deal with them in your own strength. You'll lie awake at night wracking your brain, trying to come up with ways to successfully reach them…and you'll come up empty every time.

Do you know why? Because the answer isn't in your brain. It's in your spirit. That's where the Spirit of The LORD dwells, and the Bible says that in Him are hidden *all* the treasures of wisdom and knowledge. (See Colossians 2:3.) Sometimes we read *all* in the Bible differently than we read *all* in the recipe book. When a recipe says to put *all* the sugar in the mix, it doesn't mean half the cup. It means *all!*

To spend time searching your brain for the wisdom to walk in love is like fishing in your bathtub! You're not going to catch anything because there's nothing there. So start fishing where *all* the wisdom is. Tune in to your heart by spending time in prayer and worship. Praise The LORD, and pray in tongues for awhile. When you do that, you'll start tapping into the wisdom of Jesus.

The LORD knows all there is to know about loving people. He knows how to love the sweet ones and those who have soured a little. He can give you the grace to let their critical comments roll off you like water off a duck. He can give you the wisdom to know what to say and the heart to keep reaching out to them when no one else will.

They may be so tough, they'll never let you know that you touched them. But if you follow the leading of the Spirit, in their hearts they'll know they've been loved.

Stay in the Light

"The one who loves his brother abides in the Light and there is no cause
for stumbling in him. But the one who hates his brother is in the darkness
and walks in the darkness, and does not know where he is going
because the darkness has blinded his eyes."
1 John 2:10-11, *New American Standard*

Do you ever feel like you're stumbling around in the dark, trying to find the plan of God for your life?

We've all felt like that at times. We've all had occasions when we couldn't clearly discern the direction of the Holy Spirit, and we felt we were groping in the darkness trying to find the light. When we find ourselves in that situation, one of the first things we need to do is check our love walk. Without even realizing it, we may have gotten out of love and into disharmony with others. As a result, our spiritual vision has become cloudy. Strife has blinded our eyes.

"I thought that only happened to people who hated their brothers!" you might say. "I certainly don't hate anyone."

Not according to your definition of hate. But the Bible's definition of hate is much broader than ours usually is. According to the Scriptures, if we have anything against our brother, it will hinder the effectiveness of our prayers (Mark 11:25). If we harbor any anger, unforgiveness or ill will toward anyone, we have left the arena of love and stepped into the arena of hate.

I've found it often isn't the major things in my dealings with others that trip me up. When I encounter big problems with someone, I've learned enough to seek The LORD until I'm sure my heart toward them is right. It's the minor irritations that cause me trouble. It's the attitude I have toward the waitress who got my order wrong and didn't seem to care. It's the anger I yielded to when I blasted the horn on my car at the guy who carelessly got in my way on the road. It's the sharp tone of voice I used with the telemarketer who interrupted my evening…again.

When we ignore those little attitudes and offenses, they begin to pile up and obscure the illumination of the Spirit inside us. They grieve the Holy Spirit and choke off the flow of love until we find ourselves with hardly any spiritual power at all. Usually, we don't even know how we got in that condition. We just know that when we pray, nothing seems to happen. We cannot sense the leading of God.

Don't let yourself slip into that trap. Watch carefully over your heart in the big things—and in the small. The moment you catch yourself stepping out of love and into irritation and strife, stop right then and repent. Then, take action. Do something kind. Say something uplifting to BLESS that person. Step out of the darkness and right back into love so God's light can keep shining on you.

LIMITLESS**LOVE**

Honor the Blood

"Of how much sorer punishment, suppose ye, shall he be thought worthy, who hath trodden under foot the Son of God, and hath counted the blood of the covenant, wherewith he was sanctified, an unholy thing, and hath done despite unto the Spirit of grace?"
Hebrews 10:29

When we harbor unforgiveness against fellow believers, refusing to love them because of something they've done, we actually dishonor the blood of Jesus. That is extremely serious business. It puts us in position to be judged and punished. We cannot escape that punishment by pleading for mercy because mercy comes through the blood. And when we refuse to recognize the forgiveness the blood has bought for others, we cut ourselves off from the benefit of it, too.

Think about the moment you were first born again. Think about the day you said, "Father, forgive me of my sin. I receive Jesus as My LORD. Please come into my heart." Why didn't the Father reject you? Why didn't He say, "No, I don't want you in this household of faith, messing things up. I know what you've done, and I don't want you for a son"?

I'll tell you why He didn't say that. It was because He honored the blood of Jesus more than He did your sin. He considered that blood so precious, He counted it sufficient payment for the debt you owed Him. When Jesus' blood was shed, the sin question was eternally answered as far as God was concerned. Sin had once and for all been forgiven. All anyone had to do to receive the benefits of it was to accept it.

Now that we *have* received those benefits, we are under divine command to forgive others just as God in Christ has forgiven us (Ephesians 4:32). That means we are to honor the blood of Jesus more than we do each other's sin. It means we consider the blood of Jesus to be so precious that it is sufficient payment for whatever wrong anyone might do to us. We are to extend unconditional love and forgiveness to one another, not because we've earned it or deserve it, but because we are in covenant with God and with each other through the blood of Jesus. And to do any less is to dishonor that blood.

When you realize what a serious thing that is, you won't be so quick to be swayed by your emotions when someone does you wrong. Instead of letting your foolish, carnal feelings dominate you, you'll rise up in the spirit and honor the blood of Jesus. You'll count His blood to be reason enough for you to forgive your brother. By faith in that blood, you'll offer the forgiveness to others that God has extended to you.

LIMITLESS**LOVE**

The Greatest Love Ever Known

"Greater love hath no man than this,
that a man lay down his life for his friends."
John 15:13

To truly appreciate how deeply Jesus loves us, we need to understand just how much He sacrificed—not only when He died on the cross, but every day He lived in this sin-wracked world. We need to think about the fact that He left the unspeakable glories of heaven where He had lived forever. He left a place where there is nothing but joy and peace, harmony and love to dwell in a place that is a pigsty by comparison, a place that is full of hatred, robbery, murder and every other kind of violence imaginable.

He gave up the privileges of divinity. He gave up the divine spiritual form that enabled Him to be omnipresent, omniscient and omnipotent. The Bible says He emptied Himself of those privileges (Philippians 2:7) and limited Himself to the form of flesh and blood. He, being God, became a man. Not a superman, but a real human being who felt hunger and got tired just like other men. He gave up His divine knowledge and took on the mind of a man who had to grow in The WORD just as you and I do. He had to find out who He was through prayer and by studying the Scriptures. He had to find Himself in the book of Isaiah and the Psalms. He had to stand on those words when doubts assailed, temptations came, and the devil said, "If thou be the Son of God...."

Jesus had to stand on God's WORD by faith after His crucifixion, when He was in the pit of hell paying the full price for our sins. He had to believe that God could raise Him up from that place, even though it had never been done before. No one had ever gotten out of hell! What if something went wrong? From the viewpoint of human history, Jesus was taking a risk no other man had ever taken.

What could make someone take such a risk?

Love. Only love.

Love drove Jesus to become the Son of Man—not just for 33 years, but forever! Even after His resurrection from the dead, He didn't go back to His previous form. He remained a man, a glorified man, a man who is as much God as He is man—but a man nonetheless. Even now, He ever lives to make intercession for us (Hebrews 7:25). He still has the holes in His hands and feet. He still has the hole in his side and the scars on His head. He still bears in His glorified body the marks of His eternal sacrifice. He carries them as undeniable evidence of His love for us...the greatest love ever known.

LIMITLESS LOVE

By Faith, Not Feelings

"We having the same spirit of faith, according as it is written, I believed, and therefore have I spoken; we also believe, and therefore speak."
2 Corinthians 4:13

There are times for all of us when we don't feel the love of God. There are times when we encounter such trials and difficulties that, naturally speaking, it doesn't look much like God cares about us. That's when we're tempted to say dumb things like, "Yes, I know God loves me, but I feel like He's so far away. If He'd just do something to let me know He's near, it would help me. If I could just see His face or feel His gentle touch on my fevered brow, I could believe."

That kind of thinking is wrong. Faith in God's love doesn't come from seeing Jesus' face or feeling His hand. Faith in His love comes like every other kind of faith—by hearing The WORD of God!

Once we've heard The WORD of God's love, we have no business sitting around whining about what we feel or don't feel. We have no business looking to our flesh to see if God's WORD is true. We have a responsibility to believe that WORD and speak accordingly.

Actually, when we don't feel God's love is when we had better believe in it most strongly because that's when the devil is trying to take advantage of us. That's when he is putting pressure on our flesh and our emotions, trying to get us to open our mouths and speak words that will give him license to wreak havoc in our lives.

Don't let him do it. Don't let yourself be moved by what you feel or what you see. You may feel drier spiritually than you've ever felt in your life, but that doesn't change a thing. The WORD still says God loves you. It still says He'll never leave you nor forsake you.

So instead of yielding to the spirit of doubt, maintain the spirit of faith. Believe and speak the truth about God's love. Regardless of how your flesh feels, open your mouth and start praising The LORD for His compassion. Open your mouth and say, "No matter how I may feel, the truth is, My God loves me. Jesus loved me enough to leave glory, come to earth and die for me. He loved me enough to go to hell for me. He loves me so much now, He ever lives to intercede for me! He's promised to be with me even to the end of the world, and I believe He's here right now, loving and caring for me!"

If you'll believe and speak like that, those dry feelings will begin to change. Your old fleshly emotions will be replaced by the stirrings of the spirit, and before long you'll be dancing around, not only believing and speaking, but also experiencing the truth. Your whole spirit, soul and body will be rejoicing in the light of God's marvelous love.

LIMITLESS**LOVE**

Set the Example

"Children, obey your parents in The LORD: for this is right. Honour thy father and mother; which is the first commandment with promise; that it may be well with thee, and thou mayest live long on the earth. And, ye fathers, provoke not your children to wrath: but bring them up in the nurture and admonition of The LORD."
Ephesians 6:1-4

As Christian parents, we set the example of love for our children. What they see in us is what they expect to find in God. That's one reason why we should never instill fear in them in the name of love.

Fear and love aren't a team. They're opposed to each other. The Bible says fear brings torment. According to the dictionary, *to torment* means "to agitate, terrorize, seize or paralyze in order to oppress." God is totally against those things. His love casts them out. So, never try to use them to train your children.

Instead, train them the way that God trains you. He instructs you with His WORD. He doesn't sic the devil on you and send him to terrorize you into obeying Him. He sends the Holy Spirit to guide you into all truth. If you ignore that truth and get yourself into a mess anyway, when you call out to Him for help He doesn't condemn you. He doesn't beat you like a dog and send you off with your tail between your legs. He forgives you and talks to you about how you can avoid getting hurt like that again.

Remember that the next time you are teaching your children something. If you're training them to avoid a dangerous situation, don't terrorize them. Just tell them the facts. Don't say things like, "Oh, I'm so afraid you're going to do this and mess up your life. I'm so afraid you're not going to listen to me, and you'll end up in ruin."

Speak to them in love, and believe in them the way your heavenly Father believes in you. Express your confidence in them and their ability to make right choices. Let them know you want the best for them, and you expect wonderful things for their future.

When they make a mistake, don't act as if it's the end of the world, and don't kick them when they're down. Comfort them in their pain. Let them know you understand and are there to help them. Then, teach them what The WORD says. Say, "Sweetheart, I love you. I want things to be well with you. So, let's take a look at this together and see how you can keep from making this mistake again."

Whether your children are young or older, they'll appreciate your kindness and respect. They'll find it easier to do what's right when you refuse to provoke and frighten them. They'll truly want to honor and obey you when you teach them and discipline them in love.

The High Priest of Our Confession

"Therefore, holy brethren, partakers of a heavenly calling, consider Jesus, the Apostle and High Priest of our confession." Hebrews 3:1, New American Standard

Once you realize you've been born again and given the very nature of God Himself, the question immediately arises, "How do I get that new nature within me to come out? Where do I get the power to push aside the impulses of my flesh so I can consistently walk in love?"

The answer can be found in Hebrews 3:1. You get that power from Jesus, the Apostle and High Priest of your confession.

An apostle is someone who has been sent for a purpose. If, for example, you gave someone money and sent them to the store to buy bread, that person would be your apostle to the grocery store. So the word *apostle* in itself isn't particularly holy. However, when God sends someone and equips them with power to carry out a task, being an apostle becomes a very supernatural thing. Add to that the concept of the high priest, who is one appointed by God with the authority to bring His WORD to pass on behalf of the people, and you get a glimpse of what Jesus does for us.

He has been sent by God to bring to pass our confession of faith! When we confessed Him as LORD, for example, He, as the High Priest over that confession, brought the new birth to pass in our lives. When we said, "Jesus, come into my heart! I receive You as my LORD," He administered the power necessary to make us new creatures—instantly, old things were passed away and all things became new!

Later, after we learned He had purchased our healing, we may have said in faith, "LORD Jesus, I believe that by Your stripes I was healed. I believe I receive my healing!" When we did, Jesus, as the High Priest of that confession, saw to it that those covenant words we said came to pass, and we were healed.

In the same way, once we understand that the love of God has been shed abroad in our hearts by the Holy Spirit, we can draw on that love by making the confession of faith. We can say, "LORD Jesus, I believe I've been made a partaker of the divine nature. I believe the love of God dwells in me, and I walk in that love. I receive the power to do it, now!"

When we say something like that, Jesus goes to work as the High Priest of our confession and uses His authority to bring it to pass. He looses all the grace we need to draw out His nature within us. He administers all the spiritual resources necessary to enable us to walk out our confession of faith. He gives us the power to live the life of love.

Living From the Inside, Out

"We know that we are of God, and that the whole world lies in the power of the evil one."
1 John 5:19, *New American Standard*

Why is it that so few Christians consistently walk in love? Since we are born of God and have His loving nature within us, you'd think we'd do it easily, almost automatically. But, we all know there is nothing easy or automatic about living a life of love.

The reason is simple: We live in a world driven by selfishness. We are constantly surrounded by a society full of unsaved people who are concerned only about themselves. They are born of darkness, just as we are born of the light. They have a fallen, self-centered nature that is constantly under the influence of the devil. Their attitude is, "I have to look out for myself because if I don't, no one else will! I have to grab everything I can because if I don't, I'll end up with nothing!"

In a way, they're right. Their father, the devil, isn't like our heavenly Father. He doesn't meet the needs of his children. In fact, he doesn't care for them at all. He just uses them, abuses them and throws them away.

Because we're constantly surrounded by that kind of thinking, it's easy for us as believers to think that way too. When the pressure of the world bears down on us, unless we purposely feed on God's WORD, we'll end up acting just like the people around us. We'll find ourselves thinking, *Hey, if I don't selfishly try to push ahead in this world, I won't ever get ahead at all!*

Unlike worldly people, however, we don't have any business thinking that way. We do have Someone looking out for us. We have Almighty God on our side. He is constantly BLESSING us and watching over us. He has promised to see to it that we prosper and prevail!

We don't have to seek our own. We can walk in love and focus on meeting the needs of others. We can spend our lives giving all we can to others instead of grabbing all we can for ourselves, knowing that our God has promised to give to us again, good measure, pressed down, shaken together and running over!

To do that, however, we will have to resist the external pressures that try to make us conform to the thinking of this world. We must renew our minds so thoroughly to the mindset of love that the moment a selfish thought presses itself upon us, we recognize it and reject it. By nourishing ourselves on the truths of The WORD and fellowship of the Holy Spirit, we must grow so strong on the inside that we can resist the pressure of the world, and live from the inside, out, in the nature and power of love.

LIMITLESS**LOVE**

What's So Hard About That?

"Now the just shall live by faith...."
Hebrews 10:38

Sometimes I see Christians struggling and sweating in an effort to live by faith. To watch them, you'd think that faith in God is very difficult to obtain and extremely complicated to walk in.

But, God never intended living by faith to be difficult. He meant it to be so simple that even a child could do it. We're the ones who made it hard, and we did it by separating it from love. Since faith works by love, you can quickly see what a great mistake that can be.

To have faith in God basically means to trust Him. Before we trust anyone, we have to know their heart. We have to know not only what they've promised us but why they made those promises. Unless we know their motives, we can never fully trust them. If they're under pressure, for example, and have to choose between protecting themselves or us, we're never sure exactly what they will do.

That's why it does us only a limited amount of good to rehearse God's promises over and over, trying to believe them, when we have little revelation of His love. We're continually plagued with doubts. *What if God's promises are conditional,* we wonder, *and we have unknowingly failed to meet those conditions? What if in this contract called the Bible, there are clauses and exceptions that excuse God from fulfilling these promises? What if there are qualifications we don't know anything about?*

Once we understand God's heart, however, such questions just melt away. Once we realize that He made all those promises because He loves us, we can rest assured not only that He will, but that He *wants* to do for us all that He has said.

God's motive in everything He does for us is purely and simply love. We never have to worry about Him choosing His own interests over ours because He already proved at Calvary that He was willing to sacrifice Himself on our behalf. By pouring out His very own blood, He showed us that every promise He has made us and every word He has spoken was prompted by His great love. He demonstrated once and for all that He cares so much about us that He wants to meet our every need, and He has power enough to do it.

All we have to do is give Him an open door by inviting Him into our lives, and He will rush in to do good things for us. That's how much He loves us!

The more we understand that, the easier it is for us to have faith. After all, faith is just believing what God says. Faith is simply being confident that God has told us the truth. What's so hard about that?

Nothing, when you know His love.

LIMITLESS**LOVE**

When Your Joy Slips Away

"Finally, my brethren, rejoice in The LORD. To write the same things to you, to me indeed is not grievous, but for you it is safe."
Philippians 3:1

Have you ever noticed that when the fruit of the spirit is listed in Galatians, love tops the list? That's because love is the fruit from which all the others flow. When love is present, joy, peace, longsuffering, kindness, goodness, faithfulness, gentleness and self-control always follow right behind it. When love is absent, the rest are absent, too.

That's why I've trained myself to pay close attention to not only my love life but to my joy level. Since joy is the immediate result of walking in love, I've learned that when my joy begins to wane, it's a sure sign that somewhere along the way I've stepped out of love and into selfishness.

Initially, I might have no idea when it happened. I'll just notice that although I began my day in joy, somehow a sense of sadness or irritation has set in. *What's the matter with me?* I wonder. *I felt great a while ago. What has stolen my joy?*

Inevitably, as I think back through my day, I'll remember some insignificant but unkind thing someone said to me that caused me to take offense without even realizing it. I'll recall some situation where someone aggravated me and I failed to respond in love. I'll see that from that moment on, my day began to go downhill. My joy slowly but surely began to slip away.

Once I've realized what has happened, I do whatever is necessary to correct the situation. I repent for my failure to walk in love, forgive the person who was unkind to me, and extend heartfelt grace to the person who irritated me. If I responded to them outwardly in an unloving manner, I apologize, if possible, and make things right.

Then, I purposely stir my joy up again. If I'm driving my car, I'll play a CD of praise songs and sing along. (I can't carry a tune, so I only do that when I'm alone. It wouldn't be loving to do it when others are around!) If thoughts of strife or aggravation try to persist, I just resist them. I look at the situation in the light of The WORD of God and say to myself, "That's no big deal! I'm full of love, so I'm not going to be touchy and fretful about that. I'm not going to let the devil use it to steal my joy!"

If you're serious about walking in love, I recommend you do the same thing. Watch yourself, and when you find you're getting downcast or depressed, look back and see where you stumbled and fell out of love. Then step right back in and stir your joy up again. You and everyone around you will be very glad you did!

LIMITLESS**LOVE**

Who's in Control?

"Let no one delude and deceive you with empty excuses and groundless arguments [for these sins], for through these things the wrath of God comes upon the sons of rebellion and disobedience. So do not associate or be sharers with them. For once you were darkness, but now you are light in The LORD; walk as children of Light [lead the lives of those native-born to the Light]. For the fruit (the effect, the product) of the Light or the Spirit [consists] in every form of kindly goodness, uprightness of heart, and trueness of life."
Ephesians 5:6-9, *The Amplified Bible*

If you want to get on the spiritual fast track and grow more quickly in your love walk, here's one important thing you must do: Stop making excuses. When you see you've been wrong and you've stepped out of love, don't waste any time explaining and rationalizing your behavior. Don't pass the buck and say, as one comedian did many years ago, "The devil made me do it."

The devil can't make you do anything. You're a born-again child of God. Neither the devil nor the sin he is peddling have any dominion over you (Romans 6:14)). So don't try to lay the blame on him.

Don't point your finger at the person who aggravated you, either. It's not their fault. It doesn't matter what anyone says or does, the Spirit of God who lives in you will provide you with all the power you need to respond in love. He will enable you to bear the fruit of goodness, kindness and love in every situation.

One thing He will *not* do, however, is control your flesh for you. He'll strengthen you and help you, but you're the one who must put that strength and power to work. It's your job to take authority over your mind and your mouth and make them line up with the law of love.

In a meeting some years ago, the Holy Spirit said this through a word of prophecy: *If you don't have control of your flesh, I don't have control of your flesh.* Take that revelation a step further and you'll see that if we don't have control of our flesh and God doesn't have control of our flesh, someone else will take control of it. And that someone is the devil himself. That's a sobering thought, because if we let Satan control our flesh, he will ultimately control our lives. He'll not only steal our love walk and keep us from bearing the fruit of the spirit, he'll rob us of THE BLESSING of God.

Don't let him do it. Rise up and take responsibility for yourself. Stop making excuses. When you miss it and step out of love, admit it immediately and do whatever it takes to step right back in. Take control of your flesh, and walk as a child of Light every day.

LIMITLESS**LOVE**

Reaping a Harvest of Life

"Do not be deceived, God is not mocked; for whatever a man sows, this he will also reap. For the one who sows to his own flesh will from the flesh reap corruption, but the one who sows to the Spirit will from the Spirit reap eternal life. And let us not lose heart in doing good, for in due time we will reap if we do not grow weary. So then, while we have opportunity, let us do good to all people, and especially to those who are of the household of the faith."
Galatians 6:7-10, *New American Standard*

Wouldn't it be wonderful if you were constantly receiving unexpected blessings? Wouldn't it be great if the love of God seemed to overtake and overwhelm you again…and again…and again?

Amazing as it may sound, that's exactly the kind of life that we, as believers, are meant to live. All we have to do to receive it is to sow to the spirit by continually walking in love. By taking every opportunity God gives us to do good to others and to let the forces of love, joy, peace, patience, kindness, goodness, faithfulness, gentleness and self-control flow out of us, we can set in motion a harvest of life that will bring us THE BLESSING every day.

The reverse is also true. If we spend our days in sin and strife, yielding to our flesh instead of to the promptings of the Spirit, we will reap misery as a result. If we are too lazy and self-centered to put down the remote control, get up off the couch and do some things for others, we'll find ourselves hurting and alone in times to come. If we're harsh and critical toward people who have failed us, when we need mercy, we'll get judgment from others, instead.

The Bible says that the wages of sin is death. Although, as believers, we've been redeemed by the blood of Jesus from the penalty of eternal death, this fact remains true. If we continue to live in sin by disobeying the commandment of love, the wages of our sin will still come and eat away at the quality of our lives. Those fleshly seeds we planted will spring up and corrupt our relationships, our health and success.

If you've planted some fleshly seeds in the past (and we all have) repent of them today. Receive the cleansing of the blood of Jesus, declare a supernatural crop failure, and receive the mercy of God so you won't have to eat the fruit of your ways.

Then start working on your harvest of BLESSING. Ask the Holy Spirit to help you find opportunities to reach out to others in love. Give…and give…and give again the goodness and love you'd like to receive. When due season comes, you'll reap…and reap…and reap God's richest rewards!

LIMITLESS**LOVE**

Keep Your Heart Strong

"My son, attend to my words; consent and submit to my sayings. Let them not depart from your sight; keep them in the center of your heart. For they are life to those who find them, healing and health to all their flesh. Keep and guard your heart with all vigilance and above all that you guard, for out of it flow the springs of life."
Proverbs 4:20-23, *The Amplified Bible*

Since the love of God has been shed abroad in our hearts, the most important question we, as born-again believers, can ask is this: *How can I guard my heart? How can I keep my spirit so strong that it dominates my flesh and keeps me walking in love?*

These verses in Proverbs give us the answer. We guard our hearts by attending to God's WORD. We keep it in our eyes and ears continually to help us stay in daily, living contact with Him.

We don't use the Bible like the people in the Old Testament did. We don't use it as a set of rules to follow or as a list of laws to obey in order to achieve right-standing with God. We're born of His Spirit. We already have right-standing with Him through the blood of Jesus. So, for us, reading the Bible is a way of communing with God. When we read it, the Holy Ghost within us makes it alive and full of power. It strengthens us and energizes the nature of God within us. It separates our souls from our spirits, so that our hearts can become the dominant force in our lives (Hebrews 4:12, *The Amplified Bible*).

If we'll keep The WORD in our hearts with all diligence, the spiritual forces God has put inside us—forces like love, joy, peace, patience, goodness, kindness, faithfulness and self-control—will flow forth strongly from our inner man and wash away every hindrance of the flesh that would try to stop them. But the word "diligence" is a big word. It isn't a lazy word. It isn't a casual word. People who are diligent are people who mean business about something. They are focused and determined. And they consistently apply effort to reach their goals.

That's the way we must be about attending to The WORD. We can't afford to be lazy or casual about it. We can't afford to let our WORD level slip. If we do, we'll find ourselves growing spiritually weak. We'll find our hearts being overpowered by the things of the world and the desires of the flesh. We'll find ourselves thinking, *What's happened to me? I want to walk in love in this situation but I can't find the strength to do it!*

Don't let yourself get in that condition. Spend time in the Bible every day. Listen to The LORD as He speaks to you through the truths you read there. Keep your heart strong with The WORD.

LIMITLESS**LOVE**

Keep Increasing Every Day

"May The LORD give you increase, you and your children."
Psalm 115:14, *New American Standard*

If I were to sum up the will of God for our lives in one word, I might choose the word *increase*. Throughout the Bible, God makes it clear that He desires for us to increase in every way. He wants us to increase spiritually and physically, in health and strength. He wants us to increase in blessings of every kind.

That means no matter how successfully we've walked in love up to this point in our lives, God can increase us. He can help us walk in love more and more!

Actually, I've found that when it comes to the things of the spirit, we're never stationary. We're always either moving forward or slipping back. We're either progressing or regressing, increasing or decreasing…but we're never staying the same.

That's because in the day-to-day course of life, we're either staying in living contact with God…or we're not. We're either fellowshiping with Him consistently through prayer and The WORD…or we're not. If we are, God will be continually adding to us. He'll be constantly deepening our revelation of His love. He'll be perpetually increasing our spiritual strength. As a result, our lives will bear ever-more abundant fruit and be marked with ever-increasing BLESSINGS.

On the other hand, if we go for days without feeding on The WORD or spending time in prayer, we'll start losing ground. The devil doesn't take a vacation. He puts pressure on us in some way every day. So if we're not actively keeping in contact with God, the devil begins to get the upper hand. Our flesh starts to take dominion. Old, unloving habits we've been delivered from begin to try to come back on us. The selfishness of the world begins to pull us in the wrong direction.

If we continue like that, just going about our business, not giving God any time, the first thing you know, we find ourselves in trouble of some kind. We'll pray and beg God for help, all the while feeling like He isn't even listening to us.

The problem, however, isn't in His failure to listen to us. It's in our failure to listen to Him. That's why we need to stay in living contact with Him daily. That's why we need to pray and seek His face, not just when we're in trouble, but all the time.

Maintaining our fellowship with God is the most important thing we will ever do. If we'll make it our first priority, we will experience His wonderful will for our lives. We'll keep on increasing more and more in spirit, soul and body. We'll keep growing in victory every day.

Fragrant and Free

"I am the true vine, and My Father is the vinedresser. Every branch in Me that does not bear fruit, He takes away; and every branch that bears fruit, He prunes it so that it may bear more fruit. You are already clean because of The WORD which I have spoken to you."
John 15:1-3, *New American Standard*

All the fruit of the spirit, including the fruit of love, are abiding within us if we've made Jesus our LORD. But for that fruit to come forth in its fullness, we have to be pruned. God has to cut away the dead branches of the flesh that cling to us and get in our way. He has to cleanse us from the stinking thinking we've gotten from the world.

How does He do that?

With His WORD! As Ephesians 5:26 says, He cleanses us "with the washing of water by The WORD."

He doesn't just wash us once or twice, either. He does it again and again and again. That's because spiritually speaking, we live in a dirty world. We live in a culture driven by selfishness and fear. Our minds are constantly bombarded with the lies of the devil, like *Give someone an inch, and they'll take a mile. You have to look out for yourself first. You have to push others out of the way to get ahead.*

Even when we don't realize it, that kind of thinking is trying to cling to us. It tries to contaminate our hearts and keep us from yielding to the Spirit's flow. Although selfishness isn't in us, it gets on us and it will hinder our walk of love, unless we wash it off.

That's why we need to take a spiritual bath every day. God Himself will do the cleansing, but we have to get in the water! We have to soak ourselves in His WORD and apply it to our lives as He directs. Just as we'd take a bar of soap and scrub our dirty knees after a day in the garden, we need to pay vigorous attention to what The WORD has to say about us. We need to hear it, agree with it and obey it!

Naturally speaking, most of us wouldn't dream of allowing even a day to go by without taking a bath. We certainly wouldn't put off showering for a week. Why? Because we'd get dirty, and before long, we'd start to stink!

When we neglect The WORD for a few days, the same thing happens to us spiritually. The smell of the world starts to saturate our thinking, and we begin to stink! Instead of being patient and kind, we get short-tempered and snappy. We start focusing on what others can do for us instead of what we can do for them.

So keep yourself spiritually fragrant and free of that kind of thinking. Let God continually cleanse you with the washing of the water by The WORD.

LIMITLESS**LOVE**

Be Glad-Hearted Today

"Be happy [in your faith] and rejoice and be glad-hearted continually (always)."
1 Thessalonians 5:16, *The Amplified Bible*

One of the most loving things you can do for the people around you is to be glad-hearted and joyful every day. When you're bright and happy, you lift the spirits of others. Your joy lightens their hearts. Many Christians, however, don't bother to do what it takes to stay glad-hearted. They don't draw near to The LORD each day and stir up the joy in their hearts. When the devil attacks them with "the blues," they just give in to him. When things don't go their way, they let discouragement set in. As a result, they are down and sad a lot. They're depressed themselves and an emotional burden to others.

Actually, such behavior is totally selfish, and, as believers, we have no excuse for it. We're commanded to walk in love and to be joyful and glad-hearted. The Scriptures don't tell us to be happy in our faith when we feel like it, or when things are going perfectly in our lives. They tell us to rejoice all the time. We have the ability to do it, too! If we'll just walk with God and walk in the spirit, we can walk in gladness every day!

One friend of ours who has truly learned how to do that is Jerry Savelle. I love to be around him, because he always has a glad heart. He is so full of joy that he often makes us laugh when we're with him. But Jerry didn't just accidentally stumble into that kind of joy. He actually rejoices on purpose. He cultivates the joy of The LORD.

When he travels, for example, and has to spend days alone in a hotel room away from his family, he has tremendous opportunities to feel down. Many of those times, he'd rather be at home enjoying himself with the people he loves. Instead of letting that depress him, however, he encourages himself. He'll even tell himself funny things to make himself laugh. That's one reason he brings such BLESSING to people around him. He brings them joy because he is so funny and so glad.

Some people seem to have the idea that the more spiritual we get, the sadder and more sour-faced we ought to be. But that's the furthest thing from the truth. God is the most-spiritual Being of all, and the Scripture says He laughs! Zephaniah 3:17 tells us, "The LORD thy God in the midst of thee…will rejoice over thee with joy; he will rest in his love, he will rejoice over thee with singing."

Heaven is a happy place. The people who live there aren't walking around with long faces. They're living and basking in the gladness of the joy of The LORD. We don't have to wait till we get there to join them. If we'll walk with The LORD and stir ourselves up, we can be continually glad-hearted, too!

Don't Take That Thought

"(For the weapons of our warfare are not carnal, but mighty through God
to the pulling down of strong holds;) casting down imaginations,
and every high thing that exalteth itself against the knowledge of God,
and bringing into captivity every thought to the obedience of Christ."
2 Corinthians 10:4-5

Sometimes we think of walking in love in such sweet and gentle terms that we fail to realize we have to fight the devil every step of the way. He is totally committed to keeping us from walking in love, because he knows love is the key to our spiritual success. So, he frequently bombards us with thoughts designed to draw us off course. He repeatedly reminds us of the offenses of others. He magnifies their shortcomings and pressures us to think badly of them.

If we yield to those thoughts and begin to entertain them, before long we'll find ourselves saying unloving things. We'll find ourselves "sharing" those thoughts with others. In other words, we'll find ourselves violating the law of love.

We can thwart the devil's plan, however, by resisting every unloving thought that comes our way. When we find ourselves getting aggravated and thinking unkindly about someone, we can take authority over our minds and say, "No, I refuse to receive that thought. I refuse to give it any place in my mind. I love that person, and I am committed to thinking the best of them."

Some Christians don't seem to know they can do that. They operate as if they have no control over what they think. But they're wrong. We have absolute control of our minds. That's why Jesus could give us the bold instruction we find in Matthew 6:31, "Therefore take no thought, saying...."

We can either take a thought...or we can reject it. If we take it, we'll end up saying it. If we reject it and refuse to speak it, that thought dies unborn and we will never act on it.

Our daughter, Kellie, figured that out when she was just a little girl. She absolutely hated to pick up her toys, and she did everything possible to avoid it. One day, Ken gave her a firm command. "Kellie," he said, "you go to your room right now and put your toys in the closet!"

"No," she said, "that's not my thought."

She knew as a three-year-old what many full-grown Christians still haven't learned. If she didn't want to do something, she could reject the very thought of it. Remember that. If you don't want to act in unloving ways, then reject unloving thoughts. Resist the devil by refusing to receive them. Fight him by taking every thought captive to the law of love, and you'll walk in victory every step of the way.

Don't Let the Devil Choose for You

"Choose you this day whom ye will serve…
but as for me and my house, we will serve The LORD."
Joshua 24:15

First John 3:9 tells us that if we are born again, God's nature abides within us. We have His love, joy, peace, kindness, patience, faithfulness and self-control. We may not be acting on those things, but we have them within us, nevertheless.

What we must do is make a choice. We must decide if we will yield to the nature of God within us, or the pressure of the flesh and the world around us. We must choose whether to live in love or in strife, in joy or in sadness, in peace or in turmoil.

Some Christians never bother to do that. They just drift along in life, waiting to see what happens. They wish and wonder and hope they'll somehow end up living a life of love, but it never happens.

Whenever I think about that, I remember an advertisement that ran some years ago promoting a particular long-distance telephone service. In it, the announcer said, "If you don't choose a long distance company, a choice will be made for you." That's the way the devil is with us. If we don't make a choice, he will make one for us. He will push and pressure us into yielding to the flesh so he can lock us into a life of sin.

He doesn't really have the power to do it, because the Bible says that when we were born again, sin lost its dominion over us. Our old man is dead, and we don't have to allow the flesh to rule our lives anymore. But it will, if we don't choose to act on the spiritual forces within us and a decision to serve The LORD.

That's why you're not just going to wake up some morning without any effort and discover you've accidentally started walking in love. No, day after day, you must make a conscious choice to do it.

I do that almost every morning during my prayer time. I deliberately make a choice to yield to the fruit of the spirit that day. Usually, before I ever see or speak to another person, I make it a point to draw near to The LORD and make my determination. I say, "LORD, I'm going to be love-ruled today. I'm going to let joy and peace flow out from within me. I'm going to have a good day today!"

I don't wait until I'm in trouble and facing a dilemma before I make that choice. I don't wait until I'm already half mad before I try to decide whether I'm going to walk in love or not. I make my choice ahead of time. Then, when the challenge comes, God Himself backs me up. He gives me the grace and strength to act on the choice I made that morning. He gives me the power to live out His love.

LIMITLESS**LOVE**

Develop Your Vision of Love

"Where there is no vision, the people perish:
but he that keepeth the law, happy is he."
Proverbs 29:18

If you diligently study what the Bible has to say about love, it will give you a vision for your life. It will give you an inner image of who you are on the inside so you can grow up into the person of love God designed you to be. Meditating on scriptural truths about love will do for you the same thing watching training videos of highly skilled athletes will do for the person who is a novice to a sport. Meditating on these truths gives you a picture of what success actually looks like, so you can see yourself in that light.

Those of us who didn't grow up in homes governed by love desperately need such a vision. Because we didn't see love demonstrated when we were young, we have a tough time visualizing ourselves walking in it. Even though we're born again and want to follow the promptings of our new nature, because of those old mental images, we often slip into the unloving habits we developed as kids.

That's why we must work diligently to replace those images with the images of love from the Bible. That's why we must do whatever it takes to keep The WORD in the forefront of our thinking until the vision of love is fully developed there.

When we see in ourselves something contrary to it, we must be brutally honest about it. We must let The WORD correct us while refusing to allow the devil to condemn us. When we see we're not living up to our vision of love, we must say, "LORD, I see I've been wrong there. I repent of that unloving way. Help me to change." Then we can rejoice, assured that the Holy Spirit, who is our Helper and lives within us, will enable us to make the necessary changes and do the will of God.

If you find certain unloving habits more difficult than others to break, write down that part of your vision and put it on the mirror…and the refrigerator…and the dashboard of the car. Put forth some extra effort to keep that image of love in front of you. If you've spent a lifetime being hardheaded and stubborn, you might want to write out the words, "I do not insist on my own rights or my own way. I walk in love." And post them on your nightstand so you can go to sleep with that vision in your mind at night.

That may sound extreme, but the fact is, changing a lifestyle takes some work. It takes writing things down, keeping them in your memory, and diligently imprinting them on your mind. If you'll do it, the vision of love will become such a part of you that eventually it will take over your life, and you'll begin to walk in it unconsciously. You'll happily and habitually keep the law of love!

No Substitute for Fellowship

"Do not be misled: 'Bad company corrupts good character.'"
1 Corinthians 15:33, *New International Version*

Why is it that bad company corrupts good character? It's because we are influenced by our associations. When we habitually fellowship with negative people, before long we find ourselves thinking and talking negatively. When we habitually fellowship with positive people, we soon become more positive and optimistic.

That's why if you want to walk in love, spending time in fellowship with God is the very best thing you can do. Because He is so perfectly loving, the more you associate with Him, the more loving you become. The more you listen to His voice and attend to His WORD, the more naturally kind and loving your words will be. Without your even realizing it, His nature will begin to rub off on you. His influence will bring out those qualities within you which come from Him. You will naturally begin to walk and talk and act in love.

Have you ever been around someone who was raised in an area of the country where people speak in a very distinctive way? If that person moves away after they're grown, they often lose much of their original accent. They begin to speak more like the people in the area where they're living now. But, put them in a group of people from their home town, and before long, their speech will change. That old accent will be back as strong as ever. The influence of the people from home will naturally bring out the old, familiar tones and phrases they used growing up. Suddenly, without even trying, they'll sound again like the person they used to be.

That's what happens to us when we fellowship with The LORD. His presence and His divine personality so affect us that, without even trying, we are conformed to the image of Jesus. We start acting on the outside like who we are on the inside—a new creation born with the nature of God. One author who understood that principle was Donald Gee. In his book, *The Fruit of the Spirit,* He wrote:

> Loss of communion is the explanation of most of our failure in spiritual fruit bearing, and no amount of Christian work or even exercise of Christian gifts can ever be a substitute for walking with God. It is encouraging to remember that sustained communion with Christ in our daily walk produces the fruit of the Spirit unconsciously. Others see it before we do and it is better so.[13]

Keep that in mind the next time your schedule gets hectic and you find yourself too busy to spend time with The LORD. Remind yourself that His company is what produces the fruit of the spirit. Only His fellowship can bring out His love in you.

---

[13] Donald Gee, *The Fruit of the Spirit* (Springfield: Gospel Publishing House, 2006) p. 13.

LIMITLESS LOVE

You're Not Ready for the Woodpile

"If a man abide not in me, he is cast forth as a branch, and is withered; and men gather them, and cast them into the fire, and they are burned."
John 15:6

Because our daily communion with The LORD is what keeps us abiding in Him and bearing the fruit of love, the devil works ceaselessly to hinder it. He pressures us with busy schedules and tries to convince us we just don't have time to fellowship with God. When we do sit down to read The WORD and pray, he endeavors to distract us with thoughts of other things and interruptions of every sort.

If we yield to those pressures and miss our time of prayer, the devil heaps condemnation on us. He makes us reluctant to draw near to The LORD again by convincing us that God is mad at us for neglecting Him. Instead of taking the first opportunity and jumping back into communion with God, we drag our feet, thinking He is going to punish and criticize us for the times of fellowship we've missed.

The devil may even misquote scriptures and say that God is fed up with our failures and ready to cast us into the fire. He'll tell us God has thrown us into the woodpile!

Don't listen to lies like that. God isn't mad at you when you miss your time of fellowship with Him. He doesn't want to punish you. He loves you. He is eagerly waiting for you to draw near to Him, and the moment you do, He will draw near to you. He will speak to you and help you and BLESS you because that's what He wants to do.

That's the whole reason He commands you to abide in Him! It's only through that union He can get to you the grace and strength you need to live in victory. He is the vine and you are the branch. If the branch removes itself from the vine, it will wither—not because the branch is mad at it, but because without that living contact between them, the vine cannot do for the branch what it is supposed to do.

What's more, that scripture doesn't say that *the vine* gathers withered branches and burns them—it says that *men* do. When we stop spending time with The LORD we get burned by the natural circumstances of life. When trouble comes, we don't have the divine life flowing through us that we need to overcome it. If we haven't been abiding in The LORD, we don't have our faith ready; we don't have the fruit of the spirit flowing out of us and the wisdom of God operating in us to enable us to handle the situation.

So, don't the let devil trick you into getting yourself into that condition. Don't let him distract you and deprive you of your communion with The LORD. Don't ever let him condemn you and convince you that God has thrown you on the woodpile and doesn't want fellowship with you. Resist those lies and realize it's the devil—not The LORD—who is wanting you to get burned.

LIMITLESS**LOVE**

Follow the Fruit

"Beware of false prophets, which come to you in sheep's clothing, but inwardly they are ravening wolves. Ye shall know them by their fruits. Do men gather grapes of thorns, or figs of thistles? Even so every good tree bringeth forth good fruit; but a corrupt tree bringeth forth evil fruit. A good tree cannot bring forth evil fruit, nor can a corrupt tree bring forth good fruit."
Matthew 7:15-18

We aren't called to judge and criticize Christian leaders, but we do need to be fruit inspectors. Before we wholeheartedly follow someone's teaching or imitate their lifestyle, we ought to inspect the fruit of their lives. We should see in them not just popularity, spectacular spiritual gifts or success in ministry, but evidence that they are walking in the fruit of the spirit—the first and foremost of which is love.

It doesn't matter how prophetically accurate someone seems to be, or what amazing miracles they have in their ministry. If they're not following the way of love, they're not following God, and you shouldn't follow them. They may call themselves an apostle, prophet, pastor, teacher or evangelist. They may even be called and gifted to operate in those offices. But if they don't do it in love, they'll eventually draw you off course.

The Apostle Paul had some of the most powerful ministry giftings the Church has ever seen, yet he didn't say, "Follow me because I'm an apostle." He didn't say, "Follow me because I have a worldwide ministry." He said, "Follow my example, as I follow the example of Christ" (1 Corinthians 11:1, *New International Version*).

Don't ever be so impressed by a leader's position or success that you forget to inspect the fruit of their lives. If you find good fruit, follow them. If you don't, don't criticize or condemn them. Don't gossip about them with others. Just pray for them, and look for someone who does have good fruit in their lives. Find a leader who is walking in love and bearing the fruits of joy, peace, patience, faithfulness, kindness and self-control. Find someone who has a life—not just a teaching—you can follow.

As you do, remember that you have a responsibility to lead others, too. Even if you aren't called to full-time ministry, or to hold one of the fivefold offices of the Church, you are called to be an example for younger believers. So, be a good one. Give those around you who are less mature in The LORD an opportunity to inspect your fruit. Let them find in you a life they can follow—a life that is filled with love.

LIMITLESS**LOVE**

The Greater One Is in You

"Beloved, do not believe every spirit, but test the spirits to see whether they are
from God, because many false prophets have gone out into the world. By this you
know the Spirit of God: every spirit that confesses that Jesus Christ has come in
the flesh is from God; and every spirit that does not confess Jesus is not from God;
and this is the spirit of the antichrist, of which you have heard that it is coming,
and now it is already in the world. You are from God, little children, and have
overcome them; because greater is He who is in you than he who is in the world."
1 John 4:1-4, *New American Standard*

There is no question about it, the spirit of the antichrist is at work in the world today.
We hear in the words and see in the lives of people around us great influences of evil. On
television and in magazines we see a rising antagonism toward holiness and the things of
God. It seems that society is rebelling against every restraint and the forces of the devil are
pushing people further and further into immorality and darkness.

At times, you might be tempted to say, "If God is Love, why doesn't He do something
about all this?"

He *is* doing something about it. He has put you and me and every other believer alive
on the earth today in the midst of it, and He has given us the power to overcome it. We are
lights of God in the midst of a dark world, and no matter how great the darkness becomes,
it cannot put out our light.

I remember when I first found that out, it was such a comfort to me. Ken and I were facing
so many impossible situations. Back then, it seemed like the devil had the upper hand not
just in the world around us, but in our own lives. Then we found out that God had made us
overcomers, and we began to say, "The Greater One lives in me!"

The more we believed that and the more we acted on it, the more we overcame. Little by
little, Ken and I took the power God had given us by His indwelling Spirit and His WORD and
drove the devil out of our lives, marriage, family and finances. Then, we began to reach out
with that same overcoming power, and influence the lives of others. We began to see what
God's love working in us and through us could truly do!

Next time you start to feel overwhelmed by the circumstances of life or the darkness
of the world around you, remind yourself that the Greater One lives within you. Don't let the
devil disturb you with the things he's doing. Turn the tables on him. Rise up like the overcomer
God has made you to be. Let the love of God within you shine forth, and start putting out the
darkness with God's light!

Develop a Strong Defense

> "But one whom you forgive anything, I forgive also; for indeed what
> I have forgiven, if I have forgiven anything, I did it for your sakes in the
> presence of Christ, in order that no advantage be taken of us by Satan,
> for we are not ignorant of his schemes."
> 2 Corinthians 2:10-11, *New American Standard*

The devil is continually devising plans and schemes to throw believers off course. He is constantly sending offenses, troublesome circumstances, pressures and temptations designed to trip us up and keep us from finishing our race in God.

One way we can defend ourselves against his schemes is by developing the fruit of the spirit in our lives. That fruit—love, joy, peace, patience, kindness, goodness, faithfulness, gentleness and self-control—within us always helps us overcome.

Most people think the fruit of the spirit works primarily to BLESS those around us. It does BLESS others, all right, but walking in the fruit of the spirit BLESSES *us,* too. The fruit of the spirit in operation enables us to combat the forces of darkness that surround us. It helps us rise above challenges that confront us every day of our lives.

Think about it for a moment and you can easily see why. When the devil tries to discourage us, joy will wash that discouragement away. When he tries to tempt us with the pressure of lust and fleshly indulgence, self-control will kick in and give us the strength we need to triumph. As one writer says:

> Because of His love, the Father yearns for His children to begin to cultivate every fruit of the Spirit, for He wants His sons to be overcomers. Actually, a believer cannot be a totally successful overcomer if any one of the fruit is missing in his life, because that particular area will be the very one in which the devil will concentrate his attack. Each fruit of the Spirit enables the individual believer to better cope with adverse situations in his life. Each fruit of the Spirit has a job to do in obtaining victory for you in every area of your life.[14]

Since love, for example, is not touchy, fretful or resentful and takes no account of a suffered wrong, when the devil sends someone to hurt you or treat you badly, that device won't work against you. Love will keep that offense from sticking to you. It will keep you from succumbing to the devil's strategy and stepping into strife and sin. His plan will be defeated, and he'll be left without a way to damage or destroy you. Love will be your best defense!

---

[14] *A Call for Character: Developing the Fruit of the Spirit In Your Life,* Greg Zoschak. 1991. Harrison House, Inc.: Tulsa, Oklahoma.

LIMITLESS**LOVE**

Taking the Narrow Way

"Enter through the narrow gate. For wide is the gate and broad is the road that leads to destruction, and many enter through it. But small is the gate and narrow the road that leads to life, and only a few find it."
Matthew 7:13-14, *New International Version*

Some believers seem to think that walking in love is optional. They act as if they have the right to take offence if they want to…or act rudely and unkindly when they aren't in a good mood. They do it without ever realizing they are in sin.

"Sin?" you might say. "That's a pretty strong word."

I know it is, but it's the right word, nevertheless. And, if we are going to walk in THE BLESSING and the abundant life of God, we'd better quit making excuses for it and call it what it is.

Love is God's commandment to us. It's not His suggestion. It's not His preference. It's a command. When we're not walking in love, we're in disobedience to that command. In other words, we're in sin.

We don't have to go kill someone or commit adultery to be in disobedience to God. We don't have to swear or cheat on our taxes. All the devil has to do to get us into sin is to convince us to walk in selfishness, to put ourselves first and ignore others. To put us on the road of destruction, all he has to do is get us to walk another way—any other way—than love.

I know keeping the law of love sounds difficult, and if you were doing it in your own strength it would be. In fact, it would be impossible. But you're not doing it in your own strength. You're born again. You have a Savior who shed His blood so you can have the life and love of God inside you. You have been empowered by God Himself to love as He loves.

You may have been a selfish person before you met The LORD, but He delivered you from that selfishness when you were born again. You may have been critical and unforgiving all your life, but when you received Jesus as your LORD, He made you a new creature. All those old things passed away. They don't have the power to rule you anymore.

God has called you with a high calling. He has given you a high way to live and a high law to keep. But He's given you the ability to keep it from the inside out. He's given you the nature of love, and He's given you the Holy Spirit to teach you to walk in that nature.

Sure, the way of love is narrow. To stay on it, you can't allow the pressures of the world to push you this way and that. You must let The WORD of God and the Spirit within you direct your steps. It will take some spiritual effort, but you can do it. Because you've been born of love, it's the only way for you to live.

LIMITLESS**LOVE**

More Powerful Than Feelings

"Praise The LORD! How blessed is the man who fears The LORD, who greatly delights in His commandments. His descendants will be mighty on earth; the generation of the upright will be blessed…. Light arises in the darkness for the upright; he is gracious and compassionate and righteous…. He will not fear evil tidings; his heart is steadfast, trusting in The LORD. His heart is upheld, he will not fear, until he looks with satisfaction on his adversaries."
Psalm 112:1-2, 4, 7-8, *New American Standard*

Most people think a compassionate person is one who pets and pampers people's feelings when things go wrong. They think it's loving in times of calamity to feel sorry for people, to pat their hands and say, "I just feel so bad for you. Bless your dear, little heart."

But, according to The Word of God, there are times when that is just the opposite of what a truly compassionate person will do. When evil threatens and circumstances get dark, real love refuses to be moved by the emotions of the moment. Love takes hold of The WORD of God by faith, and stands steadfast on it until the devil is defeated and the victory is won.

I know from experience that can be tough, but by the grace of God it can be done. Some years ago, we had just begun a weeklong Believers' Convention in Fort Worth when my granddaughter, Jenny, was in a car accident. She was just a toddler at the time, and so badly injured, she had to be care-flighted to a hospital. The medical personnel fully expected her to die before they got there.

When they brought me the news, I didn't fold up in tears and start feeling sorry for that baby. I didn't start worrying and weeping about how sad my daughter would feel if Jenny died. I just started confessing The WORD. I closed my heart to all the upset and bad reports and just centered on the promises of God. I kept The WORD coming out of my mouth and going back into my ears, until my heart was full of it. I wouldn't let my mind think about anything else.

I got tired of saying it at times, and I imagine the people around me got tired of it, too. But I didn't care about that. I wasn't about to let some fleshly weariness or soulish emotion weaken my stand of faith and give the devil an opportunity to steal my granddaughter.

If someone had offered me sympathy, I would have said, "Thanks, but I don't need it. My granddaughter will live and not die, and declare the works of The LORD."

She did, too. Jenny is alive and well today and living her life for God. She's walking proof that real compassion is more powerful than feelings. She's a living demonstration of what faith and love can do.

LIMITLESS**LOVE**

Don't Just Stand There, Say Something!

"In the beginning God created the heavens and the earth. The earth was formless and void, and darkness was over the surface of the deep, and the Spirit of God was moving over the surface of the waters. Then God said, 'Let there be light'; and there was light."

Genesis 1:1-3, *New American Standard*

The next time you have trouble loving someone, here's something you can do. Every time you think of that person, say that you love them. Say it out loud. Say it with faith. Say it like you mean it.

Why? Because when you speak words by faith that are in agreement with The WORD of God, the Holy Spirit moves in with His power and brings them to pass. That's one of the first things the Bible teaches us. It reveals in the very first verses of Genesis that the Holy Spirit can be present, hovering over a situation in all His wonderful power and might. He can be there, ready and willing to act, but He will not do so until The WORD of God is spoken. His work is to fulfill The WORD.

If you're born again, the Holy Spirit is within you, willing and able to help you love the most unlovely people in your life. Yet He cannot do it until you speak words He can act on. He can't do much for you when you are saying things like, "That person irritates me! I just can't seem to get along with them. Why is he so hard for me to love?" Those aren't God's words, so the Holy Spirit can't bring them to pass.

But when you get your mouth in agreement with God and say, "The love of God dwells in me, and I love that brother with the love of The LORD. I am tenderhearted toward that sister. I love her just like Jesus loves me!" the Holy Spirit can go to work on you, exerting His mighty power to help you bring your emotions and thought life in line with those confessions of faith. Just as God said, "Light be!" and the Holy Spirit brought forth light in the darkness, when you say, "Love be," that same Spirit will bring forth God's love in you.

"But, I don't feel like I love that person at all," you might argue. "I'd be a liar if I said I did."

You wouldn't be a liar, you'd be imitating your heavenly Father. The Bible says He calls things that do not exist as though they did. He called Abraham a "father of many nations," when he was a childless old man married to a barren old woman. He called Gideon a "mighty man of valour" when he was hiding in fear from his enemies. He called David a king when he was just a shepherd boy.

So, don't just stand there, say something loving! Start talking like God does, and the power that made Abraham a father, Gideon a victorious warrior and David a king will go to work on your soul. The Holy Spirit Himself will bring forth the nature God has put in you, and make you more loving than you ever dreamed you could be.

LIMITLESS LOVE

All Dressed Up
With Nowhere to Go

"For as the rain cometh down, and the snow from heaven, and returneth not thither, but watereth the earth, and maketh it bring forth and bud, that it may give seed to the sower, and bread to the eater: So shall my word be that goeth forth out of my mouth: it shall not return unto me void, but it shall accomplish that which I please, and it shall prosper in the thing whereto I sent it."
Isaiah 55:10-11

If you say what God says about love, the Bible absolutely guarantees you will see the results in your life. Stubborn personality traits you thought you could never change will start to soften. Unloving habits that seemed unbreakable will begin to disappear if you will dare to put 1 Corinthians 13 in your mouth and faithfully say, "I am patient and kind. I'm never envious or jealous. I'm not conceited or rude. I don't act unbecomingly or insist on my own way. I'm not touchy, and I don't take account of a suffered wrong...."

Speaking God's WORD activates spiritual law. When it comes out of our mouths, it accomplishes what it was sent to do. It prospers and brings forth the plan of God in our lives.

"Yes, I know," you might say. "I've heard that before."

Maybe so, but what are you doing about it? Are you acting on it? Are you doing what you know to do?

We all have to check up on ourselves in that area because it's easy to slip out of active faith and into mere mental assent. We can get the idea that just because we agree with The WORD and we want it to work in our lives, that our job is done. We get busy with other things and neglect to do what the Bible tells us to do. Eventually, we'll look up and realize we're not making any spiritual progress.

That reminds me of something that happened to Ken and me years ago that I'll never forget. We were heading from our hotel room on our way to preach a meeting. We got onto the elevator and we were so caught up in conversation, we weren't really paying attention to what we were doing. In a few minutes, we looked up to see what floor we were on and realized the elevator hadn't moved at all. We were in the same place we started, because we either hadn't pressed the button, or without thinking we had pressed the button for the floor we were already on. There we were, all dressed up and going nowhere!

Don't let that happen to you in the area of love. Don't get all dressed up with knowledge from The WORD about the love of God within you...and then end up going nowhere. Lift that WORD back up to The LORD, confess it and step out on it so it can accomplish what it was sent to do in your life!

LIMITLESS**LOVE**

Don't Think Like a Beggar

"O fear The LORD, ye his saints: for there is no want to them that fear him.
The young lions do lack, and suffer hunger: but they that seek The LORD
shall not want any good thing."
Psalm 34:9-10

Our heavenly Father loves us so much, He has promised we'll never be in want. He has given us His word that we won't lack any good thing. But, instead of believing His promise and receiving by faith its benefits, most Christians are living like orphans who have no one to take care of them and meet their needs.

We ought not to live like orphans when we're children of God. We shouldn't think like beggars. Even if we're short of funds, we shouldn't look at our financial situation and see ourselves in lack. We ought to see ourselves by faith. We ought to trust what the Bible says and see ourselves as richly BLESSED children of a loving and giving God.

When shortage rears its ugly head in our lives, we should see it for what it is—an attack of the devil who is trying to steal THE BLESSING by undermining our faith. Instead of doubting God's love and faithfulness, we should rebuke that lying devil and say, "Lack, I resist you in Jesus' Name. You get out of my life. I don't have to live with you because you're a curse, and I'm redeemed from the curse. God has redeemed me from poverty and lack. He abundantly supplies my needs."

I remember the first time I did that. Ken and I had been leasing a home and were believing God for the money to buy it. We had a year to come up with the purchase price, and in the natural it looked like we wouldn't be able to do it. Lack just kept dogging our steps.

Suddenly, as I stood in the living room of that house, looking out the window and thinking about our situation, the revelation of God hit me. I thought about how God in His great love had delivered us, through the plan of redemption, from all the oppression of the devil. I thought about how He had redeemed us from sickness and disease, poverty and lack. Then I realized I hadn't been resisting lack like I had sickness and disease. When sickness attacked our family, I fought it tooth and nail. I hit it with The WORD and with faith until it fled.

Instantly, I knew I had to do the same thing with lack. From that day on, I took an aggressive stand against it. I took hold by faith of what my heavenly Father had promised me and started declaring, "Lack, you get out of my way. My God meets all my needs according to His riches in glory by Christ Jesus."

I don't mind telling you, we paid for that house, and we've paid for several more since then. I don't live like an orphan anymore. I don't let the devil make me a beggar. I live in THE BLESSING of my Father's love.

LIMITLESS**LOVE**

When God Has a Good Time

"Let them shout for joy, and be glad, that favour my righteous cause:
yea, let them say continually, Let The LORD be magnified,
which hath pleasure in the prosperity of his servant."
Psalm 35:27

Don't ever let anyone make you feel bad for stepping out in faith and believing for God to BLESS you. Don't let people put you down for standing on God's promises and looking to Him to put food on your table, money in your bank account, and provide for you all that you need to do every good work He has called you to do.

God isn't insulted by that. He isn't offended that you would expect that of Him. (Other people might be, but He isn't.) God is honored when you believe His WORD. He is pleased by it, because your faith opens the door for Him to do good things for you. He loves you, so He takes pleasure in prospering you.

I decided a long time ago that I wanted God to get plenty of enjoyment out of me. I decided I would keep on believing Him for prosperity in every area of my life. That way He could have a really good time.

Of course, the devil has pressured me and tried to talk me out of it every step of the way. He's brought me circumstances and trials designed to make me doubt God's faithfulness and love. He's tried again and again to make me give up and quit.

He'll do the same thing to you. Why? Because he knows that if he can't make you doubt the love of God and stop you from believing His promises, you'll end up with a testimony that will inspire faith in others. People around you will see God's love at work in your life, and they'll start trusting Him, too!

Years ago, when I first read in the Bible that God would take care of me, it didn't look like I would ever be a threat to the devil. When I began to believe God for grocery money and other basics of life, I didn't know my faith would ever affect anyone but me.

But in the years since, Ken and I have had the opportunity to tell thousands of people about God's love and faithfulness. We've shared the stories of what God has done (and is still doing) for us.

Don't you know the devil hates that?

But, then, who cares what he thinks? God is the One we want to please. He is the One we love, and He loves to prosper us. So let's just keep on believing His WORD. Let's BLESS Him by letting Him BLESS us. That way, we'll all have a wonderful time!

The Best Way to BLESS The LORD

"Then The LORD saw that the wickedness of man was great on the earth,
and that every intent of the thoughts of his heart was only evil continually.
The LORD was sorry that He had made man on the earth, and He was
grieved in His heart…. But Noah found favor in the eyes of The LORD….
Noah was a righteous man, blameless in his time; Noah walked with God."
Genesis 6:5-6, 8-9, *New American Standard*

Once you begin to understand how much God loves you, your love for Him will naturally increase. You'll want to give to Him and BLESS Him. You'll want to do all that you can to express your affection and gratitude toward the One who has done so much for you.

But what can you give to God, who is already the Creator and Possessor of everything? How can you BLESS the Source of all BLESSING?

You can walk with Him by faith. You can be one of those rare people who honors Him by believing what He says, and stands fast on His WORD, even when it contradicts what is seen in the natural world. Despite the taunts of the devil and the criticism of skeptics, this person says, "I believe my heavenly Father. I have His WORD and I will trust it no matter what happens. I will not let it go!"

That's the kind of man Noah was. When God told him a flood was coming and instructed him to build the Ark, no one had ever seen rain before. The earth had always been watered from beneath. So when Noah began to preach about the coming Flood and prepare for it by constructing a boat the size of a football field, no doubt people laughed at him. They probably made fun of "crazy old Noah," and labeled him a fanatic.

Year after year went by, and Noah kept building. There were probably no storm clouds in the sky, either—no indication in the natural world that what God had said would ever come to pass. But Noah wasn't moved by that. He just kept believing and obeying God. The rest of the world was in the dark. But, when the Flood came, Noah and his family weren't in the dark—they were in the Ark!

If you truly love The LORD, that's the way you'll live. When you see something in His WORD, you'll obey it in faith. When you read, for example, that God loves a cheerful, generous, prompt-to-do-it giver and rewards them with abundance, you won't stop giving just because your bank balance doesn't skyrocket overnight. You'll just keep acting on The WORD and trusting The LORD. You'll do it because you love Him. You'll do it because you believe Him. You'll do it because you want to BLESS Him.

He'll appreciate it, too. The Bible says His eyes go to and fro throughout the earth looking for someone like that. He found one in Noah…and if you truly love Him, He will find one in you!

LIMITLESS**LOVE**

Losing Sight of Ourselves

"But God has chosen the foolish things of the world to shame the wise, and God has chosen the weak things of the world to shame the things which are strong, and the base things of the world and the despised God has chosen, the things that are not, so that He may nullify the things that are, so that no man may boast before God. But by His doing you are in Christ Jesus, who became to us wisdom from God, and righteousness and sanctification, and redemption, so that, just as it is written, 'LET HIM WHO BOASTS, BOAST IN THE LORD.'"

1 Corinthians 1:27-31, *New American Standard*

Most people think the opposite of love is hate. But it might be just as accurate to say that the opposite of love is selfishness. Love causes us to focus on others. Selfishness causes us to focus on ourselves.

That's why the very first thing we must do to successfully walk in love is to stop looking at ourselves, and start looking at God. We must cease being self-centered and start being God-centered. We must give up self-confidence and gain God-confidence, instead.

Actually, it's a great relief just to admit that what the Bible says about us is true. On our own, we're nothing. We are weak, foolish and base. What's more, that's why God called us. He likes to take people who are incapable of doing anything worthwhile on their own and enable them to do great things by His power. He likes to take ordinary earthen vessels and display His glory in them.

How does He do that? He makes us new creatures in Christ Jesus. He gives us His righteousness, holiness, wisdom and abilities. He puts His own Spirit inside us, so instead of looking to ourselves, we can depend on the Greater One who dwells within.

In the process, we lose sight of ourselves. Insecurity and self-consciousness become a thing of the past. We discover it doesn't really matter what we are. It doesn't matter how smart or talented we are. We just keep our eyes on Jesus, knowing that by His Spirit He will give us the ability to do whatever God tells us to do.

As we start centering our lives around God, we'll automatically stop focusing on what pleases us and start focusing instead on what pleases Him. We won't spend our time thinking, *What do I want? What will make me happy?* We'll be seeking The LORD to find out what He wants us to do. We'll be concerned only about what makes Him happy.

You know before I even tell you what that is. It's love. When our lives become God-centered instead of self-centered, our primary purpose will be to live the life of love, not in our own power and ability, but in His. We'll stop worrying about ourselves and let our weakness be transformed by His strength. Then, we'll give all the glory to Him.

LIMITLESS**LOVE**

A Continual Feast

"And he gave some, apostles; and some, prophets; and some, evangelists; and some, pastors and teachers; For the perfecting of the saints, for the work of the ministry, for the edifying of the body of Christ: Till we all come in the unity of the faith, and of the knowledge of the Son of God, unto a perfect man, unto the measure of the stature of the fulness of Christ."
Ephesians 4:11-13

To walk in love, we have to maintain a strong spirit. We must continually nourish our hearts with The WORD of God. Just as we deplete our natural strength when we exert ourselves physically, and have to eat natural food, when we exert ourselves spiritually by walking in love (and it does take real spiritual exertion to do it!), we deplete our spiritual strength. So, we must continually replenish it by feeding on The WORD.

One way we do that, of course, is by spending time alone reading the Bible. We don't have to wait for someone else to feed us, we can get into God's WORD for ourselves.

But it's also important for us to go somewhere where we can hear someone especially called and gifted by God to teach and preach His WORD. When we receive The WORD that way, there is an extra anointing and impartation on it. That anointing will cut through some of the mixed-up thinking we may not have previously been aware of. It will straighten out and renew our minds. The anointing God has given to that minister will add something to us that we just can't get on our own.

I know that from personal experience. That's why I go to so many church services and Believers' Conventions. That's why I have stacks of CDs and DVDs in every room in my house. Sometimes I listen to messages that are 20 years old. I may have heard them many times before, but when I hear them again, the anointing is still on them to strengthen and build me up spiritually.

Some people don't understand that. They think you just listen to ministers preach The WORD so you can get new information. But actually, you listen to them to get revelation. You might think you know all there is to know about love, for instance. But, when you hear someone preach about it under the anointing, more revelation on it will come. You'll get more light and insight about it, and you'll walk out of that meeting (or away from that CD or DVD) more empowered and equipped to walk in love than you've ever been before.

As Romans 10:17 says, "Faith cometh by hearing, and hearing by The WORD of God." So, find some good, anointed preaching, and keep your spirit strong with a continual feast of The WORD!

LIMITLESS**LOVE**

The Impossible Is Easy for God

"While the harpist was playing, the hand of The LORD came on Elisha
and he said, 'This is what The LORD says: Make this valley full of ditches.
For this is what The LORD says: You will see neither wind nor rain,
yet this valley will be filled with water, and you, your cattle and your other
animals will drink. This is an easy thing in the eyes of The LORD;
he will also hand Moab over to you.'"
2 Kings 3:15-18, *New International Version*

When you find yourself in an impossible situation, when you're in trouble and in need of a miracle, remember two things: God loves you, and miracles are easy for Him.

That's what the prophet Elisha told the three kings who were seeking The LORD'S help to defeat the army of Moab. They had made some serious mistakes. They had not done everything God wanted them to do and, as a result, they found themselves in a deadly situation. Their armies and animals were dying of thirst. They were facing a fierce foe, and had no natural strength left to defeat them.

But even though they were to blame for getting themselves in that situation, God didn't leave them there. What's more, He didn't wring His hands and say, "I don't know, fellows. This is a pretty tough problem. I'll do what I can, but I'm not sure I can help you."

No, He said, "This is an easy thing."

Isn't it good to know that the things you think are such challenges are easy for our great and loving God? It's easy for God to heal your body, fix your finances and turn impossible situations around. God has no trouble at all doing miracles. It didn't tax His strength to make the sun stand still. He didn't struggle or strain to open up a path through the Red Sea. To Him, those things are simple to do.

The only difficulty God has is getting people to trust Him and believe what He says. And when you think about it, that in itself is amazing. After all, He really has a very good reputation. For thousands of years, He has faithfully been loving and delivering His people. Why is it, then, so difficult for us to relax and rely on Him?

It's because the devil is constantly telling us lies about Him. He is continually bombarding us with thoughts that God doesn't care. He pressures us with circumstances and promotes the idea that God has abandoned us and will not help in our time of need.

Don't buy the lies. Fight them with faith and The WORD. Keep the truth of God's love and His power fresh in your heart. Then, when you face the impossible, you won't panic, because you'll know God cares and He can easily do a miracle for you.

LIMITLESS**LOVE**

A Steady Diet of Good News

"Therefore we do not lose heart, but though our outer man is decaying, yet our inner man is being renewed day by day…while we look not at the things which are seen, but at the things which are not seen; for the things which are seen are temporal, but the things which are not seen are eternal."
2 Corinthians 4:16, 18, *New American Standard*

I've been teaching for years how absolutely vital it is for us to spend time in The WORD and in fellowship with The LORD every day. I repeat it again and again. If people get tired of it, I don't care. I'm like Peter, who said, "I intend always to remind you about these things, although indeed you know them…" (2 Peter 1:12, *The Amplified Bible*).

Actually, I think it's even more important now than it's ever been before, because as the world gets darker, we are more surrounded by fear and bad news. The media make sure we hear about every tragedy, every downturn in the economy and any natural circumstance that might threaten us. They interview people who have been victimized, or lost their jobs, or those who have been traumatized in some way. But, rarely will they give much time to report about those who have overcome tragedy, or received new and better jobs, or those who have been miraculously spared some kind of trouble.

Because of the development of satellite and cable, we now have the opportunity to watch bad news 24 hours a day. (What a breakthrough!) You can watch the same depressing newscast over and over. If you do, before you know it, you'll lose heart. You'll be thinking, *I'm afraid I'm going to be laid off. I'm afraid I'm not going to have enough money to retire. I'm afraid all this trouble that is troubling the world is going to come to my house before long!*

That's why, if you want to stay strong in your faith in God's love and faithfulness to take care of you, you need to have a constant, steady diet of God's WORD. You have to continually renew your inner man by fellowshiping with Him in the spirit day by day.

You must purposely spend time focusing not on the things which are seen, but on the unseen truths of God, and remind yourself that all the bad news the media report is just temporary. Tomorrow something different will be happening. As one minister says, "Newspapers are so temporary they have to be published every day!"

But the truth of God is eternal. Your Bible will say the same thing tomorrow that it says today because God doesn't change. He just keeps on loving you. He just keeps on giving you every good and perfect gift because in Him there is "no variableness, neither shadow of turning" (James 1:17). He will—now and forever—love and take care of you.

LIMITLESS**LOVE**

In Your Heart and Your Mouth

"But the righteousness which is of faith speaketh on this wise, Say not in thine heart, Who shall ascend into heaven? (that is, to bring Christ down from above:) Or, Who shall descend into the deep? (that is, to bring up Christ again from the dead.) But what saith it? The WORD is nigh thee, even in thy mouth, and in thy heart: that is, The WORD of faith, which we preach."
Romans 10:6-8

"If God loves me, why doesn't He heal me? If God really cares about me, why doesn't He help me out of this financial mess?"

We've all heard people say things like that. We may have even said them ourselves. But the fact is, the Bible clearly answers those questions. It says God loves us so much that, through Jesus, He has already taken care of all those things for us. Before we ever needed healing or help or deliverance, God provided them for us. Then, He told us about it in His WORD, so we could receive His provision whenever we wanted to by simply putting that WORD in our hearts and in our mouths.

To me, that's exciting! It means I don't have to talk God into healing me. He loves me so much He has already said, "by whose stripes ye *were* healed" (1 Peter 2:24). I don't have to try to persuade God to help me with my finances. He has already said, "I will supply all your need according to My riches in glory by Christ Jesus" (see Philippians 4:19).

"Maybe so, but I'd just be able to receive better if Jesus would come Himself and appear to me," you might argue. "I'd just have more faith if He'd give me something more than His WORD."

No, you wouldn't because the Bible says that faith comes by hearing The WORD of God. It doesn't come by seeing Jesus in the flesh. It doesn't come by experiencing some spectacular miracle. When I was first learning about these things, The LORD showed me that His written words carry the same authority when I read them in the Bible that they would if Jesus came into my room and said them to me with His own mouth. God's WORD always carries creative power.

If you let that power go into your heart and come out of your mouth, it will straighten out your life. It will bring forth all the things God has so lovingly provided for you. I'll just be blunt: The only thing that can stop you from receiving God's promises once you find out about them is laziness or unbelief.

So, determine right now you won't ever let laziness or unbelief stop you. Decide you will never frustrate God's love and grace by failing to receive His provision. Put His WORD in your heart and in your mouth. Receive by faith all the good gifts He has ready for you.

LIMITLESS**LOVE**

When God Draws Near to You

"Draw near to God and He will draw near to you."
James 4:8, *New American Standard*

It's wonderful just to believe that God loves us. It's a great thing to be so well-grounded in the truth of The WORD that we know God is with us and cares about us every moment of every day—when we feel His presence, and when we don't. Every believer needs that assurance. Every Christian needs to be so strong in faith in that area that the devil can never shake our confidence in God's eternal love.

Even so, we all hunger for times when we can sense in our hearts the expression of that love. We desire encounters with The LORD where we become so aware of His presence that we receive, to a greater degree, what the Apostle Paul prayed for in Ephesians 3:18-19:

That you may have the power and be strong to apprehend and grasp with all the saints [God's devoted people, the experience of that love] what is the breadth and length and height and depth [of it]; [That you may really come] to know [practically, through experience for yourselves] the love of Christ, which far surpasses mere knowledge... *(The Amplified Bible).*

What can you do to experience God's presence in that way? Simply follow the instructions in the Bible. Draw near to Him and He will draw near to you.

It's not God's style to come barging into your living room while you're watching some silly television show, take the remote control out of your hand and say, "Hey, turn that off! I want to reveal My love to you, now." He is not an intruder. He won't even force His way into a church service or your daily devotional time if you don't desire and make time for Him to speak to you.

You have to make room for God's Spirit if you want Him to move. You have to seek Him, believing He will reward you by revealing Himself more clearly to you. You must let Him know with your heart, your mouth and your actions that you truly want Him to.

One thing about God is that He goes where He is wanted. So, if you want to sense His presence more strongly, you need to make the first move. Take the time to get quiet and set your mind on Him. Tell Him, simply and honestly from your heart, how much you love and appreciate Him and how grateful you are that He loves you. Don't push for some spectacular manifestation. Just worship and wait in reverence before Him.

Draw near to Him in faith. Just as He promised, He will draw near to you.

Receive a Great Reward

"Therefore, do not throw away your confidence, which has a great reward.
For you have need of endurance, so that when you have done
the will of God, you may receive what was promised."
Hebrews 10:35-36, *New American Standard*

Do you know God promises rewards to people who walk in love? Not just rewards here in this life (although there are enough of those to make living the love life worthwhile) but rewards in eternity. I don't know exactly what those rewards are, but because I know God, I know they'll be good!

Jesus said anyone who gives so much as a cup of cold water to someone in His Name would by no means lose his reward. Can you imagine, then, the kinds of rewards God has in mind for us if, for His sake, we commit ourselves to loving people every day? You probably can't. Neither can I. But one thing is for sure, we don't want to miss out on them.

We will, though, if we don't exercise patience and endurance as we walk in love. The devil will see to that. There will be times when he'll make people around us so unlovely for so long that we'll want to get mad and give up. We'll be tempted to say, "Love isn't working in this situation. The more I love this person, the more impossible they are. I just can't do it anymore."

What should you do at times like that? Just keep obeying God. Just keep doing what you know to do. Let the force of patience, which is within you as a fruit of the spirit, go to work on the problem and bring you through.

Patience, according to 1 Corinthians 13:4, is an attribute of love. It means *even temper or forbearance.* It is the quality that does not surrender to circumstances or succumb under trial. No matter how exasperating someone might be, no matter how much their attitude or behavior makes you want to throw up your hands and quit, patience simply won't let you do it. Patience will keep you walking in love even when your flesh wants to yield to the pressure of the moment and act ugly.

So let patience go to work in you. Don't let yourself get so empty on the inside that you cave in and cast away your confidence in the power of God's love within you. Keep going back to what The WORD says about love. Feed on it. Saturate yourself in it so you'll have the spiritual strength to do what you know to do. In the Name of Jesus, keep on loving…and loving…and loving even the most unlovely. He will see to it that you receive a great reward.

Strength to Win the War

"Walk worthy of The LORD unto all pleasing, being fruitful in every good work, and increasing in the knowledge of God; strengthened with all might, according to his glorious power, unto all patience and longsuffering with joyfulness."
Colossians 1:10-11

Many times we start out with great intentions to walk in love. But then someone provokes us one time too many, or aggravates us more than we expected. "I've had it!" we'll find ourselves saying. "I just don't have the patience to put up with this. I'm going to give that person a piece of my mind."

We can do something to prevent that, however. We can purposely begin to strengthen the force of patience in our lives. We can practice it in the small events of life so that when the big challenges come, we're spiritually strong, and we can win the victory.

Like every other aspect of love, patience increases with practice. The more we exercise it, the stronger it grows. Patience is important because it gives you the power to keep on loving under pressure, persecution, distress and trouble. It enables you to remain steadfast, enduring wrong and ill-treatment without anger or thought of revenge.

Sadly, most of us run out of patience when we need it most because we don't take the opportunities we have to develop it every day. I caught myself making that mistake in my own life recently in a situation that's common to us all. I had dashed into the grocery store to pick up just a couple of items. Ken was waiting out front for me in the car, because I only expected to be a few minutes.

I grabbed the things I wanted, went to check out, and chose what looked to be the fastest alternative—a line with only two people in it. But something went wrong and I waited…and waited…and waited. The longer I stood there, the more irritated I became. I started thinking sarcastic thoughts. I looked at a sign nearby that read "Express Lane," and shook my head. "They ought to have a sign over this line that says, 'Slow Motion!'" I muttered silently.

The worst part of it is, I had been listening to a message about exercising patience just a few days before. I had heard a minister tell me the same thing I'm telling you. "Exercise it and it will grow." It wasn't until I got out of the store that I realized I had missed my opportunity!

Don't make the mistake I made. Take every opportunity to develop the force of patience. Use it to win the little skirmishes in life that hardly seem to count. Then, when you face a significant battle and you're fighting for your love life, you'll have strength to win the war.

LIMITLESS**LOVE**

Resist, Endure and Triumph

"BLESSED is the man that endureth temptation: for when he is tried,
he shall receive the crown of life, which The LORD hath promised to them
that love him. Let no man say when he is tempted, I am tempted of God:
for God cannot be tempted with evil, neither tempteth he any man."
James 1:12-13

You must watch carefully over your thinking when you face times of temptation and pressure. The devil will try to take advantage of your situation and rob you of your confidence in God's faithfulness and love. Of course, he's too smart to come right out and tell you God doesn't care about you. If you know The WORD of God very well at all, the devil knows you won't fall for a blatant lie like that.

So, he disguises himself as an angel of light (2 Corinthians 11:14). He comes up with seemingly pious explanations for the pressure and pain you are experiencing. "Don't resist these things," he'll say. "Just submit to them. They're God's way of teaching you a lesson. He's the One who sent them to you."

Those are lies! The Bible says clearly that God doesn't send evil. He doesn't tempt anyone. He is the giver of every good and perfect gift. He's not the giver of things that are bad and destructive.

If you let the devil deceive you into believing God is the One harming you, even if it's for "your own good," you may initially feel more spiritually enlightened about the situation. But ultimately, that kind of thinking will undermine your confidence in God's love. You'll end up confused about what love truly is. You may even conclude that if God, in love, inflicts evil on you, you can do the same to others.

As the old saying goes, "With friends like that, who needs enemies?"

The devil knows that's where his lies will lead. That's why he tells them to you. So refuse to receive them. When you find yourself in a test or trial, don't ever say that God has brought it to you. He is not the one who put you in that place. You either got yourself in that situation or you're under a direct attack of the devil.

Either way, the last thing you should do is blame it on God and submit to it. If the trouble is of your own making, do what James 1:5 says and ask God to give you the wisdom you need to triumph over it. If it's an attack of the devil, resist him with The WORD of God. Refuse to give in to discouragement and defeat. Endure it in faith and power, remaining firm in your assurance of God's love. In the end, you'll defeat that temptation, and the devil will flee from you!

LIMITLESS**LOVE**

Buy Up Every Opportunity

"Look carefully then how you walk! Live purposefully and worthily and accurately, not as the unwise and witless, but as wise (sensible, intelligent people), making the very most of the time [buying up each opportunity], because the days are evil."
Ephesians 5:15-16, *The Amplified Bible*

When you find yourself surrendering to the pressures around you and stepping out of love, don't give up and get discouraged. Don't condemn yourself for your failures. Build yourself up! Increase your spiritual strength by improving your spiritual diet.

In other words, spend more time with God in prayer and in His WORD.

If you think you don't have time, think again. I can almost guarantee that you do. If you'll make the most of your time, buying up every opportunity to edify yourself in The LORD, you'll be amazed at the difference it will make.

When you're getting ready for work in the morning, for example, don't waste those minutes (15 or so if you're a man, probably much more if you're a woman!) letting your mind wander aimlessly. Write out some scriptures and tape them on your mirror. Meditate on them and confess them. Put melody to them and make a song.

"Talk and sing to myself?" you might ask.

Absolutely! The Bible tells us to do it. Ephesians 5:19 instructs us to sing to ourselves in psalms and hymns and spiritual songs, making melody in our hearts to The LORD. You may feel silly at first, but get over it! There's nothing silly about acting on The WORD and building yourself up the way it tells you to.

When you're driving to work, to the store or wherever else you have to go that day, use your CD player and listen to some good, anointed preaching of The WORD of God. If you don't have any CDs like that, get some. If that's not an option, spend those minutes praying in other tongues, building yourself up on your most holy faith (Jude 20).

I'll warn you, as simple as those things are, your flesh may rebel against them at first. It would rather be lazy and do nothing during those times. That's just the way flesh is. But don't let it push you around. Don't let a little fleshly laziness rob you of the spiritual strength and power that's available to you.

Get yourself in motion. Live with purpose. Be wise and make every moment count. Keep your spirit strong and your heart in top condition, so you can overcome every obstacle and live the life of love.

LIMITLESS**LOVE**

It Is Written

"For I am persuaded, that neither death, nor life, nor angels,
nor principalities, nor powers, nor things present, nor things to come, nor
height, nor depth, nor any other creature, shall be able to separate us
from the love of God, which is in Christ Jesus our LORD."
Romans 8:38-39

Some people believe that God loves them and wants to protect them, but they let the threats of the devil shake their confidence. They quake in their boots when he speaks to them through thoughts and circumstances and says, "I'm going to ruin you financially. I'm going to steal your children. I'm going to kill you." They let the devil sell them the idea that he's big enough and strong enough to separate them from the love of God.

But, the Bible tells us clearly that the devil can't do that. All he can do is come like a salesman and make his pitch to see if we'll buy it. If we do, he can steal THE BLESSING. If we don't, he can't do a thing.

He doesn't have the authority. All authority in heaven and on earth has been given to Jesus, and you've been given His Name. That means the devil has no right to ride roughshod over you. He has to get your permission—either by pressuring you or deceiving you. Don't give it to him. Do what 1 Peter 5:9 says to do instead. Resist him steadfast in the faith.

Why do you have to resist steadfastly? Because the devil is persistent. He'll just keep pestering you, and you have to keep resisting him. When he assails you with doubts and fears, you must keep answering them with The WORD of God—14,000 times a day if necessary. Keep saying what Jesus said, "It is written...."

If you do, he will eventually get scared and run away. That's right. When you resist with The WORD and in the Name of Jesus, the devil has to flee from you. Of course, odds are you aren't dealing with the devil himself anyway. He's not omnipresent. There's just one of him, and he can only be one place at one time so he has a lot of little, low-level devils working for him. Those are the imps he sends to aggravate you.

Think about that. Here you are a born-again, Holy-Spirit-filled child of Almighty God, empowered with the Name and authority of Jesus. Wouldn't it be ridiculous for you to let some minor devil intimidate you? Wouldn't it be stupid if you let him talk you into believing that God can't deliver and protect you?

Sure, it would. No devil in the world is the big shot he makes himself out to be. Remind him of that next time he threatens to do something to you. Say, "It is written, devil, nothing can separate me from the love of God—and the word *nothing* certainly includes you!"

Ask the Right Questions

*"But thanks be to God, who always leads us in triumph in Christ,
and manifests through us the sweet aroma of the
knowledge of Him in every place."*
2 Corinthians 2:14, *New American Standard*

Sometimes, God doesn't give us the answers we want because we're asking the wrong questions. When we get in trouble, for example, and something bad happens in our lives, we probably won't hear much from Him if we say, "God, why did You let this happen to me?"

If we're even tempted to ask that question, we ought to put our hands over our mouths and stop ourselves. Why? Because that question is based on a lie of the devil. It's based on the assumption that God is responsible for the evil in our lives. (See James 1:13.)

But, He isn't responsible for it. God isn't the one who lets bad things happen to us. He's the One who loves us. He is the One who BLESSES and cares for us. If we fall prey to calamity or harm, it's either because we opened the door to it ourselves through disobedience, ignorance or unbelief, or it's because the devil is attacking us, and we aren't resisting him like we should.

If you want to ask God the right questions, ones He will answer, try these: "LORD, what can I do to triumph over this trouble? How do I stop being a victim and start acting like the victor You made me to be?"

When you think about it, that's really what you need to know anyway. After all, it doesn't really matter what got you into trouble. What's important is how you get out.

If we're honest, most of the time we know how we got there. We can easily look back and see the mistakes we made. When Ken and I first got saved, for example, we were in terrible financial shape. We were so deep in debt we had no hope, naturally speaking, of ever getting out. It was no mystery how we got there. Ken had been borrowing money for years. (I think he borrowed money on his tricycle!) I married him and his debts. Then I helped him increase them.

Thankfully, we were smart enough to realize, even back then, that God didn't get us into that condition. We didn't know much, but we knew that. And we saw in The WORD that He loved us and was willing to help us out. So we said, "LORD, show us the way! Tell us what to do and we'll obey You."

You can absolutely count on God to give you that information. So start asking Him the right questions, questions based on your confidence in His love for you. He will always lead you in triumph in Christ Jesus and show you just what to do!

LIMITLESS**LOVE**

Make Excuses for Others

"I therefore, the prisoner for The LORD, appeal to and beg you to walk (lead a life) worthy of the [divine] calling to which you have been called [with behavior that is a credit to the summons to God's service, living as becomes you] with complete lowliness of mind (humility) and meekness (unselfishness, gentleness, mildness), with patience, bearing with one another and making allowances because you love one another."
Ephesians 4:1-2, *The Amplified Bible*

Most of us have no trouble making allowances for ourselves. When we're short-tempered or rude to someone, we're quick to make excuses. If someone points out our failure to walk in love, we say, "Well, you know, I didn't really mean that the way it sounded. I'm just tired, and I've been under a lot of pressure lately. It wasn't my intention to hurt anyone."

But when it comes to dealing with others, we don't usually make the same allowances. In fact, many times we're as quick to be hard on them as we were to be easy on ourselves. When someone speaks even a little unkindly to us, we're likely to jump on the slightest negative inflection. "Did you hear the tone of voice she used with me?" we might say. "It was mean! Why, she practically insulted me!"

That's just the reverse of what the Bible says we should do. It says we should make allowances for one another. In other words, we should be harder on ourselves than we are each other. Instead of justifying ourselves, we ought to just admit it when we're wrong and repent. When we're less than loving in our words or demeanor, we ought to apologize. We ought to say, "I'm sorry I spoke to you that way. There's absolutely no excuse for that. Please forgive me for being unkind."

We ought to save our excuses for others. If we're walking in love, we should believe the best of them. Real love practically makes it impossible for people to offend us because instead of accusing them of mistreating us, we'll actually defend them. We'll even make allowances for people who are intentionally ugly to us. "Oh, I don't think that person really wanted to come across like they did," we'll say. "I believe their heart is right, they just got their words wrong. They were probably having a tough day."

Some people think that kind of forbearance makes you a fool. But the scriptural truth is, it is simply part of walking in love. And there is nothing foolish about that.

LIMITLESS**LOVE**

The Healthiest Thing You Can Do

"Pleasant words are as an honeycomb,
sweet to the soul, and health to the bones."
Proverbs 16:24

These days, it seems like medical researchers are constantly discovering things we should eat (or avoid eating) and ways we can change our lifestyle so we can be healthy. Those things are fine and helpful. But, if you really want to enjoy divine health, the best thing you can do is receive and obey The WORD of God.

Personally, I'm much more interested in what God says about health and healing than what men say. He just knows more than they do. No one is more qualified than God to tell us how to keep our bodies well and in good working order. After all, He is the One who made them!

According to God's medical journal, which, of course, is the Bible, walking and talking in love will not only BLESS your soul, it will promote health in your body. Rather than getting sick and having to go to God for healing all the time, if we'll walk and talk in love, we can live continually in divine health.

John G. Lake, a minister who knew a great deal about the healing power of God wrote, "Healing is the removal, by the power of God, of the disease that has come upon the body. Divine health is to live day by day, hour by hour in touch with God so that the life of God flows into the body just as the life of God flows into the mind or the spirit."[14]

Clearly, healing is good. But divine health is better! Since it comes by staying continually in touch with God, and the Bible tells us that when we abide in love we abide in Him, we can come to only one conclusion. Walking in love is one of the healthiest things we can do!

The reverse is also true. Yielding to selfishness, unforgiveness or bitterness, and speaking unkind words will not only contaminate our souls, it will eventually make our bodies sick. The Bible is full of warnings like the one in Proverbs 14:30, "A sound heart is the life of the flesh: but envy the rottenness of the bones."

You can stay free from those things by keeping your heart filled with The WORD of God. His words are good and pleasant. They always bring you a good report and Proverbs 15:30 says, "…a good report maketh the bones fat"!

So, give your attention continually to God's WORD. Let it fill your heart and come out of your mouth in words of faith and love. Keep the pleasant words of God coming into and flowing out of you. That's the only to stay strong, healthy and free—spirit, soul and *body!*

[14] *John G. Lake: His Life, His Sermons, His Boldness of Faith* (Fort Worth: Kenneth Copeland Publications, 1994) p.9-10.

Don't Lose Your Grip

"Let The WORD of Christ dwell in you richly...."
Colossians 3:16

Sometimes, when you start to tell a fellow believer what The WORD says about love (or any other subject), they'll interrupt you. "Yes, I already know that," they'll say. "I did an entire study on the subject of love one time. I spent a whole year reading a devotional book about it."

What those people fail to understand is this. It's not The WORD you know that is affecting your life. It's The WORD that's alive in you right now. It's The WORD that is speaking to you on the inside and directing your thoughts and behavior. In short, the only WORD that's working in your life is The WORD that is dwelling richly in you.

When The WORD about love is dwelling in you richly and the devil puts pressure on you through difficult circumstances or unkind people, what God says about love is the first thing that will come to your mind. That WORD, not the pressure or the emotions of the moment, will determine your response.

As I've said before, it's not easy to keep yourself in that condition. It takes effort. Even if you're a scriptural expert on love, you must continue feeding on what The WORD says about it because you are constantly surrounded by an unloving world. You're around natural people who think selfishness is normal and right. You are continually hounded by the devil who is pushing you to agree with them.

If you don't maintain a steady intake of The WORD and keep your attention on what God has to say, your heart and mind will begin to yield to the pressure of the world around you. You'll begin to lose your grip on the power of the love of God. Before long, you'll begin to say and do unloving things. When you encounter a difficult situation that can only be solved with love, you'll have your eyes on the problem instead of the answer. You'll react to it, not like a born-again, world-overcoming child of the living God, but like a mere, unchanged man.

Amazing as it may seem, the Bible reveals that even Christians who have walked in maturity and power can slip back into that kind of immature state. Hebrews 5:11-12 says we can become spiritually dull and sluggish, needing someone to teach us over again the very first principles of God's WORD.

That will never happen, however, if you hold yourself steady on The WORD of God, continually taking in that WORD and letting it wash your thoughts and govern your actions. You'll never lose your grip on love if you'll keep God's WORD abiding richly in you.

LIMITLESS**LOVE**

Receive Correction Like a Wise Man

"Do not reprove a scoffer, or he will hate you, reprove a wise man and
he will love you. Give instruction to a wise man and he will be still wiser,
teach a righteous man and he will increase his learning."
Proverbs 9:8-9, *New American Standard*

When you read The WORD of God, receive it like a wise man. Be quick to let it correct you. If you see that you've been talking or acting in unloving ways, don't get insulted and resent God for bringing it to your attention. Don't get a chip on your shoulder. Be grateful for it.

The Bible tells us it's the grace of God that teaches us to reject ungodliness and live uprightly (Titus 2:12). It's the grace of God when we see in the Scripture or hear someone preach a word that pricks and convicts our hearts. It's the grace of God that moves a fellow believer to lovingly point out an area in our lives where we've been blindly disobeying The WORD of God and violating the law of love.

So, when it happens, we shouldn't get huffy about it. We should thank God for showing us where we're missing it, and immediately make the necessary change.

We ought to be so teachable, so pliable and quick to repent that the moment we see we've been wrong, we say, "Oh LORD, forgive me. I receive that word of correction, and I'm going to do it right from now on."

Sometimes, when correction comes, we change our behavior, but we do it with a bad attitude. We're like the little boy who kept standing up in his chair at the table, despite his mother's commands to sit down. Finally, she threatened him with such severe punishment that he did what she told him. But the glare on his face let her know that even though he was sitting down on the outside, he was still standing up on the inside.

It's easy to let that attitude slip in when it comes to walking in love. When God corrects us and instructs us to be kind and forgiving toward someone who has been mean to us, we sometimes try to change our actions without changing our attitude. It's as if we're saying, "OK, God. I'll be nice to that person, but I'm not going to enjoy it."

When we do that, we miss out on God's BLESSING. He said, "If ye be willing and obedient, ye shall eat the good of the land" (Isaiah 1:19). When God corrects us, He expects us to not just be obedient but willing, as well. Only then will we enjoy the benefits He promised.

Don't rob yourself of THE BLESSING by hanging onto an ugly attitude. When God shows you you're wrong, quickly make the adjustment. Willingly and lovingly receive God's instruction, and enjoy the rich rewards that come to the wise man!

Keep Your Doctrine Simple

"Thus have ye made the commandment of God of none effect by your tradition."
Matthew 15:6

God is Love. That truth is so widely believed by Christians that the devil knows he would never be able to steal it from us altogether. He could never convince the Church to believe that God is hateful and unloving. So, he doesn't even try to do it. What he has chosen to do, instead, is to talk people into redefining love. By fostering religious tradition, he has deceived people into believing that God expresses His love in unloving ways.

Because He loves us, tradition would say, God brings us sickness to teach us truths we couldn't learn any other way. Dear Christian people have received such lies and believed them. I remember hearing one woman give a "testimony" and say, "The cancer God gave me was a blessing in disguise. I've had it now for nine years, and I've learned a lot of things about walking with God because of this disease."

I know that lady meant well, but I have to admit, the first thing I thought was, *Nine years! Even if God were trying to teach you something through that disease, if you can't learn it in nine years, how long is it going to take?*

Traditions like that make The WORD about God's love of no effect. It robs us of what that truth is meant to do for us. It's meant to inspire our faith! It's meant to let us know God will heal us, deliver us and meet our every need!

"But doesn't the Bible also say God teaches and corrects those whom He loves?" someone might ask.

Yes! But it doesn't say He does it through sickness and disease. He does it with His WORD. As 2 Timothy 3:16-17 says, "All scripture is given by inspiration of God, and is profitable for doctrine, for reproof, for correction, for instruction in righteousness: That the man of God may be perfect, thoroughly furnished unto all good works."

God didn't appoint cancer to be the teacher of the Church. He didn't send arthritis to show you His ways. He sent the Holy Spirit and The WORD—and between them, they can get the job done!

If a parent today found a way to give a child cancer and did it purposely to teach him a lesson, he'd be arrested and put in prison. Why? Because it's wrong, it's mean and it's the furthest thing from love.

God will never do something like that. *Never!* So don't let the devil talk you into exchanging the truth of God for a lie of man. Keep your doctrine scriptural. Simply believe that God is Love.

LIMITLESS**LOVE**

Pass Up the Pity Party

"And Caleb stilled the people before Moses, and said, Let us go up at once, and possess it; for we are well able to overcome it. But the men that went up with him said, We be not able to go up against the people; for they are stronger than we. And they brought up an evil report of the land which they had searched unto the children of Israel, saying, The land, through which we have gone to search it, is a land that eateth up the inhabitants thereof; and all the people that we saw in it are men of a great stature. And there we saw the giants, the sons of Anak, which come of the giants: and we were in our own sight as grasshoppers, and so we were in their sight. And all the congregation lifted up their voice, and cried; and the people wept that night."

Numbers 13:30-33, 14:1

The next time you're tempted to indulge in a little self-pity, remember this story. When you feel small, insignificant and overwhelmed by the circumstances around you, and want to moan and cry about how no one loves you or takes care of you...beware. God calls that kind of talk an evil report.

He is not going to encourage your unbelief by patting you on the back and sympathizing with you. He won't appreciate your complaints. In fact, He'll probably say to you something like He said to the children of Israel: "How long will this people spurn Me? And how long will they not believe in Me..." (Numbers 14:11, *New American Standard*).

Once you've heard The WORD that God loves you, He expects you to believe it. He expects you to speak that WORD, and act on it. So, no matter how bad things are around you, you should never again say, "No one loves me." You should never allow that thought in your mind.

When you're tempted to see yourself as a grasshopper, overwhelmed by the circumstances around you, take charge of your thinking and turn the picture around. See yourself as a giant in The LORD! See yourself as the one God loves. Open your mouth and say, "God is good to me!"

If you do that, I can assure you, it won't be long before other people are being good to you, too. As you receive God's love and act on it, you'll naturally begin to be more loving toward other people. You'll put into motion the law of sowing and reaping. As you love others, that love will be multiplied and given back to you again.

If you take that path, you won't be overcome by the negative things around you. You'll rise up like Caleb and overcome them instead. You'll pass up your pity party, take hold of God's love and do your celebrating in the promised land.

LIMITLESS**LOVE**

Be Glad, Not Sad!

"Make a joyful noise unto The LORD, all ye lands. Serve The LORD with gladness: come before his presence with singing. Know ye that The LORD he is God: it is he that hath made us, and not we ourselves; we are his people, and the sheep of his pasture. Enter into his gates with thanksgiving, and into his courts with praise: be thankful unto him, and bless his name."

Psalm 100:1-4

I think some people have misread this verse. They believe it says we should serve The LORD with *sadness.* "Yes, I love The LORD," they say, "but the way is hard, the burdens are heavy, and the battle is taking its toll." It's almost as if they think God is pleased with the price they are willing to pay for Him, as if the more they suffer the happier He is.

That's the furthest thing from the truth! God wants us to serve Him with gladness, not sadness. He loves us. It BLESSES Him to see us happy and singing His praises. He enjoys it when we come into His presence with singing, not sighing!

When you think about it, that's easy to understand. After all, doesn't it bless you when you see your children happy and enjoying the things you've given them? Wouldn't it grieve your heart if they were always dragging around talking about how hard it is to be your child? You'd want to say, "Wait a minute. I give you far more than I ask of you. I work hard to make sure your needs are met and you have everything necessary for a good and happy life. The least you could do is appreciate it and enjoy it!"

Do for The LORD what you want your children to do for you. Cultivate an attitude of gratitude and joy. If you have to, do what the old hymn says to do and "count your blessings."

"But I don't feel like counting my blessings," you might say. "I have some serious problems. I need God to move in my life."

That's all the more reason to remind yourself how much God loves you, and thank Him for His faithfulness to you. It's easy for God to move in your heart when you're thankful. It's easy for you to have faith when you're rejoicing in Him.

It's difficult for The LORD to move in your life when you're about half mad at Him all the time. It limits Him when you're fretting and saying, "God, why did You let these bad things happen to me?" That kind of thinking leads to doubt, not faith. It will get you nowhere—fast.

So, read this scripture right. Do what it says, and serve The LORD with gladness. Sing and shout and thank Him for His wonderful love. Not only will He be BLESSED by your praises, they will open the door for Him to do even more marvelous things for you.

LIMITLESS**LOVE**

What You Say Makes the Difference

*"Death and life are in the power of the tongue, and those
who love it will eat its fruit."*
Proverbs 18:21, *New American Standard*

God has said He loves you again and again. He has said it in every conceivable way. He has promised to express that love by BLESSING you, prospering you, healing you and satisfying you with long life. There's no question about it. That's what God has said.

But it's not just what God says that counts. For His words and promises of love to come to pass in your life, you must say them, too. Jesus said, "…out of the abundance of the heart the mouth speaketh. A good man out of the good treasure of the heart bringeth forth good things: and an evil man out of the evil treasure bringeth forth evil things" (Matthew 12:34-35).

So many believers miss out on the wonderful promises and provisions of God because they ignore this principle. They literally put themselves beyond the reach of God's goodness by speaking evil words. They don't usually realize what they're speaking is evil. They think of evil speech only in terms of profanity or saying things that are ugly and unkind. But according to the Bible, words of doubt and unbelief also qualify as evil. (See Numbers 13:32.) In fact, any words we speak contrary to The WORD of God are evil words.

It deeply grieves the heart of God when we put ourselves in that position. He never stops loving us. He never stops wanting to BLESS and deliver us. But even so, He cannot break His own spiritual laws to do so. And, the fact that we have what we say is an eternal, spiritual law.

It's not a bad law, either. It's a good law! That's the law that enabled us to be born again by simply saying, "Jesus, I receive You as my LORD." It's the law that enables us to put The WORD of God in our hearts and our mouths and overcome every attack of the devil. But, if we misuse it, it will work just as mightily against us as it does for us.

One minister tells the story of a man in a coma he was asked to pray for. The man was born again, yet despite the minister's prayers, did not awaken. As the minister continued to pray about it, The LORD spoke to him and said, "Spiritual laws were set in motion long ago. They cannot be reversed at this time."

Later, the man's mother and brother told the minister that ever since he was a teenager, this man had been saying, "I'll never live to see 40." He said it again and again. In fact, he had said it the last time his mother had seen him before he slipped into the coma. Sure enough, he died just four months before his 40th birthday.

That dear man probably just didn't know any better. But, you do. So, act accordingly. Don't let the loving words God has spoken about you go unfulfilled. Agree with Him. Put those words in your heart and in your mouth, and bring forth good things all the days of your life!

LIMITLESS**LOVE**

The Truth Will Make You Free

"Jesus was saying to those Jews who had believed Him,
'If you continue in My WORD, then you are truly disciples of Mine;
and you will know the truth, and the truth shall make you free.'"
John 8:31-32, *New American Standard*

God loves us and wants us to be BLESSED with good things in every area of our lives. He wants us to be free from all the evil and oppression of the devil. He wants us to enjoy BLESSED, abundant lives.

But, there is only one way for Him to get His goodness to us—through the knowledge of the Truth. The more of His Truth we know and act on, the freer we will be to walk in more of THE BLESSING. The less of His Truth we know and act on, the less freedom and BLESSING we'll experience.

There is no way around it. That's just the way it is.

If there's any area of our lives where the love and goodness of God is not abounding, it's not God's fault. It's ours. We are either in disobedience, or we lack revelation of the truth in that area. Sometimes people who have failed to receive healing or some other aspect of THE BLESSING of God will come to me complaining. They'll try to lay the blame on God. "I did everything I know to do!" they'll say. "But I still didn't get what I needed!"

"Then you just didn't know enough," I answer.

That may not be what people want to hear, but it's right, anyway. And if we'll pay attention to it and act on it, it will help us because the fact is, we can always learn more. As the old saying goes, "It's not a sin to be ignorant, but it is a sin to stay that way!"

We have absolutely no excuse for staying ignorant of God's Truth. After all, He's given us a whole Bible full of His Truth. He has given us the Holy Spirit to teach us and explain it to us. He has given us a born-again spirit with the capacity to learn from Him and hear His voice. On top of it all, He has given us an open invitation to come to Him and receive ever-increasing knowledge of the Truth. "Call to Me, and I will answer you, and I will tell you great and mighty things, which you do not know," He promises in Jeremiah 33:3 *(New American Standard)*.

There is no way for you to increase God's love for you. There is nothing you can do to make Him want to BLESS you any more than He already does, and there's no need to. His desire to BLESS you is absolutely boundless. There is no limit to His love!

What you *can* do, however, is increase your capacity to receive by increasing your knowledge of His Truth. You can put God's WORD first place in your heart and in your life. With the Holy Ghost as your Guide, you can daily search the Bible and "seek [Wisdom] as for silver and search for skillful and godly Wisdom as for hidden treasures" (Proverbs 2:4, *The Amplified Bible)*. He will surely reveal it to you.

LIMITLESS**LOVE**

Eternal Expressions of God's Love

*"Wherefore it shall come to pass, if ye hearken to these judgments,
and keep, and do them, that The LORD thy God shall keep unto thee
the covenant and the mercy which he sware unto thy fathers:
And he will love thee, and BLESS thee, and multiply thee....
And The LORD will take away from thee all sickness...."*
Deuteronomy 7:12-13, 15

If you believe the Bible, you simply can't separate the love of God from healing and prosperity. Throughout the Scriptures, from first to last, God makes it clear that it is His will to heal, prosper, protect and deliver all His obedient people.

We ought to meditate on that fact until, in our thinking, THE BLESSING is so bound to God's love for us that no one can ever talk us out of them. We should have it so settled in our hearts that we simply laugh at the old religious lies about God keeping us sick to teach us something, or leaving us in poverty because He loves us. With all due respect to those who have been unwittingly deceived by them, I must say that, in the light of God's WORD, doctrines like that are just plain dumb.

I can say that with compassion because I once believed them myself. I was raised in a church where they taught that miracles had passed away. (I'll admit, I wasn't a very good member, but I did attend sometimes.) They taught that God stopped healing when the last apostle died. I just assumed they were right, because I didn't know any better. But, now that I know what the Bible says, those ideas sound downright silly to me.

Since God has always healed and worked miracles for His people, those things couldn't pass away without God undergoing a major change. We know that's not possible because the Scripture says there's no shadow of turning with Him. He is always the same. God healed all the way through the Old Testament, all the way through the ministry of Jesus, and all the way through the book of Acts.

Can you imagine Him just making this announcement one day? *Tonight at midnight, healing passes away. Everyone better get another health plan, because I'm going out of the healing business. I know I said I'm the God that healeth thee in Exodus 15:26, but I've decided I'm not going to be that kind of God anymore.*

That's ridiculous, isn't it? How could the God who has always healed, prospered and BLESSED His people ever stop doing those things? He couldn't! He didn't! And He never will! THE BLESSING is an eternal expressions of His unchanging love.

LIMITLESS**LOVE**

Loaded With Benefits Every Day

*"Blessed be The LORD, who daily loadeth us with benefits,
even the God of our salvation. Selah."*
Psalm 68:19

Some people always put THE BLESSING of God off until another day. Instead of believing to receive it right now, they say, "One of these days, God is going to prosper me. One of these days, God is going to heal me. One of these days, God is going to BLESS my life."

But the Bible tells us something different. It says He loves us so much, He loads us with benefits *every day!*

What kinds of benefits does He give us? The benefits of salvation, which include the new birth, freedom from sin, healing and prosperity. The word *salvation* actually means "soundness or wholeness in every area of life." It means "deliverance from both temporal and eternal danger."

People often get excited when they go to work for a company that has an especially good employee-benefits plan. They're thrilled when they can get a good health or a retirement plan. But no matter how good those kinds of plans are, they just provide benefits every now and then—and they're always limited.

Worldly people have to be satisfied with that, but you don't! You're a child of God. You don't have to live like the world does. You have something they don't have. You have a covenant in the blood of Jesus with a God who loves you and wants to be good to you. He has provided for you the best plan in the history of man. And, you can load up on its benefits not just now and then, but every day.

Just think! No matter how many of God's children draw on those benefits at once, they never run out. He always has enough to take care of every believer. He always has enough to meet every need.

If you doubt it, read how God brought the Israelites out from the bondage of Egypt. They'd been living as slaves, mistreated and overworked. They were poor and, no doubt, many of them were sick and hurting.

But when they applied the blood of the Passover lamb to their houses, they instantly became beneficiaries of God's great BLESSING plan. Within hours, they were not only free, they were healed and prosperous. The Bible says, God "brought them forth also with silver and gold: and there was not one feeble person among their tribes" (Psalm 105:37).

That was no small feat. There were more than a million of those people! But God had enough to take care of them all. He had more than enough power to load every one of them with benefits. So, stir up your faith and lay claim, daily, to what your loving God has provided. He will surely do the same for you.

LIMITLESS LOVE

What Happens Next Is Up to You

"Having disarmed the powers and authorities, he made a public spectacle of them, triumphing over them by the cross."
Colossians 2:15, *New International Version*

"Why do bad things happen to good people?" It seems every time a tragedy takes place, people start asking that question. They act as if it's some deep, unfathomable mystery. But the fact is, it's a question with a very simple answer.

Bad things happen because of the devil. He is mean and ruthless. He comes to steal, kill and destroy. He comes to good people and bad, and brings evil to anyone who will let him.

"But if God loves us," someone might ask, "why doesn't He do something about that?"

He already has. He sent Jesus to the earth to defeat him on our behalf. He sent him to disarm the devil and bring him to nothing (Hebrews 2:14). And through His death, burial and resurrection, that is exactly what Jesus did. Jesus defeated the devil in his own domain. He stripped from him all his rights and authority in the earth. He canceled all the devil's legal claims by paying the price of sin so that he no longer has any power over any person who receives Jesus as LORD.

Why, then, is the devil still giving believers so much trouble? Because he is an outlaw. Think of it in natural terms and you can easily understand it. In our country, we have laws against murder, drug dealing and theft. But if the law is not enforced, criminals still do those things, don't they? They will do every rotten thing they can get away with.

The devil is the same way. He is a murderer. He is a thief. He takes what doesn't belong to him. So, even though he has no legal right to do bad things to good people, he will do it anyway if we let him get away with it. He'll steal our authority and use it against us with the words of our mouths. He'll pressure us into saying things that legally open the door to his destructive plans.

Even though God loves us dearly and paid a high price to secure our freedom, if we don't enforce His WORD in our lives, Satan will continue to dominate us, anyway. He'll put sickness on us if we don't enforce God's WORD about healing. He'll put poverty on us if we don't enforce God's WORD about prosperity.

We cannot simply sit around waiting for God to do something about the devil. That's unscriptural. The Bible says God has already done His part. What happens next is up to us. We can continue to let the devil operate illegally in our lives, or we can do what the Bible says and resist him. We can drive him out of our lives with The WORD of God. We can personally see to it that he doesn't get away with a thing.

LIMITLESS**LOVE**

Let Jesus Touch Others Through You

"And as you go, preach, saying, 'The kingdom of heaven is at hand.'
Heal the sick, raise the dead, cleanse the lepers, cast out demons.
Freely you received, freely give."
Matthew 10:7-8, *New American Standard*

Those are the instructions Jesus gave to His disciples during His earthly ministry. He told them to do much the same thing He commissioned us as believers to do in Mark 16. He told us to tell the good news about Jesus. Cast out devils. Lay hands on the sick and they shall recover.

Why did Jesus give us those instructions? Did He do it because He wanted us to go out and show the world how much spiritual power we have? Did He want us to do supernatural things just to prove to people that we're right and they're wrong?

Certainly not! Jesus told us to do those things for the same reason He told those first apostles to do them—because the multitudes were weary and scattered like sheep without a shepherd, and when He saw them "He was moved with compassion on them..." (Matthew 9:36).

Jesus instructed us to minister to people because He loves them, and the only way we will effectively carry out that ministry is as we love them, too. It won't work for us to be short-tempered and insensitive to people and then try to pray for them or lay hands on them for healing. We won't be able to operate in much of God's power with that attitude.

On the other hand, if we'll go out every day with our hearts full of God's love, and be kind and compassionate toward people in the natural affairs of life, we'll also be able to minister to them with the supernatural power of God. Our love will draw them to Jesus, and they'll be eager and willing to receive.

"But, I'm just a believer," you might argue. "I'm not an apostle or an evangelist. I can't minister to people like that!"

The Bible says you can. It says *believers* will minister healing. It doesn't say just apostles will do it. It doesn't say evangelists will do it. It says *believers* shall lay hands on the sick, and they shall recover. That's your job. It's what you're supposed to do!

If you'll just begin to lay hands on people in simple faith because you love them and want them to be BLESSED, you'll be amazed at how many people will get healed. Jesus is still as moved by compassion for the multitudes as He was 2,000 years ago. He still wants to teach them, touch them and heal them. All He needs is for you to step out in love and in faith, and He will do those things for them through you.

LIMITLESS LOVE

Give God Some Real Glory

"Jesus departed from thence, and came nigh unto the sea of Galilee; and went up into a mountain, and sat down there. And great multitudes came unto him, having with them those that were lame, blind, dumb, maimed, and many others, and cast them down at Jesus' feet; and he healed them: Insomuch that the multitude wondered, when they saw the dumb to speak, the maimed to be whole, the lame to walk, and the blind to see: and they glorified the God of Israel."

Matthew 15:29-31

It's amazing to me that any sane person could ever think that our wonderful, loving God could get glory from the sickness, poverty or pain of His children. But, the fact is, some people do. So when the devil comes along and attacks them, robbing them of THE BLESSING of their inheritance in Jesus, instead of fighting him, they just lie down and let him run over them.

"I guess I'm just suffering for The LORD," they'll say. "I'll just try to be sweet and grateful for it so I can show the world how much I love God and bring glory to Him."

Don't ever let that kind of thinking get a hold on you. It's not only unscriptural, it totally maligns the character and nature of God. Instead of portraying Him as a tender and infinitely loving Father who wants to do nothing but good for His children, that kind of theology presents God as a cruel, unfeeling tyrant who somehow gets pleasure out of the suffering of His own, obedient people. It not only grieves the heart of God, it drives the unbelieving world even further away from Him.

The world is not impressed with how we suffer. They aren't looking for a God who will help them suffer sickness more gracefully. They aren't looking for a God who will afflict them with poverty and pain...and then give them strength to endure it.

The world is looking for a way out of those things. They're looking for healing. They're looking for deliverance. They're searching desperately for a way to live and be BLESSED.

If you want to glorify God, allow His healing, delivering and prospering power to work fully in you. When the devil comes to steal God's BLESSING, fight him hard with faith and The WORD. Hold on tightly to what belongs to you in Jesus. Resist the devil, and he will flee from you.

Hold your ground until the full manifestation of God's BLESSING breaks through in your life, and your body is healed and whole, your family is happy and BLESSED, and your finances are flowing abundantly. Become a living demonstration of the love of God so that others can see it, and God can truly be glorified in you.

LIMITLESS**LOVE**

You're Supposed to Be BLESSED Today

"O taste and see that The LORD is good:
BLESSED is the man that trusteth in him."
Psalm 34:8

Once you begin to see in The WORD that God truly loves you…once your heart begins to grasp how good He really is, all you must do to receive THE BLESSING is simply trust His love.

Trust Him instead of fussing and worrying about the circumstances that threaten you. Trust Him instead of trying to figure out how He's going to deliver you. Trust Him instead of striving and struggling with those around you who are causing you trouble. Trust Him completely with confidence that somehow He will get THE BLESSING to you.

That kind of childlike faith in God's love is the most powerful force on earth. The devil can't defeat it. People can't stop it from working. It absolutely cannot be denied.

Some years ago, Oral Roberts told the story of an 11-year-old boy who came to one of his meetings with that kind of faith. Oral Roberts didn't even see him until the meeting was over. By that time, he had laid hands on so many people he was almost depleted of strength. As he was walking out of the building, however, that boy who was sitting with his crutches beside him happened to catch his eye. "What are you doing here, son?" asked Brother Roberts.

The boy answered simply, "I am supposed to be healed today."

Sadly, Oral Roberts began to apologize. "I wish I could help you," he said. "But I don't have the strength to pray for one more person."

"I don't know about that," the boy answered. "All I know is I'm supposed to be healed today."

Oral Roberts knew from experience what that kind of simple trust in God could do. So, weary as he was, he laid his hand on the little boy and prayed while the boy believed and received his healing. The last time I heard, that young man had grown up and is still healed and whole.

Just think what wonderful things God could do for us if we all trusted Him that way! Imagine what miracles would happen if we shook off the complexities and questions that weaken our faith, and simply expected God to do for us what He said He would do. Even the devil himself couldn't stop us from receiving the benefits of God's love. When he threatened us with calamity or suggested God might not be able to come through for us this time, we would answer much like that young boy did.

We would say, "I don't know about that. All I know is that my Father loves me, and I'm supposed to be BLESSED today."

LIMITLESS**LOVE**

The Comprehensive Plan of Love

"Surely He has borne our griefs (sicknesses, weaknesses, and distresses) and carried our sorrows and pains [of punishment], yet we [ignorantly] considered Him stricken, smitten, and afflicted by God.... But He was wounded for our transgressions, He was bruised for our guilt and iniquities; the chastisement [needful to obtain] peace and well-being for us was upon Him, and with the stripes [that wounded] Him we are healed and made whole."
Isaiah 53:4-5, *The Amplified Bible*

When the prophet Isaiah wrote those verses, he was looking ahead by the spirit, foreseeing what Jesus would do for us one day on the cross. He saw then what many believers even now haven't yet seen. He saw that Jesus, by His sacrifice, would BLESS every part of man's being. He would BLESS us spiritually by bearing the punishment for our sins. He would BLESS our souls by paying the price for our peace, and He would BLESS us physically by taking upon Himself our sicknesses and diseases, so we could be healed and free.

That's one of the things I appreciate most about the love of God. It is comprehensive. God doesn't just care about one or two isolated parts of our lives. He isn't concerned only about our spiritual well-being. His love covers every part of us—spirit, soul and body.

Think about that. Jesus didn't pay the price for your spirit and leave your body under the dominion of sickness and disease. He didn't pay the price for your body and leave your mind to be tormented with anxiety and guilt. Jesus paid the price for the whole man. When He went to the Cross, He obtained righteousness for your spirit, peace for your mind and healing for your body. He didn't leave any part of you out of the plan of redemption.

That's what we call the "full gospel"! The only reason more people aren't enjoying the benefits of it is because it hasn't been widely preached. Religion has convinced us to preach a partial gospel, instead. As a result, most Christians think the plan of redemption is much like the insurance or health plans devised by man.

Those plans are exclusive. They're full of stipulations that leave a great many things in your life uncovered. They contain lots of fine print that tells you if you get yourself in this situation or that situation, this plan won't help you. The benefits will be denied.

God would never give us a redemption plan like that. He cares so deeply about every detail of our lives that He was compelled to provide us with a comprehensive plan that would meet our every need in every possible situation. A plan that would keep us forever completely covered—spirit, soul and body—by His unfailing love.

LIMITLESS**LOVE**

The Secret of Supernatural Success

"But when Herod's birthday was kept, the daughter of Herodias danced before them, and pleased Herod. Whereupon he promised with an oath to give her whatsoever she would ask. And she, being before instructed of her mother, said, Give me here John Baptist's head in a charger. And the king was sorry: nevertheless for the oath's sake, and them which sat with him at meat, he commanded it to be given her. And he sent, and beheaded John in the prison."
Matthew 14:6-10

Fear of failure. It has haunted all of us at some time in our lives. Popular psychology advises us to adjust and learn to live peaceably with it. After all, failure is, to a certain extent, inevitable—isn't it?

Not according to The WORD of God. It tells us there is a failure-proof way to live. It is the way of love. First Corinthians 13:8 says it plainly: Love never fails.

To those who think love expresses itself only through emotion, that may sound silly. Emotion can't turn failure into success! But real love isn't expressed only through emotion—it shows up in action. And the right action can make all the difference.

Read the story recorded in Matthew 14, and you can see that for yourself. There, Jesus faces one of the toughest situations in His earthly life—the murder of His beloved cousin, John.

What would you do in such a painful situation? Initially, you would probably do the same thing Jesus did. When He heard the news, He went out to be alone. But the masses of people, insensitive to His personal distress, simply followed Him.

Most people would have responded to them in anger. Most would have rebuked them and said, "Can't you people ever leave me alone?" But that's not what Jesus did.

On the contrary, the Bible says that He was moved with compassion and healed their sick. Jesus refused to give in to self-pity or react in anger. Instead, He focused on the real enemy He was facing. He retaliated against the devil himself.

He attacked Satan in the spirit realm by destroying his works of sickness and disease. He attacked pain and suffering with the compassion of God by healing and delivering those who were oppressed by the devil.

When, through the murder of John, the devil lashed out at The LORD with a cruel and tragic blow, Jesus overcame him with the power of compassion. He turned a potential failure into a supernatural success. He did what every believer who wants to live in perpetual victory must do. He defeated hatred with love.

LIMITLESS**LOVE**

Recognize Your Real Enemy

"For we wrestle not against flesh and blood, but against principalities,
against powers, against the rulers of the darkness of this world,
against spiritual wickedness in high places."
Ephesians 6:12

Have you ever wondered how Jesus was able to look at those who were crucifying Him—the ones who mocked Him, spit on Him and sentenced Him to death—and pray, "Father, forgive them for they know not what they do" (Luke 23:34)? How was it possible in the midst of such suffering to respond in such love? Why wasn't He angry and bitter at the people for behaving so wickedly toward Him?

Because He knew those people were not His real enemies. Jesus walked in the spirit. He understood the spiritual realm is more real than the one which can only be seen with the physical eye. That's the realm where His true enemies, the devil and all his demonic forces, were operating. They were the ones pushing and inciting the people to cry, "Crucify Him!" They were simply using men as puppets to get their evil job done.

So Jesus moved against them with the most effective weapon in the arsenal of heaven. He moved against them with the power of love.

Had Jesus allowed Satan to pressure Him into responding in bitterness and unforgiveness toward those who were crucifying Him, the devil would have thwarted the whole plan of salvation. He would have succeeded in getting Jesus to sin and disqualified Him from serving as the spotless, sacrificial Lamb.

But Jesus didn't fall into that trap. He recognized His warfare was not against flesh and blood, but against principalities, powers, rulers of the darkness and wicked spirits in heavenly places. And He won that war with the compassion of God. He won because instead of allowing Himself to be moved by the emotions of the moment, He was moved by the Holy Spirit of God who is Compassion Himself. As always, Jesus obeyed His Father and thus, He acted in love.

"But that was Jesus!" you say. "He had a direct line to the Father. I don't!" Yes, you do. You have the ability, through the same Holy Spirit that indwelt Jesus, to be moved with compassion just as He was. Romans 5:5 says the love of God is shed abroad in our hearts by the Holy Spirit. All we have to do is make the decision to be motivated by His love rather than our own, human feelings.

No matter how fiercely the devil rages against us, we can overcome him by wielding the weapons of the spirit—not against the people who hurt us, but against the forces of darkness themselves. We can rise up as more than conquerors and win the victory with the power of love.

LIMITLESS**LOVE**

Obey The WORD of Love

"But whoever keeps His WORD,
in him the love of God has truly been perfected...."
1 John 2:5, *New American Standard*

Many people, believers included, think love means having warm feelings about people. They think of love as an emotional thing. But love is not a feeling, and feeling is not the evidence of love. Love is a Person and action is the evidence.

God is Love (1 John 4:8). So to be moved by Love is to be moved, not by feelings, but by God Himself. What does God move us to do? He moves us to obey His WORD because whoever keeps God's WORD, in him the love of God is perfected.

What does keeping God's WORD have to do with living in love? Think about it for a moment. The WORD of God is the expression of God Himself. Since God is Love, everything The WORD tells us must be loving. So if we want to walk in love, all we have to do is act on The WORD. Whatever it says to do, we just do it.

If we'll follow that simple guideline and put God's WORD first, we can come through the most complicated, challenging situations in victory. We can overcome every scheme of the devil because love never fails. It can't fail because God is Love, and God cannot fail.

Love people unconditionally by acting on God's WORD, and you'll see miracles take place around you. You'll not only see others BLESSED, you'll find yourself stepping into greater BLESSING than you've ever known before.

Walking in love by obeying God's WORD will even cause your finances to increase. A friend of mine experienced that years ago when he went into the television and radio business. He wanted to buy a station from a Jewish man and told him, "The WORD of God says that if I will BLESS you, God will BLESS me. So I'm going to see to it that you get the better part of this deal." Most people would be afraid to say such a thing. They'd be afraid of being taken advantage of.

But that deal turned out to be exceptionally profitable for both of them. My friend was a tremendous Christian witness to his Jewish friend, and they ended up preaching the gospel of Jesus Christ together on radio. When love rules, prosperity can flow.

So commit to living the life of the love of God today by determining to obey The WORD, no matter what. Then, watch God turn failure into success again and again. At home, at work, in any situation, you can prove it for yourself—love never fails!

LIMITLESS**LOVE**

The Miraculous Realm of Love

"Verily, verily, I say unto you, He that believeth on me,
the works that I do shall he do also; and greater works than these
shall he do; because I go unto my Father."
John 14:12

Every true believer at some time in his life longs to walk in the realm of the miraculous. He hungers to operate in supernatural power to fulfill the words of Jesus by doing the works that He did—and even greater works than those! He longs for that because it is the divinely ordained destiny of every born-again child of God.

The LORD let me know years ago, however, that for us to step into the fullness of that destiny, we must first have a greater revelation of the love of God. He said to me, *A revelation of My love is the highest revelation of the Church because I am Love.* To have a revelation of love is to have a revelation, not of what God has or what He can do, but of God Himself.

That's why God is revealing His love as never before to His people today. The day of His coming is approaching, and it is time for us to step into our destiny. I believe with all my heart that it is the revelation of God's love in the Church that will usher in the Great Resurrection.

When the Spirit of The LORD spoke to me about this, He said, *My people must learn to walk in love. They must realize that My love is alive and powerful, that faith works by love and that in love there is no occasion for stumbling. They must understand they can walk and be perfected in love before they come to heaven and that as they do, that love will protect them. I want them to know the reality of My WORD that says, "Above all things, have a fervent love for one another."*

The Greek text of that scripture in 1 Peter 4:8 says, "Above all things, have a white-hot love for one another." The Bible says we are baptized with the Holy Ghost and fire (Luke 3:16). That fire is the all-consuming love of God. God's love will consume sin and death. It will consume the work of Satan and absolutely swallow it up.

Today, there is a vast army of men and women who have made the decision to do the works of Jesus. They have committed themselves to live and walk in the realm of the miraculous. The love of God is the key to walking in that realm. There are things available to us as we walk in the love of God that are not available any other way.

In this day and hour, we, as God's people, are taking our rightful position, dedicating ourselves to God and renewing our minds with The WORD. We are setting ourselves apart from the carnal ways of the world and committing ourselves to walk in the love of God. We are moving toward our divine destiny through a revelation of God's love.

LIMITLESS**LOVE**

For Love's Sake, Take Care of Yourself

"For, brethren, ye have been called unto liberty; only use not liberty for an occasion to the flesh, but by love serve one another. For all the law is fulfilled in one word, even in this; Thou shalt love thy neighbour as thyself."
Galatians 5:13-14

The life of love is a life of continually giving of yourself to others. It is God-centered and others-centered, instead of self-centered. When we're walking in love and we face a decision, our first thought is not, *What do I want to do in this situation? What will make me happy?* but *What does The LORD want me to do here? What choice will enable me to be the greatest BLESSING I can possibly be?*

That doesn't mean we neglect to take care of ourselves, however. It doesn't mean we ignore our own spiritual and natural needs. It is not loving and right to go on and on working endlessly on behalf of others, until you work yourself to exhaustion. If you do that long enough, you will reach a place physically that makes you ineffective spiritually. You'll end up bankrupt with nothing left to give. Instead of being a BLESSING to others, you'll become a burden to them.

There is nothing loving about that.

Years ago, I made that mistake in ministry. I had such a drive and desire to serve The LORD and preach The WORD to those who were hungry to hear it that I overcommitted myself. I wound up preaching seven days a week. I didn't even take a day to rest. That's not scriptural. And anything that is unscriptural cannot possibly be done in love.

After a while, I got so tired I could hardly make it up the steps of the airplane to fly to my next meeting. I remember thinking, *I must be the most tired man in the world.* The reason? I was drawing strength from my spirit, giving out all the time, without taking the time to rest and replenish myself. I really believe if I had kept it up, it would have killed me at an early age.

But, thank God, the Holy Spirit showed me my mistake. I repented and made the change. It's been years since then, and I'm still going strong, serving The LORD and ministering to people today.

As you learn to walk in love, remember that you can only be a BLESSING to others if you take good care of yourself. Take the time to maintain a strong spirit, a refreshed soul and a healthy body. Do it not out of selfishness but out of your desire to be a BLESSING to others. Because you love your neighbors, be sure to love yourself. That way you'll not only be willing but able to keep on serving them for many years to come.

LIMITLESS**LOVE**

Stay Connected to the Spirit

"These be they who separate themselves, sensual, having not the Spirit.
But ye, beloved, building up yourselves on your most holy faith,
praying in the Holy Ghost, keep yourselves in the love of God...."
Jude 19-21

The Bible lets us know clearly just how secure we are in God's love. It says that love is so strong that neither death, nor life, nor angels, nor principalities, nor powers, nor things present, nor things to come, nor height, nor depth, nor any other creature shall be able to separate us from it (Romans 8:38-39).

That's a powerful statement. Yet, even so, there is one person—and only one—who's not included in that list. That person is you.

God will never fall out of love with you. The devil will never be able to keep God's love from reaching you. But you can separate yourself from it—and that is exactly what many believers do.

How? By remaining sensual or carnal. Most people associate sensuality with gross moral sin. But actually, to be sensual, in its most basic form, simply means to be moved or led by the natural, fleshly senses rather than by The WORD and the Spirit of God. When we begin to let our senses, or our flesh, govern our behavior, we always get off into sin. What's more, we open ourselves to deception because we are basing our lives on the natural world around us. Satan, who is the god of this world, can easily work his wiles on us there.

When we let our fellowship with God slip and don't maintain our spiritual walk by spending time in The WORD and in prayer, we often begin to attribute thoughts to God when they actually originate in our carnal minds. I've seen men base their ministry on such errors. They stand up in the pulpit and say, "After I had my heart attack and was lying in the hospital, God told me He gave me that heart attack to slow me down and teach me something."

God doesn't give people heart attacks! But when we get drawn into sensual, carnal thinking, we can be deceived into believing He does. And when we start thinking that way, we can find ourselves separated from the love of God! We can end up cutting ourselves off from His BLESSING and power, being led by our own, natural, stinking thinking instead of by His Spirit and His faith-building WORD.

Don't let that happen to you. Keep yourself in God's love. Stay connected to His Spirit and His truth by praying in the Holy Ghost and abiding in His WORD. Be spiritual, not sensual, and you'll stay connected with God's love. Then no one will be able to steal THE BLESSING from you.

A Vessel Fit for the Master

"Let every one that nameth the name of Christ depart from iniquity. But in a great house there are not only vessels of gold and of silver, but also of wood and of earth; and some to honour, and some to dishonour. If a man therefore purge himself from these, he shall be a vessel unto honour, sanctified, and meet for the master's use, and prepared unto every good work."

2 Timothy 2:19-21

Some believers who are well-trained in the Scriptures and in the operations of faith think they are ready to do great things for God. Yet, they consistently find themselves on the spiritual sidelines, waiting for ministry opportunities and wondering why they never come.

Very often it's because they haven't yet departed from iniquity. They haven't cleansed themselves from the invisible sins of unkindness and unforgiveness in their lives. They haven't consecrated themselves to walk in love.

The worst part is, they don't even realize it. They would be shocked if anyone even suggested they had sin in their lives. Yet the Bible says clearly that God considers unforgiveness over even the most minor offenses to be wickedness on our part. The little debts we don't forgive are what give Satan place in our lives—the small things we do and say, the cutting words and sarcastic remarks. Many times, these incidents of aggravation occur with people in the world we don't know personally. They are easily forgotten, but never forgiven.

As I was praying about this one day, the Spirit of God showed me what happens when we allow such things to build up in our spirits. I saw a pipe stretching between God and me. The pipe was a funnel for the power of God. At God's end, there was a surge of power going in. At my end, there was only a trickle flowing out.

The pipe was clogged with dirt and filth. He explained that the filth was unforgiveness and unloving attitudes. It had been put in the pipe (which represented my spirit) one grain at a time. God was not holding back His power from me. It was flowing. The pipe was just so clogged that His power could not get through it.

In order for us, as believers, to effectively minister the gospel—the good news of The LORD Jesus Christ—to the world, the power of God must be allowed to flow through us unhindered. We cannot be fully used by the Holy Spirit when our spirits are clogged with bitterness, resentment and unforgiveness.

To be vessels fit for the Master's use, we must open our hearts to God and purge ourselves of all those things. We will only be prepared to minister to others when we ourselves are walking in God's love.

LIMITLESS**LOVE**

Strife Will Stop the Power

"Make every effort to keep the unity of the Spirit through the bond of peace. There is one body and one Spirit...."
Ephesians 4:3-4, *New International Version*

Strife is the primary strategy Satan uses against the Body of Christ. A group of believers working together in faith and love, operating in the gifts of the Spirit, and moving in the power of God have the potential to destroy Satan's works. To stop them, he has to stop the move of the Holy Spirit in their midst.

How can he do that? He could send nine different evil spirits to come against each gift of the Spirit, but that is unnecessary. There is really only one thing he has to do: interrupt the unity of the spirit that keeps believers in harmony and agreement, by stirring up strife. If he can do that, he can stop the power of God from operating through the Church. He can render the Body of Christ totally ineffective.

That's why, as members of the Body of Christ, getting into strife is the most dangerous thing we can do. It makes a mockery of everything spiritual that we do. When love is not operating in a congregation, the gift of tongues, for example, has no value. There may be a manifestation of it, but it will have no power. It will be as sounding brass—just empty noise. Without love, the gifts of prophecy, wisdom, knowledge and faith are for nothing. Even our giving becomes unprofitable. To give without love is a waste. There will be no return. The supply line has been cut.

The amazing thing to me is how often the devil succeeds in using seemingly spiritual things to get congregations into strife. Most church folks aren't fighting with each other because one of them stole the other's car or because one of them punched the other in the nose. The devil divides believers over spiritual issues. He gets them taking sides, trying to control each other and saying things like, "If you don't agree with me on every point, I'm not going to fellowship with you." Or, "This is my area of the church. I've heard from God about it, and we're going to do things my way no matter what you want to do."

I don't care how we might try to dress those things up spiritually, they're nothing but strife. Selfishness and possessiveness don't run together with the love of God. His love allows people to be free. It never oppresses them. The Spirit of God never creates a possessive, dominating atmosphere. The spirit of the devil does that.

So don't open the door to strife in your church. It's deadly. It is born of the mind of Satan. Do whatever it takes to maintain the unity of the Spirit with your fellow believers. If we'll harmonize and walk in faith as a Body—nothing shall be impossible to us.

God Has You Surrounded

"To which of the angels did God ever say, 'Sit at my right hand until I make your enemies a footstool for your feet'? Are not all angels ministering spirits sent to serve those who will inherit salvation?"
Hebrews 1:13-14, *New International Version*

One of the great things that God, in His love, has provided for us is the angelic host assigned to minister on our behalf. We may never see them with our natural eyes, but we know from the Bible that as we walk in faith and in love, they are always with us carrying out God's commands in our lives. As Psalm 34:7 says, "The angel of The LORD encamps around those who fear Him…" *(New American Standard)*.

Just think, your Father loves and treasures you so much, He has surrounded you with an unseen army of heavenly beings to move with you at all times. They are working constantly to protect you, bring you favor, and see to it that as you speak The WORD of God in faith, every enemy that rises up against you falls for your sake. Their job is to help bring THE BLESSING to pass in your life. Whether you realize it or not, as a born-again child of God you don't go anywhere without a heavenly entourage!

When you face danger or trouble, you ought to be as confident as the Old Testament prophet Elisha when he was surrounded by the armies of the enemy in 2 Kings 6. His servant panicked and said, "Alas, my master! how shall we do?" Elisha's answer was, "Fear not: for they that be with us are more than they that be with them" (verses 15-16).

Then, he prayed that The LORD would open the servant's eyes so he could see into the spirit realm. "And The LORD opened the eyes of the young man; and he saw: and, behold, the mountain was full of horses and chariots of fire round about Elisha" (verse 17). Those angels didn't suddenly come into existence when the servant saw them with his eyes. They were there all the time. Angels followed Elisha around everywhere he went because he was a precious servant of God.

That's why Elisha wasn't afraid. He knew the armies of God would be there when he needed them because God had promised they would be. He was walking by faith in The WORD of The LORD.

Yeah, but I'm not Elisha! you might be thinking. *I'm not some big-time prophet or preacher. I'm just an ordinary believer.*

There is no such thing in the eyes of God as an ordinary believer. Jesus said the "least" person who has been born again through faith in Jesus is greater in God's eyes than the greatest prophet who ever lived (Matthew 11:11). That means you and I are just as loved and treasured as Elisha was. So, we can rest assured that God has us surrounded by angels, too.

Go Out in a Blaze of Glory

"Let us therefore follow after the things which make for peace, and things wherewith one may edify another."

Romans 14:19

As believers, we are supposed to be constantly searching for ways to build each other up. As Ephesians 4:16 says, we should be continually increasing as we edify each other in love. The Greek word translated *edify* means "to charge, as you would charge a battery." As we edify one another, we pump ourselves full of power. We grow up in strength and maturity, and start talking and acting like Jesus.

The closer we get to the end of this age, the more we're going to do that because Jesus is not coming back for a weak, sickly strife-ridden Church that has been defeated and beaten down by Satan. He is coming back for a victorious Church that is walking in the divine love and supernatural power of God. When we leave this earth in the Rapture, we're going out in a blaze of glory!

But, we're not going to step into that kind of glory without first receiving the commandment of love as exactly what it is—*the commandment of God!* It is just as wrong to break it as it is to break the commandment that says, "Thou shalt not steal" or "Thou shalt not kill" or any of the other commandments of God. In fact, keeping the commandment of love will keep you from breaking the others. Therefore, this one is more important than all the others combined.

As long as in our thinking the commandment of love is just a "take it or leave it" proposition, we'll never truly walk in it. The pressure is too great. The moment we attempt to step into the love life, Satan will throw so many obstacles in our path, we'll never stay with it. That's why God gave us the instruction to love in the form of a command. He knew that in order for us to do it, we'd have to know that we had no other acceptable choice.

When we accept love as a command, it becomes a bit in our mouths that keeps us going in the right direction in times of pressure. It takes love out of the realm of convenience where we love only when we're treated fairly or our feelings aren't hurt, and into the realm of commitment where we walk in love, no matter what happens.

When we receive love as a command, we love whether anyone else does or not. No matter what the devil brings against us, we draw on the grace of God and the wellspring of love within us, and obey that great command. The more we do that, the more we'll be charged up with the power of God. We'll rise up like a new breed of believers and walk in the miraculous power and authority God has given us in the Name of Jesus. We'll become the victorious Church God designed us to be, marching forward triumphantly in a blaze of the glory of God.

LIMITLESS**LOVE**

Whosoever Will Means Me

"And when he had called the people unto him with his disciples also, he said unto them, Whosoever will come after me, let him deny himself, and take up his cross, and follow me. For whosoever will save his life shall lose it; but whosoever shall lose his life for my sake and the gospel's, the same shall save it."
Mark 8:34-35

"Whosoever will...." Jesus said those two words again and again in the New Testament. He let us know that when it comes to making difficult choices, it's our will that makes the difference. No matter how our minds might fight us and our bodies might rebel, if we keep our wills steadfastly set, we can make the right choices. We can obey The LORD.

Our wills determine everything we do. They determine our success or our failure and open or close the door to the power and grace of God in our lives. Our wills determine everything we have been and will be in the future. We will be what we *will* to be.

As born-again believers, if we set our wills to walk in love, we can do it. That's why God made love a command and not a recommendation. I asked The LORD one time, "What is Your definition of a commandment?" He said, *A commandment is an order from Me, from which there is no retreat and about which there is no choice.*

It takes a commandment to affect our wills strongly enough to overcome our emotions. But once we fully receive that commandment and set our wills to keep it, all of hell itself cannot stop us.

Whenever I think about the power of the human will, I'm reminded of times when I was a boy and my father promised to take me fishing. I'd spend the evening the night before straightening up my tackle box, and even before my dad woke up the next morning, I'd get up, get dressed and lay down on top of the covers so I'd be ready to go when he called for me. When he did, I would jump out of bed, even though it was 4 a.m., grab my fishing stuff, and off we'd go.

On the other hand, if my father came to me the night before and said, "I'm going to get you up early tomorrow to work in the yard," it would be a different story. He'd have to call me at least three times to wake me up. Even then, I'd feel so tired, I could hardly move. My mind would be fuzzy and my body would be dragging. Why? Because I was willing to go fishing—but I wasn't willing to work in the yard!

Remember this: Your mind and body respond to your will. They will do whatever it tells them to do. So set your will to walk in the love of God, because it is His commandment to you. Dare to say to Jesus, *"Whosoever will means me!"*

LIMITLESS**LOVE**

All Things Are Possible

"All things are possible to him who believes."
Mark 9:23, *New American Standard*

Although we often refer to our New Testament commandment as simply the command to love one another, the fact is, our instruction is twofold. We are to believe in The LORD Jesus Christ *and* walk in love (1 John 3:23). Since faith works by love, when you put both of those commands into operation in your life, all things are possible for you.

A man or woman of faith who is moved and motivated by the love of God cannot be stopped by anyone or anything. They do things that, naturally speaking, are literally impossible to do.

A close friend of mine shared this testimony with me some years ago. He and his son were working together clearing some land. They were driving a little tractor and pulling a log behind it. The log got caught on something and the tractor flipped over on its back, trapping both father and son beneath it. Eventually, the father managed to struggle free and crawl out from the wreckage.

As he did, the tractor burst into flames with his son still trapped underneath it. He ran around to the back of the tractor, grabbed the fender and tried his best to lift it, but with no success. The situation looked hopeless, but suddenly, that father's love for his son and his faith in God roared to life within him. "All right, God," he said, "if You've ever helped me, You are going to help me now!" Then he grabbed that tractor, picked it up and got his son out.

Had that father not been a man of faith, he would never have been able to save his son. He probably would have stood there helplessly while his son died—and God would have gotten the blame for it. People would have said, "I wonder why God didn't save that boy? I wonder why God let him die like that?"

Love alone wouldn't have gotten the job done in that situation. It took both faith and love. But thank God, that father had both of them. He was ready to face trouble and triumph over it because he walked in The WORD of God, not just that day but every day. He believed in Jesus, not just as his LORD, but as THE LORD over every situation. He believed that all authority both in heaven and in earth have been given to him. So he stepped out on that authority, and expected God to give him all the power necessary to save his son that day.

It was love that motivated him to step into the flames and put his hand on that tractor. It was faith in God that enabled him to lift it. Together, those two became an unbeatable force and turned tragedy into triumph. If you'll put them to work, they'll do the same in your life—and all things will be possible to you.

LIMITLESS**LOVE**

Don't Turn Out the Light

"This I say therefore, and affirm together with The LORD, that you walk no longer just as the other Gentiles also walk, in the futility of their mind, being darkened in their understanding, excluded from the life of God, because of the ignorance that is in them, because of the hardness of their heart."
Ephesians 4:17-18, *New American Standard*

As believers, we're simply not supposed to live like worldly people do. For them, things like selfishness, bitterness, anger, strife and gossip (Ephesians 4:31) are just a normal part of life. Their understanding is darkened and their hearts are blinded, so they can't see any other way to live. As Christians, we know better. The light of God has shined in our hearts and revealed God's truth and love. When we willingly step back into those old ways of thinking and behaving, however, our minds are blinded again. When we let those old attitudes come back in, we end up walking in darkness until we repent.

Then, having alienated ourselves from the life of God, when we need healing in our bodies, we find ourselves unable to receive it. When we need divine wisdom to solve a problem in our lives, we just can't seem to lay hold of it. We've cut ourselves off from the light of God so His WORD—His revelation—cannot flow from our spirits up into our minds or out into our bodies.

"Wait a minute," someone might say, "how can that be? I thought that God within us is absolute light, that in Him there is no darkness at all."

That is absolutely the truth. There is no amount of darkness that can overcome the light of God in your spirit. No matter how dark the world around you might become, it can never dim the light you have in Him. When you make a decision of your will to walk in that light, no amount of darkness can penetrate it.

But when you choose to turn out that light by walking in strife instead of in love, you'll find yourself stumbling around in darkness again. When you step over into unforgiveness, disharmony or envy, those things interrupt the spiritual power current that is flowing from God to you. Although He still wants to BLESS you and help you, His hands are tied. His power cannot get through. You are left without His light and without His protection, so the devil can come crashing into your life to steal, kill and destroy.

The choice is yours. You can choose to walk in the light, or you can choose to walk in the darkness. God has "set before you life and death, blessing and cursing," light and darkness (Deuteronomy 30:19). Choose to walk in the light!

LIMITLESS**LOVE**

When Love Drives Us to Our Knees

"If any man see his brother sin a sin which is not unto death,
he shall ask, and he shall give him life...."
1 John 5:16

Notice, that verse doesn't say that if we see our brother sin, we should call one of our friends and tell about it. It doesn't say we ought to get together at the coffee shop after church and criticize that brother for his bad behavior. It says we should pray for him, and God will give him life.

Real, heartfelt prayer offered on behalf of a fellow believer who has stumbled and fallen into sin is one of the most powerful expressions of love. It opens the door to the Spirit of God and gives Him access to people the devil has bound through ignorance and deception. Our prayers of intercession can destroy the works of the devil in the lives of our brothers and sisters in Christ so that the full and perfect plan of God can be fulfilled. Our prayers can set them free.

If we'll make ourselves available to the Holy Spirit to pray for each other in love, He'll bring us to the point where we know by the spirit when someone needs prayer. Even if we don't specifically know what to pray for them, we can pray perfectly in other tongues until we have the assurance in our hearts that the will of God has been done. That's what the Apostle Paul was referring to in Romans 8:26-28 when he wrote:

> Likewise the Spirit also helpeth our infirmities: for we know not what we should pray for as we ought: but the Spirit itself maketh intercession for us with groanings which cannot be uttered. And he that searcheth the hearts knoweth what is the mind of the Spirit, because he maketh intercession for the saints according to the will of God. And we know that all things work together for good to them that love God, to them who are the called according to his purpose.

Many people think that passage is saying that even the things the devil does will work for the good of those who are called of God. But Paul didn't mention the devil there. He was talking about the things of God: the Name of Jesus, the gifts of the Spirit, The WORD of God, and all the other spiritual weapons of warfare sent into the earth by Jesus to make the Body of Christ strong and victorious.

If we will begin to use those weapons in prayer for one another, they'll all work together and bring forth God's good plan for our lives, and the evil schemes of Satan will not work at all. When love drives us to our knees to intercede for our sinning brother instead of to the telephone to tell on him, we will all step into the greatest victories we have ever known.

Armed and Dangerous

"But if we walk in the light, as he is in the light, we have fellowship one with another, and the blood of Jesus Christ his Son cleanseth us from all sin."
1 John 1:7

The more we learn to walk in God's commandment of love, the more brightly the light of God will shine in our lives. The blood of Jesus will keep us cleansed from all sin, and when the devil tries to trip us up, we won't stumble and fall into his traps. The light of God will rise up inside us and show us exactly what to do and the right way to go. We will know just how to handle every situation.

The only thing that stands between us and all of God's glory in this earth is our commitment to walk in the commandment of His love. When we become determined to walk in love, we can be trusted with more and more of God's anointing power. God can trust us with greater degrees of material prosperity when love is our total way of life.

The abundance of God's provision and power we experience in every area of life will be directly determined by how we love when the pressure is on and the going is rough. That's why we must be determined to walk in love whether anyone else does or not. That's why we must receive the commandment of love as the mandate of God in our lives and make a quality decision to walk in the fullness of it.

We must say to ourselves, "There is no other way. I will live by the commandment of love."

The moment we wholeheartedly make that decision, the very power of God Himself comes to back us up and enable us to carry it out. Then, even in times of natural weakness, the grace of God will be sufficient for us. We will find that even when our own strength fails, God's strength enables us to keep right on walking in love.

That's when we become truly dangerous to Satan. When we are armed with love, he trembles every time we step out in faith because he knows our faith will work. When we walk in love, we control his works. We take from him the very spoils he has plundered, and we topple spiritual strongholds he has worked years to establish. The life, light and love of God operating in us destroy the devil's works, and leave him totally helpless.

When we walk in God's love, we enforce the law of life. So let's do it. Let's become the mighty force that God intended us to be. Let's take love out of the natural realm, where our feelings get in the way, and into the realm of the spirit, where we love one another because God loves us and for no other reason. Let's move into the miraculous realm of love where together, we can operate fully in the supernatural power of God.

LIMITLESS**LOVE**

A Kinder, Gentler You!

"Speak evil of no man…be no brawlers, but gentle,
showing all meekness unto all men."
Titus 3:2

Some people just naturally have a sharp tongue and an abrupt personality. They're often harsh with others and hurt their feelings. "I can't help it," they'll say. "That's how I am. I don't sugar-coat things. I just tell it like it is. If people get offended, that's their problem."

That kind of thinking isn't acceptable, however, once we are born again. God expects us, as His children, to walk in love. He expects us to be kind because He is kind and He has put His very own Spirit of kindness within us. Even if we've been sharp and abrasive all our lives, God says we should override those old habits by releasing our new nature and "be…kind one to another" (Ephesians 4:32).

Exactly what does it mean to be kind?

In my studies, I've found some wonderful definitions. If you'll meditate on them and let the Holy Spirit imprint on your heart the picture they present, they'll help you learn to yield to the personality of God within you and behave in ways that are truly kind.

According to *Vine's Expository Dictionary of Biblical Words*[15] [and/or *Strong's Exhaustive Concordance of the Bible*[16]], *kindness* can also be translated *goodness* "in the sense of what is upright, righteous; it signifies not merely goodness as a quality, rather it is goodness in action expressing itself in deeds, in grace and tenderness and compassion; in sweetness of disposition, gentleness in dealing with others, benevolence, affability. The word describes the ability to act for the welfare of those taxing your patience."

Webster's dictionary says *kindness* is "the state, quality or habit of being kind, sympathetic, friendly, gentle, tenderhearted, generous, affectionate, well dispositioned, courteous."

I particularly like *Webster's* use of the word *habit* because when we're truly walking in the lovingkindness of God, it will just flow out of us habitually. We won't have to try to think up kind things to do. We can just let the kindness of God be expressed through us, moment-by-moment. In other words, we can simply give in to our new nature instead of the flesh.

If you were harsh and abrasive before, that might require a total personality change for you. But that's OK. God is up to the job. His Spirit within you can get it done. He can empower you to shake off the old man and put on the new. As you yield to Him, He can bring forth a kinder, gentler you!

[15] W.E. Vine, *Vine's Expository Dictionary of Biblical Words*, ed. Merrill F. Unger, William White (Nashville: Thomas Nelson Publishers, 1985) p. 343.
[16] James Strong, *The New Strong's Exhaustive Concordance of the Bible* (Nashville: Thomas Nelson Publishers, 1984) G 5543.

LIMITLESS**LOVE**

Protect Your Heart

"I will set no worthless thing before my eyes; I hate the work of those
who fall away; It shall not fasten its grip on me. A perverse heart
shall depart from me; I will know no evil."
Psalm 101:3-4, *New American Standard*

A majority of what you will find on television and in the movies will not enhance your love walk. Secular entertainment is absolutely full of filthy language, selfishness and strife. And if you want to develop your love life, the Spirit of God will lead you more and more to turn that ugly stuff off.

Why? Because when you feed your mind on it, watching and hearing it again and again, you become desensitized to it. It works its way down through your mind and into your heart… and sometime, when you least expect it, it will come right back out.

The Bible tells us to rid ourselves of filthy communication, of "anger, rage, bad feeling toward others, curses and slander, and foulmouthed abuse and shameful utterances…" (Colossians 3:8, *The Amplified Bible*). It doesn't take a rocket scientist to figure out that means we'll have to rid ourselves of all the soap operas, most of the talk shows, and a lot of the other programs worldly people watch. There is so much in them that is unloving and perverse that we should give them absolutely no place in our lives. We need to see them for what they are—the devil's attempt to pull people further into darkness. And, we need to say the same thing the psalmist said, "I will set no worthless thing before my eyes"!

I realize simply changing the television channel won't protect you from all those kinds of things. As long as we live in this world, there will be people around us talking and behaving in unloving and ungodly ways. But, by the power of God, we can rise above those influences. We can, as one minister said, "shut the door of our nature to it." God will help us close our hearts to it so that it won't get in.

If we purposely put ourselves in position to witness ungodly things, however, that's another matter altogether. We're making a choice to open the door of our nature to the devil's trash. We're consciously choosing to sow to the flesh, and the Bible says that when we do that we'll reap corruption (Galatians 6:8). That's the unchangeable law of God, and it is going to work in our lives whether we like it or not.

Don't give the devil a free shot at you. Don't willingly give him the opportunity to corrupt your love walk and sow strife into your life. When something comes on television that violates your born-again spirit, turn it off. If you're in a theater, dare to walk out. Refuse to give the wicked ways of the world an opportunity to cling to you.

LIMITLESS**LOVE**

Make an Active Effort to Be Kind

"Rejoice not when thine enemy falleth, and let not thine heart be glad
when he stumbleth: Lest The LORD see it, and it displease him...."
Proverbs 24:17

The Bible tells us that God has "good will toward men" (Luke 2:14), and if we're going to walk in His love we'll have goodwill toward them, too. Not just toward the ones who are nice to us and do what we like, but toward those who have done us wrong. We won't allow ourselves the fleshly luxury of hoping someone will hurt them the same way they hurt us. And we certainly won't rejoice when we hear they've fallen upon hard times.

The Bible says God is displeased with that kind of attitude. He'll disapprove if He sees us rejoicing over the calamity of our enemies and saying, "Well, I don't feel sorry for them a bit. After all, they've done plenty of bad things to others, and what goes around comes around!"

The LORD expects us to have the same attitude He has and the Bible says He takes no pleasure in the calamity of the wicked, but continually desires for even the most wicked person to turn from his way so that he can live and be BLESSED (Ezekiel 33:11)!

God expects us to be the same way. That means instead of hoping they get what they deserve, we're to extend goodwill toward them. We're to pray for them to be helped and BLESSED of The LORD.

Having goodwill toward someone means more than just forgiving them and refusing to be bitter or wish them harm. Goodwill starts with those things, of course, but then goes even further.

When we have goodwill toward someone, we make a choice to behave kindly toward them. We willfully choose to take satisfaction and delight in seeing them blessed. Webster's dictionary refers to goodwill as "having understanding toward a person; to offer a gesture of conciliation; to show courtesy or respect; to express enthusiasm over benefits received by another; to make an active effort to be friendly, peaceable and compatible."

Remember this: Real love isn't just the absence of negative things like hatred, resentment and unforgiveness. Love is the presence of goodness, kindness and THE BLESSING. So check up on yourself every now and then. Ask the Holy Spirit to reveal to you if you have ill will toward anyone. If so, don't be content just to forgive them and let the matter drop. Take another step. Let The LORD show you something loving and kind you can say or do for that person. Make an active effort to be courteous and friendly to them. Be like your Father and extend goodwill toward your enemies—not just your friends.

LIMITLESS**LOVE**

Acting in Love Will Set You Free

"Then Jesus said to His disciples, 'If anyone wishes to come after Me,
he must deny himself, and take up his cross, and follow Me.
For whoever wishes to save his life shall lose it; but whoever
loses his life for My sake shall find it.'"
Matthew 16:24-25, *New American Standard*

I've noticed a great number of people—even Christian people—are having trouble with depression these days. That in itself may not be anything new. What is new, however, is that professional, worldly voices are now putting fancy names on it, calling it a "condition," and making people think it's OK for them to have it.

They're not just doing that with depression, either. They're doing it with things like anger, too. These days, if someone lets their anger get out of control, we excuse him and say he has "road rage" or "airplane rage," and act as if they're victims of something that just can't be helped.

As believers, we need to reject those kinds of rationalizations. We shouldn't take those names the professionals are giving us. We shouldn't just submit to them and say, "Well, I guess I'm just a victim of clinical depression or chemical imbalance, and there's nothing I can do about it."

Certainly, there's something we can do about it! First, we can get honest about where those things come from. Depression and rage of every kind are of the devil. They are signs that the devil is coming to steal, kill and destroy our lives. And we can stop him by digging into The WORD of God—attending to it and obeying it—and by spending time fellowshiping with The LORD in prayer. We can rise up, resist the devil and, according to the Bible, he will flee from us.

One way to resist the devil is to stop focusing on ourselves and focus, instead, on The LORD and the good things He has done for us. We can also get busy with our minds and bodies, tending to someone besides ourselves. Most people who are depressed have tunnel vision. All they can see is themselves. *Things just aren't right for me,* they think. *I don't feel good. I'm not doing well. I'm a failure. I'm unloved. I've been mistreated…I…I…."*

Anyone can get depressed if they think about themselves long enough. So stop thinking those kinds of thoughts. If you're having trouble with depression, make yourself get up and go do something to help someone else. Start giving of yourself and listening to The WORD of God day and night. Actively release your faith and expect God to make you whole, spirit, soul and body. Attend to and act on the truth of God's love, and that truth will make you free!

Keep the Inner Fire Burning

*"Never lag in zeal and in earnest endeavor; be aglow and
burning with the Spirit, serving The LORD."*
Romans 12:11, *The Amplified Bible*

Most of us start our spiritual walk with a fervent passion for The LORD. We're so grateful to be delivered from hell and headed toward heaven, cleansed from sin and given hope for our future, that we're aglow with love for the One who made it all possible. All we want to do is serve Him.

But as time passes, the fire within us can begin to dim. We can get busy with other things and begin to lose our interest in Him. That happened to me after I'd been saved a few years. I'd hardly even noticed it until I heard a minister I highly respect prophesy about the mighty end-time army of The LORD. He said, "Rise up and become on fire…and you can be part of that army." As I thought about his words, it began to dawn on me that I wasn't as zealous as I used to be.

I wasn't in sin. I wasn't doing anything bad. I'd just become distracted with the natural things of life. At that time, Ken and I had been walking with The LORD about five years, and we weren't destitute anymore as when we were first saved. We were comfortable and BLESSED. In the early days, our desperation had driven us into a determined pursuit of God. He was our only hope. But, after we had served Him awhile and began to prosper, that initial desperation faded, and some of my inner fire faded with it.

Although I was still reading The WORD every day, I wasn't attending to it with the enthusiasm I had before. So I said to The LORD, "I want to change that! I want to get spiritually fired up with the desire I had for You before. What's more, I want that desire to increase!"

I acted on that decision by giving The LORD some extra time each day. I began to read some inspiring books The LORD led me to read. I began to watch over my inner fire. When it needed to be stoked, I'd check with The LORD and find out what to do to add some spiritual fuel and make it burn brighter.

You can do the same thing—and you'll have to if you want to be a part of God's mighty end time army. Why? Because that group isn't going to be made up of believers who are only mildly interested in the things of GOD. It's not going to be composed of Christians who have let their affections be drawn away from The LORD and have fallen in love with the things of this world, instead.

Those who step into the supernatural and get in on this great last-days ministry of signs and wonders will be those whose passion for The LORD has consumed their lives and kept them earnestly serving Him. I've made up my mind to be among them. How about you?

LIMITLESS**LOVE**

In Everything, Give Thanks

"Rejoice always....in everything give thanks;
for this is God's will for you in Christ Jesus."
1 Thessalonians 5:16, 18, *New American Standard*

When we talk about walking in love, we usually think about how we behave toward other people. But the One who deserves our love first and foremost is our heavenly Father. We should treat Him, above all, with courtesy, appreciation and respect. We shouldn't just do it on Sundays, either. We shouldn't be content to lift our hands and tell The LORD how much we love Him and honor Him when we're in church…then walk out the door and start griping to each other about how lousy things have been.

We've all done that at times. We've said a hearty "amen!" during the sermon when the preacher talked about how God meets all our needs according to His riches in glory by Christ Jesus (Philippians 4:21). Then, when we got home, we turned to our husband or wife and said, "I don't know why God isn't taking care of us! We have all these bills piling up, and He hasn't done anything to help us. Sometimes I wonder if He even remembers we're here!"

Do you know what that kind of talk is? It's called "murmuring" or "complaining," and the Bible says God doesn't appreciate it. In fact, 1 Corinthians 10:10 tells us that when the Israelites did it, they were destroyed. That in itself is reason enough to avoid an attitude of ingratitude. But the best reason to do it is simply because we desire with all our hearts to treat our God with love.

One of the primary ways we do that is by rejoicing continually and giving thanks in everything. That means we don't allow ourselves to be depressed and downhearted. We purposely maintain a positive outlook and expectant faith.

When something negative happens, we give thanks to God right in the midst of it. We don't thank Him *for* bad things—because He isn't the author of them, the devil is. But we can stay grateful and thankful to God as we go through them.

No matter how bad things are, we always have something to be thankful to God for. If nothing else, we have life and breath in our bodies. We have The WORD of God to teach us how to get through any situation and come out in victory. So we can say, "LORD, this is a tough place, but I'm thankful to You that I don't have to stay in it. I can stand on Your WORD, and things will turn around! I'm grateful that You'll never leave me or forsake me. You'll stay with me and see me through!"

Those are the kinds of words The LORD appreciates. When we speak them, we are treating Him with the love He so richly deserves.

LIMITLESS**LOVE**

A Very Dumb Thing to Do

"And when the sabbath day was come, he began to teach in the synagogue: and many hearing him were astonished, saying, From whence hath this man these things? and what wisdom is this which is given unto him, that even such mighty works are wrought by his hands? Is not this the carpenter, the son of Mary, the brother of James, and Joses, and of Juda, and Simon? and are not his sisters here with us? And they were offended at him.... And he could there do no mighty work, save that he laid his hands upon a few sick folk, and healed them."
Mark 6:2-3, 5

You know it's impossible to maintain your love walk when you get offended with other people. But, have you considered the fact that you can also wreck your love life by getting offended at *God*? The moment you begin to blame Him for the things that go wrong in your life, saying things like, "I just don't know why God let this happen to me..." you've stepped out of love into strife, and you're headed nowhere—fast.

When you think about it, getting mad at God is one of the dumbest things we could do. The Bible tells us clearly, He is perfect in all His ways (Deuteronomy 32:4). God never misses it. He's always good. He is always right on time. So if things aren't working, we need to look at ourselves. We need to listen to the words that have been coming out of our mouths because usually when there's a problem, we can find it right there. We'll find that we've yielded to the pressure of our situation and begun speaking doubt and fear instead of confessing The WORD of God. We'll find we've actually stopped The LORD from doing mighty works on our behalf by our own words of unbelief.

That's what the people at Nazareth did when Jesus was there. Instead of loving Him and appreciating the power of God working in Him, they became offended with Him. He didn't fit their idea of who the Messiah ought to be. He didn't do and say everything exactly like they thought He should. So, they became offended and refused to trust Him.

No doubt, that grieved The LORD, but do you know who paid the highest price in that situation? The people of Nazareth. They missed out on their healings and the miracles Jesus wanted to do among them. They failed to receive the deliverance they needed. All because they took offense!

The next time you're tempted to get mad and blame God for something bad that has happened to you, refuse the temptation to take offense. Instead, just keep on loving and trusting The LORD. Keep confessing His goodness, believing His WORD and He will do mighty works for you!

LIMITLESS**LOVE**

That's What Our Loving God Can Do!

"I shall not die, but live, and declare the works of The LORD."
Psalm 118:17

I've noticed that when we start talking about the goodness and love of The LORD (especially in secular or traditionally religious company), it always seems as if someone always has a story to tell that puts God in a bad light. "I don't know," they'll say. "If God is such a loving God, why did He let dear old Sister Supersaint die of that terrible disease? Why didn't He do something to save her?"

Don't ever let stories like that shake you. Just stick with The WORD. Stand strong on your faith in the loving nature of God…and start accumulating some inspiring stories of your own.

Collect stories like the one about Sister Pearl. She's a lady who attended one of our healing meetings in Denver a few years ago. She didn't come to get healed. She came with her daughter and granddaughter to give her testimony about what The LORD had already done for her.

It seems some months before, Pearl had been rushed to the emergency room and diagnosed with spinal meningitis. Even before her daughter was able to get her there, Pearl had slipped into a coma. "All I can remember is that I closed my eyes. I didn't feel any pain, and I went to this beautiful place that was just peace and rest."

Left to herself, Pearl might have been just as happy to go home to heaven and be with The LORD. But her daughter and granddaughter weren't about to let that happen. Pearl had raised them on The WORD of God. She had taught them the truth about God's love and His healing power. She'd seen to it they were trained to walk in faith.

So at that critical moment, that training kicked in! When the doctors told them Pearl's heart wasn't functioning properly, they refused to be afraid. When they were told that her lungs were failing and her brain was filling up with fluid, they just kept believing Pearl would not die but live and declare the works of The LORD. The doctors were confounded. "Don't you see the reports?" they asked. "Don't you understand what the results of the tests and the MRIs mean?"

"We don't look at things that are seen," that daughter and granddaughter said, "we look at The WORD of God, and it says by the stripes of Jesus, she is healed!"

Within days, Pearl's condition turned around. Her heart, her lungs and her brain returned to normal. Despite the doctors' dire predictions, she doesn't walk with a cane. She has no brain damage and she was functioning better when she left the hospital than she ever did.

When someone dares to believe and act on The WORD, that's what our loving God can do!

LIMITLESS**LOVE**

Love...and Be Happy

"There is nothing better for a man, than that he should eat and drink,
and that he should make his soul enjoy good in his labour.
This also I saw, that it was from the hand of God."
Ecclesiastes 2:24

One of the reasons The LORD commands us to walk in love is because He wants us to be happy. He wants us to enjoy our lives, and the more we love, the more we do!

It's when we get out of love and into strife, unforgiveness and offense that misery sets in. When we operate in those things, we put out a welcome mat for the devil. We give him an open invitation to come torment us and wreak havoc in every area of our lives. We open the door to sickness, weakness and all kinds of mental and emotional distress. Instead of enjoying our lives, we find ourselves struggling just to get through them.

God doesn't want that to happen to us. He wants us to enjoy ourselves! He doesn't want us to be under the thumb of some devil who is telling us what to do. He doesn't want some ugly demon driving us and ruining our lives. He doesn't want us to be stressed and depressed! He wants us to be free.

He wants us to wake up every day with a song in our hearts saying, "This is the day The LORD has made. I will rejoice and be glad in it!"

Some people think God doesn't care about our comfort and happiness, but He does. He cares about the big things in our lives...and the small. The Bible says He pays such close attention to us that He even numbers the hairs on our head!

God revealed how truly eager He is to bless us and help us, through the ministry of Jesus. You can read through the Gospels and see how much He wanted to help people. They didn't have to coerce Him or have to have an appointment. They could just run up to Him on the street and say, "LORD, heal me!" and He would. He might be walking down the road, see a mother crying at the funeral of her son, and He'd raise that boy up from the dead, just so the mother wouldn't be grieved. When He saw people hungry, He worked a miracle just so they wouldn't have to go away to eat!

He's still the same today. He hasn't changed—except for the fact that He's more powerful now than ever. Now He is the resurrected LORD of the whole earth, seated at the right hand of the Father. All power and authority is His.

He is not only willing, but eager, to make that power available to us and through us. He'll see to it that we are a BLESSING to others and that we enjoy His goodness all the days of our lives—if we'll only walk in love.

LIMITLESS**LOVE**

Remember Them No More

"For I will be merciful to their unrighteousness,
and their sins and their iniquities I will remember no more."
Hebrews 8:12

God loves us so much that when He cleanses us from our sins, He doesn't just forgive us—He remembers our sins no more! And, if He doesn't remember them, neither should we. We should never let the devil keep us down by making us look at the sins of our past.

He will try to do that, you know. He'll try hard! The minute he sees you're making progress in your life and walking in the righteousness God has given you, the devil will bring up your history. He'll say, "How can you expect to do anything for God after all the bad things you've done?"

When that happens, stand fast in faith. Once you've repented and put a sin under the blood, leave it there. Don't let the devil beat you over the head with it. Refuse to let him make you look back.

Instead, do what Jesus said in Luke 17:32. Remember Lot's wife!

In that passage Jesus was referring to the time when God sent an angel to bring Lot and his family out of the city of Sodom, where they'd been living, because it was wicked and destined for destruction. The angel gave them instructions that would get them safely to their chosen destination. He said, "Don't look back" (Genesis 19:17, *New International Version)!*

Lot's wife, however, disobeyed. She turned, looked back at the sinful place behind her and got stuck in that place. There, the Bible says, she became a pillar of salt. Lot's wife never reached the place where God was taking her, because she refused to leave the past behind.

Years ago, Ken and I heard a story about a little boy in Sunday school who responded to that story with great excitement. After his teacher told how Lot's wife looked back and turned into a pillar of salt, he raised his hand eagerly. "That's nothing!" he exclaimed. "When my mom was driving down the road the other day, she looked back and turned into a *telephone pole!"*

Clearly, the little boy misunderstood the scriptural story, but oddly enough, the message is the same. When we let our past distract us and get our eyes on past events, we get off course and run into trouble. We end up stuck in yesterday, unable to fulfill the will of God for our lives today.

Don't let that happen to you. Take full advantage of God's loving forgetfulness. Follow His example and remember your sins no more. Steer clear of pillars of salt and telephone poles, fixing your eyes on Jesus, and keep moving toward your destiny in Him!

LIMITLESS*LOVE*

Rise and Be Healed

"[Jesus] his own self bare our sins in his own body on the tree, that we, being dead to sins, should live unto righteousness: by whose stripes ye were healed."
1 Peter 2:24

For thousands of years, the devil has used sickness and disease to make people doubt God's love. Again and again, he has pointed the finger of accusation and said, "If God cares about His people so much, why does He let them suffer sickness and disease? When they pray for healing, why does He so often delay or even refuse to send it?"

The scriptural fact is, He doesn't.

"Now, wait a minute," someone might say. "My dear old granny prayed for healing from her arthritis, and God told her she'd have to wait awhile. He said that arthritis was teaching her something."

With all due respect to Granny, I can assure you God didn't say any such thing. He couldn't have possibly said it because He provided healing for Granny, and everyone else, over 2,000 years ago. That's when He sent Jesus to bear our sicknesses and carry away our diseases (Isaiah 53:5). God couldn't possibly delay our healing because, as far as He is concerned, it's already been done. The only thing left is for us to believe and receive it. And if we haven't, it's not because we're waiting on God—it's because God is waiting on us!

Ken and I know that, not only from The WORD, but from our own experience. When we first began to walk with God, we learned right away that God was doing miracles. We saw them firsthand. We heard Oral Roberts preach about them—and we believed. But we continued to struggle with sickness ourselves.

Then, one day, we heard Kenneth E. Hagin preach on 1 Peter 2:24. We found out that when Jesus went to the cross, He purchased for us not only salvation for our spirits and souls, but healing for our bodies. When we believed that, it changed our whole outlook. We no longer saw ourselves as the sick trying to get God to heal us. We saw ourselves as the healed of The LORD. We realized healing was already ours, and when the devil came to steal it by attacking us with sickness and disease, we resisted him and flatly refused to receive it!

As a result, not only did Ken and I begin to walk in divine healing and health, we never once had to take our children to the doctor because of sickness and disease. We would have, had it been necessary, but it never was. Every time they'd start to get sick, we'd just pray and receive what God had provided, and they'd be healed!

If you're wishing that were true for you, stop wishing and start believing. Receive by faith what God in His great love has already provided for you. Rise and be healed in the Name of Jesus!

LIMITLESS**LOVE**

The Truth Will Make You Free

"Grace and peace be multiplied unto you through the knowledge of God,
and of Jesus our Lord, According as his divine power hath given unto us all things
that pertain unto life and godliness, through the knowledge of him that hath called
us to glory and virtue: Whereby are given unto us exceeding great and precious
promises: that by these ye might be partakers of the divine nature,
having escaped the corruption that is in the world through lust."
2 Peter 1:2-4

Do you ever long to be absolutely free of selfishness? Do you yearn to throw off every fleshly bondage and hindrance so you can walk fully in love?

As amazing as it seems, we can do it!

Jesus told us how: "...If you continue in My word, then you are truly disciples of Mine; and you will know the truth, and the truth will make you free'" (John 8:31-32, *New American Standard*).

That's why, again and again, we must meditate on the truths in The WORD that tell us we've been made partakers of God's divine and loving nature. We must continually grow in our revelation of the fact that God's love has been shed abroad in our hearts. The more fully and deeply we come to know that truth, the freer we will be!

It simply doesn't work for us to try to free ourselves out of sheer, human self-discipline from our unloving habits and behaviors. It doesn't work when, by the force of our own efforts, we try to make ourselves "act nice." When we do that, we inevitably fail, and get frustrated and discouraged with ourselves. As a result, we end up more irritable and short-tempered than we were before!

The only way we can truly succeed at walking in love is by drawing on the grace of God within us. The only way we can truly love like Jesus loves is by letting His nature, which dwells within our reborn human spirits, flow out through us. The more we know about His nature, the more we can do that.

As 2 Peter 1:2 says, God's grace is multiplied to us through the knowledge of God and of Jesus our LORD! That's true in every area of the Christian life. We can't receive something from God that we don't know about. We have to hear the truth about it. Then, when we hear it, faith comes. As we believe and begin to act on that truth, we see the power of it go to work in our lives.

So dig into The WORD and find out more about the loving nature of God that abides in you. Meditate on it. Confess it and say, "God's love lives in me!" Then, begin to act by faith, and the bondages of the flesh will be broken. You will know the truth, and it will make you free!

LIMITLESS**LOVE**

See Yourself Through God's Eyes

"For if these things be in you, and abound, they make you that ye shall neither be barren nor unfruitful in the knowledge of our LORD Jesus Christ. But he that lacketh these things is blind, and cannot see afar off, and hath forgotten that he was purged from his old sins."

2 Peter 1:8-9

The verses preceding these scriptures list many of the fruit of the spirit—the foremost of which is *love*. They let us know that if God's love isn't abounding and increasing in our lives, there is one central reason: We have forgotten we were cleansed from our old sins.

Spiritually speaking, we've forgotten who we are.

How would it be possible for us to do such a thing? Actually, it's easy. All we have to do is get so caught up in the day-to-day details of living that we don't have time to sit down and look into the mirror of The WORD. (See James 1:23-25.) All we have to do is lose touch with our born-again spirits and begin thinking of ourselves as just natural, human beings.

It doesn't take years to do that, either. It can happen in just a day.

You see, the devil is working constantly to blind us to truths of the spirit. He continually endeavors to fill our minds with the facts of this physical realm. He wants us to get so absorbed in this temporal world, we lose sight of the eternal and invisible. When we do that, we forget who God has made us and yield instead to what the natural, external evidence tells us we must be.

When we stumble and act unlovingly, we begin to think that we are, in fact, unloving and unkind. When we experience natural feelings of selfishness and irritation, we start to assume we are selfish and irritable by nature, instead of seeing ourselves as The WORD says we are— like our Father—compassionate, tender and patient.

The solution? It's simple! Never let yourself forget who you are in Jesus. Never let a day go by without drawing near to God in His WORD and in prayer so He can remind you who He made you to be.

It's easy to abound in love when you've been freshly reminded that the God of love has re-created you in His image. It's a cinch to shake off selfish habits and sin when you're living in the awareness that He who knew no sin was made to be sin for you, so that you could be made the righteousness of God. You won't walk in worldly and unloving ways when you keep your mind on the truth that you are filled with the Spirit of your heavenly Father, and destined to be like Him.

If you forget those things, your love life will be barren. So, don't do it! Open your Bible often, and look into the mirror of The WORD. See yourself through God's eyes every day.

LIMITLESS**LOVE**

Win the World With Love

"Honour all men. Love the brotherhood. Fear God. Honour the king."
1 Peter 2:17

The reason we, as God's children, are living on this earth is so that we can advance the kingdom of God. Certainly, God wants to bless us and give us wonderful lives, but if that's all He wanted to do, He would take us to heaven the minute we made Jesus The LORD of our lives. After all, the least that heaven has to offer beats the best we have on earth.

But God left us here so we can influence others for Him. He told us to share the gospel with lost people so that they can get born again. One of the most powerful ways we can do that is by simply loving them.

The love of God is one of the most evangelistic forces of all. The whole world is looking for love all the time, everywhere they go. You may not realize that if you've been a Christian for a while. You may almost take love for granted. I know I sometimes do. My whole family is saved, all my friends are saved, everyone I work with is saved…and since they all have the love of God flowing through them, I'm surrounded by love almost all the time.

Worldly people don't have that experience. They're surrounded by a selfish, dog-eat-dog society. They're not exposed to the love of God very much, and they're starved for it.

If you'll just let God's love within you flow out to them, you'll be amazed how it will minister to them. If you'll just honor them and respect them, treat them like they're the most precious, valuable beings in the world, God's love will touch them and open their hearts. Then, when you have the opportunity to share the gospel with them, they'll be eager to hear it. They'll be prepared and ready to receive.

In times past, the Church missed it in this area in a big way. We focused so much on the sinfulness of sinners that we began to disregard and look down on them. We developed an inner attitude of disdain toward those who were in rebellion against God and weren't born again.

But, the Bible doesn't teach us to do that. It says we should honor *all* men. It says we should be like our Father who loved not just the righteous but the whole world so much, He sent Jesus to die for their sins. Even in our fallen and dishonorable state, God still saw in us the wonderful beings He created us to be. He recalled what we were before the Fall, looked through the eyes of Love, and saw what, through His redemption, we could once again be.

When we start seeing the lost in that same light, we will love them just as He does…and that love will draw them to Him.

LIMITLESS**LOVE**

A Sure Spiritual Cure

"This I say then, Walk in the Spirit, and ye shall not fulfil the lust
of the flesh. For the flesh lusteth against the Spirit, and the
Spirit against the flesh: and these are contrary the one to the other:
so that ye cannot do the things that ye would."
Galatians 5:16-17

Have you ever heard the old saying, "Stuff a cold and starve a fever"? Some people say that helps overcome symptoms of sickness in your body. I don't know if that's true or not, but I can give you a similar formula that's a sure cure for what ails you spiritually. It will help you overcome the symptoms of selfishness and walk in love.

Stuff your spirit and starve your flesh!

That may not sound very poetic, but it is absolutely scriptural. And, I can tell you from experience, it works!

Here's why. Once you're born again, you have a pure, reborn spirit within you. Inside, you're a new man, re-created in Christ Jesus, made to walk in love. But outside, you're wearing the same old flesh you always had. And until you renew your mind with The WORD of God, you're going to think the same old thoughts.

Clearly, there is going to be a conflict. The flesh (which is composed of your unrenewed mind and your spiritually dead body) will pull you one way—*the wrong way*—and your spirit will pull you the other. As the Bible says, they are "contrary to one another," and until we go to heaven or get raptured, they always will be.

If your spirit takes dominion, you'll overcome those fleshly desires. You'll conquer selfishness and walk in love. If your flesh takes dominion, you'll do the same old things you did before you were born again. The question is: Which side is going to win?

The answer is obvious. The side that is stronger will always have the advantage.

That means if you renew your mind with The WORD of God, if you stuff your heart full of spiritual nourishment and build it up by praying in tongues, fellowshiping with God and going to a strong, anointed church, your spirit will rise up and conquer your flesh. If you give yourself an extra edge by separating yourself from worldly indulgences—yes, things like those ugly movies you used to watch and those gossip sessions at the office—your flesh will get weaker and weaker and your spirit will win the battle, easily, every time.

Remember that, when you start suffering symptoms of selfishness and stumble in your walk of love. Take the cure. Stuff your spirit and starve your flesh. You'll be spiritually strong and healthy very soon!

LIMITLESS**LOVE**

Say *Yes* to the Spirit and *No* to the Flesh

"Therefore, brethren, we are debtors, not to the flesh, to live after the flesh.
For if ye live after the flesh, ye shall die: but if ye through the Spirit
do mortify the deeds of the body, ye shall live. For as many as are
led by the Spirit of God, they are the sons of God."

Romans 8:12-14

If we'll learn to be led by the Holy Spirit, we will live a life of love. In fact, we can measure just how truly Spirit-led we are by the love that flows forth from us in our day-to-day lives. Because God Himself is Love, His Spirit will always lead us to be kind and gentle to people. He will cause us to notice them, to smile warmly and say hello, instead of rushing past them rudely on our way to "serve The LORD."

The Holy Spirit will also enhance our love life by leading us to deny (or as this passage says "put to death") our flesh when it rises up and wants to act selfishly and unlovingly. When our bodies are tired and we feel like being short-tempered and irritable with others, the Holy Spirit will lead us to deny those feelings the right to rule us. He'll give us the wisdom and the strength to subdue our bodies and make them obey the law of love.

Some people don't seem to realize that. They think all that's necessary to walk successfully in the spirit is to say a wholehearted *yes* to God. "Oh, LORD," they pray, "I truly want to live a life of love. I totally submit myself to You. Help me, LORD, to be more loving today."

That's wonderful and good…but it's just half the picture. If we're going to walk in love, we must not only say *yes* to The LORD, we must, by His grace, say an equally powerful *NO!* to the pressures of the flesh. Once we've asked The LORD to help us, that's the first thing He'll lead us to do!

The WORD tells us the desires of the flesh are contrary to the desires of the spirit. That means if you let your flesh do what it wants to, you'll never consistently walk in love. So when our carnal nature begins to put demands on us, we have to rise up in the spirit and subject it to The WORD. We must say, "No, flesh! You're not going to do that! You stop it, in the Name of Jesus!"

We must follow the example of the Apostle Paul who said, "I discipline my body and make it my slave, so that, after I have preached to others, I myself will not be disqualified" (1 Corinthians 9:27, *New American Standard*). By saying *yes* to the spirit and *no* to the flesh, we will be qualified to minister to others, and we will live the life of love.

LIMITLESS**LOVE**

Build on the Rock

"Whosoever cometh to me, and heareth my sayings, and doeth them, I will show you to whom he is like: He is like a man which built an house, and digged deep, and laid the foundation on a rock: and when the flood arose, the stream beat vehemently upon that house, and could not shake it: for it was founded upon a rock. But he that heareth, and doeth not, is like a man that without a foundation built an house upon the earth; against which the stream did beat vehemently, and immediately it fell; and the ruin of that house was great."
Luke 6:47-49

I love the truths of God's WORD! I treasure revelation knowledge. But just knowing what the Bible says about love—or any other area of life for that matter—is not enough. We can know every scripture about love, and be confident that the love of God dwells in us. We can be fully aware that, as believers, our great commandment is to walk in love. It's possible for us to know all those things and still be the meanest thing on two legs. That's right. With all that knowledge, we can still end up living like prisoners of our selfish flesh.

"How can that be?" you might ask. "Didn't Jesus say that the truth would set us free?"

Yes, but in the verse right before that He put a condition on that statement. He said, "If you abide in My WORD [hold fast to My teachings and live in accordance with them], you are truly My disciples. And you will know the Truth and the Truth will set you free" (John 8:31-32, *The Amplified Bible*).

It's not just knowledge of The WORD that sets you free. It's acting on what you know and keeping The WORD of God alive in you continually that does it. The more of God's WORD you hear and act on, the more unshakable you'll become. You'll be like the man who built his house on the rock. Then when the storms of life come, you'll stand strong and solid on The WORD, and you'll be BLESSED.

If you fail to act on what you hear, however, you'll start thinking you're strong and solid because you have a head full of knowledge but, in reality, you'll be on very shaky ground. Then, when the pressures of life hit or the devil takes a swipe at you, the tower of knowledge you built will come crashing to the ground.

So, as you continue to study and meditate on The WORD of love, be sure you're acting on what you learn. Check up on yourself regularly to see what you're doing differently as a result of your study on love. Ask yourself, "What unloving habits and tendencies am I actively overcoming these days? What am I doing that I haven't done before?" Don't just be a hearer...be a doer. Build your house on the Rock. Listen *and live* in accordance with the law of love.

LIMITLESS**LOVE**

More Than Enough

"O magnify The LORD with me, and let us exalt his name together."
Psalm 34:3

Sometimes, when you tell people that God loves them (especially when they're in the midst of trouble or a trial), they act like it's no big deal. They aren't comforted or encouraged because they've let their problems become bigger in their mind than God. They've magnified their circumstances instead of The LORD, so they don't think His love is enough to get them through.

But the Bible says we should do just the opposite. It says we should magnify The LORD! How? By focusing our hearts, minds and mouths on Him until He is the biggest thing in our lives. We make Him big in our own sight by talking about His great power and love.

The fact is, no matter how much we magnify God, we'll never be able to make Him as big as He really is. We'll never be able to overestimate His love. God's love is so great, we'll spend eternity exploring it. He's so good that no matter how good we think He is…we'll continually discover He's better than we thought!

Some time ago, Ken and I received a letter from a little lady in Russia who had been watching our television broadcasts. Her letter blessed me tremendously. Even though she had more problems than most of us ever will, she was happy because she was confident in God's love, and she believed He could do anything for her.

She told us how God had put food on her table and given her a place to live. She wrote about how greatly her life had improved since she'd found out about God's goodness and made Jesus her LORD. Then she said something that made me laugh out loud. Apparently on one of the broadcasts she watched, one of the ministers had said something about God being able to give you an airplane. (To those of us who are called to preach all over the world, an airplane is a great help!)

In response, she wrote something like this. "I like everything you say and agree with it. But I don't know what I would do with an airplane. It would be so much trouble for me. I'd have to hire a pilot and find a hangar where I could keep it. You have no idea how complicated that would get for me. If you don't mind, I think I'll just pass that blessing by. I don't think I want it."

Isn't that wonderful? It never even occurred to this faith-filled little lady that God might not be willing or able to give her an airplane. She knew how big and loving He is. She had magnified Him greatly in her heart and life. In her mind, her problems were no big deal because she had magnified The LORD, and she knew He is more than enough!

LIMITLESS**LOVE**

Speak God's Language of Love

*"Through Him, therefore, let us constantly and at all times offer up
to God a sacrifice of praise, which is the fruit of lips that thankfully
acknowledge and confess and glorify His name."*
Hebrews 13:15, *The Amplified Bible*

To God, praise is *the language of love.* So, if you really want to let God know you love Him, do what this verse says and praise Him constantly…at all times. Don't be grateful one day and griping the next. Continually rejoice and thank The LORD for what He's done for you.

According to Ephesians 5:18-20 that's not just a nice idea, it's God's will for us. He tells us to be continually filled with the Spirit, "speaking to one another in psalms and hymns and spiritual songs, singing and making melody with your heart to The LORD; always giving thanks for all things in the name of our LORD Jesus Christ to God, even the Father" *(New American Standard).* We should be expressing our love to God by singing and speaking His praises—in the shower, in our cars, and even as we go about our work. Whether we're doing it aloud or quietly in our hearts, we should be praising Him all the time.

That's the way God wants us to be. He wants us so full of victory that we overflow with gratitude to Him. He wants us to be so full of His praises that no one has to lead or urge us, we just praise Him because we can't help ourselves.

"I don't see how I can do that," you might say. "I have so many problems, I don't feel like praising The LORD. I'm just not very happy right now."

Then you might have to begin by simply choosing to do it. You might have to say, "I'm going to praise The LORD whether I feel like it or not." But if you'll do it wholeheartedly, before long you *will* feel like it. You'll start remembering how bad things were when God found you. You'll start thinking about what He's done for you since then. You'll get excited about what He's going to do for you in the days ahead…and you'll want to sing and shout!

The more you keep on praising The LORD and walking with Him, the more reasons you'll have to praise Him. And, one of these days, you'll look around yourself and see the love of God poured out in every area of your life. You'll see His goodness everywhere you turn. You'll be living out His plan, enjoying His provision and dwelling in the place He prepared especially for you.

You'll be living proof that "happy is that people, whose God is The LORD" (Psalm 144:15). You'll be glad when times were rough you chose to offer up the sacrifice of praise.

Don't Look Back

"But this one thing I do, forgetting those things which are behind, and reaching forth unto those things which are before, I press toward the mark for the prize of the high calling of God in Christ Jesus."
Philippians 3:13-14

The devil will always try to steal your confidence in God's love by tempting you to look backward. He'll draw your attention off God's wonderful provisions and promises by reminding you of yesterday's failures, pains and disappointments.

But looking back is not the way to get ahead in the kingdom of God. It's not the way to lay hold of the heavenly prize. So don't let the devil talk you into it!

Get out your Bible instead, and look at what God says about your future. He says you're the healed, so enjoying a healthy body is in your future. He says you're more than a conqueror, so victory in every area of life is in your future. God says He loves you, and you have a glorious life ahead of you right here on this earth—and an even better life awaiting you after that!

Always remember, this earthly life we're living is just a temporary situation. If we live to be 120 years old, that's just a moment in eternity. We are on our way to heaven! We ought to live healthy, BLESSED and prosperous lives while we're here because that's the will of God. But, even so, we need to remember we're just passing through.

We always need to be aware that during this lifetime we're on temporary assignment for God. We're here to work for Him and build His kingdom on the earth. Right now, we're laying up rewards for heaven. We won't be able to earn the same kinds of rewards once we get there because there won't be any pressure up there. There won't be a devil up there trying to knock our heads off, make us sick and steal our resources.

Right now, we have a fleeting opportunity to give glory to God by standing strong on His WORD and walking in love right in the face of all the pressure and lies the devil can bring. We have the opportunity to say, "That's OK, devil, give it your best shot. When you're finished, I'll still be standing here believing God loves me. I'll still be praising Him and pressing forward toward the prize!

If we'll start thinking like that, we'll be able to stand more successfully against the devil's attempts to stop us. When he tries to turn our eyes toward the past, we'll just keep looking forward in faith. Knowing how much Jesus loves us, we'll step boldly into a future full of the promises and provisions of God!

Prayer for Salvation and Baptism
in the Holy Spirit

Heavenly Father, I come to You in the Name of Jesus. Your Word says, "Whosoever shall call on the name of the Lord shall be saved" (Acts 2:21). I am calling on You. I pray and ask Jesus to come into my heart and be Lord over my life according to Romans 10:9-10: "If thou shalt confess with thy mouth the Lord Jesus, and shalt believe in thine heart that God hath raised him from the dead, thou shalt be saved. For with the heart man believeth unto righteousness; and with the mouth confession is made unto salvation." I do that now. I confess that Jesus is Lord, and I believe in my heart that God raised Him from the dead.

I am now reborn! I am a Christian—a child of Almighty God! I am saved! You also said in Your Word, "If ye then, being evil, know how to give good gifts unto your children: HOW MUCH MORE shall your heavenly Father give the Holy Spirit to them that ask him?" (Luke 11:13). I'm also asking You to fill me with the Holy Spirit. Holy Spirit, rise up within me as I praise God. I fully expect to speak with other tongues as You give me the utterance (Acts 2:4). In Jesus' Name. Amen!

Begin to praise God for filling you with the Holy Spirit. Speak those words and syllables you receive—not in your own language, but the language given to you by the Holy Spirit. You have to use your own voice. God will not force you to speak. Don't be concerned with how it sounds. It is a heavenly language!

Continue with the blessing God has given you and pray in the spirit every day.

You are a born-again, Spirit-filled believer. You'll never be the same!

Find a good church that boldly preaches God's Word and obeys it. Become part of a church family who will love and care for you as you love and care for them.

We need to be connected to each other. It increases our strength in God. It's God's plan for us.

Make it a habit to watch the *Believer's Voice of Victory* television broadcast and become a doer of the Word, who is blessed in his doing (James 1:22-25).

About the Authors

Kenneth and Gloria Copeland are the best-selling authors of more than 60 books. They have also co-authored numerous books including *Family Promises,* the *LifeLine* series and *From Faith to Faith—A Daily Guide to Victory.* As founders of Kenneth Copeland Ministries in Fort Worth, Texas, Kenneth and Gloria have been circling the globe with the uncompromised Word of God since 1967, preaching and teaching a lifestyle of victory for every Christian.

Their daily and Sunday *Believer's Voice of Victory* television broadcasts now air on more than 500 stations around the world, and the *Believer's Voice of Victory* magazine is distributed to nearly 600,000 believers worldwide. Kenneth Copeland Ministries' international prison ministry reaches more than 20,000 new inmates every year and receives more than 20,000 pieces of correspondence each month. Their teaching materials can also be found on the World Wide Web. With offices and staff in the United States, Canada, England, Australia, South Africa, Ukraine and Singapore, Kenneth and Gloria's teaching materials—books, magazines, audios and videos—have been translated into at least 26 languages to reach the world with the love of God.

Learn more about Kenneth Copeland Ministries
by visiting our website at **kcm.org**

US IS L

We're Here for You!®

Your growth in God's WORD and victory in Jesus are at the very center of our hearts. In every way God has equipped us, we will help you deal with the issues facing you, so you can be the **victorious overcomer** He has planned for you to be.

The mission of Kenneth Copeland Ministries is about all of us growing and going together. Our prayer is that you will take full advantage of all The LORD has given us to share with you.

Wherever you are in the world, you can watch the *Believer's Voice of Victory* broadcast on television (check your local listings), the Internet at kcm.org or on our digital Roku channel.

Our website, **kcm.org,** gives you access to every resource we've developed for your victory. And, you can find contact information for our international offices in Africa, Asia, Australia, Canada, Europe, Ukraine and our headquarters in the United States.

Each office is staffed with devoted men and women, ready to serve and pray with you. You can contact the worldwide office nearest you for assistance, and you can call us for prayer at our U.S. number, +1-817-852-6000, 24 hours every day!

We encourage you to connect with us often and let us be part of your everyday walk of faith!

Jesus Is LORD!

Kenneth & Gloria Copeland

Kenneth and Gloria Copeland